Monks and Nuns, Saints and Outcasts

MONKS & NUNS, SAINTS & OUTCASTS

RELIGION IN MEDIEVAL SOCIETY

ESSAYS IN HONOR OF LESTER K. LITTLE

EDITED BY

SHARON FARMER & BARBARA H. ROSENWEIN

CORNELL UNIVERSITY PRESS

ITHACA AND LONDON

First Published 2000 by Cornell University Press
First printing, Cornell Paperbacks, 2000

Printed in the United States of America

Library of Congress Cataloging-in-Publication Data

Monks and nuns, saints and outcasts: religion in medieval society:
essays in honor of Lester K. Little / edited by Sharon Farmer and Barbara H. Rosenwein.
p.   cm.
Includes bibliographical references and index.
ISBN 0-8014-3445-9 (cloth : alk. paper) — ISBN 0-8014-8656-4 (pbk. : alk. paper)
1. Church history—Middle Ages, 600–1500.   2. Civilization, Medieval.
3. Europe—Church history—600–1500.   I. Little, Lester K.
II. Farmer, Sharon A.   III. Rosenwein, Barbara H.
BR252.M575   2000
274.03—dc21   99-056454

Cornell University Press strives to use environmentally responsible suppliers and materials to the fullest extent possible in the publishing of its books. Such materials include vegetable-based, low-VOC inks and acid-free papers that are recycled, totally chlorine-free, or partly composed of nonwood fibers. Books that bear the logo of the FSC (Forest Stewardship Council) use paper taken from forests that have been inspected and certified as meeting the highest standards for environmental and social responsibility. For further information, visit our website at www.cornellpress.cornell.edu.

Cloth printing   10 9 8 7 6 5 4 3 2 1
Paperback printing   10 9 8 7 6 5 4 3 2 1

Lester K. Little

CONTENTS

PREFACE

This collection of essays honors Lester K. Little on the occasion of his sixty-fifth birthday. Even without this preface, it would be hard for readers to miss how much of this book is inspired by Lester's writings on religious movements, on monastic cursing, and on the social meaning of disease. What might be less obvious is Lester's personal impact as a teacher, colleague, and correspondent. Many of the contributors, including the two editors, were once Lester's students. We were transfixed in his classes, not by anecdotes (though there were certainly some of those), but by the intensity, passion, high seriousness, and downright good humor that Lester brought to his subject. He was (he is) a connoisseur of the human condition and its vicissitudes. He was not exactly the Ancient Mariner, fixing us with his glittering eye—for one thing he was much too young, and still is. Yet we felt much the same immediate grip: we were about to hear the most important thing in the world. "Listen to this!" It's doubtful that he ever *said* that; but that's what we heard as Lester launched into the history of the pilgrimage to Santiago or unraveled a knotty text by St. Anselm.

We were drawn into these classes as equals, not in expertise (of course) but in worth. Our ideas counted, and not just as "good student responses," but as contributions to a common enterprise. We were creators of history: "Write it as if you're going to publish it," Lester told one of the editors as she started a paper. She did. And it *was* published.

These experiences were—must have been—magical. How else explain this largely undergraduate teacher producing so many Ph.D.'s? They rival the number of Joseph Strayer's progeny—those students who, like Charles Radding, William Chester Jordan, Robert Lerner, and Lester himself, constitute so significant a part of the medieval professoriate in the United States. Lester's offspring certainly outdo Strayer's in the number of women professors. There is no denying that women would have entered the profession even if Lester had not been at Smith College. But so many? One suspects that if Lester had taught at a men's school, there would now be an even more disproportionate number of men teaching medieval history.

Not that Lester's influence was or is limited to his students. Consider the ways in which medievalists interact: at conferences, whether at formal meetings, in the corridors, or over drinks; through e-mail; as visiting professors; as guest lecturers; as fellow laborers in libraries and archives. Lester was (is) active in all of these ways; and through them he became important to many of his colleagues and *their* students, not only because of his ideas but because of his warmth, wit, passion, and compassion.

But also, of course, because of his ideas. Lester's specific theses are very important, and we discuss some of them below. But to understand Lester's influence, it is important to realize that above all there has always been one idea: allow your curiosity to get the better of you. Ask what happened—and cast the net wide. Ask why, and cast it wider. For answers, don't be afraid to read anthropology, philosophy, psychology, and anything else that may shed light. Pursue your interests because there is delight in doing so. Such delight is ever-present in Lester's classes.

In the introduction we trace the historiography of medieval religious studies, showing how, in the 1960s, historians began to link religious, political, and social movements. Lester was not interested simply in "links." He was interested in the "social meaning" of religion: the elements of religious phenomena that expressed a society. In his first book, *Religious Poverty and the Profit Economy in Medieval Europe* (1978), he traced the growth of the new European money economy and the religious and moral crisis, then resolution, that it provoked. In *Liberty, Charity, Fraternity: Lay Religious Confraternities at Bergamo in the Age of the Commune* (1988), he brought to center stage some little-studied lay religious organizations of the thirteenth and fourteenth centuries. These were lay initiatives, the product of profound religious, political, and social upheavals. In *Benedictine Maledictions: Liturgical Cursing in Romanesque France* (1993), he studied ritual cursing as a cultural artifact of multiple significance in a society of monks and malefactors.

The contributors to this collection draw upon and discuss these and other studies by Lester Little in the essays that follow. Our debt is clear. It is only fitting that we thank Lester and offer him this gift.

Sharon Farmer
Santa Barbara, California

Barbara H. Rosenwein
Evanston, Illinois

Abbreviations

AASS	*Acta Sanctorum quotquot toto orbe coluntur,* ed. Joannus Bollandus et al., 66 vols. (Venice, 1734–1770)
Annales: ÉSC	*Annales: Économies, Sociétés, Civilisations*
Annales: HSS	*Annales: Histoire, Sciences Sociales*
BF	*Bullarium franciscanum,* ed. Joannes Hiacintus Sbaralea (Rome, 1759)
BHG	*Bibliotheca Hagiographica Graeca,* 3 vols. (Brussels, 1957)
BHL	*Bibliotheca Hagiographica Latina* (Brussels, 1898–1901)
CCCM	Corpus Christianorum, Continuatio Mediaevalis
CCSL	Corpus Christianorum, Series Latina
CSV	*Cartulaire de l'abbaye de Saint-Victor de Marseille,* ed. M. Guérard, Collection des cartulaires de France 8–9 (Paris, 1857)
DACL	*Dictionnaire d'archéologie chrétienne et de liturgie,* ed. F. Cabrol, 15 vols. (Paris, 1907–53)
MGH	*Monumenta Germaniae Historica*
AA	*Auctores antiquissimi,* 15 vols (Hannover, 1877–1919)
Capit.	*Capitularia, Legum Sectio II, Capitularia Regum Francorum,* 2 vols. (Hannover, 1883–97)
Concilia	*Concilia, Legum Sectio III,* 3 vols. (Hannover, 1893–1984)
Epp.	*Epistolae,* 8 vols. (Hannover, 1887–1939)
Necr.	*Necrologiae Germaniae,* 5 vols. (1888–1920)
SSrerMerov	*Scriptores Rerum Merovingicarum,* 7 vols. (Hannover, 1885–1920, alt. ed. vol. 1, 1951)
SRG	*Scriptores Rerum Germanicarum.* Nova Series, 13 vols. (Berlin, 1922–1967)
SS	*Scriptores,* 30 vols. (Hannover, 1824–1924)
PG	*Patrologiae Cursus Completus, Series Graeca,* ed. J.-P. Migne, 161 vols. in 166 (Paris, 1857–87)
PL	*Patrologiae Cursus Completus, Series Latina,* ed. J.-P. Migne, 221 vols. (Paris, 1841–66)

Monks and Nuns, Saints and Outcasts

Introduction

Sharon Farmer and Barbara H. Rosenwein

Why another book about medieval religion? Because this is where medievalists are doing some of their most serious rethinking. Indeed, formulated as part of social history, the topic is relatively young. The articles in this collection represent some of the most forward-looking, even cutting-edge, work in the field of medieval history.

RELIGION AND SOCIETY

Cast out of Enlightenment thought as the unwanted child of "superstition," the topic of medieval religion was generally avoided by medieval historians—with the exception of those connected with religious orders—until the second half of the twentieth century.[1] Sources connected with the topic gathered dust in manuscript form or were tucked away in old and rare Latin editions; lives of saints were tidily categorized (and marginalized) as "hagiography."[2] Textbooks on the Middle Ages were written without a word about beliefs. The Church figured, to be sure, but only as a political player.

The editors would like to thank John G. Ackerman, director of Cornell University Press, Laura Wilson Baird, Loyola University Chicago research assistant, Nancy McLoughlin, University of California, Santa Barbara research assistant, and Cornell University Press's two anonymous readers.

1. For a recent survey, on which many of the following historiographical observations are based, see Lester K. Little and Barbara H. Rosenwein, eds., *Debating the Middle Ages: Issues and Readings* (Oxford, 1998), part 4.
2. Felice Lifshitz, "Beyond Positivism and Genre: 'Hagiographical' Texts as Historical Narrative," *Viator* 25 (1994): 95–113. See esp. pp. 108–9, where she discusses the way in which nineteenth-century scholars redefined the term "hagiography" to contrast with scientific "history."

The separation of religion from the rest of medieval history ended in the 1960s, but the way had been paved thirty years before that. Herbert Grundmann's 1935 study, *Religious Movements in the Middle Ages,* looked at the connections (*Zusammenhänge*) between heretics, mendicants, and mystics.[3] Hitherto, religious historians, most practicing believers themselves, had treated heretical and orthodox religious movements as utterly separate. Grundmann's great breakthrough was to see links. This he was able to do in part by looking at the common social origins of the adherents of heretical and mendicant groups.

Hard on the heels of Grundmann came Gerd Tellenbach's 1936 study of eleventh-century church reform, *Church, State, and Christian Society at the Time of the Investiture Contest.*[4] This was largely an exploration of high ideals. But because it treated the religious zeal of monks as a serious matter with practical political implications, it breached the barriers between religious and other kinds of history.

In France, Marc Bloch's *Feudal Society,* published in 1939–40, approached society from the theoretical position of Emile Durkheim, who taught that societies were organic, cohesive entities. Bloch's viewpoint marginalized linear narratives of political events and personalities, placing mental categories and economic structures at the center. "A society, like a mind," Bloch argued, "is woven of perpetual interactions. For other researchers, differently oriented, the analysis of the economy or the mental climate are culminating points; for the historian of the social structure they are a starting point."[5] It was impossible, in this vision, to ignore religion's constitutive role in society. Bloch not only discussed "religious mentality" in *Feudal Society* but also revolutionized political history in *The Royal Touch* by examining the role of a "miracle" (the kings' supernatural ability to cure scrofula) in sustaining over centuries the legitimacy of the French and English monarchs.[6]

In the aftermath of World War II, these approaches began to take root. In Eastern Europe, Grundmann's consideration of "social origins" was

---

3. Herbert Grundmann, *Religiöse Bewegungen im Mittelalter: Untersuchungen über die geschichtlichen Zusammenhänge zwischen der Ketzerei, den Bettelorden und der religiösen Frauenbewegung im 12. und 13. Jahrhundert und über die geschichtlichen Grundlagen der deutschen Mystik* (Berlin, 1935), now in English: *Religious Movements in the Middle Ages: The Historical Links between Heresy, the Mendicant Orders, and the Women's Religious Movement in the Twelfth and Thirteenth Century, with the Historical Foundations of German Mysticism,* trans. Steven Rowan (Notre Dame, 1995).

4. Gerd O. Tellenbach, *Libertas: Kirche und Weltordnung im Zeitalter des Investiturstreits* (Stuttgart, 1936), published in English as *Church, State, and Christian Society at the Time of the Investiture Contest,* trans. R. F. Bennett (New York, 1970).

5. Marc Bloch, *Feudal Society,* trans. L. A. Manyon (London, 1961; French edition, 1939–40), 1:59; idem, *The Royal Touch,* trans. J. E. Anderson (London, 1973; French edition, 1924).

6. On the significance of Bloch's work, see Peter Burke, *The French Historical Revolution: The Annales School, 1929–1989* (Stanford, Calif., 1990), chap. 2.

taken up—and radically recast—by Marxist historians who wanted to show how the dominant feudal classes of medieval society employed religion both to placate and to oppress the masses.[7] In the West, particularly in Italy, liberal Catholic historians welcomed Grundmann's approach for their own explorations of such communal movements as the Patarines of Milan, which mingled economic demands with religious programs.[8] Meanwhile, Gerd Tellenbach and his students published important studies on the social relations between monks and nobles.[9]

In the United States, Marc Bloch's *Feudal Society*, coupled with Richard Southern's *The Making of the Middle Ages*, first published in 1953, became the staples of undergraduate medieval history courses in the 1960s and 1970s. Many American medievalists who are active today, and indeed, many British and European scholars as well, can trace their own interest in the social meaning of religion to these two seminal texts. Southern's book opened up whole fields of inquiry: the history of devotional beliefs and practices, of emotions, of perceptions of God, self, and other. There were important differences between Bloch's view of history and that of Southern. Bloch was more interested in peasants; Southern, in intellectuals. Bloch's school of history tended to erase the subject, or actor, in history; Southern, by contrast, told a story about individual actors who gave birth to conscious subjectivity. Nevertheless, there were also similarities. Both Bloch and Southern wrote works that appeared to be synchronic (that is, they were not structured as linear accounts of change over time); both nevertheless described Western history as a story of progress, beginning not with the Renaissance of the fifteenth century but rather with the cultural flowering of the eleventh and twelfth centuries.[10] Like Bloch, Southern refused to compartmentalize cultural phenomena. Ever since Southern, it has been impossible to talk about the rise of the cult of the Virgin without also recalling the birth of scholastic thought and the emergence of romance literature.

Meanwhile, developments within Catholic historiography brought religious *sources* into mainstream historical discourse.[11] The early twentieth century saw a renewed interest in the original texts of medieval theology. The handy editions *cum* translations of patristic texts in *Sources chrétiennes*

7. See, for example, Ernst Werner, *Die gesellschaftlichen Grundlagen der Klosterreform im 11. Jahrhundert* (Berlin, 1953).

8. For example, Cinzio Violante, *La Pataria milanese e la Riforma ecclesiastica* (Rome, 1955).

9. Gerd Tellenbach, ed., *Neue Forschungen über Cluny und die Cluniacenser* (Freiburg, 1959).

10. Patrick J. Geary, *Phantoms of Remembrance: Memory and Oblivion at the End of the First Millennium* (Princeton, N.J., 1994), p. 23.

11. Some of the points in the following section derive from a lecture on the development of the discipline of theology given in November 1998 by Professor Dennis Martin (Loyola University) in a course entitled "Medieval Studies Today."

came out of this movement, as did Étienne Gilson's pioneering rereading of the original *summae* (treatises) of Thomas Aquinas and other scholastics. Marie-Dominique Chenu was a young member of this group when he began to work out a historical theology of his own. In his view, very few truths of the Christian religion were constant; the rest depended on society and culture—that is, on the historically specific needs of men and women. Theology changed as society changed. It was the task of the historian to tease out the threads that tied together seemingly disparate phenomena "by making an impassioned search for internal points of contact, for half-conscious relationships." [12]

Chenu marked a major shift. Giovanni Miccoli, a recent historian of the Gregorian church, has highlighted the importance of his own reading of Chenu as a student. In 1978, Lester K. Little professed in the preface of his first book, "I was never in any formal sense a student of Père Chenu, but ever since that day in 1960 when we first met and we talked for an hour, I have claimed him as my teacher." [13] In 1982 Caroline Bynum was calling Chenu's 1957 book on twelfth-century theology "recent," not, to be sure, because it had just been published but because it represented the most up-to-date approach. [14]

Opening religion to society meant opening it to new groups. In the technical sense, the "religious" of the Middle Ages were the monks. Priests, bishops, and popes were "secular" clergy. Most of society, however, was composed of men and women who belonged to neither of those orders. They were laypeople. Chenu's essays touched on the laity, but that was not his focus. In the 1970s, however, the laity came into its own with the work of André Vauchez, Emmanuel Le Roy Ladurie, and Jean-Claude Schmitt. Vauchez, a liberal Catholic historian, endeavored to write the history of what laypeople believed, regardless of what the Church told them to think or do. [15] Le Roy Ladurie and Schmitt, who identified with Marc Bloch's "Annales School," turned to sources that revealed the religious beliefs and practices of medieval peasants. [16]

12. Marie-Dominique Chenu, *Nature, Man, and Society in the Twelfth Century: Essays on New Theological Perspectives in the Latin West,* ed. and trans. Jerome Taylor and Lester K. Little (Chicago, 1968), p. xix.

13. Giovanni Miccoli, "Gli 'Incontri nel Medio Evo' di Arsenio Frugoni," *Studi Medievali* 24 (1983): 469–86 at 470, cited in Little and Rosenwein, *Debating the Middle Ages,* p. 303, n. 7; Lester K. Little, *Religious Poverty and the Profit Economy in Medieval Europe* (Ithaca, N.Y., 1978), p. viii.

14. Caroline Walker Bynum, *Jesus as Mother: Studies in the Spirituality of the High Middle Ages* (Berkeley, 1982), p. 60, citing (n. 4) Chenu's *La théologie au douzième siècle* (Paris, 1957).

15. See the discussion of Vauchez's work in Little and Rosenwein, *Debating the Middle Ages,* p. 304.

16. Jean-Claude Schmitt, *The Holy Greyhound,* trans. Martin Thom (Cambridge, 1983; French edition, 1979); Emmanuel Le Roy Ladurie, *Montaillou: The Promised Land of Error,* trans. Barbara Bray (New York, 1978; French edition, 1975).

At the same time that it was opening to embrace the laity, medieval religious history expanded its own parameters. For example, with the seminal article by Peter Brown on the significance of holy men in Late Antique society, the whole field of saints and relics became part of the new social/religious history.[17] Now hagiography and miracle stories were dusted off and given pride of place on the medievalist's desk.

OLD HISTORY AND NEW

What did medieval historians write about in the period before they put religion and society together? Politics and institutional history. Medieval historians wanted to know how kings ran their monarchies, how parliamentary institutions came into being, how feudalism worked in theory and practice.[18] If politics was not their focus, other major institutions certainly were: medieval universities, cities, guilds, commercial enterprises. These historians argued for the importance of the medieval past by seeing in it the origins of "the modern": in the United States, Haskins wrote about the twelfth-century "renaissance," Lopez about the "commercial revolution" of the middle ages, and Strayer about the medieval origins of the modern state.[19] In Europe, medievalists were "relevant" because their investigations helped to explain national identities and institutions. Lot and Fawtier wrote a two-volume *History of French Institutions in the Middle Ages;* Fasoli wrote about the early Italian kings; Lamprecht wrote the first volume of his four-volume history of Germany.[20]

Much of this work was facilitated by critical editions of primary sources and depended on meticulous readings of those texts. The "sciences" of

17. Peter Brown, "The Rise and Function of the Holy Man in Late Antiquity," *Journal of Roman Studies* 61 (1961): 80–101; reprinted in *Society and the Holy in Late Antiquity* (Berkeley, 1982), pp. 103–52. This was followed by Brown's equally pioneering *The Cult of Saints: Its Rise and Function in Latin Christianity* (Chicago, 1981). For bibliography on the explosion of studies in this area, see Patrick J. Geary, "Saints, Scholars, and Society: The Elusive Goal," in his *Living with the Dead in the Middle Ages* (Ithaca, N.Y., 1994), pp. 9–29.

18. For fuller particulars, see Paul Freedman and Gabrielle Spiegel, "Medievalisms Old and New: The Rediscovery of Alterity in North American Medieval Studies," *American Historical Review* 103 (1998): 677–704. On the current sensitivity to the meaning of "feudalism," see Little and Rosenwein, *Debating the Middle Ages*, pp. 107–13.

19. Charles Homer Haskins, *The Renaissance of the Twelfth Century* (Cambridge, Mass., 1927); Robert S. Lopez, *The Commercial Revolution of the Middle Ages, 950–1350* (New York, 1971); Joseph R. Strayer, *On the Medieval Origins of the Modern State* (Princeton, N.J., 1970), based on a series of lectures given in 1961.

20. Ferdinand Lot and Robert Fawtier, *Histoire des institutions françaises au moyen âge,* 2 vols. (Paris, 1957–58); Gina Fasoli, *I re d'Italia, 888–962* (Florence, 1949); Karl Lamprecht, *Deutsche Geschichte,* vol. 1 (Berlin, 1920).

diplomatics, paleography, and codicology gave historians the tools to winnow authentic documents from those that had been forged, to date manuscripts with precision, to analyze the production of books, and to understand the organization of scriptoria. At the time, in the nineteenth and pre-1960s twentieth century, these tools were thought to be value free, unencumbered by any but the most objective and rational agendas.[21] Historians maintained that intelligent, rational use of such tools enabled them to construct objective, scientific narratives about the past "as it really was."

After World War I, some historians began to question the possibility of objective history, coining the pejorative term "positivist" to refer to those historians who had thought, and who continue to think, that primary source texts—if read critically and carefully—could give them an unobstructed view of the past. Most medievalists, however, did not (and do not) count themselves among the relativists.[22] In other fields, however, many intellectuals began to reject the possibility of objectivity in the aftermath of the social changes of the 1960s; by the late 1980s this stance was fully articulated. Within the academy at large, this change has been given the name "postmodernism"; within the historical profession it is frequently referred to as the "linguistic turn."[23]

Postmodernism is no one thing. Nevertheless, some generalizations are possible. It posits that there is no Truth but rather many truths; that all norms imply by definition the existence of non-norms (the "other"); that all texts (both those that we study and those that we write) are "interested"; that texts do not merely represent reality but also constitute, or shape, it; that all categories—such as "women," the "poor," the "sane"—are socially constructed; that history is the story not of progress but of jagged discontinuities. Postmodernism also questions the existence of the self-conscious subject: identities are fragmented; they are constituted not by an organic "me" but by "discourses"—sets of cultural rules about how things are discussed.[24] When we write history—or anything else—

21. This is no longer the case. See, for example, *The Politics of Editing Medieval Texts: Papers Given at the 27th Annual Conference on Editorial Problems, University of Toronto, 1–2 November 1991*, ed. Roberta Frank (New York, 1993).
22. For the relativists, see Freedman and Spiegel, "Medievalisms Old and New," p. 687.
23. Good accounts of the linguistic turn are John Toews, "Intellectual History after the Linguistic Turn: The Autonomy of Meaning and the Irreducibility of Experience," *American Historical Review* 92 (1981): 879–907; and Gabrielle Spiegel, "History, Historicism, and the Social Logic of the Text in the Middle Ages," *Speculum* 65 (1990): 59–86; reprinted in Spiegel, *The Past as Text: The Theory and Practice of Medieval Historiography* (Baltimore, 1997), chap. 1.
24. The notion of "discourse" is largely Michel Foucault's. For an introduction to the concept, see Michèle Barrett, *The Politics of Truth from Marx to Foucault* (Stanford, 1991), chap. 6, and Edward Said, "Michel Foucault, 1926–1984," in Jonathan Arac, ed., *After Foucault* (New Brunswick, N.J., 1988). Said explains: "What enables a doctor to practise medicine or a historian to write history is

it is the dominant discourses, rather than our "selves," that shape the new text.

On the whole, medievalists have been wary of embracing postmodernism wholeheartedly.[25] But that is in part because they have been posing similar questions all along—and without the jargon. Consider, for instance, Bloch's observation in *Feudal Society:* "social classification exists, in the last analysis, only by virtue of the ideas which men form of it."[26] Or again, consider the first two pages of *The Royal Touch,* in which Bloch explores a single, possibly mythological, and certainly minor event of the fourteenth century: a report that the king of England challenged the king of France to prove he was the true king by submitting to some supernatural tests. Bloch was well aware of the possibility that the English king never made this challenge; nevertheless, he built his entire book around one of the supernatural tests in the account.[27]

Thus already in the 1920s, Bloch had the idea that representations give shape to reality. Small wonder, then, that in the 1960s and 1970s, even before the coining of the expressions "postmodern" and "linguistic turn," Caroline Bynum, Georges Duby, Patrick Geary, Lester Little, Michel Mollat, Gabrielle Spiegel, and others began to explore the rituals and texts that shaped, legitimized, and sustained noble, monastic, mercantile, and marginal identities in the Middle Ages.[28] Unlike Bloch,

---

not mainly a set of individual gifts, but an ability to follow rules that are taken for granted as an unconscious *a priori* by all professionals. . . . More than anyone before him Foucault specified rules for those rules, and even more impressively, he showed how over long periods of time the rules became epistemological enforcers of what (as well as how) people thought, lived, and spoke" (ibid., p. 10, cited by Barrett, *Politics of Truth,* pp. 126–27). Joan Scott is one historian who has employed Foucault's ideas to question organic notions of identity, in "Experience," in Judith Butler and Joan Scott, eds., *Feminists Theorize the Political* (New York, 1992), pp. 22–40.

25. Spiegel, *The Past as Text,* p. 72.

26. Bloch, *Feudal Society,* 1:268 and quoted by M. M. Postan in his introduction, p. xv.

27. Bloch, *The Royal Touch,* pp. 1–2.

28. Caroline Bynum, "Did the Twelfth Century Discover the Individual?" *Journal of Ecclesiastical History* 31 (1980): 1–17, reprinted in eadem, *Jesus as Mother,* pp. 82–109; eadem, "Jesus as Mother and Abbot as Mother: Some Themes in Twelfth-Century Cistercian Writing," *Harvard Theological Review* 70 (1977): 257–84; reprinted in *Jesus as Mother,* pp. 110–69; Georges Duby, "Remarques sur la littérature généalogique en France aux XIᵉ et XIIᵉ siècles," *Comptes rendus des séances de l'année 1967* (April–June 1967), Académie des Inscriptions et Belles-Lettres (Paris, 1967), trans. in Duby, *The Chivalrous Society,* trans. Cynthia Postan (Berkeley, 1977), pp. 149–57; idem, *The Three Orders: Feudal Society Imagined,* trans. Arthur Goldhammer (Chicago, 1980; French edition, 1978); Patrick J. Geary, *Furta sacra: Thefts of Relics in the Central Middle Ages* (Princeton, N.J., 1978); Lester K. Little, "La morphologie des malédictions monastiques," *Annales: ÉSC* (1979): 43–60; idem, *Religious Poverty and the Profit Economy in Medieval Europe* (Ithaca, N. Y., 1978), pp. 173–82; Michel Mollat, *The Poor in the Middle Ages,* trans. Arthur Goldhammer (New Haven, Conn., 1986; French edition, 1978); Gabrielle Spiegel, "The Reditus regni ad stirpem Karoli Magni: A New Look," *French Historical Studies* 7 (1971): 145–74, reprinted in eadem, *The Past as Text,* pp. 111–37; eadem, "The Cult of St. Denis and Capetian Kingship," *Journal of Medieval History* 1 (1975): 43–60, reprinted in eadem, *The Past as Text,* pp. 138–62.

however, these later historians stressed conflict rather than cohesion. Unlike Southern, their investigations moved away from the notion of cohesive, self-constituted individuals. Caroline Bynum made this clear: medieval identities and "discoveries" of interior selves were constructed in accordance with cultural models.[29] In other words, medieval identities were embedded in the cultural milieu.

In the 1980s and 1990s medievalists continued to investigate similar questions, but we also expanded the field of inquiry to include gendered constructs and categories of exclusion. Like others who entered the academy in the 1960s, 1970s, and 1980s, we did so because we felt compelled to investigate a past which spoke to our particular positions in the present.[30] Writing a history of the Middle Ages that included women, Jews, heretics, Muslims, and those who deviated from sexual norms required that we rethink the entire picture.

MONKS . . . AND OUTCASTS

The present book unabashedly draws on some of the latest of these developments while remaining, in each essay, firmly rooted in the *methods* of rigorous historical scholarship. It begins in Part 1 with what might appear to be the most "conservative" approaches. These articles clearly draw upon the traditional tools of the medievalist—paleography, codicolgy, diplomatics, philology, careful reading of texts. Nevertheless, each complicates the old narratives.

In Chapter 1, Patrick Geary's discussion of monastic memory compels us to rethink the way in which the Middle Ages has come to be divided into periods. Geary shows that, far from writing "value free" texts, monks remembered and represented their past in such a way as to construct their present identity. Primary source texts that *appear* on their surface to tell us about rapacious lords and a wholesale social "mutation" around the year A.D. 1000 could be, as Geary shows in the instance of a text from the monastery of St. Victor of Marseille, late confections that constructed a certain version of the past in order to constitute present realities.

What makes Geary's argument exceptionally important is that part of

29. Bynum, "Did the Twelfth Century Discover the Individual?"
30. Important works include John Boswell, *Christianity, Social Tolerance and Homosexuality: Gay People in Western Europe from the Beginning of the Christian Era to the Fourteenth Century* (Chicago, 1980); R. I. Moore, *The Formation of a Persecuting Society: Power and Deviance in Western Europe, 950–1250* (Oxford, 1987); Caroline Bynum, *Holy Feast and Holy Fast: The Religious Significance of Food to Medieval Women* (Berkeley, 1987).

his story is not new. Historians have realized for a long time that monks of the eleventh and twelfth centuries invented a past in order to legitimize their claims in the present.[31] But Geary is the first to register the full implications of those inventions for the way in which we conceive of the story of the Middle Ages. Geary uses the monastic invention of the past to speak to a controversy that rages today, in the waning years of the second millennium, about the reality and extent of the "transformation of the year 1000" and its importance for our understanding of the social and political history of Europe. Geary argues that the mutationist controversy was in effect created by monks in whose interest it was to construct a caesura between the ninth and the eleventh centuries. In Geary's hands, texts that other historians have interpreted as transparent windows onto a major historical break become mirrors that reflect back the original inventors of that break.

Geary's essay challenges us to ask why so many of us at the end of the twentieth century remain invested in this narrative about a radical rupture between the ninth and the eleventh centuries. Is it—as he himself has suggested—the continuing influence of a discourse created for us by Bloch, Southern, Duby, and others?[32] Are we imposing a modernizing assumption that "order" can exist only when there is a well-organized bureaucratic "state"?[33]

In Chapter 2, Barbara H. Rosenwein looks at a monastery, Saint-Maurice of Agaune, that had been neatly tucked away for years, far from the historiographical mainstream of Western monasticism. Until now, medieval historians who have bothered to look at Agaune at all have categorized it as a *laus-perennis* cloister, a monastery practicing the perpetual liturgy of a group of Byzantine monks. Through a thoroughly traditional study of the primary sources (informed, however, by postmodern doubt), Rosenwein discovers that the term "laus perennis" is a relatively recent creation; that the liturgy practiced at Agaune was a product of Western practices and traditions right in the Rhône Valley where Saint-Maurice

---

31. See, for instance, Albert D'Haenens, *Les invasions normandes en Belgique au XIᵉ siècle,* Recueil de Travaux d'Histoire et de Philologie, ser. 4, 38 (Louvain, 1967), pp. 164–68; Giles Constable, "Forgery and Plagiarism in the Middle Ages," *Archiv für Diplomatik* 29 (1983): 20–21; Sharon Farmer, *Communities of Saint Martin: Legend and Ritual in Medieval Tours* (Ithaca, N.Y., 1991), chap. 6.

32. Geary, *Phantoms of Remembrance,* p. 23. See also Stephen D. White's discussion of the influence of Richard Southern in his review of the second edition of M. T. Clanchy's *From Memory to Written Record* in *Speculum* 72 (1997): 131–32.

33. Much recent work on dispute settlement in the Middle Ages makes this point implicitly. For bibliography, see Little and Rosenwein, *Debating the Middle Ages,* pp. 111–12, to which should be added Richard E. Barton, "Power and Lordship in Maine, c. 890–1110" (Ph.D. diss., University of California, Santa Barbara, 1997), pp. 272 ff.

was situated; and that its highly organized, ceaseless liturgy must be understood in the context of local interests, piety, and power. Rosenwein's article unhinges earlier accounts of the derivative nature of this particular religious practice, emphasizing instead the creative innovations of "local cultures."[34] In so doing, it complicates our narratives about the history of Western monasticism, revealing its astonishing variety and nonlinear developments. It thus functions as a brief for reexamining old categories.

A parallel reexamination is at the heart of Chapter 3. Even in the perspective of recent, gender-conscious conceptualizations, the twelfth-century reformed monastery is male, and women are strictly cloistered. Moreover, with the notable exceptions of Heloise and Hildegard of Bingen, analyses of the intellectual efflorescence of twelfth-century monasticism leave us with the impression that it was a decidedly male phenomenon.[35] Alison Beach gives a different picture by peeking into the one room of the monastery about which we can know something: the scriptorium. There, through a meticulous examination of paleographical and codicological evidence from two double monasteries in Germany, Beach discovers that the official norms of strict separation of the sexes sometimes gave way. "When books needed to be produced," she writes, "intellectual and social barriers came down." Indeed, Beach shows the variety of collaborative forms possible in the twelfth century. One monastery, Admont, respected and encouraged women's education and intellectual contributions; women scribes and editors played an active role there in the construction of the male "voice." At the monastery of Schäftlarn, by contrast, the monks exploited women's copying as a form of manual labor while ignoring women's intellectual growth.

While the articles in Part 1 focus on particulars within texts—or on the surface of the velum upon which those texts were written—they nevertheless suggest that we must move outside of the texts in order to understand their full meaning. The relationship between texts and contexts has been posited by proponents of the linguistic turn as a fundamental dilemma for historians. How do we get beyond the texts that purport to

---

34. Borrowing terms loosely from Clifford Geertz, *Local Knowledge: Further Essays in Interpretive Anthropology* (New York, 1983).

35. In Giles Constable, *The Reformation of the Twelfth Century* (Cambridge, 1996), the reformed monasteries under discussion are almost always male. In Janet Burton, *Monastic and Religious Orders in Britain, 1000–1300* (Cambridge, 1994), p. 87, women's monasticism is characterized by strict enclosure. Bruce Venarde, *Women's Monasticism and Medieval Society: Nunneries in France and England, 890–1215* (Ithaca, N.Y., 1997), shows that women's monasteries proliferated in the period 1080–1170, but one gets no sense that nuns and monks made regular contact.

represent the reality outside of themselves?[36] The articles in Part 2 offer various ways of approaching this dilemma. They build on and expand the contextual approach to religion pioneered by Grundmann, Southern, and Chenu, but they also reflect more current postmodern debates.

In Chapter 4, Robert Brentano examines various sources concerning the city of Sulmona and the life of Peter of Morrone (who became Pope Celestine V), sources which survive in Sulmona and Rome. Among them is the intensely personal and interior text that has come to be known as Peter's autobiography and which shows the kind of holy man Peter seemed within the inner group at his Abruzzi mountain hermitage on the Maiella. Another of the sources, one of which was prepared for the process of Peter's canonization, shows what people in Sulmona, particularly some men and women from professional families, wanted and expected from Peter, and how the hermit, as they saw him, could be helpful to them, and why he should be drawn geographically closer to them. With the help of texts that surround these two, the observer can see how the Peter of each text fits the other. Brentano's goal is not to write a "firm biographical" study; he makes no effort to construct a metanarrative out of fragmentary, perspectival sources. He tries not to elide representations with external reality. The sources, in Brentano's treatment of them, are narratives that tell their own stories. The identities that they purport to represent are textual identities, although, of course, textual identity in the autobiography has a substance and relation to the physical world different from that in the canonization process. Brentano is careful to qualify that the Peter represented in the autobiography is just that—"the autobiography's Peter." The text may be "anxious to show . . . the real Peter," but Brentano is anxious to heighten our awareness of the distance that always exists between texts and external reality.

In Chapter 5, Luigi Pellegrini resolves the relationship between texts and contexts in a different way, one which challenges us to push beyond the smokescreens of the sources. In a study of the interactions of the institutional Church with religious women in Italy, he listens through the "male voice" of the church (the only voice that we have, in most instances) in order to hear the echoes of female initiatives that male institutions, and male-authored texts, attempted both to harness and to sup-

---

36. See Spiegel, *The Past as Text*, chaps. 1, 2, and 3; see also Kathleen Canning, "Feminist History after the Linguistic Turn: Historicizing Discourse and Experience," *Signs: Journal of Women in Culture and Society* 19 (1994): 368–404. Both Spiegel and Canning advocate a "middle" position, one that would recognize the insights of postmodern theory while positing the possibility that historians can and should attempt to write about the reality beyond the texts.

press. His approach thus differs in important ways from the work of
Georges Duby, who insisted that the male voice predominanted in medieval sources, and that the near absence of the female voice was indicative of women's lack of agency in medieval society.[37] Pellegrini argues that
in thirteenth-century Italy women's religious and social needs led to the
unprecedented bending and reshaping of official institutions. It is well
known that the papacy allowed St. Francis and his followers to practice
new forms of religious life based on wandering, voluntary poverty, and
preaching. But it has been thought that women could not participate
in this new movement.[38] Pellegrini challenges this view by focusing on
small groups of religious women (*mulieres religiosae*) who were able to
carry out lives of "radical poverty" through a dynamic and creative use of
traditional institutional channels.

In Chapter 6, Lisa Bitel approaches the issue of texts and contexts by
seeking the broader cultural codes that help to explain the phenomenon
of saintly curses in Irish hagiography. Bitel argues that Irish saintly cursing "shared the theology of Continental maledictions." At the same time,
however, she emphasizes that Irish cursing took root in a distinct political culture, with a vibrant oral tradition, a literary memory of pagan word-
smiths, and a reverence for the literary models of the Old Testament.
Bitel evokes this vivid oral culture, which "maneuvered between pronouncement and inscription," by recounting the lively stories that illustrate the ubiquity of cursing in Ireland and the hierarchical dominance
granted to saints in that tradition.

The articles in Part 3 go beyond text and context to focus on the construction of social categories in medieval Christian society, categories such
as male and female, elite and lower status, insider and outsider. Because
the sacred was so central to this society, the binary saint/outcast represents the construction of those who were most central to it as well as
those who were defined as either outside (for example, heretics and Muslims) or at its lowest levels (for example, beggars and lepers). The essays
in this section make clear that the identity of saints was often constructed
against or even intermingled with the identity of outcasts. But the essays also suggest that binary oppositions—whether saint/outcast, male/

---

37. See especially *Women of the Twelfth Century*, 3 vols. (Chicago, 1997–98; French edition, 1995–
96). For a critical discussion of this aspect of Duby's work, see Sharon Farmer, "La voix des femmes.
Une réception américaine," *Clio*, no. 8 (1998): 161–77.
38. John Moorman, *A History of the Franciscan Order from Its Origins to the Year 1517* (Oxford,
1968), pp. 32–39, 207. Brenda Bolton, "Mulieres Sanctae," in *Women in Medieval Society*, ed. Susan Mosher Stuard (Philadelphia, 1976), pp. 141–58.

female, rich/poor, Christian/Muslim, or saint/leper—were inherently unstable. They could mutate and multiply.

In Chapter 7 Sharon Farmer draws on the insights of feminists of color and postcolonial feminists to challenge the simple binary oppositions that recent gender-sensitive historians have established for the Middle Ages. In so doing she reveals the complex ideas that medieval commentators (clerics, all) had about such categories as "male," "female," "rich," and "poor." Soon enough, in the fourteenth century, voices would be raised to declare hard labor honest and holy.[39] But in thirteenth-century Paris the involuntary poor were associated with flesh, while the "poor in Christ," the members of the mendicant orders, especially the Franciscans and Dominicans, were associated with spirit. The category of poverty, then, was labile: in the context of involuntary beggars it evoked base images—the body rather than the soul, appetite rather than reason—while in the context of holy mendicants it implied incorporeality and spirituality. Indeed, the idea of poverty was so indeterminate and associational that, as Farmer shows, stereotypes used for women, especially lower-status women, attached themselves as well to stereotypes of un- and underemployed men. Farmer suggests that medieval elites did not construct clearly delineated binaries, such as male/female and elite/poor. Rather, they constructed a grid of differences that included poor Christian men, poor Christian women, elite Christian men, and elite Christian women.

Thus medieval clerics struggled with the question of how to "place" and categorize the poor vis-à-vis other members of society. In Chapter 8 Catherine Peyroux shows how the leper, too, "occupied a highly charged and profoundly ambiguous position in medieval society." On the one hand, lepers were cut off from normal social activities, barred from transacting business, relegated to leprosaries, and sometimes put to death after being accused of heinous crimes against humanity. On the other hand, they were the focus of lavish charity and, by the same inversion that we saw with the poor, they were understood as models of holy suffering. By the High Middle Ages, kissing them—according to the hagiographical texts that represented such kisses—was a redemptive act, but it is unclear whether or not the lepers themselves benefited from these kisses: Peyroux ends her essay with the disturbing insight that in the *Life of St. Francis,* the spiritually poor and outcast saint displaces and appropriates the bodily suffering of real lepers. Peyroux's examination of hagio-

---

39. See, for example, the dignity given to labor in Langland's *Piers Plowman,* as in Walter W. Skeat, ed., *The Vision of William concerning Piers the Plowman,* 2 vols. (Oxford, 1886; reprint, 1969), 1:216–17. We thank Allen J. Frantzen for this reference.

graphical texts reminds us of the degree to which medieval identities and behaviors were shaped by deeply embedded cultural codes, but she also shows us how those codes changed over time.

The possibilities of transformation from profane into holy are equally the theme of Chapter 9. Here, Amy G. Remensnyder focuses on "the appropriation and conversion of sacred space": how Christian Spanish soldiers turned Muslim mosques and, later, Mexican temples into Christian churches. The key, as she points out, was rededication of the structure to the Virgin. In Spain, the original building remained and continued to look like a mosque; in the New World, at first, a cross and a statue of the Virgin sanctified a formerly pagan temple as Christian. The presence of Mary, whose power was enlisted on the battlefields and whose womb signified inviolability, sufficed to reconceptualize them as sacred spaces. But, Remensnyder reminds us, cultural meanings and transformations are not always clear-cut; boundaries and differences can be blurred. In reconquest Spain, mosques were deliberately left intact when they were intended as places of worship for Christian conquerors. But when these sacred spaces were intended for people newly conquered and converted, their subversive potential was deemed too potent. In both Spain and the New World, new churches were built for converts; moreover, in the New World, where the conquered peoples had their own traditions of female sacred images, the uses of the Virgin's image were carefully safeguarded.

Remensnyder's "postcolonial" examination of the meanings and uses of the cult of the Virgin takes us a long way from Richard Southern's benign depiction of the rise of the cult of the Virgin and its significance. In addition, much like Geary's work on the early Middle Ages, Remensnyder's investigation of cultural practices that spanned the medieval and early modern periods calls into question conventions of periodization.

Thus the outcast mosque was sanctified and the outcast leper redeemed. The category of saint, too, was pitched against another category or image. In Chapter 10, Thomas Head demonstrates the internal logic that linked the physical bodies of dead saints to their bodies in the afterlife. The same reasoning contrasted those "two-tiered" bodies with the two-tiered bodies of damned heretics. Head discovers a liturgical rite—the ordeal by fire—that was used to authenticate saints' relics: the potentially sacred bits were subjected to fire in a highly controlled ritual procedure. When they did not burn, they were vindicated as the relics of true saints. Head argues that this ritual "had meaning only within an eschatological framework": like their bodies in heaven, which were subjected neither to purgatorial fires nor to the eternal fires of hell, the physical remains of saints did not burn. Conversely, when heretics were executed by fire, their bodies burned "completely," thus demonstrating to the living the punishments that the bodies of the damned would suffer in the afterlife. Head thus skillfully demonstrates the links between the testing of relics, judicial ordeals, and the use of fire in executions. In so doing, he suggests an eschatological perspective that sheds new light on the much-debated topic of judicial ordeals.

Writing nuns, burning bones, cursing saints, conquering Virgins: the essays in this volume bring us face-to-face with the exuberant variety of medieval culture and its religious expression. By stressing careful reading of sources, sensitive exploration of contexts, and critical rethinking of categories, the articles here show their indebtedness to two historiographical streams: that of medieval history in general and that of medieval religion in particular. The questions that they ask, however, and the ways in which they approach the answers, speak to epistemological and social issues of the late twentieth and early twenty-first centuries.

I

New Paradigms, Traditional Tools

Monastic Memory and the Mutation of the Year Thousand

Patrick J. Geary

Monastic culture sought to control the future through the proper performance of liturgy. Prayer, for the living and the dead, was the primary function of the monastic community, a function understood and cherished by all orders of lay society. Moreover, ritual actions showed the proper social hierarchy, they acted out the proper order of the world, or, when necessary, they dramatized the failure of human society to conform to the divine order.[1] Monastic culture's control of the past through the written word was if anything even more effective. By determining what was worthy of memory and how these memorabilia would be recalled, monks effectively established what the past was and would be. In no period was this more true than in the eleventh century, when monastic recording established the broad outlines of the past, outlines that have endured until the present. Among the fundamental legacies of this creative spirit is the transformation of the year thousand itself, which is once more at the center of scholarly debate.

THE ISSUE OF A.D. THOUSAND

Until a few decades ago, when scholars thought of the millennial transformation, they were inclined to think in terms of the nineteenth-century debate about the terrors of the year thousand, the millenarian

---

1. For a particularly striking monastic ritual of order, see Lester K. Little, *Benedictine Maledictions: Liturgical Cursing in Romanesque France* (Ithaca, N.Y., 1993).

and apocalyptic fears and hopes that some eleventh-century texts present as crucial to the millenarian generation. These issues have not disappeared. Indeed, with the approach of the start of a new millennium, interest in these issues has, if anything, intensified among the general public. American and European scholars, first Richard Landes,[2] then Johannes Fried[3] and, more recently, Jean-Pierre Poly,[4] have reopened the question of the terrors of the year thousand that generations of positivist historians thought they had put to rest almost a century ago. True, the original fascination with the year thousand grew from a French romantic tradition of historiography, and both the extent of millenarian expectations and the explanations of these expectations were colored by the romantic movement. However, the arguments that sought to banish the possibility of apocalyptic expectations in the last decades of the tenth and the first decades of the eleventh centuries were, if anything, even more distorted by an urgency to create a scientific history in place of a history more interested in human emotions and psychology.

Still, while the concerns about the dawn of the new age were a feature of the mental and social terrain of the generation that preceded ours by one thousand years, most recent discussion of the millennial generation has focused on quite different issues, which have clustered around the debate over the putative feudal mutation or revolution of the year thousand. Radical political change between the middle of the tenth and the third quarter of the eleventh century cannot be denied. First and most obvious is evidence that, within a few generations on either side of the year thousand, new polities appeared in Italy, Germany, France, and England.

In Italy, the claims of the new rulers met serious objections from various sectors of the aristocracy for whom the novelty of the new dynasties provided the opportunity to challenge their legitimate right to control the spheres of justice and defense that were traditionally the prerogative of the public order. The result in Lombardy was the demise of the Pavian kingdom as a meaningful source of power.[5] In the south, disgruntled

2. Richard Landes, *Relics, Apocalypse, and the Deceits of History: Ademar of Chabannes, 989–1034* (Cambridge, Mass., 1995); "Sur les traces du Millennium: La via negativa," *Le Moyen Âge* 99 (1993): 5–26; "Lest the Millennium Be Fulfilled: Apocalyptic Expectations and the Pattern of Western Chronography, 100–800 C.E.," in *The Use and Abuse of Eschatology in the Middle Ages*, ed. W. D. F. Verbeke, D. Verhelst, and A. Welkenhuysen, Medievalia Lovaniensia ser. 1, studia XV (Louvain, 1988), pp. 137–211.
3. Johannes Fried, "Endzeiterwartung um die Jahrtausendwende," *Deutsches Archiv für Erforschung des Mittelalters* 45:2 (1989): 385–473.
4. Jean-Pierre Poly, "Le sac de cuir: La crise de l'an mil et la première renaissance du droit romain," in *Droits savants et pratiques françaises du pouvoir (XIᵉ–XVᵉ siècles)*, ed. Jacques Krynen and Albert Rigaudière (Bordeaux, 1992), pp. 48–62.
5. See, for a brief overview, Chris Wickham, *Early Medieval Italy: Central Power and Local Society, 400–1000* (London, 1981).

Lombards enlisted Norman adventurers who soon swept away the last vestiges of Lombard and Byzantine rule.[6]

In the Empire, the new Ottonian dynasty vacillated between models of aristocratic collegiality and royal-imperial command under its early kings. Otto III's visit to the tomb of Charlemagne in 1000, whether evidence of an aborted attempt to establish a saint's cult or a more secular attempt to identify the new emperor with his almost-mythic predecessor, is but the most visible sign that these leaders felt a great need to reaffirm their continuity with an earlier age.[7]

The new Capetian dynasty in France saw a rapid erosion of royal power as the offices of count and bishop, traditionally within the prerogative of royal grant, were transformed into hereditary familial titles. Families maintained the form of royal subordination while appropriating the prerogatives of royal power within the territories they controlled.[8] Finally, the most profound changes of all occurred in England, where in the aftermath of the Norman conquest of 1066 an entire ruling elite was swept aside in the interests of a new and predatory Norman aristocracy.[9]

However, contemporary historians are less concerned with these major dynastic changes than they are with the deeper social and economic transformations of Europe that may underlie these dramatic events. The most extreme proponents of deeper transformations, such as the Marxist historians Pierre Dockès and Guy Bois, have argued that the decades around the millennium saw a profound transformation in the organization of agricultural labor, perhaps the most profound since the Romanization of Gaul in the first centuries of the Roman empire.[10] Bois has argued, from a study of a single Burgundian village, that until the late tenth century, chattel slavery continued to be the dominant form of labor organization. His vision of the economic structures of Europe prior to the

---

6. Patricia Skinner, *Family Power in Southern Italy: The Duchy of Gaeta and Its Neighbours, 850–1139* (Cambridge, 1995).

7. The opening of Charlemagne's Tomb in 1000 by Otto III, long interpreted as a millennial act on the part of Otto, has been the subject of considerable revisionist history. See in particular Johannes Fried, *Otto III und Boleslaw Chrobry: Das Widmungsbild des Aachener Evangeliars, der "Akt von Gnesen" und das frühe polnische und ungarische Königtum: Eine Bildanalyse und ihre historischen Folgen* (Stuttgart, 1989); Knut Görich, *Otto III, Romanus Saxonicus et Italicus: Kaiserliche Rompolitik und sächsische Historiographie* (Sigmaringen, 1993); and Gerd Althoff, *Otto III* (Darmstadt, 1997).

8. For a general survey, see Jean Dunbabin, *France in the Making, 843–1180* (Oxford, 1985).

9. The literature on the Norman Conquest is enormous. On the particular aspects of the memory of this event in post-conquest England, see Elisabeth van Houts, "The Memory of 1066 in Written and Oral Traditions," *Anglo-Norman Studies* 19 (1996): 167–79.

10. Pierre Dockès, *La libération médiévale* (Paris, 1979); translated by Arthur Goldhammer, *Medieval Slavery and Liberation* (Chicago, 1982); Guy Bois, *La mutation de l'an mil: Lournand, village mâconnais de l'Antiquité au féodalisme* (Paris, 1989), trans. Jean Birrell as *The Transformation of the Year One Thousand: The Village of Lournand from Antiquity to Feudalism* (Manchester, 1992).

"mutation féodale" consists basically of large landowners owning property and labor on their domains, the successors of the Roman latifundia. Surplus is still drawn off the land through a state system in which towns continue their parasitic relationship with the countryside as centers of control and consumption, not as centers of production or distribution. At the start of the eleventh century, this ancient system undergoes a sudden, revolutionary change. The disappearance of the Carolingian-style state with its ability to protect free small landowners and to coerce slave labor to the benefit of landowners creates a window of opportunity for lower and middling elements of society. The economy becomes increasingly monetized, making possible the growth of an increasingly active land market and with it a new relationship between land ownership, production, consumption, and diffusion. Towns, long stagnant centers of exploitative consumption, become for the first time centers of economic exchange and even production. For a brief period, labor is able to negotiate for its services, escaping the legal status of slavery and realizing a new value and self-worth. This period of freedom does not, however, long endure: within a generation landowners are able to regain control of labor by depriving freeholders of access to allodial land and by forcing peasants under their protection and domination to be serfs within a feudal system that characterized European economic and social structures for centuries.

While this extreme vision of a revolution at the end of the first millennium is easy to set aside,[11] more judicious historians have long argued that between the early tenth and later eleventh centuries, fundamental transformations did indeed appear in European society. This perception can be traced back at least to Marc Bloch,[12] although Georges Duby and his students emphasized the more rapid transformations that they termed, if not a revolution, then at least a "mutation."[13]

While not positing the disappearance of chattel slavery in the eleventh century, these scholars saw the existence, into the eleventh century, of a free peasantry protected if often also exploited by the Carolingian state. Their work has focused primarily on the argument that the demise of the

11. For a discussion, see "L'an mil: Rythmes et acteurs d'une croissance," *Médiévales* 21 (1991): 5–114.

12. Marc Bloch, *Feudal Society* (Chicago, 1961), which first appeared as *La société féodale* (Paris, 1939–40).

13. Georges Duby, *La société aux XIe et XIIe siècles dans la région mâconnaise* (Paris, 1953). The most significant refinements of this view are those of Pierre Bonnassie, *La Catalogne du milieu du Xe à la fin du XIe siècle: Croissance et mutations d'une société*, 2 vols. (Toulouse, 1975–76); and Jean-Pierre Poly and Éric Bournazel, *La mutation féodale, X^e–XIIe siècle*, 2d ed. (Paris, 1991). Unfortunately the English edition, *The Feudal Transformation: 900–1200* (New York, 1991) was made from the first edition.

coercive authority of the traditional state gives rise to a new class of warriors, the milites, or knights, who break free from the old order of royal
and comital authority and succeed in imposing their "malae consue-
tudines," or novel customs, on society. This class is characterized by extreme levels of violence and of independence. Its members work to control the economic production of the areas in which they operate through
the process of incastelization or *incastellemento,* obliging peasants to break
with centuries-old forms of habitation and social organization and to
move into fortified or nucleated communities in which they can be "protected," or rather, more efficiently exploited. The emergence of this class
of warriors is coincidental with attempts to control their violence, led by
the threatened representatives of the old order, especially counts, who,
having transformed their offices into hereditary family property, see the
other free warriors in their jurisdictions escape from their control in the
same way that they had escaped the control of kings.[14]

The rise of banal lordship that was centered on fortified centers of familial control brought with it transformed social and cultural relations:
endogamous marriages contracted to preserve patrimonies and kinship
conceptualizations emphasizing the vertical transmission of land and office replaced Carolingian traditions of exogamous marriage and horizon-
tal kin solidarity that had helped to form and maintain alliances within
a system of royal manipulation and intervention.

These concomitant transformations are familiar to most of us as the
model of the feudal transformation, which, in its complex aspects, reaches
throughout the entire social structure from top to bottom. But did such
transformations actually occur? Recently, French historians, most notably Dominique Barthélemy, have challenged the very notion of a feudal
transformation.

Barthélemy first announced his objection in a short review article focusing on the second edition of *La mutation féodale* by Jean-Pierre Poly
and Eric Bournazel.[15] His argument against the mutationists, not only

14. The argument has been taken up by American medievalists. See Thomas N. Bisson, "The 'Feudal Revolution,'" *Past and Present* 142 (1994): 6–42, and the response by Stephen D. White in "Debate: The 'Feudal Revolution,'" *Past and Present* 152 (1996): 205–23. See also the responses of the
English historians Timothy Reuter and Chris Wickham in *Past and Present* 155 (1997): 177–208.
Thomas Bisson's reply appears in *Past and Present* 155 (1997): 208–25. For another survey of the debate within the context of the work of Georges Duby, see Theodore Evergates, "The Feudal Imag-
inary of Georges Duby," *Journal of Medieval and Early Modern Studies* 27 (1997): 641–60,
esp. 647–48.
15. Dominique Barthélemy, "La mutation féodale a-t-elle eu lieu?" *Annales: ÉSC* 47 (1992): 767–
77. Barthélemy's essays on the year thousand have now been collected and published as *La mutation de l'an mil a-t-elle eu lieu? Servage et chevalerie dans la France des Xe et XIe siècles* (Paris, 1997).

the more extreme proponents such as Guy Bois, but also the moderates, including Poly and Duby, is based on two approaches. First, he argues that the image of eleventh-century society as more violent and anarchistic than that of the Carolingian and immediately post-Carolingian worlds was incorrect. Basing his approach on the work of Americans who apply insights of legal anthropology to their study of conflict, he recognizes that the conflicts, feuds, and disputes that other historians of the period saw as evidence of the breakdown of social order were in fact traditional constituent elements of that order. He argues that European society had operated for well over a century according to certain kinds of negotiations, compromises, and balances between local interests which were at least as important as the formal institutions of delegated authority. The fundamental balance of power, he insists, had not changed. The idea that vigorous Carolingian public institutions and the survival of Roman law were the foundation of a public order in the Carolingian era is a myth.

Second, he argues that the class of free peasants that supposedly survived until the millennium is also a myth. These free land-holders did not exist, nor did a new subclass of milites. The popularist image of the Peace of God and its connections with millenarianism he likewise rejects. Instead, he sees both of these as the continuation of conservative legislation developing out of the Carolingian tradition. Finally, he argues that historians looking for a radical transformation of society were seduced by their sources. The change in the eleventh century that produced an image of increased violence was in fact simply a change in documentation.

In place of the conventional notion of feudal transformation, Barthélemy suggests a model that owes much to the pre-Marc Bloch schema of political historians who saw the decisive change in European society beginning between 843 and 888 and completed by 890 with the disappearance of a unitary political system in the Carolingian world and the appearance of non-Carolingian successor kingdoms. However, even before that point, the Carolingian polity was a complex interpenetration of public and private power, in which a military aristocracy virtually identical to the "knightly" society of the eleventh century exercised its authority through a combination of public office and private lordship. For Barthélemy, the next decisive change in European (read French) society occurred between 1070 and 1130, when the reform of the Church and the expansion of urban power and wealth coincided with the systematic submission of independent lordships and castle holders to princely authority.

This assault both on the model of feudal transformation developed by Georges Duby and his successors as well as on the more radical thesis that classical antiquity survived until the year thousand has predictably generated considerable debate. Barthélemy's principal objects of attack, Poly and Bournazel, replied to his review in the *Revue historique de droit français et étranger*.[16] In the United States, Thomas Bisson has jumped into the fray, while a number of other American scholars have tried to come to terms with the implications of the debate, which raises significant questions that are ideological as well as conceptual and methodological.[17] Nevertheless, the mutationist debate provides an excellent opportunity to explore how one can read and interpret texts, and in particular to see how monastic reformers, masters of the text and thus those most able to speak the past for their contemporaries and successors, were able to set the parameters within which almost a thousand years of historiographical debate would take place.

Opponents of the view that European society changed significantly in the tenth and early eleventh centuries must come to terms with the contemporary and near-contemporary reports of widespread disorder, violence, and political discontinuity. Already in the eleventh century, the very attempts to tie Ottonian, Capetian, Hungarian, Italian, and Danish monarchies to previous traditions indicate the potency of the perception of discontinuity against which new political elites had to struggle. As I have argued elsewhere, monastic writers in the tenth and eleventh centuries restructured and re-created the pasts of their institutions and their regions for very specific purposes. This massive revisionist undertaking was at the heart of what we call the reform movement which demanded a new and more acceptable past on which to base a new and radical future.[18]

A Text and Its Readings

This process largely created the mutationist tradition, not simply by identifying a radical break in social and political tradition, but by claiming that such a break indeed took place. Small wonder that nine hundred years later, conscientious historians would discover the mutation of the year thousand: it had already been created in the eleventh century. In the following pages I will discuss a document that illustrates this point (see page 33). It is found in the cartulary of St. Victor of Marseille, a manu-

16. Jean-Pierre Poly and Éric Bournazel, "Que faut-il préférer au 'mutationnisme'? ou le problème du changement social," *Revue historique de droit français et étranger* 72 (1994): 401–12.
17. Bisson et al., as in note 14.
18. Patrick J. Geary, *Phantoms of Remembrance: Memory and Oblivion at the End of the First Millennium* (Princeton, N.J., 1994).

script compiled between 1080 and 1100.[19] One can explore this document in a variety of ways, giving it both a mutationist reading and a continuity reading. Our purpose is less to decide whether the image it presents is "reality or fiction" than to see how the broad outlines of the mutationist tradition had already been created by a religious community eager to establish a social meaning for their imagined past.

One interpretation of the text would support the mutation thesis to an extraordinary extent. Indeed, this is how Marc Bloch used it in his *Feudal Society:*[20] in 972 Count William the Liberator expels the Saracens from Garde le Freinet.[21] The reconquered land is made part of the royal fisc. The King, Conrad of Burgundy-Arles, grants this fiscal land to Count William the Liberator. William is charged with establishing the territories of the fisc and settling disputes over its possession among the region's magnates. He grants a certain portion of the properties, specifically in the *villa* of La Cadière, to St. Victor in the presence of William, viscount of Marseille, Bishop Honoratus of Marseille, and others, including Abbot Adalard (977–984). The abbot then establishes a contract with two free cultivators, Theodericus and Noe, *ad medium plantum*—that is, they are to bring the land into cultivation by planting vines. When the vines begin to produce, the monastery and the cultivators are each to own half of the property.

The abbot also begins to cultivate his land to establish a seigneurial reserve. The two workers object to this, saying that he is reneging on the agreement that they were to obtain half of the property. They expel the abbot's plowman. The abbot appeals to Viscount William of Marseille for justice. The viscount, however, surrounded by his knights, asks the abbot to invest him with the property for life, during which time he will expel the abbot's enemies, defend him against all opponents, and extend his property. Once this is done, however, William gives the property of La Cadière to his wife Ermengarde. Likewise, a certain Arnulfus Seben-

---

19. *Cartulaire de l'abbaye de Saint-Victor de Marseille* (hereafter cited as CSV), ed. M. Guérard, Collection des cartulaires de France 8–9 (Paris, 1857), 1:104–6, no. 77. On the cartulary of St. Victor of Marseille see Monique Zerner, "L'élaboration du grand cartulaire de Saint-Victor de Marseille," *Les Cartulaires: Actes de la Table ronde organisée par l'Ecole nationale des chartes et le G.D.R. 121 du C.N.R.S. (Paris, 5–7 décembre 1991),* ed. Olivier Guyotjeannin, Laurent Morelle, and Michel Parisse (Paris, 1993), pp. 217–46; and Zerner, "La capture de Maïeul et la guerre de libération en Provence: Le départ des Sarrasins vu à travers les cartulaires provençaux," *Millénaire de la mort de Saint Mayeul 4e abbé de Cluny 994–1994* (Digne-les-Bains, 1997), pp. 199–210, esp. pp. 208–10. Zerner assumes that the document was written "vers l'an mil," but does not discuss her reasons for the date. The section in which it appears was probably copied between 1080 and 1090.

20. Bloch, *Feudal Society,* 1:39.

21. See the text and translation, p. 33, first paragraph.

cus fraudulently obtains a quarter of the property. Abbot Pons, successor of the unfortunate Adalard, records the event for future reference in the hope that eventually the monastery might recover its rights.

What this seems to suggest is the classic image of the mutation: at the beginning, we have a royal authority intact. Fiscal land is granted to the count. However, already public authority is beginning to erode, as local powers begin to act "each according to his own power" (*unusquisque secundum propriam virtutem*). The count attempts to settle this situation through his intervention, making the viscount of Marseille the defender of the monastic interests in the region. But public order cannot protect the settlement he establishes. Local independent cultivators such as Theodericus and Noe can enter into contracts with the owners, but when a conflict arises, the viscount takes advantage of it for his own purposes: surrounded by his knights, he manages to turn the situation against both parties to his own profit. Here is no public justice but simply a power play by the viscount. The small landowners are simply expelled, the abbey is defrauded of its property, and the viscount, the monastery's defensor, becomes its predator. Here is a perfect example of the breakdown of public authority in the last decades of the tenth century, of the suppression of the small landowners who arose from the confusion at the time of the reconquest, and the establishment of the viscount's familial lordship at the expense of the count, the monastery, and the independent landowners.

This reading would support the mutationist tradition in the strongest possible way: a breakdown of public order in the last decades of the tenth century; the disappearance of public justice; the exploitation of monks and of ordinary freemen by a predatory aristocracy strengthened by their new bands of armed warriors who turn church and fiscal land into their hereditary property.

But there are other possible readings. I would like to propose some of the aspects that might lead to slightly different interpretations.

First, one must ask at what remove from the events it purports to describe was the account written. Jean-Pierre Poly is convinced that it is a genuine text of circa 1000 and describes events that took place circa 978.[22] Perhaps. But if so, it was still written approximately twenty years after the events it purports to relate—after the deaths of the principal ac-

---

22. Jean-Pierre Poly, *La Provence et la société féodale, 879–1166: Contribution à l'étude des structures dites féodales dans le Midi* (Paris, 1976), p. 38, n. 42. Poly is correct that the events in the document are for the most part datable, but this does not establish the accuracy of the account in which they are embedded.

tors and thus subject to the possibility of considerable transformation. Moreover, circumstantial evidence suggests that it may have been written later than the year thousand. One hint at a later date is the nature of the document itself. Jean-Pierre Poly has called it "a genuine fragment of a chronicle" ("un véritable fragment de chronique").[23] It is in a sense, but how does such a document find its way into a cartulary? It is not a confirmation, a vidimus or subsequent authentication by an official, or any other sort of traditional diplomatic document. Its closest analogues are so-called *queremoniae* which appear in Southern French and Catalan cartularies and charter collections from the eleventh and twelfth centuries.[24] At St. Victor itself, its closest analogue is an even longer account, written probably in the 1080s to preserve the perspective of the monastery in another long and ongoing dispute.[25] Its form, then, might be more appropriate to the end of the eleventh century than to the beginning.

A second problem with the document is that the other documents it mentions, including the gift of the king (*donatio regis*) and the charter (*carta*) in the charter collection of St. Victor, do not exist. It is of course possible that they did at some time, but it is worth noting that the cartulary of St. Victor groups its charters concerning La Cadière, all of which indicate that in the later eleventh century the monastery was involved with property in this location, but it does not include any record of this alleged earlier donation.[26]

The vocabulary used in the notice is most unusual for the late tenth or early eleventh centuries. In particular, references to milites antedate other such references in the region by almost half a century.[27] Moreover, the earliest designations of military retainers in the area, which date from 1029, use the term *caballarii*[28] rather than milites. Of course, it may simply be that this document contains a very precocious use of the term, but it may alternatively be that the document is a very late composition.

---

23. Ibid, p. 38, n. 42.
24. The best known of these queremoniae is that concerning Hugh of Lusignan and William V of Aquitaine, ed. Jane Martindale, *English Historical Review* 84 (1969): 528–48. This document has generated a large literature. The most extensive, and controversial, is George Beech, Yves Chauvin, and Georges Pon, *Le Conventum (vers 1030): Un précurseur aquitain des premières épopées* (Geneva, 1995). On Catalan queremoniae, a similar type of literature, see Thomas N. Bisson, *The Tormented Voices: Power, Crisis, and Humanity in Rural Catalonia, 1140–1200* (Cambridge, Mass., 1998).
25. CSV 1: 555–64, no. 1089. For a discussion of this document, see Patrick J. Geary, "Vivre en conflit dans une France sans état: Typologie des méchanismes de règlement des conflits (1050–1200)," *Annales: ÉSC* 41 (1986): 1107–33; revised English version, "Living with Conflicts in Stateless France: A Typology of Conflict Management Mechanisms, 1050–1200," in Geary, *Living with the Dead in the Middle Ages* (Ithaca, N.Y., 1994), chap. 7.
26. CSV 1, nos. 30, 75, 76, 77, 78, 80, 81, and 82.
27. Poly, *La Provence*, p. 139.
28. Ibid., pp. 137–39.

The way that individuals are designated in the document raises equally troubling although perhaps insoluble questions. The use of topographics for names of individuals—such as Pontius de Fossis (Pons de Fos)—or of double names such as Arnulfus Sebencus are unusual in this area for the turn of the millennium. Normally, individuals were known by a single name until well into the eleventh century. The Pons de Fos who appears in the text as one of the most powerful men of the area (along with Viscount William) was probably the individual known as Pons the Elder in other later documents,[29] but nowhere else is he called Pons de Fos. This designation de Fos is first carried by Pons IV of Fos in the 1080s.[30] Recent studies on the chronology of onomastic change in the tenth and eleventh centuries suggest that such designations are much more likely to date from the later eleventh century than from the late tenth.[31]

The identity of a number of individuals who appear in the document is also problematic. Other than Viscount William, Abbot Adalard, and Count William, it is very difficult to identify the principals in the document. This is particularly true for the alleged author, Abbot Pons. This is the only document that mentions him. As for Abbot Gisfredus (Gisfredo, necnon abbate), who is said to have witnessed Count William's gift to St. Victor, we are at a loss to identify this figure, although St. Victor had an abbot of this name in 1005. However, if one is to assume that this is the same individual, Abbot Pons was indeed prescient to be able to identify his successor as abbot five years before his own supposed death.

This series of apparent anachronisms and inconsistencies must lead one to ask if it might be possible that this document, rather than being the "smoking gun" demonstrating the feudal mutation in this region, is not simply the first historical interpretation of the events and people of the millennial generation, seen from the perspective of anywhere between

---

29. Ibid., p. 50.

30. On the Fos, see Poly, *La Provence*, p. 96, and in greater detail in the appendix to his thèse, *La société féodale en Provence du 10ᵉ au 12ᵉ siècle* (Thèse du doctorat en droit, Université de Paris II, 1972; Paris Publications de l'A.U.D.I.R. Microéditions Hachette, 1973), "Lignées et domaines en Provence," partie C.

31. For onomastic transformations, see Monique Bourin and Pascal Chareille, eds., *Genèse médiévale de l'anthroponymie moderne* (Tours, 1989–1992) and *L'anthroponymie: Document de l'histoire sociale des mondes méditerranéens médiévaux. Actes du colloque international, Rome, 6–8 octobre 1994*, ed. Monique Bourin, Jean-Marie Martin, and François Menant, Collection de l'École française de Rome 226 (Rome, 1996). However, according to Pierre Bonnassie, the appearance of such name forms in Catalonia is attested from the period prior to 1031. If this pattern found in Catalan sources can be generalized to Provence at this early period, then the onomastic evidence is inconclusive, although even so it may suggest that the account was written, if not a century after the events, then at least about fifty years after the reconquest of the region. See Pierre Bonnassie, "Les inconstances de l'An Mil," *Médiévales*, no. 37 (1999). I am grateful to M. Bonnassie for allowing me to see his criticisms and valuable corrections before their publication.

fifty years and a century later. If it is an interpretative history of the events following the reconquest of Le Freinet, then one might ask if there are other ways that one might interpret these events, ways that present a different sense of the rhythm of change in the later tenth and early eleventh centuries.

Let us first return to the expulsion of the Saracens in 972. Since the publication of Marc Bloch's *Feudal Society* in 1939, the expulsion of the Saracens, the defeat of the Normans, and the defeat and conversion of the Magyars has been presented as the point of departure for a new European history. These alien intruders had destroyed traditional bonds in European society and were at the heart of the radical caesura separating the Carolingian world from that of the first feudal age.

True, the Saracens established a base in the region where they controlled passes, going so far as to capture Maieul, abbot of Cluny, on his way to Rome in 972. However, these Saracens had become an integral part of the political constellation of the region, and their expulsion had more to do with shifting internal politics than with a Christian reaction against an alien body. The lands, contrary to contemporary images presented by Christian authors, were not abandoned. In fact, the region was described by Arab geographers as fruitful and productive. Apparently it was controlled and cultivated by Saracens. Christians who were captured were put to work in the region, not primarily exported to the slave markets of Spain. William the Liberator's predecessor but one, Hugh of Arles, apparently made a treaty with the Saracens, using them (and they him) in the balance of power in the lower Rhône. After Hugh's departure for Italy, he was succeeded by Count Boso, an ally of Hugh of Arles and the husband of Hugh's niece, Bertha. Boso abandoned Hugh and divorced Bertha to remarry, thus becoming an enemy of Hugh and his allies still in Provence. This divorce may also have created problems with Hugh's traditional Saracen allies. At any rate, William the Liberator, son of Boso and conqueror of Le Freinet, was acting less as a defender of Christianity than as a count pursuing a new policy against the allies of his family's enemy.[32]

Certainly, the conquest of Le Freinet seems to have introduced new dynamics into the exercise of power in the region. William the Liberator's victory was his own, not that of King Conrad. It was the successful expansion of his power which could be ratified by the king, but the king actually had no particular role in the events. However, one could ar-

---

32. Concerning Hugh of Arles and the expulsion of the Saracens, see Geary, *Phantoms of Remembrance*, pp. 135–46.

gue that the kings of Burgundy-Arles never had such a role, nor had the Carolingians before them. Hugh of Arles had been an autonomous ruler, and before him the nominal kings of Burgundy were distinguished by their lack of authority outside a very small range of monasteries such as St. Maurice d'Agaune. This was an old story even by the 880s, when the kingdom was established. Provence had been ruled by *patricii* in the Merovingian period, and the Carolingians had accorded extraordinarily wide powers to their counts of Arles, who were already acting, in the ninth century, in extremely independent ways. Thus one can hardly talk about a revolution of authority following the defeat of the Saracens. Rather, one must consider it business as usual.

The situation of the viscounts of Marseille, the nominal agents of the counts, is perhaps similar. Their origins are from a comital family in the Viennois to the north. Their position in Marseille was not of independence-seeking agents of the counts but was the result of intervention by King Conrad, who granted them important fiscal rights in Provence during the lifetime of Count Boso and when Hugh of Arles, with whom they may have been allied, still exercised considerable authority in Provence.[33] In Marseille, the family obtained hereditary control of the offices of both viscount and bishop: we see Viscount William beside his brother Honoratus in our document. This pattern will endure for several generations.

Moreover, in the tenth century, St. Victor of Marseille had no existence independent of the cathedral. The ancient monastery was restored in 977 by none other than Honoratus; however, his family dealt with it as a proprietary church through the end of the tenth century. It had no more than five monks, and its first "abbots," including the Adalard and Pons of our document, are so obscure that the historian of St. Victor, Paul Amargier, prefers to consider the first genuine abbot Gisfredus, installed in 1005, at a time when the monastery actually began an independent existence, with twenty-one monks.[34] The alleged confiscation of monastic property by the protector is thus attributed to a time when the monastery may not have actually existed. Certainly there was no sense of a distinction between the lands of the viscomtal family and those of its religious institution. The actual restoration of the monastery only occurred in 1005, and this at the instigation of the family of the viscounts.

33. On the origins of this important family see Poly's appendix, "Lignées et domaines en Provence," partie I, as in note 30 above.
34. Paul A. Amargier, *Un âge d'or du monachisme: Saint-Victor de Marseille, 990–1090* (Marseille, 1990); Poly, *La Provence*, p. 73.

Rather than seeing Honoratus and William as the destroyers of the monastic property, it would be proper to see them as the reformers.

However, this reform was only a beginning. In the 1030s, inspired by other reform movements, under Abbot Isnard of St. Victor, the monastery began a familiar process of reform that was much more radical than that experienced at the start of the century.[35] In the course of the 1060s through the 1080s, the monastery under Abbot Richard undertook a much more systematic program of demanding autonomy and rights to its lands and estates. Those involved in this more radical reform looked to the traditional supporters of the institution, the viscomtal family, as enemies, not as protectors. It is in the context of this new and radical reform that the image of the viscounts and their knights as rapacious, violent usurpers was created. Our document may confirm the image of the "feudal mutation," then, because its author, long before Poly or Duby, was among the generation that created the myth of the mutation which subsequent historians have accepted for almost a millennium. Not, of course, that the world was static in the tenth century: important gradual changes had indeed been taking place since the ninth century, but these changes were only incorporated into a new vision of the world as part of the reform, a reform based as much on creating a different understanding of the past as on creating a new future.

35. Amargier, *Un âge d'or.*

APPENDIX

Cartulaire de l'abbaye de Saint-Victor de Marseille, ed. M. Guérard, Collection des cartulaires de France, VIII (Paris: Typographie de Ch. Lahure, 1857), vol. 1, no. 77, pp. 104–6.

Notitia conventionum villę Cathedrę inter Adalardum, abbatem sancti Victoris, et Wilelmum, vicecomitem Massilię, quam ego Pontius abba, successor predicti, volo scribere, precipiente et cogente mihi patre meo, Inguilberto, quatinus presentes et futuri cognoscant quid credere debeant, vel quid refutare. Igitur cum gens pagana fuisset e finibus suis, videlicet de Fraxeneto, expulsa, et terra Tolonensis cępisset vestiri et a cultoribus coli, unusquisque secundum propriam virtutem rapiebat terram, transgrediens terminos, ad suam possessionem. Quapropter, illi qui potentiores videbantur esse, altercatione facta, inpingebant se ad invicem, rapientes terram ad posse, videlicet Wilelmus vicecomes et Pontius de Fossis.

Notice of the agreement of the villa of La Cadière between Adalard, Abbot of St. Victor [ca 977–ca. 984] and William, viscount of Marseille, which I, Pons, abbot, successor of the above mentioned, wish to write, on the order and encouragement of my father Inguilbertus so that the present and future [generations] may know how much they should believe or what they should deny. Therefore, when the pagan people had been expelled from their territories, that is, from Le Freinet, and the land of Toulon [972] began to be invested and to be cultivated by farmers, each one was crossing boundaries and seizing land for himself according to his own power. For this reason, those who were seen to be the more powerful when they had started a dispute were pushing against each other, stealing land as much as they could, that is, Viscount William and Pons of Fos.

Qui Pontius pergens ad comitem, dixit ei: "Domine comes, ecce terra, soluta a vinculo paganę gentis, tradita est in manu tua, donatione regis. Ideo rogamus ut pergas illuc, et mittas terminos inter oppida et castra et terram sanctuariam, nam tuę potestatis est eam terminare, et unicuique distribuere quantum tibi placitum fuerit." Quod ille ut audivit, concessit, et continuo ascendens in suis ęquis perrexit. Cumque fuisset infra fines Catedre villę, cępit inquirere nomina montium et concava vallium et aquarum et foncium. Que cum audisset, misit terminos in terra sanctuaria, qui

This Pons went to the count [William II the Liberator, ca. 970–993] and said to him "Lord count, behold this land that has been redeemed from the bonds of the pagan people has been handed over into your hands by a gift of the king. Therefore we ask that you go there and establish boundaries between the towns and the castles and the land of the sanctuary, for it is in your power to establish it and to distribute to each the amount that is pleasing to you." When the count had heard this he agreed, and immediately mounting his horse he went there. And when he was within the

sunt in carta quę est in cartulario sancti Victoris, ita dicendo: "Quantum ego habeo infra istos terminos donatione regis, hoc est fiscum regalem, dono sancto Victori et monachis ibidem excubantibus." Haec donatio facta est coram Wilelmo vicecomite, et fratre suo episcopo, et Theoderico atque Noe, fratribus, sive Gisfredo, necnon abbate, et Ranganardo monacho.

boundaries of the villa of La Cadière he began to ask the names of the mountains and hollows of the valleys and the waters and springs. When he had heard them he established the boundaries in the sanctuary's lands that are in the charter that is in the charter collection of St. Victor, saying: "As much as I have within these boundaries by royal donation, that is the royal fisc, I give to St. Victor and to the monks who keep watch there." This donation was made in the presence of Viscount William and his brother the bishop [Honoratus, bishop of Marseille] and Theodericus and Noe, brothers, and Abbot Gisfredus and the monk Ranganardus.

Is ita gestis, venerunt Theodericus et Noe, fratres, ad Adalardum abbatem, rogantes eum, verbis blandis, ut concederet eis Catedram vestire ad medium vestem. Quod et factus est. Abbas vero, missis bobus, cępit terram, quę est ante aecclesiam sancti Damiani, ambienter excolere, et huc illuc rumpere terram, ad faciendas condaminas. Noe vero et Theodericus dixerunt ad alterutrum: "Isti monachi semper habebunt totam terram ruptam; et nos, qui dicimur vestitores, quandoque erimus illusi, nichil habentes!" Et, invidia ducti, ejecerunt boves arantes, flagellantes bubulcum; insuper, quandam concam marmoream, quę satis videbatur apta officiis monasterialibus, confregerunt ante aecclesiam supradicti sancti. Abbas vero et monachi, haec audientes, nimium irati, pergentes ad Wilelmum, vicecomitem Massilię, complanxerunt se, ita dicentes: "Domine, terram, quam comes terminavit et in tua defensione misit, nescimus quid opus habeat monachis, nisi justitiaveris nobis Theodericum et Noe, qui nostros boves expulerunt, et bubul-

When these things had been done, Theodericus and Noe, brothers, came to Abbot Adalard, asking him, with seductive words, that he would grant to invest them with La Cadière ad medium vestem. This was done. The abbot, after sending a plowman, eagerly began to work the land that is before the church of St. Damian and to break the land here and there in order to establish a demesne. Noe and Theodericus said to each other: "These monks still have all of the plowed land and we, who call ourselves the holders, we will be mocked because we will have nothing." And, led by envy, they drove out the plow animals, beating the plowman and, moreover, they broke a marble vessel before the church of the above-mentioned saint which was most appropriate for the use of the monastic personnel. When the abbot and monks heard this they were extremely angry and, going to Viscount William of Marseille, they complained to him, saying, "Lord this land for which the count had set boundaries and placed under your protection, we do not know

cum ciciderunt; insuper quoddam vas nobis utile confregerunt.

Qui audiens, dixit: "Ite, et tali die sitis ibi, quia ego ero, et habeamus placitum cum illis." Interea, cum pergerent ad placitum, et abbas cum suis monachis multum complangeret se ad vicecomitem de supradictis fratribus, ait ille: "Domine abba, colligite me in medietatem terrę et vestite me, in tali convencione, ut, quandiu vixero, teneam et possideam, et, post discessum meum, reverta[tu]r ad sanctum Victorem; et ego expellam omnes inimicos foras, non solum istos qui talia vobis fecerunt, sed et de omnibus defendam vos, et dilatabo terminos illos." Milites vero cuncti, causa adolationis, ita laudaverunt, ut abbas vestiret eum. Adolardus vero, vicarius Massilię, fraudulenter dixit abbati: "Domine abba, isti vestri vestitores exibuerunt vobis unquam mel aut ceram?" Respondentibus monachis: "Nunquam."

"Juro per Deum omnipotentem, ait, quia, alio die, obviavi Salomonem judeum, ducentem quattuor asinos onustos melle. Quem cum percontatus essem unde venisset, et, respondente illo: de vestro Sancto Damiano,—et quis tibi vendidit, aio, tantum mel?—Audivi ilico: 'Theodericus et Noe.'" Cumque multi multa dicerent, abbas, nimium credulus promissionibus vicecomitis et suorum, apprehendens virgam suam, dixit: "In tali convencione ut loquuti estis, audiente me, vestio vos." Et ita ves-

what value there might be for the monks unless you give us justice against Theodericus and Noe, who expelled our cattle and cut down our plowman and besides they destroyed a vessel that was useful to us."

When he had heard this he said, "Go, and on a certain day be there, and I will be there also, and we will have a meeting with them." Then, when they had come to the meeting, and the abbot with his monks had made many complaints against the above-mentioned brothers to the viscount, the viscount said, "Lord Abbot, admit me as a joint proprietor of this land and invest me with the provision that as long as I shall live I shall hold and possess it, and after my death, it will return to Saint Victor; and I will expel all of your enemies, not only those who are doing these things to you, but I will defend you against all, and I will extend your boundaries." All of the knights, because of flattery, approved of the plan that the abbot should invest him. Adolardus, the vicar of Marseille, fraudulently said to the abbot, "Lord abbot, have these your cultivators ever delivered any honey or wax?" The monks answered, "Never."

"I swear by the almighty God," he said, "the other day, I met the Jew Salomon, leading four donkeys loaded with honey. When I asked him from whence he was coming he answered, 'from your Saint Damianus.' 'And who sold you so much honey?' I asked. I heard directly, 'Theodericus and Noe.'" And when many had said many things, the abbot, greatly believing the promises of the viscount and of his men, taking up his crozier, said, "In such an agreement as you have spoken, hear me, I invest you." And

tivit eum, presente episcopo fratre suo, et Deodato canonico, Adalardo, et Gisfredo, et Ranganardo monacho.

Nunc intentis auribus audiatur et mente figatur, idcirco scripsisse me hanc noticiam, instigante patro meo, quoniam terram sancti Victoris videbamus membratim carpere et ceu a beluis particulatim dilaniare, ab Arnulfo scilicet Sebenco, qui fraudulenter adquisivit sibi quartonem Cathedrę ab antecessore meo Bernardo, necnon et a Wilelmo vicecomite, qui nuper professus est se esse terrę sanctuarię defensorum. Mortua uxore sua, dotavit Cathedram uxori suę Ermengarde, quam postea duxit, et hęc omnia consiliante Arlulfo, filio suo.

thus he invested him in the presence of the bishop his brother, and the canon Deodatus, Adalardus, and Gisfredus, and the monk Ranganardus.

Now incline your ears that it might be heard and fixed in your mind: therefore I have written this notice, urged by my father, how we have seen the land of St. Victor ripped to pieces and torn to shreds as if by wild beasts, that is by Arnulfus Sebencus, who fraudulently acquired for himself a quarter of La Cadière from my predecessor Bernardus [abbot ca. 965] and by Viscount William, who not long ago had proclaimed himself to be the defensor of the lands of this sanctuary. When his wife [Belielda] died, he gave La Cadière as a dower to his wife Ermengarde, whom he then married, and all of this he did with the advice of his son Arlulfus.

C H A P T E R   T W O

Perennial Prayer at Agaune

Barbara H. Rosenwein

Perhaps no moment was so crucial to the formation of the Christian West as the turn of the sixth century. It was then that the king of the Franks, Clovis (481–511), converted to Catholic Christianity; that Pope Gelasius (492–96) shaped the near-final form of the Roman Mass; and, just a bit later, that Saint Benedict (ca. 480–550) wrote his *Rule* for monks. By the end of the same century, Gregory the Great could draw upon its legacy with stunning virtuosity, sending missionaries to convert the Anglo-Saxons (by working through their king), putting the finishing touches on a few Mass chants, and writing up the *Life* of St. Benedict in one of his *Dialogues.*[1]

The foundation of Saint-Maurice d'Agaune is never invoked in this litany of achievements. It ought to be. The story of the Christianization of the West and the monasticism that accompanied it, as historians generally tell it, leads straight past Agaune. It starts at Monte Cassino, goes up the Italian Peninsula, on through Gaul, over to Kent, then back again to the Continent via the Anglo-Saxon reformers of the eighth century. Even when the monasticism of the fierce Irish reformer Columbanus (ca. 540–615) is added to the picture, it remains extraordinarily tidy. We are only

This paper owes its existence to two colleagues: Lester K. Little, to whom it is dedicated, and Ian N. Wood, whose encouragement and generosity will be evident throughout. I am grateful to Sharon Farmer for her comments on an earlier draft. Bryon White and Laura Wilson Baird were able research assistants. I thank as well Loyola University Chicago Research Services for a grant to carry out research in Switzerland in connection with this project.
1. On Gelasius, Gregory, and the Mass, see Josef A. Jungmann, *The Mass of the Roman Rite: Its Origins and Development (Missarum sollemnia),* trans. Francis A. Brunner, 2 vols. (New York, 1951), 1:55–63. For Gregory's *Life* of Benedict, see Grégoire le Grand, *Dialogues,* vol. 2, ed. Adalbert de Vogüé and Paul Antin, Sources chrétiennes 260 (Paris, 1979), pp. 126–249.

Map 1: The Central Rhône Valley in the Sixth Century

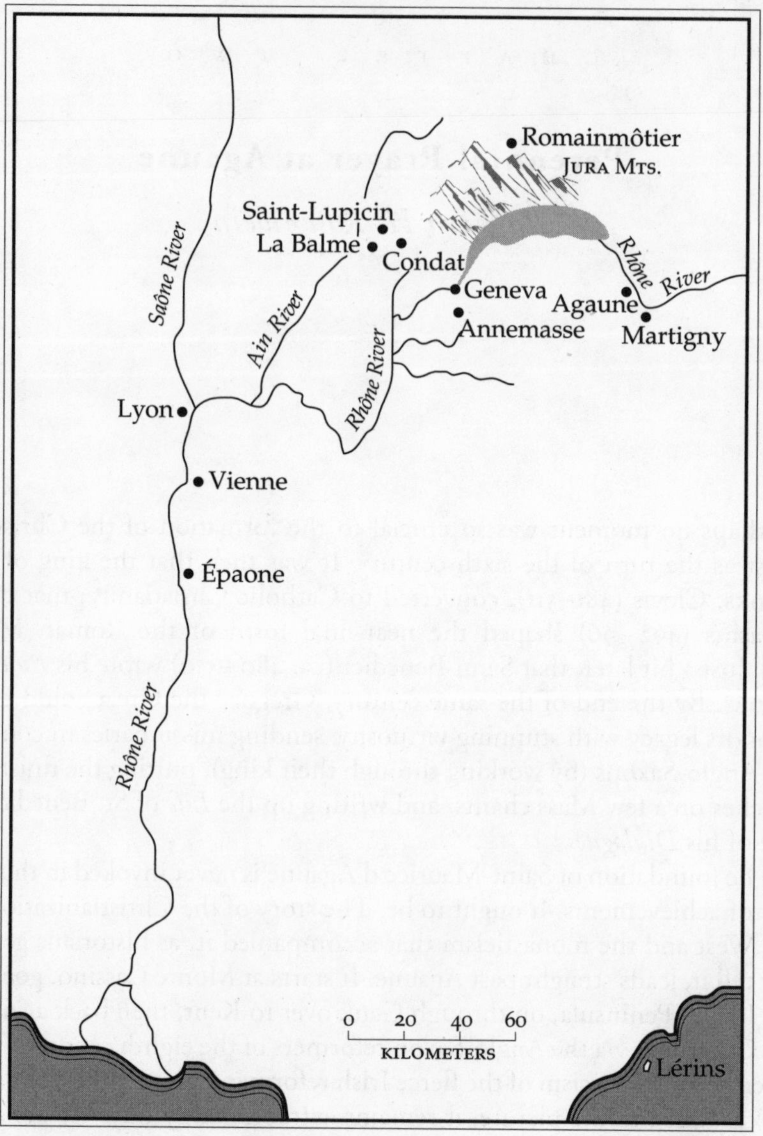

now discovering how much this trim linearity owes to omission: it leaves out regional variants that tellingly reflected and at the same time modified Western religious identity.[2]

Saint-Maurice is a case in point. Though it has sometimes received at-

2. Even the relatively recent appreciation of the so-called mixed rule of Columbanian monasteries does not do justice to the immense variety of religious life in the Merovingian West. For the mixed rule, see Joseph Semmler, ed., "Ordines aevi regulae mixtae," in *Corpus consuetudinum monasti-*

tention, its monasticism has seemed derivative—a pale imitation of Byzantine monasticism and for this reason not really part of the Western tradition.[3] We shall see that this is a misconception.

Rather, Saint-Maurice is a compelling and revealing counterpart to Frankish monasticism. The monastic life that was instituted at Agaune, rather than telling us about Byzantium, teaches us instead about the cultural gaps between East and West. Like Clovis, Sigismund, prince of Burgundy and founder of Saint-Maurice, broke with his father's religion, allied himself with Catholic bishops, and devoted himself to the cult of saints.[4] By founding a monastery, rather than acting simply as a monastic patron, Sigismund committed himself to his new religion in ways especially pleasing to his episcopal advisors. Indeed, the foundation of Saint-Maurice reveals graphically a little-recognized aspect of the sixth-century Church: episcopal-monastic symbiosis in the form of liturgy. The "social meaning" of Saint-Maurice lies in large measure in the lives and concerns of the bishops who participated in its foundation.

SLEEPLESS MONKS IN THE WEST?

Sigismund, recently converted from Arian to Catholic Christianity, founded the monastery of Saint-Maurice in 515.[5] Perched above the

---

carum, vol. 1: Initia consuetudinis benedictinae (Siegburg, 1963), pp. 3–91. For the "linear" view, see C. H. Lawrence, Medieval Monasticism: Forms of Religious Life in Western Europe in the Middle Ages (2d ed., London, 1989). For exceptional studies that emphasize regional variety, see Ian N. Wood, "A Prelude to Columbanus: The Monastic Achievement in the Burgundian Territories," in Columbanus and Merovingian Monasticism, ed. H. B. Clarke and Mary Brennan, BAR International Series 113 (Oxford, 1981), pp. 3–32, and Alain Dierkens, "Prolégomènes à une histoire des relations culturelles entre les îles britanniques et le continent pendant le Haut Moyen Âge. La diffusion du monachisme dit colombanien ou iro-franc dans quelques monastères de la région parisienne au VIIᵉ siècle et la politique religieuse de la reine Bathilde," in La Neustrie: Les pays au nord de la Loire de 650 à 850. Colloque historique international, ed. Hartmut Atsma, 2 vols. (Sigmaringen, 1989), 2:371–94.

3. Friedrich Prinz, Frühes Mönchtum im Frankenreich: Kultur und Gesellschaft in Gallien, den Rheinlanden und Bayern am Beispiel der monastischen Entwicklung (4. bis 8. Jahrhundert) (2d ed.; Munich, 1988), pp. 102–12, is well aware of the importance of Saint-Maurice as a model for other monasteries, but he too derives its unique liturgy from Byzantium, and he largely assimilates its impact to that of Lérins.

4. On Sigismund, see Ian N. Wood, "Avitus of Vienne: Religion and Culture in the Auvergne and the Rhône Valley, 470–530" (Ph.D. diss., Corpus Christi College, Oxford, 1979). At the time of Agaune's foundation, Sigismund in fact already had the title rex, though King Gundobad, his father, was still alive. See Fredegar, Chronicle 3.33 MGH SSrerMerov 2:104: "Gundebadi filius Sigymundus apud Genavensim urbem [i.e., Geneva] villa Quatruvio [Carouge] iusso patris sublimatur in regnum." [At Carouge, near Geneva, Sigismund, son of Gundobad, was raised to the kingship by order of his father.] Yet, according to Marius of Avenches, Chronicle a. 516, this elevation to royalty occurred in 516, after the death of Sigismund. See La chronique de Marius d'Avenches (455–581): Texte, traduction et commentaire, ed. and trans. Justin Favrod, Cahiers Lausannois d'histoire médiévale 4 (2d ed., Lausanne 1993), p. 70.

5. The conversion may have been as much as a decade earlier. See Wood, "Religion and Culture," p. 210.

Rhône river about 64 kilometers due east of Geneva, its site is even today replete with numerous water springs; in the Roman period, it had been dedicated to the nymphs. By 515, however, it had come to be known as the burial place of the "Theban martyrs"—Saint Maurice and his fellow soldiers. A chief feature of the new monastery was its distinctive liturgy—the "laus perennis," as every modern historian who writes about the matter puts it. To carry it out, the monks were divided into squadrons—called *turmae*—and spelled one another throughout the day and night.[6] There had been nothing like it in the West before, and ever afterward it would be associated with Agaune. Only a decade or so later, Saint Benedict's *Rule* would allot about four hours a day to the liturgy. To historians, Saint-Maurice's round of prayer seems an aberration. Indeed, they consider it an import. Friedrich Prinz's view fairly represents the general consensus:

> [The *laus perennis*] came from Constantinople, where it was at home in the monasteries of the "Akoimetoi". The question of how it came to Burgundy may be answered quickly: Avitus [bishop] of Vienne exchanged letters with the Patriarch of Constantinople and also wrote to the Emperor Anastasius at the behest of King Sigismund.[7]

Prinz, like other recent historians, here follows the pronouncement made in 1954 by the archivist and pre-eminent historian of Agaune, Jean-Marie Theurillat. In fact, however, Theurillat was simply repeating a historiographical commonplace that he considered perfectly reasonable: hadn't the *Life* of Anthony been translated into Latin? Were not the monastic fathers of the West eager to visit Eastern hermits? Had Westerners not made the arduous pilgrimage to Palestine? The *laus perennis* was simply one more prestigious Eastern institution to take root in the West.[8]

Nevertheless, there are problems. No contemporary sixth-century source dealing with Agaune speaks of its *laus perennis;* those words were simply never used. Contemporaries spoke instead of its psalmody, which lasted through both night and day: it was "assiduous psalmody" or

---

6. The best "working hypothesis" about the way that this liturgy worked in practice is in François Masai, "La 'Vita patrum iurensium' et les débuts du monachisme à Saint-Maurice d'Agaune," in *Festschrift Bernhard Bischoff zu seinem 65. Geburtstag,* ed. Johanne Autenrieth and Franz Brunhölzl (Stuttgart, 1971), pp. 43–69 at p. 66, n. 85. Masai suggests that all the monks sang the canonical hours, but the intervals were filled, each in turn, by one *turma.* The seven intervals thus required seven *turmae.* I thank Chanoine Olivier Roduit, archivist at Saint-Maurice, for his help on this and other issues.

7. Prinz, *Frühes Mönchtum im Frankenreich,* p. 103.

8. Jean-Marie Theurillat, *L'Abbaye de St.-Maurice d'Agaune des origines à la réforme canoniale, 515–830 environ = Vallesia* 9 (1954): 103–4. The argument in favor of the Akoimetoi had been made quite strongly in 1907 by Henri Leclercq in *DACL* I, s.v. Agaune, esp. col. 859, but even then it was not new. See below, n. 12.

"hymns of psalmody day and night" or "divine songs by day and night" or "psalmody by *turmae* both night and day," and so on.[9] Moreover, no Western source at the time of Agaune's foundation nor for centuries afterward breathed a word about the Eastern origins of its unique liturgy. If we wish to understand perennial prayer at Agaune, we shall have to put away preconceptions about an institution called *laus perennis* and look at the few facts that remain.

Avitus of Vienne is certainly the right starting point, as he was a confidant of Sigismund, and his homily on the dedication of the church of Agaune in 515 proves that he was intimately involved with the new monastic foundation.[10] Others—such as Bishop Maximus of Geneva—were involved as well. But with Avitus we have a whole corpus of authentic texts—letters, poems, homilies—that we do not have for the others; and with Avitus, too, we clearly have someone who knew something about what was happening at Constantinople. What precisely did he know about the Akoimetoi? What did anyone know? These are our first questions.

We are not in a terribly good position to answer them, for modern scholars themselves know rather little about the Akoimetoi. Had Avitus known what we do, he would have had the following information to hand:

The Akoimetoi were founded circa 405 in Constantinople by a monastic leader named Alexander (d. ca. 430). Persecuted as social deviants and heretics, they soon moved outside the capital but made their presence felt there at crucial moments. Akoimetoi means Sleepless Ones, and the *Life* of Alexander details how the saint created his liturgy (which was, however, revised several times even during his lifetime) by trying to adhere literally to various biblical phrases—in particular Psalm 1.2 "and on his law he shall meditate day and night"—and by interpreting various bibli-

---

9. Gregory of Tours, *Libri historiarum decem* [henceforth *Historiae*], 3.5, MGH SSrerMerov 1/pt. 1, p. 101: "psallentium . . . assiduum"; Eucherius, *Passio acaunensium martyrum,* Appendix 1, MGH SSrerMerov 3:40: "die noctuque psalmorum hymni decantatio non desistit"; *Vita abbatum acaunensium,* c. 3, MGH SSrerMerov 3:176: "die noctuque . . . cantionibus divinis insisterent"; *ChLA* 13:37, no. 558 (a privilege of Clovis II for Saint-Denis drawn up in 654): "psallencius per turmas . . . die noctoque." In a text probably drawn up in the ninth century (see Theurillat, p. 55), it is "ut . . . norma psallentii perenniter ageretur ibi imperpetuo juges laudes constituit."

10. The works of Avitus have been edited a number of times but are differently organized; here reference will be made to the two most accessible publications: Avitus, *Opera quae supersunt,* ed. Rudolf Peiper, MGH AA 6/pt. 2; and *Oeuvres complètes de saint Avit, évêque de Vienne,* ed. Ulysse Chevalier (new ed., Lyon, 1890).

Avitus's works will be abbreviated thus:

> *Contra Eutychianam haeresim* = *CE*
> *Epistolae* = *Ep.*
> *Homiliae* = *Hom.*

All quotations here are from the Chevalier edition.

cal numbers as injunctions. He set up a monastic round of twenty-four offices to fill every hour; the monks were divided into choirs and took turns at the psalms and hymns. Alexander's biographer calls the result (in modern Latin translation) *assidua hymnodia* or *perennis hymnologia*.[11] This is fundamentally equivalent to *laus perennis,* since a hymn was a song of praise. But the precise term "laus perennis"—at least when used to re-fer to a liturgical round, even to that of the Akoimetoi—seems to be a modern construct.[12]

By the middle of the fifth century, the Akoimetoi comprised a whole group of monasteries and were renowned for their orthodoxy. This was the period at Constantinople when doctrines about the nature of Christ were both matters of political strategy and issues of the deepest personal significance.[13] The Akoimetoi were vocal opponents of the Monophysite heresy of Eutyches (ca. 378–after 451), a monastic leader who denied that Christ existed in two natures, insisting rather that He was pure Godhead. By the same token, the Sleepless Ones were known as ardent supporters

11. *Vie d'Alexandre l'Acémète,* c. 43 and 50, ed. E. de Stoop in *Patrologia orientalis,* vol. 6, fasc. 5 (Paris, [1911]), pp. 692, 698. For the Akoimetoi, see *DACL* 1:107–21 s.v. Acémètes and *The Oxford Dictionary of Byzantium* 1:46. In the *Vita et conversatio . . . Marcelli,* c. 4 (PG 116, col 710) = BHG 1028, the young saint discovers Alexander's monastery: "In quo novam quidem, sed longe omnium pulcherrimam, legem imposuit, ut hymnorum ad Deum nunquam interrumperetur perpetuitas." [Where, indeed, he imposed a new law (but the finest of all by far) to ensure that their perpetual hymns to God would never be interrupted.] There is a modern critical edition of an even earlier version of the Vita (= BHG 1027) in Gilbert Dagron, "La vie ancienne de saint Marcel l'Acémète," *Analecta Bollandiana* 86 (1968): 271–321.

12. Obviously, in the East the liturgy of the Akoimetoi would not be referred to in Latin. But *laus perennis* in the medieval West did not refer to monastic liturgy. Note its use, for example, in a poem by Venantius Fortunatus, *Opera,* pt. 1, c. 8 (PL 88, col. 96): "Tibi laus perennis, auctor / Baptismatis sacrator/." A search of the words *laus perennis* and their permutations in the volumes of the PL via the Chadwyck-Healey on-line database turned up only modern editors using the term to refer to the liturgy at Agaune. A search of MGH SSrerMerov 1–7 glossaries shows no use of the term in Merovingian materials. The term *laus perennis* seems to be a neo-Latinism of the sixteenth or sev-enteenth century. The earliest source in which I have found it is Antonio de Yepes, *Crónica gen-eral de la orden de San Benito* (1609), a. 557, where it is associated with both Irish monastic practice and the Akoimetoi. In an extended argument, Carolus Le Cointe, in *Annales ecclesiastici franco-rum,* 8 vols. (Paris 1665–1683), 1:534–44, challenged the apparently widespread view that Agaune's liturgy was the *laus perennis* because (he argued) it was not continuous but rather conformed to the canonical hours. Jean Mabillon took issue with Le Cointe, however, and his view has prevailed to the present day: see Johannes Mabillon, *Praefationes in Acta Sanctorum Ordinis Sancti Benedicti* (Trent, 1724), pp. 381–86, and, more briefly, idem, *Annales ordinis Sancti Benedicti occidentalium monachorum,* vol. 1 (Paris, 1739), pp. 26–27. Albrecht Diem independently noted the modern ori-gins of the term *laus perennis* in his Utrecht Ph.D. dissertation-in-progress. I thank him for shar-ing his observations and bibliography with me.

13. See the discussion in Peter Brown, *The Rise of Western Christendom: Triumph and Diversity,* A.D. 200–1000 (Oxford, 1996), pp. 70–71, and the detailed account in W. H. C. Frend, *The Rise of the Monophysite Movement: Chapters in the History of the Church in the Fifth and Sixth Centuries* (Cambridge, 1972).

of the Council of Chalcedon of 451, which solemnly declared the two natures—divine and human—of Christ. Because Chalcedon accepted the
Tome of Pope Leo I—which propounded "two natures united without
change, without division, and without confusion in Christ"—adherence
to Chalcedon came (in the West) to be equated with right Catholic doctrine. What might have been even more important to Westerners such as
Avitus, who lived in considerable anxiety about the possible triumph of
Arianism, was the fact that the Akoimetoi were opponents of the Arians
as well. While Monophysitism tended to swallow Christ into the Godhead, Arianism tended to emphasize His humanity at the expense of His
divinity. In the *Life* of Saint Marcellus, a monastic leader who became
head of the Akoimetoi, the hero is depicted as publicly besting one of the
Empire's most powerful military officers, the Arian Aspar, and his ambi-
tious son Ardaburius.[14]

Some of this may have been known in the West. Around 460, a man
named Studius, possibly of Roman origin, founded a monastery in Constantinople and populated it with a contingent of Sleepless monks.[15]
More certain evidence of Western contact comes in 484, when a Roman
synod excommunicated Acacius, a patriarch of Constantinople who urged
rejecting Chalcedon in the hopes of obtaining religious unity in the East.
It was a Sleepless monk who pinned the papal "charter of damnation" to
the patriarch's pallium as he celebrated the Mass at Constantinople.[16]

In the early sixth century the Akoimetoi continued their active role
in the controversies that roiled the capital. They demonstrated on behalf
of the patriarch of Constantinople, Macedonius, around 510, supporting
his opposition to the Monophysite attempt to add the doxology "Who
was crucified for us" to the Trishagion—or Sanctus—of the Masses celebrated in the capital. "Holy God, holy and mighty, holy and immortal,"
the Monophysites chanted and then interposed, "Who was crucified for

---

14. *Vita et conversatio . . . Marcelli,* c. 34 (PG 116, col. 742). See also Gilbert Dagron, "Les moines
et la ville: Le monachisme à Constantinople jusqu'au concile de Chalcédoine (451)," *Travaux et Mémoires* 4 (1970): 229–76, esp. 237; Raymond Janin, *Les églises et les monastères des grands centres byz-
antins* (Paris, 1975), p. 14.

15. Theodore Lector, *Ecclesiastica historia* 1.17 (PG 86.1, col. 174): "Studius ecclesiam Sancti Joannis exstruxit, et monachos ex Acoemitensibus in ea collocavit." See Dagron, "Les moines et la ville,"
pp. 236–37, n. 46. On the likely sequence—foundation of St. John's as a church in 453/4, subsequent incarnation as a monastery for Sleepless monks—see Cyril Mango, "The Date of the
Studius Basilica at Istanbul," *Byzantine and Modern Greek Studies* 4 (1978): 115–22. But Mango
(p. 121) doubts the tradition of Studius's Roman origins.

16. Liberatus (deacon at Carthage), *Breviarium,* c. 17 (PL 68, col. 1028): "per quemdam mona-
chum Acimaetensem ipsam chartam damnationis, dum ingrederetur [sc. Acacius] ad celebranda
sacra, suspendere in ejus pallio, et discedere."

us," making Christ crucified as God (rather than as man in the flesh).[17] The Sleepless Ones were also probably among those who took to the streets again when, two years later (with Macedonius now in exile), the Emperor Anastasius himself had the inflammatory doxology added to the Mass at Santa Sophia.[18]

The Akoimetoi were thus well known, but not particularly for their liturgy.[19] Obviously their very name recalled it to mind. But the Sleepless monks seem to have stood out more for their politics than for their prayers.

What did Avitus know of the Akoimetoi, let alone of Eutyches, Acacius, and Macedonius? Recently Ian Wood and Danuta Shanzer have suggested that he learned about events at Constantinople from an interested and highly biased source: Celer, Emperor Anastasius's "master of the offices," and a key political and military figure.[20] Working for Anastasius, a devout Monophysite, Celer in effect engineered Macedonius's downfall by inducing him to repudiate the two councils that mattered most to his supporters: both the 431 Council of Ephesus and the 451 Council of Chalcedon.[21]

We have correspondence between Avitus and Celer from the period after Macedonius's deposition.[22] If their communications began earlier, they may help to account for what Avitus knew and did not know—and also help us see what he cared about. One thing is clear: in all of the extant materials connected with Avitus, there is not a word about Sleepless monks. The bishop of Vienne did have some interest in the doctrinal mat-

---

17. This is the implication of Zachariah of Mitylene, *Chronicle* 7.7 in *The Syriac Chronicle Known as That of Zachariah of Mitylene*, trans. F. J. Hamilton and E. W. Brooks (London, 1899), p. 168.
18. They may well have been the ones referred to as "alii quidem, ceteris die noctuque hymnum trinitatis Christo deo psallentibus, totam peragrant civitatem" in *Chronicon Marcellini comitis*, a. 512 MGH AA 11:97–98.
19. For other political/religious events in which they were involved, see Evagrius Scholasticus, *Historia Ecclesiastica* 3.19–21 (PG 86.2 cols. 2635–42). Yet it is odd that this same historian does not mention them explicitly when speaking of the events surrounding the addition to the Trishagion; see ibid. 3.44 (cols. 2698–99).
20. Ian N. Wood and Danuta Shanzer, trans., *The Prose Works of Avitus of Vienne* (Liverpool, forthcoming). I am extremely grateful to these scholars for allowing me to consult a draft of their work as I prepared this study.
21. Ernest Stein, *Histoire du bas-empire*, vol. 2: *De la disparition de l'empire d'occident à la mort de Justinien (476–565)*, ed. Jean-Remy Palanque (Paris, 1949), p. 170; J. R. Martindale, *The Prosopography of the Later Roman Empire*, vol. 2 (Cambridge, 1980), p. 276.
22. Avitus, *Ep.* 48, ed. Peiper, p. 77; 40, ed. Chevalier, p. 195. At around the same time (515/16), Avitus wrote a letter to the patriarch (*Ep.* 9, ed. Peiper, pp. 43–44; 7, ed. Chevalier, pp. 141–42); to Emperor Anastasius (*Ep.* 46A, ed. Peiper, p. 76; 38F, ed. Chevalier, p. 193); and to Vitalian, an army officer who led a military revolt, in which he presented himself as a champion of Chalcedon and gained the upper hand (temporarily) over Anastasius in 514 (*Ep.* 47, ed. Peiper, pp. 76–77; 39, ed. Chevalier, p. 194).

ters important to the Akoimetoi, however. At the behest of Sigismund's father, the Arian king of Burgundy Gundobad, Avitus wrote two treatises against the heresy of Eutyches, ca. 512/13. But he was mistaken—probably misinformed—about key events and debates. What interested him about doctrine was the nature of Christ as both God and man—a matter that spoke as much to Arianism as it did to Monophysitism.[23] What interested him about events at Constantinople was the relationship between a good people and a misguided emperor. Thus he wrote that Acacius "died not only unpunished, but even uninvestigated," spared by a remiss emperor, even though Pope Felix had in fact issued an excommunication which (as we have seen) a Sleepless monk then had hung on the condemned patriarch's pallium.[24]

Avitus was also interested in the liturgy of the capital. He said nothing about any ceaseless liturgy carried out by Sleepless monks; but he knew there had been controversy over the phrase "Who was crucified for us." He believed it to be a traditional supplication offered up at the beginning of the Mass in the churches of major cities of the empire. The problem, in his view, lay with those who wanted to do away with it! This mistake alone demonstrates that Avitus had no direct knowledge of the Akoimetoi. But once that point is made, it is important to know what Avitus thought, and to see what really moved him—the image of the people of the empire (*plebs*) chanting "Who was crucified for us" with such devotion and alacrity that they rightly believed their prayers would be granted. How unsatisfying, he wrote, to be forced to truncate it! Macedonius's error, Avitus thought, had been to excise the doxology. *That* was the cause of the riots and ultimately of Macedonius's exile. In Avitus's view, all this once again formed a cautionary tale about a bad emperor and a weak and vacillating churchman.[25]

Avitus's interest in the East and its affairs, though ill requited, must mean that he would have been keen to hear the news brought by delegations to and from the Burgundian kingdom and Constantinople. Yet even if these messengers met up with the Sleepless Ones, it is likely that what they learned had less to do with the monks' liturgical round than with their expertise at street demonstrations. Certainly we have no basis

---

23. At the end of Avitus, *CE* 2, ed. Peiper, p. 29; ed. Chevalier, p. 269, the bishop turned to the *sectatores*—that is, the Arians (see Wood and Shanzer, *The Prose Works*)—around King Gundobad to warn them against their own heresy and its commonality with that of Eutyches.
24. Avitus, *CE* 2, ed. Peiper, p. 22; ed. Chevalier, p. 258: "non impunitus tantummodo, verum et indiscussus interiit." "Uninvestigated" is Wood and Shanzer's clarifying translation of *indiscussus*.
25. Avitus, *CE* 2, ed. Peiper, pp. 22–29; ed. Chevalier, pp. 258–69.

to imagine that the details of their monastic life were either sought by their Western visitors or displayed in their public activities.

TRADITIONS OF THE CENTRAL RHÔNE VALLEY

Thus it is unlikely that, at least in detail, the nonstop liturgy of Agaune came from Byzantium by way of Avitus. And if not Avitus, then via no one; for Avitus was Burgundy's Catholic "contact man" with the East. It makes sense, then, to look closer to home. There were reasons for elaborating a night-and-day liturgy right in the central Rhône valley. And there were traditions there which, cobbled together with some vague ideas about Sleepless monks as the keepers of orthodoxy (for it would be wrong to deny any role to Byzantium), made such a liturgy possible.

Vienne is the obvious place to begin. It was not only the episcopal see presided over by Avitus but was also in every way his "home base." The bishop who had preceded him was his own father, Hesychius, while the one before that, Mamertus, had been his godfather.[26] Avitus's sister was a nun at the convent of Saints Gervasius and Protasius in Vienne, while another relative was abbess there. The relationship between bishop and local monasteries went deeper than familial interest. Indeed, the bishops of Vienne paid particular attention to other monasteries there, especially Grigny and its patron saint, the soldier-martyr Ferreolus (d. ca. 304). As we shall soon see, Grigny was central to the foundation of Agaune. Here, however, we need simply to note that Grigny was an important religious center for the bishops of Vienne. In a letter written to Maximus, the bishop of Geneva who was involved in advising Sigismund on the foundation of Agaune, Avitus reported that he was busy tending to matters at Grigny.[27] We learn from the *Life* of Saint Clarus, admittedly a Carolingian text speaking of a saint of the mid seventh century, that the bishops of Vienne had been the founders of Grigny.[28] It was a monastic complex consisting of several houses of both monks and nuns scattered on both sides of the Rhône. Around 473 Bishop Mamertus translated the bones of Saint Ferreolus to a new basilica of Grigny built for the purpose.[29]

26. Avitus, *Hom.* 6, ed. Peiper, p. 110; 5, ed. Chevalier, p. 295; Ian Wood, *The Merovingian Kingdoms, 450–751* (London, 1994), p. 24.

27. Avitus, *Ep.* 74, ed. Peiper, p. 91; 67, ed. Chevalier, p. 222. For Avitus's relatives, see Wood, "Religion and Culture," p. 86.

28. *Vita Clari* in *AASS*, January 1, pp. 55–56 = BHL 1825.

29. *Vita Clari*, c. 2, p. 55. On the location of the new basilica, see Auguste Longnon, *Géographie de la Gaule au VIe siècle* (Paris, 1878), pp. 424–25 and May Vieillard-Troiekouroff, *Les monuments religieux de la Gaule d'après les oeuvres de Grégoire de Tours* (Paris, 1976), pp. 339–40, with map on p. 338.

Sidonius Apollinaris, in a letter full of praise, claimed that the translation made Mamertus the equal of Saint Ambrose.[30]

An account of Saint Ferreolus's deeds (his *Acts*) was probably written in the fifth century and would have been known by Avitus.[31] Positivist scorn has been heaped on this text, which gets almost nothing historically right.[32] But as a type, Ferreolus of Vienne represents a precursor of the Theban soldiers of Agaune. In the *Acts* he is presented as a military man forced to choose between his worldly stipend and his eternal beliefs. When told by the provincial governor that he had to sacrifice to the gods, the saint replied: "I have fought for the emperors as long as it was possible without harming my religion. When I obeyed you, I owed my actions to just laws; I have never served impieties. I meant to fight against criminals, not against Christians."[33]

What this shows is that already before Sigismund's foundation there was a monastery complex at Vienne dedicated to a martyr soldier-saint. Sidonius Apollinaris suggests that the monastery was the source of a rule; he speaks of "statutes of the fathers of Lérins or Grigny."[34] The phrase implies that Grigny's way of life rivaled that of the most important monastery of the Rhône valley, Lérins. There were other houses at Vienne as well. According to the *Life* of Saint Clarus, "there were many clerics holding to the Apostolic life in the major house (*domo maiori*) of the holy martyrs, living in common and arranged in squadrons (*turmis dispositis*), so that they might carry out the [divine] mysteries."[35] Here we have, then, a local example—though we cannot be sure if it already existed in the time of Avitus—of a liturgy organized by *turmae* within a house dedicated to martyrs. We shall have occasion to return to other liturgical innovations at Vienne.

At Agaune itself there had been, even before Sigismund's monastery, ascetic groups which tended the relics of the martyred legion. However, a great effort seems to have been made to obliterate their memory. It is true that we still have the report of the *Passion* of the Theban martyrs, written by Bishop Eucherius of Lyon (d. 450/54), which claims that the

---

30. Sidonius, *Epistola* 7.1 (7) in *Sidoine Apollinaire,* vol 3: *Lettres, livres VI–IX,* ed. André Loyen (Paris, 1970), p. 33.

31. Elie Griff, *La Gaule chrétienne à l'époque romaine* 3 vols. (Paris, 1947–65), 1:107; Martin Heinzelmann, "Gallische Prosopographie 260–527," *Francia* 10 (1982): 531–718 at p. 608.

32. Griff, *Gaule chrétienne,* 1:107, calls it "de peu de valeur."

33. *Acta de S. Ferreolo martyre viennensi in Gallia,* c. 1, *AASS,* September 18, V, p. 765: "Imperatoribus, quamdiu salva religione licuit, militavi. Opera mea, cum tibi parui, justis legibus debui; sacrilegis numquam servivi, adversus noxios, non adversus Christianos mi[l]itare proposui."

34. Sidonius, *Epistola,* 7.17 (3), p. 78: "statuta lirinensium patrum vel grinnicensium."

35. *Vita Clari,* c. 2, §3, p. 55.

cult of Saint Maurice and his men attracted pilgrims immediately after it was established by the local bishop, Theodore of Martigny. Eucherius even tells us of a basilica that was built in honor of the martyrs right under an outcrop of rock, which still looms over the present monastic buildings on the site.[36] The archaeologist Louis Blondel, whose team excavated the spot in the 1940s, thought he had found the remains of important pre-sixth-century edifices.[37] However, new work on the site begun in 1994 suggests otherwise.[38] For example, what Blondel interpreted as a funerary chapel built for the Theban martyrs was nothing of the sort: it was a construction of the Romanesque or Gothic period! A few walls are all that remain from the pre-515 period. What archaeology tells us in this instance, then, is how thoroughly Sigismund's foundation tried to obliterate the remains of the old in order to present itself as something new.

The same point may be made about texts. The *Life* of the abbots of Agaune, written in praise of the abbots of the new foundation, tried to hide the fact that a religious community had existed at Agaune beforehand. The author says that Sigismund displaced a mixed group of common people.[39] But later the author slips, making clear that it was in fact *women* who were ejected to make way for the monks with their perpetual prayer: "it seemed right that all the women from that place should be removed and, remote from their secular families, a family of God be located there, that is, a community of monks who, imitating celestial things both night and day, would spend their time in divine singing."[40] That the new monastery would be exclusively male may well have been a significant change. But this does not mean scandal had reigned before-

---

36. Eucherius, *Passio acaunensium martyrum,* c. 16–19, MGH SSrerMerov 3:38–39.

37. Louis Blondel, "Les anciennes basiliques d'Agaune. Étude archéologique," *Vallesia* 3 (1948): 9–57, esp. 18–23; idem, "Le baptistère et les anciens édifices conventuels de l'Abbaye d'Agaune," *Vallesia* 4 (1949): 15–28, esp. p. 24, where he affirms that "il existait un baptistère, déjà modifié au VIe siècle, mais qu'il est plus ancien que nous ne l'avions tout d'abord estimé, sans doute du Ve siècle."

38. Hans-Jörg Lehner, "Saint-Maurice," in "Chronique des découvertes archéologiques dans le canton du Valais en 1995," ed. François Wiblé, *Vallesia* 51 (1996): 341–44. I thank Charles Bonnet and François Wiblé for discussing the new findings with me and am very grateful to Alessandra Antonini for a tour of the site and helpful explanations.

39. *Vita abbatum acaunensium,* c. 3, MGH SSrerMerov 3:176: "promiscui vulgi commixta habitatio tolleretur." Frederick S. Paxton, "Power and the Power to Heal: The Cult of St. Sigismund of Burgundy," *Early Medieval Europe* 2 (1993): 95–110, at p. 106, explains the silence regarding the earlier community: there was "a contest for authority between an earlier generation of abbot-ascetics and a new generation of bishops. . . . Monasteries would no longer be rural retreats for aristocratic contemplatives, but central institutions in the governance and protection of the realm." The *Vita abbatum acaunensium* represented the bishops.

40. *Vita abbatum acaunensium,* c. 3, MGH SSrerMerov 3:176: "visum est, ut omnes mulieres de loco eodem tollerentur, et remotis familiis secularibus, Dei inibi, hoc est monachorum, familia locaretur, qui die noctuque caelestia imitantes, cantionibus divinis insisterent."

hand: we have seen at Grigny that fifth-century monastic complexes could quite properly be mixed. This may have been the case at the cult site of Saint-Maurice before 515. We know that one of the nuns there discovered the body of the martyr Innocentius washed up by the Rhône; this is hardly the stuff of gossip.[41]

The *Life* of Saint Severinus, the short version of which probably dates from circa 515, tells of an abbot at Agaune who died in 508. The focus of the *Life* is the saint's healing of Clovis. Nevertheless, it may be useful to point out that Severinus is introduced by his hagiographer as a man of virtue who "applied himself to assiduous prayer . . . pouring forth abundant groans and tears."[42] These are commonplace characteristics for any saint; but at least we can conclude that there was a tradition of "assiduous prayer" already on the spot before 515. Another text, the *Life and Rule* of the Jura abbots, as we now know from the remarkable detective work of François Masai, was written for two men—John and Armentarius— who lived by the tomb of Saint Maurice just before Sigismund set up his foundation.[43] The author of this *Life,* possibly Viventiolus, who would thus have been writing as both a monk of Condat (one of the monasteries founded by the Jura fathers) and a candidate for the episcopacy of Lyon, seems to have wanted to convince these ascetics to follow a different rule—the one represented by Condat or perhaps Lérins.[44] Viventiolus may well have been involved in the 515 foundation of Agaune.[45]

Avitus, Sigismund, and the other bishops who participated in Agaune's reform—for that, we may now say, is what it was, not a new foundation—knew these traditions, and Eucherius's *Passion* was their basic text: Sigismund's monastery was dedicated to the martyrs' cult.[46] Avitus's

41. Eucherius, *Passio acaunensium martyrum*, Appendix 2, MGH, SSrerMerov 3:40 (the Appendix, however, was not by Eucherius and represents a later interpolation).

42. Faustus, *Vita sancti Severini Abbatis Agonensis a Fausto Presbitero eius discipulo* in Theurillat, p. 26, who suggests the date.

43. Masai, "La 'Vita patrum iurensium,'" pp. 43–69. For the *Vita vel regula* see *Vie des Pères du Jura,* ed. and trans. François Martine, Sources chrétiennes 142 (Paris, 1968).

44. For Viventiolus see Wood, "Prelude to Columbanus," p. 28, n. 118. Viventiolus became bishop of Lyon in 516/17.

45. As reported by the so-called Foundation charter, which includes a subscription by Viventiolus: see Theurillat, *L'Abbaye de St.-Maurice d'Agaune,* p. 81. Though this document was constructed in the Carolingian period, it is just possible that its confector was here drawing upon some authentic materials; see Wood, "Prelude to Columbanus," p. 15.

46. Bruno Krusch in MGH SSrerMerov 7:322–24 disparaged the historians who naively accepted the testimony of hagiographical texts and could thus believe that Sigismund's foundation was a "reformatio" rather than an "innovatio." But Krusch was too quick to declare forgeries; see Ian N. Wood, "Forgery in Merovingian Hagiography," in *Fälschungen im Mittelalter: Internationaler Kongreß der MGH, München, 16–19 September 1986,* Teil 5: *Fingierte Briefe, Frömmigkeit und Fälschung, Realienfälschungen,* MGH Schriften 33, pt. 5 (Hannover, 1988), pp. 369–84.

homily to celebrate the monastery's restoration (*innovatio*) was given on the feastday of the martyrs' passion. The text—not just the fact—of the *Passion* was important; Avitus began his homily by citing it.[47] He used the story of the "happy army" (*felix exercitus*), which transformed persecution and hatred into blessed and eternal life, as the preface to a paean to the basilica, "whose entry-way is not closed at night because it has no night"—a reference to the monks' nonstop prayer. Thus, for Avitus, the text was father to the monastery. Can we make more of this?

Eucherius's narrative in the *Passion* set up a contrast between the impious "squadrons of soldiers" (*militum turmae*) under emperor Maximian, who persecuted those who worshipped the true God, and the single "legion of soldiers" (*legio militum*) who would become martyrs rather than kill Christians.[48] As Philippe Buc has recently shown, it was the nature of Late Antique martyr accounts to subvert key terms—to give them Christian meaning and thereby disrupt and make ironic their old (and consensual) significance.[49] Eucherius laid the groundwork for this subversion; and Avitus seems to have delighted in it as well. Certainly in a homily at Annemasse, delivered a few days after the one at Agaune, Avitus dwelled on just such inversions, rejoicing in the fact that the new basilica—this one near Geneva—had been constructed on the site of a pagan temple. For Avitus, it illustrated sanctity sprung from sacrilege, new from old, nobility from confusion.[50] Similarly at Agaune he reveled in connecting the martyred army to the eternal monastery.

Among other things, Avitus knew it to have been an eloquent army. Just as the author of the *Acts* of Saint Ferreolus had his own hero engage in principled dialogue with his persecutor, so Eucherius put a statement of Christian soldiery and—this was new—anti-Arian piety into the mouths of his Theban legionnaires. Though ostensibly taking on a pagan emperor, Eucherius's soldiers seemed more to be facing off against an Arian. This is remarkable, considering that the Arian church was hardly threatening in Burgundy until after 476, when it apparently was established as a propertied institution—on property confiscated from Catholic churches—

---

47. Avitus, *Hom.* 25, ed. Peiper, p. 145; 24, ed. Chevalier, p. 338: "series lectae passionis explicuit." To what, if not the *Passio,* could Avitus be referring? No other accounts are known; see Franz Stolle, "Das Martyrium der thebaischen Legion" (Ph.D. diss., Münster, 1891), pp. 28–37.
48. Eucherius, *Passio acaunensium martyrum,* c. 2–3, MGH SSrerMerov 3:33: "Si qui tunc Dei veri cultum profiteri audebant, sparsis usquequaque militum turmis, vel ad supplicia vel ad necem rapiebantur . . . Erat eodem tempore in exercitu legio militum, qui Thebaei appellabantur."
49. Philippe Buc, "Martyre et ritualité dans l'antiquité tardive. Horizons de l'écriture médiévale des rituels," *Annales HSS,* no. 1 (1997): 63–92.
50. Avitus, *Hom.* 20, ed. Peiper, p. 133; ed. Chevalier, p. 326: "de sacrilegio sanctitas, de vetustate novitas, de confusione nobilitas."

by King Gundobad.[51] But by 515 the anti-Arian speech of the legionnaires would certainly have been noticed and appreciated by churchmen
like Avitus:

> We have always fought for justice, for piety, for the safety of the in-
> nocent [the pious troops told Maximian]. Up to now these were our
> rewards for dangers. . . . You order us to seek out Christians for pun-
> ishment. Now you won't have to look for others; you hereby have our
> confession. We believe in God the Father, Author of all things, and
> God his son, Jesus Christ. . . . Behold! We carry arms and yet we do
> not resist, for we wish rather to die than to kill; and we prefer to per-
> ish as innocents than to live as criminals.[52]

Then they offered their necks to their persecutors, making their martyrdom, as Eucherius remarks, an explicit example of imitating Christ.

But how did Sigismund and the others get from this *Passion* to perpetual prayer? A later interpolation of Eucherius's text would make the connection by tacking a few more miracles onto its last section, then opin-
ing that such things needed not be written down, for

> these things are known as facts in the hearts of the faithful [even] with-
> out a text, namely how many and what sort of miracles the Lord cease-
> lessly performs through His saints to the honor and glory of His name.
> For that [very name] the singing of the hymn of psalms by day and
> night never ends; it was instituted by order of the holy and outstand-
> ing martyr of Christ, Saint Sigismund the king, and has been preserved,
> under God, up to the present day.[53]

This was clearly written after Sigismund's murder in 523 and the return
of his bones to Agaune as holy relics in 535–36.[54] Yet its invocation of the

51. Wood, "Religion and Culture," pp. 150–54. On the significance of the late date for Burgundian Arianism, see Ian Wood, "Ethnicity and the Ethnogenesis of the Burgundians," in Herwig
Wolfram and Walter Pohl, eds., *Typen der Ethnogenese unter besonderer Berücksichtigung der Bayern:
Berichte des Symposions der Kommission für Frühmittelalterforschung, 27. bis 30. Oktober, 1986, Stift
Zwettl, Niederösterreich*, 2 vols. (Vienna, 1990), 1:53–69.
52. Eucherius, *Passio acaunensium martyrum*, c. 9, MGH SSrerMerov 3:36: "Pugnavimus semper pro iustitia, pro pietate, pro innocentium salute. Haec fuerunt hactenus nobis pretia periculo-
rum. . . . Christianos ad poenam per nos requiri iubes. Iam tibi ex hoc alii requirendi non sunt,
habes hic nos confitentes: 'Deum patrem auctorem omnium et filium eius Iesum Christum deum
credimus . . . Tenemus, ecce! arma et non resistimus, quia mori quam occidere satis malumus, et
innocentes interire, quam noxii vivere praeoptamus.'"
53. Ibid., Appendix I, p. 40: "Tamen fidelium cordibus absque lectione cognita esse noscuntur,
quae quanta et qualia miracula hic per sanctos suos ad honorem et gloriam nominis sui Dominus
operare non desinit. Pro id ipsum die noctuque psalmorum hymni decantatio non desistit, quae,
iubente sancto et praeclaro Christi martyre beato Sigismundo rege, est institutum hac usque hodie,
Deo protegente, est conservatum."
54. On the cult of St. Sigismund see Paxton, "Cult of St. Sigismund."

"day and night psalmody," which it connected not with Sigismund's virtues but rather with those of the soldier-martyrs, already figured in Avitus's homily on the foundation of the monastery. In praise of the new edifice, Avitus had pointed out that it would always resound with Christian voices and that the monks' petitions would always be heard.[55] Indeed, the very benefits that Avitus attributed to the doxology "Who was crucified for us" were made manifest in the liturgy of Agaune—a liturgy instituted as appropriate to the cult site of Christian soldiers.

Predating Sigismund's foundation at Agaune was a tradition of support for the Theban Martyrs within the Burgundian royal family. Sigismund's aunt and cousin, Catholics both, had already before 515 founded monasteries dedicated to the martyrs Victor and Ursus, soldiers in the Theban legion who suffered a separate martyrdom a few days after Maurice's death.[56] Sigismund, a soldier himself, must have found a cult site dedicated to soldiers apt for his purposes, particularly one far from the center of his father's power yet perched strategically at the pass to Arian Italy.[57]

The *Life* of the abbots of Agaune suggests another inspiration for Sigismund: his episcopal advisors. It says that Bishop Maximus suggested the very idea of founding the monastery.[58] Other bishops soon joined the effort: "In the meanwhile, a rule instituted for psalm-singing and a way of living was given to St. Hymnemodus [the first abbot of the new foundation] by the group of bishops who came there to set up the monastery." [59]

We have seen that bishops had been key players in the monasticism of the region before Sigismund's foundation: Bishop Theodore of Martigny set up the cult site at Agaune; Bishop Eucherius of Lyon wrote about Saint Maurice and his martyrs; and Viventiolus, angling for an episcopal post, was likely the author of the *Life* of the Jura Fathers, which was written for the monastic community at Agaune. Avitus and his predecessors at Vienne also interested themselves in liturgy. Mamertus was famous not only for orchestrating the translation of Ferreolus's bones but also for instituting the three-day penitential rite known as Rogations. In Avitus's homily on the Rogations, he invoked the very special relationship he had with Mamertus, "my spiritual father in baptism," then described how the

55. Avitus, *Hom.* 25, ed. Peiper, p. 145; 24, ed. Chevalier, p. 338.
56. *Passio Victoris et sociorum* in *AASS*, September VIII, pp. 292–93 = BHL 8584; they already figured by name in Eucherius, *Passio acaunensium martyrum*, c. 14, MGH SSrerMerov 3:38; see Wood, "Religion and Culture," p. 209.
57. Wood, "Prelude to Columbanus," pp. 15–16.
58. *Vita abbatum acaunensium* c. 3, MGH SSrerMerov 3:176.
59. Ibid., c. 7, p. 178: "Psallendi interim vel subsistendi regula instituta sancto Hymnemodo a coetu episcoporum, qui illic ad constituendum monasterium venerant, traditur."

bishop had conceived the new liturgy out of whole cloth, specifying the precise psalms and prayers to go with special processions during the three days before Ascension. Some senators at the time had complained that people should not modify or add to what was customary; but Mamertus convinced them not only to institute the new practice that year but to adopt it permanently.[60] The fact that Avitus reported the whole episode reveals how much he valued episcopal liturgical innovation.[61]

The bishops supported local monastic traditions. The first two abbots of Agaune came from Vienne (at Grigny) and from Lyon (at Île-Barbe). The latter fact—along with the role of Bishop Eucherius and the probable one of Viventiolus—highlights the traditions of Lyon. We have from later evidence names for some of the seven original *turmae* at Agaune. Four are significant here: *Granensis,* which referred to Grigny; *Islana,* that is, Île-Barbe; *Iurensis,* which may well have meant a group of monks drawn from those who were already at Agaune before 515; and *Meluensis,* which may have been an error for *Valdensis* and thus refer to Romain-môtier, an offshoot of Condat, Viventiolus's monastery.[62]

SOCIAL MEANING

Thus the monks at Agaune were organized as groups of local men conscripted into squadrons named (as had been Roman legions) by their place of origin. Lengthy liturgy was in this way associated with inverted

60. On the conservatives, Avitus, *Hom.* 6, ed. Peiper, p. 110; 5, ed. Chevalier, pp. 295–96: "Putabatur a quibusdam Viennensis senatus . . . inventis non posse adjici, cum vix acquiesceret legitimis inclinari."

61. On why bishops at this time engaged in extraordinary liturgical innovations, see Bernhard Jussen, "Zwischen Römischem Reich und Merowingern: Herrschaft legitimieren ohne Kaiser und König," in Peter Segl, ed., *Mittelalter und Moderne: Entdeckung und Rekonstruktion der mittelalterlichen Welt. Kongreßakten des 6. Symposiums des Mediävistenverbandes in Bayreuth 1995* (Sigmaringen, 1997), pp. 15–29, esp. 24–26 and idem, "Liturgie und Legitimation, oder: Wie die Gallo-Romanen das römische Reich beendeten," in *Institutionen und Ereignis: Über historische Praktiken und Vorstellungen gesellschaftlichen Ordnens,* ed. Reinhard Blänkner and Bernhard Jussen (Göttingen, 1998), pp. 75–136, esp. 106–22.

62. Theurillat, *L'Abbaye de St.-Maurice d'Agaune,* p. 102, analyzing the so-called Act of Foundation. Meluensis is elsewhere alternately Medlensis and Valdensis, likely the same place (the letters "ua" and "me" being interchanged by the scribe): see Marius Besson, "La donation d'Ayroenus à Saint-Maurice (mardi 8 octobre 765)," *Zeitschrift für schweizerische Kirchengeschichte: Revue d'histoire ecclésiastique suisse* 3 (1909): 294–96 at 295 n. 1. In 941 Alberic of Mâcon received a church and land in precarial tenure from the monks at Agaune and in particular from the *turma Iurense;* see *Historiae patriae monumenta* 6, *Chartarum* vol. 2 (Turin, 1853), col. 35, no. 19. Thus the *turma* of the Jura, possibly originally composed of Agaune ascetics from the pre-515 period, persisted into the tenth century; see also Masai, p. 68. It may be worthwhile to note that Alberic was related to Saint Maieul, the third abbot of Cluny; see Dominique Iogna-Prat, *Agni immaculati: Recherches sur les sources hagiographiques relatives à saint Maieul de Cluny (954–994)* (Paris, 1988), pp. 118–19 and n. 201. For a different sort of link between Agaune and Cluny, see below, n. 63.

militarism.[63] But prayer at Agaune had a more immediate meaning as well. Toward the middle of his dedication homily, Avitus turned to address the monks themselves: "You who will now live here: your secular labor invites you to hope in eternal repose. By your happy employments, all occasion for sin is denied you."[64]

Sin was a great episcopal obsession—and not just theoretically. Bishops were political figures in the fifth and sixth centuries, and they were often the butt of factional opposition clothed in the vocabulary of treason or sin.[65] The parishioners at Embrun and Gap accused their bishops of pillage, slaughter, homicide, and adultery. When the bishops reformed, though, they "never ceased to sing psalms, to undertake fasts, to do works of charity, to perform the book of David's songs by day, and to spend their nights in hymns and meditating on Scripture."[66] Clearly the day-and-night liturgy of the monks at Agaune was cast in this mold. It represented for the bishops an image of their own perfection.

Bishops were accused of sins in part because they were busybodies. They poked into people's affairs. Avitus rebuked a fornicator at Vienne —and was accused right back of fathering bastard children![67] At another time, he told a suffragan bishop to separate a couple that had been married for thirty years and have them do penance because he judged their relationship to be incestuous.[68] The issue came up before the bishops assembled at the Council of Épaone in 517. The same council insisted that aristocratic lay people travel to their bishops for a personal blessing every Christmas and Easter.[69]

Consequently, bishops were exceedingly busy. At Geneva, Lyon, Martigny, and Grenoble they presided over huge episcopal complexes.[70] Al-

63. See the present author's first published scholarly endeavor, which had its beginning, appropriately enough, in a seminar on monasticism taught by Lester Little: "Feudal War and Monastic Peace: Cluniac Liturgy as Ritual Aggression," *Viator* 2 (1971): 129–57. The present project was admittedly meant to be a pendant to that "first assignment." But only well into the research for this article did I realize that Cluniac liturgy was in effect drawing upon a *topos* already at least four centuries old.

64. Avitus, *Hom.* 25, ed. Peiper, p. 146; 24, ed. Chevalier, p. 338: "Vos nunc habitaturos hic ... saeculi labor ad spem perpetuae quietis invitat, quibus occupatis actione felici omne peccandi tempus excluditur."

65. Wood, "Religion and Culture," pp. 130–36.

66. Gregory of Tours, *Historiae* 5.20, p. 228: "numquam a psallentio cessare, celebrare ieiunia, aelemosinas exercere, librum Davitici carminis explere per diem noctesque in hymnis ac lectionibus meditando deducere."

67. Avitus, *Ep.* 55, ed. Peiper, p. 84; 47, ed. Chevalier, p. 209.

68. Avitus, *Ep.* 18, ed. Peiper, p. 49; 16, ed. Chevalier, pp. 152–53.

69. For the case of incest, *Concilium Epaonense*, c. 30 in *Concilia Galliae*, CCSL 148A (Turnhout, 1963), pp. 31–32; for episcopal blessings, ibid., c. 35, p. 33.

70. For Martigny, see Hans-Jörg Lehner and François Wiblé, "Martigny VS: De la première cathédrale du Valais à la paroissiale actuelle: La contribution de l'archéologie," *Helvetia Archaeo-*

ready before the time of Sigismund, Geneva boasted two very differently conceived cathedrals separated by a baptistery that sported a monumental *ciborium.*[71] The bishop received his visitors in an elegant reception room fitted out with a startlingly beautiful mosaic floor. At 60 square meters, it was large enough to accommodate a considerable crowd. Just before Saint-Maurice was founded, Avitus went to Geneva to dedicate the reconstructed north cathedral, which had burned during the battles between Gundobad and his brother.[72]

For all their hopes of having great impact on their flock, bishops knew that they actually exercised control mainly by instituting and enforcing the religious cult.[73] This is why there were two basilicas within a few meters of one another at Geneva, the north one so arranged as to accommodate an elaborate liturgy, the southern one set up for lecturing and teaching.[74] It is also why baptisteries so proliferated in the fifth and sixth centuries: baptism expressed the bishop's most intimate and fundamental power over each individual, regardless of rank or order.

The importance of the cult explains why Avitus was so put out with Macedonius: the patriarch had missed his chance to correct the emperor and take responsibility for the beloved liturgy of the capital. No wonder that it was the episcopal advisors around Sigismund who gave Hymnemodus his rule. And it was appropriate for them to construct a liturgy whose very busy-ness was a counterpart to the wearying cares of the pastor—yet immune from calumny.

It is just possible that traces of the architecture of the 515 church point to the importance of the liturgy at Agaune. Its southern flank was fitted out with a ramp fairly clearly meant to bring pilgrims into the church.[75] What did they find there? They must have found martyrs' tombs, though their precise locations are suddenly very much in doubt. But we can be quite certain that when they arrived within the church, they heard the chant. In his dedicatory homily, Avitus emphasized how accessible the sanctuary was; and (thus far) archaeologists have not detected barriers be-

logica 25 (1994–98): 51–68 at pp. 60–64; for Grenoble, see Renée Colardelle, *Grenoble (Isère) aux premiers temps chrétiens: Saint-Laurent et ses nécropoles* (2d ed., Paris, 1992); for Geneva, see n. 71 below.

71. Charles Bonnet, *Les fouilles de l'ancien groupe épiscopal de Genève (1976–1993),* Cahiers d'archéologie genevoise 1 (Geneva, 1993). I thank Professor Bonnet for an extraordinary tour and subsequent discussion of the site.

72. Avitus, *Hom.* 19, ed. Chevalier, p. 323.

73. Wood, "Religion and Culture," p. 136.

74. See the drawings in Bonnet, *Les fouilles,* pp. 38–39.

75. It used to be thought that the ramp led to martyrs' tombs under the rock, but this now seems unlikely. See Lehner, "Saint-Maurice," p. 342.

tween the choir and the west end of the church, structures that were otherwise routine in the region.[76]

Organized as heaven's answer to worldly troops and as the vicarious expression of the piety of bishops too busy to pray themselves and too vulnerable to be sinless, the monks at Agaune carried out a liturgy that needed only the whisper of an idea of Sleepless monks to inspire it. In essence, it was homegrown.[77] As such, it reveals (as the old Benedictine trajectory cannot do) some of the extraordinary variety, creativity, and meaning in Western monasticism.

76. For example, Bonnet, *Les fouilles,* pp. 38–39; Charles Bonnet and Béatrice Privati, "Les origines de Saint-Gervais: Recherches archéologiques," in *Le temple de Saint-Gervais* (Geneva, 1991), p. 21. In Gregory, *Liber in gloria martyrum,* c. 75, MGH SSrerMerov 1, pt. 2, p. 88, a mother is invited to come to Saint-Maurice as often as she likes to hear the voice of her dead son chanting in the choir with the other monks.

77. Masai, "La 'Vita patrum iurensium,'" p. 69, seems ready to come to this conclusion as well. Wood, "Religion and Culture," p. 100, has observed that the Lyon-Vienne region in fact formed a sort of "pocket" where the Eastern devotions of men like Cassian passed by with barely a trace. Rather, "it is fair to see monasticism in the central Rhône valley as a product not so much of the major traditions of Tours or Lérins, but rather of the devotional readings of the aristocracy."

Claustration and Collaboration between the Sexes in the Twelfth-Century Scriptorium

Alison I. Beach

The monastic renaissance of the twelfth century was vitally connected to the work of the scriptorium. As the intellectual life of reformed and newly founded monasteries expanded, interest in libraries and demand for books surged.[1] Many religious houses worked to enlarge collections that were outdated or lacking the basics—biblical and liturgical texts, patristic sermons and commentaries, saints' lives, histories, grammars, and legal texts—while others moved beyond mere copying, and devoted new energy to composing original texts.[2] In both cases, the scriptorium functioned as an intellectual nerve center, collecting and transmitting texts to the community and beyond.

During the twelfth century it was generally a monastery's own scribes who did the work. This fact tends to bring to mind the image of a monk-copyist seated before a book with a writing instrument in his hand. But if we stop here in the monks' scriptorium, our image is incomplete, and our understanding of the monastic renaissance flawed. Religious women also worked as copyists in a variety of institutional settings—in the se-

1. Wilhelm Wattenbach, *Das Schriftwesen im Mittelalter,* 3d ed. (Leipzig, 1896), p. 441. Bernhard Bischoff credited the new monastic orders—the Cistercians, the Premonstratensians, and the Carthusians in particular—with a rise in scribal activity during the twelfth century. See Bernhard Bischoff, *Latin Paleography,* trans. Dáibhí Ó Cróinín and David Ganz (Cambridge, 1990), p. 216. Raymund Kottje makes this same connection between monastic revival and book production for the monastic reforms of the eleventh century. See Raymund Kottje, "Klosterbibliotheken und monastische Kultur in der zweiten Hälfte des 11. Jahrhunderts," *Zeitschrift für Kirchengeschichte* 80 (1969): 145–62.
2. Charles Homer Haskins, *The Renaissance of the Twelfth Century* (Cambridge, Mass., 1927), pp. 78–82.

clusion of the recluse's cell, at monasteries for women only, and in monasteries for both women and men. Female scribes worked alone, in teams of women, and in collaboration with their male counterparts.

Our vision of female participation in creating books during the twelfth century, though, has been limited primarily to a few outstanding books and individuals, particularly Herrad of Hohenbourg and her *Hortus deliciarum* and Hildegard of Bingen and the Wiesbaden Codex of her *Scivias*.[3] But the more ordinary women who did more ordinary work have largely escaped modern notice.[4] Female copyists produced texts on a less grand scale at Admont, Lamspringe, Lippoldsberg, Mallersdorf, Münsterbilsen, Regensburg, Niedermünster, Schäftlarn, Schwarzenthann, Wessobrunn, and an unidentified monastery in the Middle Rhine region.[5] Women certainly worked as scribes at other centers, and the list will grow as fragments of evidence are reconnected.

Manuscripts produced at two of these houses—Benedictine Admont and Premonstratensian Schäftlarn—offer us an extraordinary glimpse into the intellectual and institutional lives of religious women in two twelfth-century double monasteries.[6] At both of these Bavarian monas-

3. For a reconstruction and discussion of Herrad's compendium, which was destroyed during the bombardment of Strassburg during the nineteenth century, see Rosalie B. Green, ed., *Hortus deliciarum* (London, 1979). On Hildegard's *Scivias* and the Wiesbaden Codex (Wiesbaden, Hess. LB, Hs. I), see *Hildegardis Scivias,* eds. Aldegundis Führkötter and Angela Carlevaris, CCCM 43 (Turnhout, 1978), and Antonius Van der Linde, *Die Handschriften der Königlichen Landesbibliothek in Wiesbaden* (Wiesbaden, 1877), pp. 22–28. On Hildegard's role in the design of the Rupertsberg *Scivias* illustrations, see Madeline Caviness, "Artist," in *Voice of the Living Light. Hildegard of Bingen and Her World,* ed. Barbara Newman (Berkeley, 1998), pp. 110–24.

4. Of the approximately 1,615 pre-twelfth-century scribal subscriptions listed in Bénédictins du Bouveret, *Colophons de manuscrits occidentaux des origines au XVIe siècle,* Spicilegii Friburgensis Subsidia 2–7 (Fribourg, 1965–1982), only roughly 1 percent (16) are female. Women may have been less likely to sign their names to their work than men, making female scribes less visible than their male counterparts. See Alison I. Beach, "The Female Scribes of Twelfth-Century Bavaria" (Ph.D. diss. Columbia University, 1996), pp. 2–3. It is important to note that the names of scribes—female or male—were seldom recorded before the fifteenth century. For a discussion of the factors that led to the increase in the use of scribal colophons after the fourteenth century, see Pamela R. Robinson, *Catalogue of Dated and Datable Manuscripts c. 737–1600 in Cambridge Libraries* (Cambridge, 1988), pp. 5–12.

5. My doctoral dissertation provides both a general survey of female scribal contributions from the Carolingian period through the twelfth century and a detailed study of female scribal activity in twelfth-century Bavaria. For early medieval female scribes, see Rosamond McKitterick, "Frauen und Schriftlichkeit im Frühmittelalter," in *Weibliche Lebensgestaltung im frühen Mittelalter,* ed. Hans-Werner Goetz (Cologne, 1991), pp. 70–73. On the role of female copyists before the Middle Ages, see Kim Haines-Eitzen, "'Girls Trained in Beautiful Writing': Female Scribes in Roman Antiquity and Early Christianity," *Journal of Early Christian Studies* 6:4 (1998): 629–46.

6. Recent scholars have called into question the use of this term, which has traditionally been used to describe a variety of institutional arrangements at religious communities with both female and male members. See Penelope D. Johnson, *Equal in Monastic Profession: Religious Women in Medieval France* (Chicago, 1991), p. 7; Penny Schine Gold, *The Lady and the Virgin: Image, Attitude, and*

teries we see women contributing at many levels to a community effort to produce and reproduce texts. Patterns of collaboration in books produced at both houses reflect differing levels of claustration and degrees of tolerance for contact between the sexes, complicating our picture of strict enclosure. When books needed to be produced, intellectual and social barriers came down.

Collaboration between men and women to produce texts was an invention neither of the twelfth century nor of Bavaria. We learn from Eusebius, for example, that female copyists assisted Origen in transmitting his work.[7] In the eighth century, the missionary Saint Boniface relied on Eadburga, abbess of the Anglo-Saxon monastery Minster-in-Thanet, to provide books for his missionary work on the German frontier. In one case, Boniface sent her the materials she needed to copy the Pauline Epistles in gold letters.[8] The nun-scribes of Chelles, working in the late eighth or early ninth century, produced a six-volume copy of Augustine's *Commentary on the Psalms* for Archchancellor Hildebald of Cologne.[9] During the twelfth century, Idung of Prüfening addressed the preface of his *Dialogue between Two Monks* to Kunigunde, abbess of Niedermünster, a Benedictine monastery in the diocese of Regensburg. He requested that the sisters there make a legible, carefully corrected copy of his text.[10] The collaboration between Hildegard of Bingen and Volmar of St. Disibod, the monk who was both her teacher and her secretary, is well known. After Hildegard composed the *Scivias* on tablets (assisted within the monastery by the nun Richardis von Stade), Volmar transcribed the text onto parch-

Experience in Twelfth-Century France (Chicago, 1985), pp. 101–2; Sharon Elkins, *Holy Women of Twelfth-Century England* (Chapel Hill, 1988), pp. xvii–xviii; while the term may be so broad as to include many diverse types of dual-sex communities, it is a convenient description that can be bolstered with a discussion of the precise institutional relationship between male and female members. I use it here to indicate a community of both male and female religious organized under one superior and sharing a common endowment.

7. Eusebius, *Ecclesiastical History* 6.23, ed. and trans. Philip Schaff and Henry Wace, in *A Select Library of Nicene and Post-Nicene Fathers of the Christian Church*, 2d ser., vol. 1 (Grand Rapids, Mich., 1976), p. 271. See Haines-Eitzen, "Girls," pp. 631–34.

8. Boniface, *S. Bonifatii et Lulli epistolae*, ed. E. Dümmler, MGH Epp. 3:285–86; Ephraim Emerton, ed. and trans., *The Letters of Saint Boniface*, (New York, 1940), pp. 64–65.

9. The nuns may have produced these on commission for Hildebald. On the nun-scribes of Chelles, see Bernhard Bischoff, "Die Kölner Nonnenhandschriften und das Skriptorium von Chelles," *Mittelalterliche Studien* 3 vols. (Stuttgart, 1966–1981), 1:16–34; McKitterick, "Frauen und Schriftlichkeit," pp. 70–73.

10. R. B. C. Huygens, "Le moine Idung et ses deux ouvrages: 'Argumentum super quatuor questionibus,' et 'Dialogus duorum monachorum,'" *Studi Medievali*, 3d series, 13/1 (1972): 320 and 376; Jeremiah F. O'Sullivan, Joseph Leahey, and Grace Perrigo, trans., *Cistercians and Cluniacs: The Case for Cîteaux: A Dialogue between Two Monks and an Argument on Four Questions by Idung of Prüfening* (Kalamazoo, 1977), pp. 21–23; Wattenbach, *Schriftwesen im Mittelalter*, pp. 445–46.

ment.[11] There were no doubt other collaborative efforts for which no manuscript or documentary evidence has survived.[12]

What makes Admont and Schäftlarn unique in this context is, first, the
survival of substantial physical evidence of male-female collaboration,
and second, the close relationship between men and women that this material reflects. Let us now turn to the two monasteries, the manuscripts,
and the stories they tell about men and women working together in the
context of claustration.

ADMONT

On March 11, 1152, a fire broke out at Admont.[13] The flames quickly
swept through and destroyed all of the buildings belonging to the community's monks. As the fire reached the women's enclosure, the senior
monk—guardian of two of the three keys required to unlock the bolts
that secured the only door—panicked and was unable to find them. A
desperate Abbot Gottfried (1138–1165) gave the order to break down the
door and rescue the women. The nuns, once outside their familiar quar-
ters, were uncertain where to go—being outside the cloister seems to
have been as upsetting and disorienting as the fire itself.[14]

We hear this story from the monk Irimbert, who would serve as abbot
of Admont from 1172 to 1176. He states that the three-lock door that
caused such distress during the fire was, under normal circumstances,
opened only for the entrance of a sister making her profession, the ad-
ministration of last rites, and burial.[15] All communication with the out-

---

11. Barbara Newman, *Sister of Wisdom: St. Hildegard's Theology of the Feminine* (Berkeley, 1987),
p. 6.

12. Joan Ferrante, *To the Glory of Her Sex: Women's Roles in the Composition of Medieval Texts* (Bloomington, 1997) provides a discussion of collaboration between men and women in the composition
of Latin texts.

13. Admont is located in a valley on the Enns River in the twelfth-century archdiocese of Salzburg
(modern Graz-Seckau). For a general history, see Jakob Wichner, *Geschichte des Benediktiner-Stiftes
Admont*, 4 vols. (Graz, 1874–80); Rudolph List, *Stift Admont. 1074–1974. Festschrift zur 900-Jahrfeier*
(Reid im Innkreis, 1974); and Walter Steinböck, "Die Gründung des benediktinischen Reform-
klosters Admont," *Studien und Mitteilungen zur Geschichte des Benediktiner-ordens und seiner Zweige*
84 (1973): 52–81. On the women's community at Admont, see Jakob Wichner, "Das ehemalige
Nonnenkloster O.S.B. zu Admont," *Wissenschlaftliche Mittheilungen aus dem Benediktiner-orden* 2
(1881): 75–86 and 288–319.

14. See Bernard Pez, *Bibliotheca ascetica antiquo-nova* (Regensburg, 1725), 8:454–64. Fire that
threatens nuns locked in their enclosure is a literary topos in medieval writing about holy women.
See Johnson, *Equal in Monastic Profession*, pp. 154–55. We know from monastery records, including the report of the consecration of the rebuilt abbey church, that a fire did, in fact, destroy a number of buildings at Admont in 1152.

15. Pez, *Bibliotheca*, p. 459.

side world, Irimbert claims, took place through a single small window in the enclosure. This opening, and the bolted door, provided the only physical link to the world beyond the cloister.[16] Irimbert's account is interesting for its reflection of contemporary concern about the proximity of men and women in double monasteries. He makes it clear that no such improprieties were possible at Admont.[17] Still, even if we allow for enthusiastic exaggeration, it appears that the monastery's nuns and monks were physically segregated and did not interact freely.[18]

Given this clear preoccupation with claustration, it is surprising that nuns were not marginal figures at Admont. In fact, they played a particularly active role in the lively intellectual life of the monastery.[19] The author of a contemporary *Life* of one unnamed *magistra,* or abbess, praises this highly educated woman for her ability to write both German and Latin, and for her mastery of sacred Scripture as well.[20] The *Life,* written after 1137, presents the author's vision of the ideal Admont nun: pious and highly literate.[21] Irimbert himself later testifies that the sisters conducted their own daily chapter meeting under the leadership of the *magistra.* Many, he says, were highly literate and skilled biblical exegetes, and a few could preach in place of the abbot when he was unable to deliver

16. The abbot did not refer to the arrangements for necessities such as food, materials for making clothes, and other essential supplies passing into the women's enclosure. Clearly, these must have entered through something other than the small window in the chapter house. Refuse, clothing made by the nuns for the monks, and other materials must likewise have found their way out.

17. The nuns maintained written contacts with the outside world, as evidenced by fragments of extant correspondence preserved in Admont's archives. See Admont, Stiftsarchiv Ii/1, fragments of twelfth-century parchment containing a collection of letters written by the nuns. Admont librarian Jakob Wichner transcribed two of these letters and published them in the appendix to his article, "Das ehemalige Nonnenkloster," pp. 318–19. My article "Voices from the Cloister: A Nuns' Letter-Book from Twelfth-Century Admont" is forthcoming.

18. The issue in this context is not active enclosure—that is, whether nuns occasionally left the cloister to defend their interests, visit ailing family members, or tend to other pressing business—but that when they were in residence, a strict separation between men and women was maintained. On the types of enclosure, see Johnson, *Equal in Monastic Profession,* p. 151, and Jane Tibbetts Schulenburg, "Strict Active Enclosure and Its Effects on the Female Monastic Experience (ca. 500–1100)," in *Distant Echoes, Medieval Religious Women,* vol. 1, ed. John A. Nichols and Lillian Thomas Shank (Kalamazoo, 1984), pp. 51–52.

19. As both Suzanne Wemple and Jane Schulenburg point out, claustration in the early Middle Ages tended to isolate women from educational opportunities. See Wemple, *Women in Frankish Society: Marriage and the Cloister, 500–900* (Philadelphia, 1985), pp. 187–88, and Schulenburg, "Strict Active Enclosure," p. 78.

20. "*Vita, ut videtur, cuiusdam magistrae monialium Admuntensium in Styria,*" *Analecta Bollandiana* 12 (1893): 356–66.

21. While scholars debate the precise identity of the author, she was certainly a nun at Admont. See Frederick Ohly, "Ein Admonter Liebesgruß," *Zeitschrift für deutsches Altertum und deutsche Literatur* 87 (1956): 13–23.

his daily sermon.[22] Some of the nuns may even have written down their own sermons or composed their own biblical commentaries.[23]

In spite of their physical restrictions, the women were well integrated into the community's intellectual life, which was a defining feature of twelfth-century Admont. Under abbots Wolfhold (1115–1137) and Gottfried, the monastery became one the most important centers of learning in Bavaria. Wolfhold, who had been a monk at the reformed monastery of St. George in the Black Forest, introduced the customs of Hirsau to Admont upon his arrival in 1115.[24] Medieval monastic reform tended to rekindle interest in book copying and library building, and this was especially true of monasteries affiliated with Hirsau, where an upswing in book production often paralleled the composition of original texts.[25] The wealth of surviving manuscripts copied by the community's twelfth-century scribes, as well as the number and variety of original texts copied by community members, testify to the intellectual revival that followed the advent of this reform.[26]

The degree to which monks and nuns worked together to compose and copy the fruits of that revival, in view of the women's alleged strict enclosure, is also surprising. We hear first of collaboration from Irimbert, who states in the prologue to his sermon-commentary on 2 Kings, one in a series of sermons originally preached through the window in the nuns'

---

22. Pez, *Bibliotheca,* p. 460.

23. Stephan Borgehammar, "Who Wrote the Admont Sermon Corpus—Gottfried the Abbot, His Brother Irimbert, or the Nuns?" in *De l'homélie au sermon: Histoire de la prédication médiévale,* ed. Jacqueline Hamesse and Xavier Hermand (Louvain-La-Neuve, 1993), p. 49.

24. Hirsau was a Benedictine monastery in the Black Forest, reformed following the model of Cluny during the eleventh century. The monastery soon became a powerful center of reform in Germany. See Stephanus Hilpisch, *Benedictinism through Changing Centuries,* trans. Leonard J. Doyle (Collegeville, 1958), pp. 62–63, and Hermann Jakobs, *Die Hirsauer. Ihre Ausbreitung und Rechtsstellung im Zeitalter des Investiturstreites,* Kölner historische Abhandlungen 4, (Cologne, 1961). Some scholars have argued that the connection between Hirsau and Admont predated the arrival of Wolfhold. See Helmut J. Mezler-Andelberg, "Admont und die Klosterreform zu Beginn des 12. Jahrhunderts," *Zeitschrift des Historischen Vereines für Steiermark* 47 (1956): 28–42.

25. Kottje, "Klosterbibliotheken," pp. 145–62. See also Karin Dengler-Schreiber, *Scriptorium und Bibliothek des Klosters Michelsberg im Bamberg* (Graz, 1979), for a study of scribal culture at Michelsberg, a community that joined the Hirsau Reform in 1112. Dengler-Schreiber documents the increased output of the scriptorium there between 1112 and 1114. Michelsberg may have had close ties to Admont, since Irimbert was Abbot of Michelsberg for many years before returning to Admont to serve as abbot there in 1172. Romuald Bauerreiss, *Kirchengeschichte Bayerns,* 7 vols. (Munich, 1958), 3:132–74, provides a survey of the blossoming of interest in theology, historical writing, poetry, and drama that characterized monasteries affiliated with the Hirsau Reform.

26. These include a large corpus of biblical commentaries and sermons, several biographies, and an historical chronicle. See Beach, "Female Scribes," pp. 72–81. For a general description of the form and content of the Admont sermon corpus, see Stephan Borgehammar, "The Admont Sermon Corpus" (paper presented at the International Congress for Medieval Studies, Kalamazoo, Mich., 8 May 1993).

enclosure between 1151 and 1152, that the nuns secretly and without his knowledge recorded his words on parchment. Perhaps his claim of ignorance was no more than a formulaic expression of modesty. Maybe he was trying to shift the responsibility for initiating what may have been a rather unconventional collaborative effort onto the nuns. It is also possible that Irimbert truly did not know that the nuns were taking notes, since he probably could not see his entire audience as he preached.[27] In any case, his comments draw our attention to the presence of female collaborators.

In the prologue to his sermon-commentary on 4 Kings, Irimbert again acknowledged the help he received from the women's community:

> In the very great difficulty of this work, I was refreshed thoroughly by the liberality of the aforementioned sisters, since they appointed me two sisters free from every occupation, who continually and diligently transcribed my spoken words onto tablets.[28]

From this account, it seems that the work that began spontaneously had become an official collaborative project. Two nuns were now primarily engaged in helping Irimbert with his work. These women must have been skilled writers, for taking dictation is a complex task requiring simultaneously careful listening and fast writing. To this, we must add the need for thorough comprehension, since the nuns probably did some editing of the dictated material in the process of converting their notes, necessarily written in haste and abbreviated, into a manuscript draft.[29] The cumbersome nature of the materials they used—in this case a stylus and wax tablets—further complicated their task. The collaboration between preacher and scribe cannot have been made easier by Irimbert's need to speak, or even shout, loudly and clearly enough to be heard and understood through a small aperture in the wall.

This was not, however, the nuns' first involvement with Irimbert's corpus of commentarial works, and their interest, whether hidden or not, in

27. Johann Wilhelm Braun, "Irimbert von Admont," *Frühmittelalterliche Studien* 7 (1973): 288. It would not have been unusual for the nuns to have access to parchment for this project since they operated their own scriptorium within the enclosure. It is also possible that one of the monks, or even Irimbert himself, provided the needed materials, casting doubt on the secrecy of the project and the sincerity of Irimbert's ignorance.

28. ". . . difficultate earundem sororum utrimque recreatus sum liberalitate, ut duas michi sorores ab omni occupatione liberas deputarent, que continue ac diligenter transscriberent, que a me dicta in tabulis excipi potuissent." Braun, "Irimbert von Admont," p. 320.

29. Nicole Bériou, *La prédication de Ranulphe de la Houblonnière: Sermons aux clercs et aux simples gens à Paris au XIIIe siècle*, 2 vols. (Paris, 1987), 1:59–64, examines the process of recording "live" sermons, stressing the impact of the recorder's own interests and understandings on the form and content of the resulting written text.

his Kings sermons must not have come as a complete surprise to him. A few years earlier, between 1140 and 1149, as many as eleven women helped to copy, and possibly to edit, his commentaries on the book of Ruth and on Judges 19–21.[30] Two primary hands appear consistently through-out the early redactions of these texts. These two scribes, who may have been the two who would later help Irimbert with his Kings commen-taries, worked together to turn preliminary versions of the text (Vorau MS 193, Admont MS 650, Admont MS 682) into the final version of the text (Admont MS 17). The rubricator of MS 17 identified them as Irmin-gart and Regilind.[31]

The execution and construction of the "draft" volumes containing the Ruth and Judges texts provide important clues to the circumstances of their production. The small (octavo) format of these books reduced the amount of parchment required for each gathering. There are fre-quent hand changes, and the scribes often appear to have been writing quickly. This implies that speed of execution was important, and copy-ists working cooperatively could produce faster results. Practical consid-erations took precedence over aesthetics, although an effort was made to use a uniform book hand and parchment with the same characteristics throughout. A more elegant script, illuminated initials, and a larger for-mat distinguish the manuscript containing the final recension of the texts (Admont 17) from the earlier recensions.[32]

If we look at the physical structure of the early manuscripts, we see what may have been a strategy for facilitating collaborative production. The basic subunit of most medieval manuscripts is the quire or gather-ing. Once filled with text, gatherings were stitched together to produce a book. The most common type of gathering is the quaternio, comprising four sheets of parchment folded to form eight folios.[33] The scribes of Ad-mont's early commentary manuscripts, though, used a different approach. Instead of using uniform gatherings as the basic subunit of their books, they used booklets: independent subunits made up of one or more quires tailored to the text contained.[34] Most of these booklets contain just one

---

30. Admont, Stiftsbibliothek MS 650 and MS 682; Vorau, Stiftsbibliothek Ms 193.
31. Admont, Stiftsbibliothek MS 17, p. 393 and p. 420; Braun, "Irimbert von Admont," p. 288; Beach, "Female Scribes," p. 67.
32. Significant modifications were made to the texts from recension to recension, indicating that the commentary was still a work-in-progress. A collation of the various manuscripts and an analy-sis of the textual changes made, while clearly beyond the scope of the present study, would likely yield interesting information about the genesis of both works.
33. For a full treatment of gatherings, see Jacques Lemaire, *Introduction à la codicologie* (Louvain-la-Neuve, 1989), pp. 39–67.
34. Pamela R. Robinson, "The 'Booklet': A Self-Contained Unit in Composite Manuscripts," in *Codicologica* 3 (Leiden, 1980): 46–69.

text. Many contain one or more irregular gatherings (i.e. other than the common four-bifolium gathering or quaternio) to provide exactly the space for that text.[35]

Admont MS 650, for example, is a composite of three independent booklets.[36] For booklet one, Irimbert's *Commentary on the Book of Ruth,* Irmingart used three regular quires and two single folios (quires one through three in Table 1). For the *Commentary on Judges 19–21,* contained in booklet two, Irmingart and Regilind first filled three regular gatherings (quires 4–6). To accommodate the short piece of text remaining after completing quire six, they added an irregular gathering of two bifolia and two single leaves to provide a total of six folios. Had Irmingart and Regilind copied this text in a standard quire, two folios would have remained unused. Booklet three contains an anonymous commentary on Exodus that was nine folios long—too long to fit in a single quaternio. Irmingart and Regilind added a single leaf to a regular gathering of four bifolia to provide the nine folios needed. If the nuns had used a standard quire to accommodate the last folio of text, they would have left seven folios blank. The women thus produced three independent booklets, each containing a single text. These may initially have circulated as individual units, but they were combined into composite volumes at an uncertain date.

Table 1. Use of Booklets in Admont, Stiftsbibliothek MS 650

Booklet	Text	Scribe	Location in Manuscript
One	Irimbert of Admont, *Commentary on the Book of Ruth*	Irmingart	fols. 1v–25r [quire 1 = III + 1] [quire 2 = IV] [quire 3 = IV + 2]
Two	Irimbert of Admont, *Commentary on Judges 19–21*	Regilind	fols. 26r–47v [quire 4 = IV] [quire 5 = IV] [quire 6 = IV]
		Irmingart	fols. 48r–49v [completes quire 6]
		Regilind	fols. 50r–55r [quire 7 = II + 2]
Three	Anonymous, *Commentary on Exodus*	Irmingart	fols. 56r–64r [quire 8 = IV + 1]

35. The distinction between quire-based and booklet-based book construction is analogous to the distinction between a standard book (even today composed of gatherings) and a series of offprints bound together to form a single volume.

36. I used the tables in Johann Wilhelm Braun, "Die Überlieferung der Schriften Gottfrieds und Irimberts von Admont mit einem Lebensabriß Irimberts" (Ph.D. diss., Universität Gießen, 1967), pp. 207–11 and pp. 215–18 as a base for my analysis of Admont MS 650 (Table 1) and Vorau MS 193 (Table 2) respectively. In the course of my work with the manuscripts, I made numerous changes to Braun's analysis.

The use of booklets may have served two purposes. First, because each subunit contained a complete text with little or no unused parchment, there was no need to coordinate space between texts. When the text ended, the booklet ended.[37] Another booklet was constructed to accommodate the next text. This was an efficient and economical strategy for accommodating the monastery's rapidly growing corpus of sermons and commentaries. As Irimbert and others wrote new texts, scribes copied them into independent booklets.

Second, the nuns' use of booklets could have facilitated collaboration between Admont's segregated scriptoria. While it was only the nuns who worked on the three booklets that comprise Admont MS 650, booklets in other composite volumes may have been copied by either male or female scribes. Table 2 contains a description of Vorau, Stiftsbibliothek MS 193, a collection of biblical sermons and commentaries, including Irimbert's Judges and Ruth texts, at least part of which was copied at Admont during the 1140s.

Only the sections containing Irimbert's Ruth and Judges texts can be attributed to nun-scribes. These were added to the work of an unidentified scribe who copied the entire first section of the book (fol. 3r–80r, quires 1–11), a collection of anonymous sermons.[38] Five other unidentified scribes copied section two, which itself can be divided into five subunits. None of the six unidentified hands is among the eleven female hands that I have identified at Admont. It is possible that these scribes were monks.[39] The composite approach may thus have eased coordination between the products of the monks' and nuns' scriptoria.

In the commentary manuscripts from Admont we do not see a group of individuals acting independently, but a team of scribes working in close coordination to produce a manuscript that appeared a unified whole. Two elements help to link the individual booklets. First, the careful training of the community's copyists to write a uniform bookhand helped to minimize the negative aesthetic impact of frequent alternation of scribes. Second, using a standard parchment format, with standard dimensions and ruling patterns, also helped to minimize visual differences

---

37. In the case of very short texts (one or two folios), booklets sometimes contain two or more.
38. The scribe of section 1 used a bookhand distinct from any other seen in the commentary manuscripts, and the parchment contains a unique ruling pattern, suggesting that this section was copied at another time or at a different monastery. The sermons in this section have been attributed to Abbot Gottfried, Irimbert's brother, with no clear justification. See Borgehammar, "Who Wrote the Admont Sermon Corpus," p. 48. For an overview of Admont's twelfth-century biblical sermons and commentaries, including the issue of authorship, see Fritz Peter Knapp, *Die Literatur des Früh- und Hochmittelalters in den Bistümern Passau, Salzburg, Brixen und Trient von den Anfängen bis zum Jahre 1273*, Geschichte der Literatur in Österreich 1 (Graz, 1994), pp. 74–79.
39. Beach, "Female Scribes," pp. 95–96.

Table 2. Composition of Vorau, Stiftsbibliothek MS 193

Section/Booklet	Text	Scribe	Location in Manuscript
One	Anonymous, Sermones de tempore et de sanctis; Sermones de tribus sapientibus	unknown #1	fols. 3r–80r [quire 1–11 = II, IV, V]
Two	Anonymous, Sermo de duobus ducibus et oblatione eorum	unknown #2	fols. 81r–83v [quire 12 = III]
	Anonymous, Sermo in dominica palmarum	unknown #3	fols. 84r–91v [quire 13 = III quire 14 = II]
	Anonymous, various short sermons	unknown #2 and unknown #4	fols. 92r–104v [quire 15 = IV quire 16 = II]
	Anonymous, various short sermons	unknown #5	fols. 105r–120v [quire 17 = IV quire 18 = IV]
	Anonymous, various short sermons	unknown #6	fols. 121r–156r [quires 19–22 = IV quire 23 = II]
Three	Irimbert of Admont, *Commentary on Judges 19–21*	Irmingart, Regilind, and nun-scribe A	fols. 157r–185r [quire 24 = IV quire 25 = V quire 26 = IV quire 27a = II]
Four	Irimbert of Admont, *Commentary on the Book of Ruth*	Irmingart, Regilind, and nun-scribes A and B	fols. 186r–214v [quire 27b = IV quire 28 = IV quire 29 = IV]

among the booklets. This facilitated the rapid production of manuscripts that were, nevertheless, harmonious in appearance.

SCHÄFTLARN

The scribes of the Premonstratensian double monastery of Schäftlarn developed different strategies to facilitate male-female collaboration.[40] Like their counterparts at Admont, Schäftlarn's women lived within the boundaries established by regulations for female claustration. The stat-

40. The priest Waltrich founded Schäftlarn, located south of Munich on the Isar River in the diocese of Freising, as a Benedictine community of men in 760. The community was destroyed by the Magyars and the secularization of its property early in the tenth century. Religious life was restored at Schäftlarn by the end of the century when a chapter of secular canons was established. This community was on the verge of extinction in 1140, when Bishop Otto of Freising (1138–1158) refounded it as a Premonstratensian house. See P. Leo Abstreiter, *Geschichte der Abtei Schäftlarn* (Schäftlarn, 1916); Paul Ruf, ed., *1200 Jahre Kloster Schäftlarn* (Schäftlarn, 1962); Josef Hemmerle, *Die Benediktinerklöster in Bayern* (Munich, 1951), pp. 115–16.

utes that the Premonstratensian order issued in 1134 demanded the strict enclosure of all professed sisters, or *sorores*.[41] Only priests were permitted to enter the women's cloister, and then only in groups of two or three to deliver a sermon, to hear confession, to administer communion, to perform last rites, or for other sacred duties.[42] Travel to other religious communities was permitted only for groups of at least ten women.[43] The door to the canonesses' enclosure was, in theory, opened only in the presence of two or three mature sisters, and conferences with visiting abbots or other religious persons took place through a window in the presence of witnesses.[44] A woman who left the cloister without following proper procedure was to be refused readmission.[45]

The statutes, however, tell only part of the story. We know from entries in the community's necrology that Schäftlarn housed a number of lay sisters, or *conversae*.[46] The term *conversa*, as used in the context of twelfth-century religious orders, is ambiguous and difficult to define precisely, and it is unclear how these women differed, if at all, from *sorores*.[47] Practice probably varied with time, location, and order. The distinction is especially unclear for Premonstratensian women, for whom manual labor in the service of an associated male community, a role that we have come to associate with lay sisters, was universal. While the *conversae* and *sorores* probably lived within a single community, we do not know whether the two groups were subject to the same strict cloister regulations.

Schäftlarn differed sharply from Admont in its assessment of the value of female education. While Admont operated a school for nuns and praised their abilities, Schäftlarn, as far as we know, provided no school for canonesses and was silent about their intellectual potential. Because Premonstratensian women lacked pastoral duties and did not, before the double monasteries were separated, participate in the celebration of the

41. Raphael Van Waefelghem, "Les premiers statuts de l'ordre de Prémontré," *Analectes de l'Ordre de Prémontré* 9 (1913): 65.
42. Ibid., p. 65.
43. Ibid., p. 66.
44. Ibid.
45. Ibid.
46. See Johnson, *Equal in Monastic Profession*, pp. 178–80, for a description of French *conversae*.
47. On the vexed issue of the distinction between *conversae* and *sorores*, see Sally Thompson, *Religious Women* (Oxford, 1991), p. 147, who argues that there was little practical distinction between the two types of women within the early twelfth-century Premonstratensian order. See also Brian Golding, *Gilbert of Sempringham and the Gilbertine Order* (Oxford, 1995), pp. 119–26, for a useful synthesis of current scholarship on the distinction between *conversae* and *sorores*, especially at Gilbertine, but also at Cistercian, Arrouaisian, and Premonstratensian houses in England. The issue has not been settled and requires further examination.

opus Dei,[48] the order felt no need to educate them.[49] The head of the female community was the prioress, and she assigned manual tasks, such as sewing, washing, and weaving.[50] These activities, which occupied most of the canonesses' daily life, required neither reading nor writing.[51] The statutes did not mandate the operation of schools for the order's women, and in fact specifically limited devotional reading to a few psalms and prayers. Female reading was merely tolerated, with special concessions sometimes made for those who arrived at the monastery better educated.[52] The lack of evidence of a canonesses' library (in the form of, for example, *ex libris* entries indicating that manuscripts belonged to the women, lending lists, or other records of book use by the women) suggests that the community heeded this limiting directive. There is no evidence to suggest that Schäftlarn held a more positive view of the intellectual potential of women than did the larger order.

Yet women were a significant component of the monastery's exceptionally visible scribal work force.[53] Three of the thirteen named scribes of the house were female.[54] How did women come to copy manuscripts

48. The *opus Dei*, or Divine Office, is the daily liturgical cycle of seven chanted services mandated by the *Rule of Saint Benedict*.

49. The Premonstratensian governing body ordered the separation of the women's and men's communities in 1141, and although the decree was not immediately or uniformly obeyed, this move reflects both an ongoing discomfort with the presence of women within the order and the contemporary distrust of double monasteries. See A. Erens, "Les soeurs dans l'ordre de Prémontré," *Analecta Praemonstratensia* 5 (1929): 5–26. In newly divided houses in which women began to sing the liturgy, a distinction between those who specialized in manual jobs (*conversae*) and those who specialized in liturgical ones (*sorores cantantes*) may have emerged with greater clarity. This argument, however, cannot be made for Schäftlarn, where the male and female communities were not separated.

50. The ultimate earthly authority in the monastery, however, was the prior, and he was responsible for monitoring the canonesses' activities and administering the sacraments to them. See Hugues Lamy, *L'abbaye de Tongerloo* (Louvain, 1914), p. 94, and Clifford Hugh Lawrence, *Medieval Monasticism: Forms of Religious Life in Western Europe in the Middle Ages* (London and New York, 1989), p. 223.

51. Manual work was central to the canonesses' daily life, and they formed a kind of manual labor corps, primarily in the service of the male community. The statutes list sewing, repairing, and washing clothing for the canons as possible occupations, suggesting that these activities were among the most common for Premonstratensian women. See Van Waefelghem, "Les premiers statuts," pp. 64–65, and Lamy, *Tongerloo*, p. 93. See also Erens, "Les soeurs," p. 14.

52. "[A sister] may have a Psalter or individual psalms, or the prayers or vigils of blessed Mary according to the provision of the abbot, but then she may learn nothing else. If any one shall have greater learning from outside the community, she shall be able to examine another book on feast days with the permission of the Abbot." Van Waefelghem, "Les premiers statuts," p. 66.

53. An exceptionally large number of Schäftlarn's scribes identified themselves in subscriptions under both Henry and his three predecessors. Almost one fifth of Schäftlarn's approximately sixty-six surviving twelfth-century volumes contain the name of a scribe or scribes. Schäftlarn alone accounts for eleven of the thirty-four named scribes who emerge from the manuscripts cataloged by Elisabeth Klemm, *Die romanischen Handschriften der bayerischen Staatsbibliothek*, 3 vols. (Wiesbaden, 1980).

54. Two female copyists, Sophia and Irmingart, are identified in colophons, and a third, Adelhait, in the house necrology. See notes 58–60 below.

in this restrictive environment? The answer may be simple community need. When Bishop Otto of Freising (1138–1158) refounded Schäftlarn in 1140 as a Praemonstratensian monastery, the library was insignificant.[55] A scriptorium was immediately established to produce texts needed for the central work of training priests.[56] Under priors Englebert (1140–1153) and Henry (1164–1200), book production was especially vigorous.[57] During this time of active book production, competent copyists of both sexes would have been welcomed into the community and its scriptorium. Recruits with previous scribal training could be assigned to the scriptorium for their primary manual work.

The first female scribe we meet at Schäftlarn is Sophia, who names herself in two signatures in the surviving volumes of what was originally a three-volume copy of Augustine's *Commentary on the Psalms*.[58] Sophia was active in the scriptorium as early as the 1160s, and it is possible that she was still producing books as late as 1180. The house necrology identifies two lay sisters (*conversae*) named Sophia. Although we can only speculate, it is possible that Sophia was a lay, rather than a professed, sister.[59] Schäftlarn's necrology names a second scribe, Adelhait, as both *conversa* and *scriptrix,* proving that the scriptorium did, in fact, employ lay sisters.[60]

Sophia worked under Adalbertus, who was master of the scriptorium under Prior Henry. In the two volumes of Augustine's *Commentary on the Psalms* (Clm 17052 and Clm 17053) the two worked closely together—and probably even in the same workshop.[61] Their hands alternate throughout both volumes. Adalbertus wrote the titles and portions of the text and made corrections, while Sophia copied the bulk of the text. Tables 3 and 4 detail the hand changes in these manuscripts, and illustrate the extent

55. Ruf, "Handschriften des Klosters Schäftlarn," pp. 29–39.

56. Hugues Lamy characterized Premonstratensian monasteries as "veritable seminaries," where the canons pursued a practical course of study geared toward the pastorate rather than one intended to foster literary productivity. See Lamy, *Tongerloo,* p. 289.

57. Beach, "Female Scribes," pp. 304–7.

58. The first signature—*scripsit Sophya*—is found at the bottom edge of fol. 214v of Codex latinus monacensis (Clm) 17052. The second—*sophia scripsit*—is found at the bottom edge of fol. 108v in Clm 17053. For a complete description of these signatures and Sophia's hand, see Beach, "Female Scribes," pp. 312–17 and 330–32.

59. "Sophia cv." See *Necrologium Sheftlariense,* ed. F. L. Baumann, MGH Necr. 3:116.

60. "Adelhait cv. nra. scriba." See *Necrologium Sheftlariense,* p. 116; Penelope Johnson has observed that *conversae* in France were generally unlettered. See Johnson, *Equal in Monastic Profession,* p. 178, This was not the case with Adelhait or Sophia, if the latter was also a lay sister.

61. Schäftlarn's booklist, compiled between 1160 and 1162 includes an "Exposition of Augustine on the Psalter in Three Volumes." See Klemm, *Die romanischen Handschriften* vol. 2, pt. 1, pp. 97–98, and Günter Glauche and Hermann Knaus, eds., *Mittelalterliche Bibliothekskataloge Deutschlands und der Schweiz,* vol. 4, pt. 2, p. 726.

Table 3. Hand Changes in Clm 17052

Location in Manuscript	Scribe	Comments
fols. 1r–1v (to line 7) [quire 1]	Adalbertus	
fols. 1v (line 8)–41r (to line 10) [quires 1–6]	Sophia	Corrections and titles by Adalbertus.
fols. 41r (line 11)–44v (to line 20) [quire 6]	Adalbertus	
fols. 44v–60r (to line 26) [quires 6–8]	Sophia	Corrections and titles by Adalbertus.
fols. 60r–94r (to line 21) [quires 8–12]	Adalbertus	
fols. 94r–129v [quires 12–17]	Sophia	Corrections and titles by Adalbertus.
fols. 130r–146r (to line 21) [quires 17–19]	Adalbertus	
fols. 146r–214v [quires 19–27]	Sophia	Corrections and titles by Adalbertus. Contemporary subscription on 214v, probably written by Sophia (scripsit Sophya).

Table 4. Hand Changes in Clm 17053

Location in Manuscript	Scribe	Comments
fols. 1r–28v [quires 1–4]	Sophia	Corrections and by Adalbertus.
fols. 29r–35r (to line 11) [quire 4–5]	Adalbertus	Hand change in middle of line 11.
fols. 35r–115r [quires 5–15]	Sophia	Corrections and titles by Adalbertus. Contemporary subscription (f.108v), probably written by Sophia herself (sophia scripsit).
fols. 115v–139r [quires 15–18]	Adalbertus	
fols. 139v–150r (to line 31) [quires 18–19]	Sophia	Corrections and titles by Adalbertus.
fols. 150r–177r (to line 5) [quires 19–22]	Adalbertus	
fols. 177r–277r [quires 22–35]	Sophia	Corrections and title by Adalbertus. "SOPHYA" scratched into parchment on fol. 269v.

to which the two worked together, often changing in the middle of a folio or, in places, in the middle of a line.

How was such close collaboration between a male and female scribe possible at Schäftlarn? One answer may lie in Sophia's status at the monastery. If she was, in fact, a lay sister, her close cooperation with Adalbertus reflects a somewhat relaxed policy regarding the enclosure of such women in order to facilitate book production—an important piece of information that sheds light on the elusive category, *conversa.* The 1134 statutes specified that *sorores* were to be cloistered, but this document makes no specific mention of lay sisters and no documents of practice have survived to fill in the gaps. Here manuscript evidence offers a unique insight: whatever the official policy may have been regarding the segregation of the sexes, women and men could interact within the context of the scriptorium.

The logistics of this interaction are uncertain. Perhaps lay sisters had access to the men's scriptorium. Alternatively, Adalbertus may have had permission to enter the residence of the women to copy and to oversee book production. A third, less likely, possibility is that there was no direct interaction between Sophia and Adalbertus. To argue that Sophia and Adalbertus worked in two separate facilities is to accept an elaborate scenario of exchange of materials. At each hand change—sometimes in the middle of a line—the scribe stopped work, marked the stopping point in the exemplar, cleaned up his or her materials, and passed the parchment on to the collaborating scribe in a separate workshop. The second scribe would have to reverse the process, setting out the parchment, preparing the ink, and locating the starting point in the exemplar before beginning work anew. Such a transfer would have occurred thirteen times in the two surviving volumes alone and perhaps an additional six or seven times in the third, lost volume. It seems much more likely that the materials remained stationary while the scribes themselves changed places. This supports the theory that the two worked in the same scriptorium, although not necessarily at the same time. Either Sophia left her enclosure and went to work in the monk's scriptorium or Adalbertus left his and entered the women's enclosure.

Sophia was also the main scribe of Clm 17054, a copy of Augustine's *Commentary on the Gospel of John,* which contains the hand of two male scribes: Adalbertus and Marchwardus. As in Clm 17052 and 17053, Adalbertus executed the titles and the beginning of the text and made corrections to the entire manuscript. His hand does not reappear in the body of the text. This was not a joint copying effort such as that seen in the psalm commentaries. Adalbertus, rather, seems to have directed Sophia's work without functioning as a co-scribe. He copied the prologue to the commentary on folio 1r, and Marchwardus copied the next section of the text. Sophia completed the volume, and both Adalbertus and Marchwardus corrected her work.

This limited collaboration did not require the extensive interaction evident in Clm 17052 and 17053; at no point did Adalbertus and Marchwardus and Sophia collaborate within a quire.[62] The canons may have

Table 5. Hand Changes in Clm 17054

Location in Manuscript	Scribe	Comments
fol. 1r [quire 1]	Adalbertus	
fols. 1v–8v [quire 1]	Marchwardus	
fols. 9r–200v [quires 2–25]	Sophia	31v, col. 1 contains an 11-line correction made by Marchwardus. Other corrections and titles by Adalbertus.

62. On collaboration within a quire as evidence of close contact between scribes, see Beach, "Female Scribes," pp. 15–16.

written the first quire for Sophia to use as a model for the layout of the remaining text.

Perhaps this change in the pattern of collaboration reflects Sophia's growing scribal experience and maturity.[63] As time passed, she may have been able to work faster and with less supervision, factors that could have encouraged Adalbertus to assign her jobs to complete by herself. It is also possible that claustration at Schäftlarn was tightened after the completion of the earlier volumes. Sophia and Adalbertus copied Clm 17052 and 17053 between 1165 and 1170, while Clm 17054 may have been completed as late as 1180. The community may have tightened claustration for lay sisters during the intervening years.

A third scribe, Irmingart, who was a professed sister at Schäftlarn between 1164 and 1200, is named both in the community necrology and in two contemporary colophons.[64] A moderately skilled scribe, she seemingly worked alone; there is no evidence that Irmingart participated in team copying. She, like Sophia later in her career, may have been prevented from team collaboration by the requirements of claustration. As a professed sister, Irmingart was probably subject to the strict cloister regulations set down in the Premonstratensian statutes.

Also like Sophia, Irmingart worked under Adalbertus's direction. Adalbertus copied the first column of text in Clm 17087, a collection of patristic homilies on the Epistles and Gospels, to establish a pattern for Irmingart to follow before the parchment was passed into the enclosure for her to complete (see Table 6). Given this limited exchange, Irmingart could easily have worked for Adalbertus without having any direct contact with him.

Irmingart's hand also appears in a copy of Palladius's treatise *On Agri-*

Table 6. Hand Changes in Clm 17087

Location in Manuscript	Scribe	Comments
fol. 1r (column 1) [quire 1]	Adalbertus	
fols. 1r (column 2)–223v [quires 1–28]	Irmingart	Corrections and titles by Adalbertus. Cruciform colophon on f. 223v.

63. Elizabeth Klemm dated Clm 17052 and 17053 to 1165–70, and Clm 17054 to 1175–80. Klemm, *Die romanischen Handschriften*, vol. 2, pt. 1, pp. 97 and 104. I disagree with Klemm's attribution of Clm 17054 to Irmingart.

64. The necrology entry reads "Irengardis scriba." See *Necrologium Scheftlariense*, p. 121; Clm 17087, fol. 223v contains a cruciform colophon in Irmingart's own hand: this colophon reads, "Iste liber pertinet ad sanctum Dyonisium Schleftlaren quem scripsit soror Irmingart obtentu Domni Hainrici prepositi." ("This book, which was written by sister Irmingart with the permission of Prior Henry, belongs to Saint Dionysus, Schäftlarn."). Clm 17116, fol. 129v contains a similar colophon by a second hand. A colophon is a scribal notation that records information about the production of the text. A colophon can include one or more identifiers such as the name of a copyist, the name of the person who commissioned the copy, the place of production, or the date of completion.

culture (Clm 23478). A single hand change occurs on folio 52v of this volume, and a second scribe steps in and completes the text. It is impossible at this point to say whether this second scribe was a canon or a canoness. Irmingart copied Clm 17116, Rupert of Deutz's *On the Divine Offices*, without collaborators, and was also the sole scribe of an alphabetical glossary (Clm 17151).

Although Schäftlarn's copyists frequently produced texts collaboratively, they did not use a standard bookhand. This resulted in manuscripts with a rather careless appearance. Indeed, the wide variation in scribal hands in evidence in the products of Schäftlarn's scriptorium suggests that individual scribes learned to write in diverse settings, before arriving at this monastery. In contrast to Admont, we can identify no single bookhand as typical of Schäftlarn's workshop. We can attribute this difference to the presence of a school for scribes, male and female, at Admont. There was no analog at Schäftlarn, where women were not taught to write, and scribes simply used the hand that they had previously learned.

Although none of the texts copied by Schäftlarn's female scribes was, according to the statutes, available for their reading, this apparently was not an impediment to participation in book production. The drive to produce more books for the library probably cleared the way for female copyists' activity. Reading and copying are two distinct activities, and it is possible that appropriately trained women were assigned to copy books without encouragement—or even permission—to explore their contents. The formula used in two colophons identifying Irmingart's work—"Sister Irmingart copied this book for the monastery of Schäftlarn *with the permission of* [emphasis mine] Prior Henry"—suggests that she needed Henry's approval to make the copy. The community's large book collection, which the canonesses helped to create, probably had little impact on their intellectual life. An intellectually stimulating environment evidently was not an essential prerequisite for scribal activity.

CONCLUSION

The traditional tools of paleography and codicology, when applied to surviving manuscripts from Admont and Schäftlarn, reshape our understanding of the nature of interaction between men and women within the twelfth-century monastery. From these books emerge extraordinary glimpses of ordinary women at work—alone, with other women, and with men.

Female scribes worked in a variety of institutional settings, and patterns of collaboration between men and women in the production of manuscripts reflect varying degrees of tolerance for contact between the sexes. At Admont, Irimbert and the nuns worked together to compose original sermons and biblical commentaries, and if Irimbert is telling us the truth, they did so within the bounds of very strict enclosure. But their collaboration was not limited to dictation; the nuns' scriptorium helped to transform the dictated words—starting with the wax tablets—first into draft manuscript, and then into final deluxe edition. Their approach to assembling manuscripts may have enabled scribes of both sexes to contribute to a single volume with minimal visual disruption and wasted parchment. Manuscript evidence seems to support Irimbert's claim that Admont's nuns were strictly enclosed: while collaboration between men and women was close, it remained indirect. The nuns remained in their enclosure, and the monks, including Irimbert, stayed out.

At Schäftlarn, however, there may have been contact between the sexes in the scriptorium. Although the statutes of the Premonstratensian order call for the strict enclosure of women, Sophia and Adalbertus apparently worked within a single workshop to produce at least two manuscripts. If Sophia was a lay sister, as the necrology suggests, we may see in these volumes evidence that nonprofessed women in the community were permitted some contact with men. Do the changes in this pattern, which seem to reflect reduced contact between male and female scribes, reflect changes in Schäftlarn's practice of claustration? The manuscripts leave us here to speculate.

II

Texts and Contexts

II

Texts and Contexts

Sulmona Society and the
Miracles of Peter of Morrone

Robert Brentano

The city and diocese of Sulmona are oddly rich in the fourteenth-century documents descriptive of them which are preserved in the city archives. The richness is odd because of the singularity of the documents. Sulmona does not retain the sort of thick net of various records from the later Middle Ages that one finds, for example, at neighboring Rieti, although there is a nice collection from a confraternity housed within the archivio di stato, and in the archivio della cattedrale there is a miscellany of documents including some quite interesting wills—normal things. But the striking survivals from the fourteenth century are three: the earliest known (I believe) record of an episcopal visitation in the south of Italy, made by a Franciscan bishop of Sulmona in 1356; the earliest known (I believe) surviving catasto from the south of Italy from 1376; and the Sulmona codex, which contains an incomplete record of the *processus informativus,* the local inquisition, made by the papal (Clement V's) inquisitors seeking, in 1306, evidence for the canonization process of Peter of Morrone who had become in 1294 Pope Celestine V.[1]

1. That I have been worrying the autobiography of Peter of Morrone for some time Lester Little and Lella Gandini know too well; they have had to listen to me try to cope with it publicly and privately in Massachusetts and California repeatedly, and probably also in Rome and Venice. I apologize for not bringing them a fresher hermit. The autobiography is helping to form a book that I am trying to write about autobiographical presentations in thirteenth-century chroniclers. At present I have in preparation a considerably shorter essay, complementary to this one, "Peter of Morrone, Space, and the Problem of Relics," which approaches the material from a rather different angle. For the episcopal visitation see G. Celidonio, "Una visita pastorale della Diocesi Valvense fatta nel 1356," *Rassegna Abruzzese* 3 (1899):155–81, 167–78; I should like to thank the late Don Antonino Chiaverini for having brought the manuscript of the visitation to the study of his home and having there let me check Celidonio's edition against it. Although I have examined the catasto I am

The 1356 visitation record's little stories, the questions of the visitor and the answers given to them, show, in the questions, some patterns of contemporarily understood, relatively official Christianity, and, in the answers, the failures of that Christianity: the Christocentric church of the Eucharist and the corporal works of mercy (the echoes of Innocent III)— the little windows to be installed in walls for the keeping of the "Corpus Christi" and the clergy ordered to learn by heart, and to be able to explain exactly, the articles of the faith, the sacraments, the commandments, the corporal works, the deadly sins. Beyond lurks the scent of darker sins and more venal activities: the cleric with a sort of wife in his house; the deacon and his woman whose son had died, or been killed, unbaptized; the two clergymen who had run a cattlemarket and a woolmarket.[2] It is a rude enough countryside with its sometimes decaying and ill-kept churches, supporting not too well its not too well instructed clergy. But within the decade after the Great Death it is still recognizably Christian.

In the center of this rudeness, and not too far from its dirt farmers and mountain herdsmen, lay the city of Sulmona. For it, from 1376, twenty years after the visitation, and ten more years after the Great Death, comes the early catasto, the tax list. The catasto exposes a city rich with doctors, notaries, judges, paper millers, saffron and silkworm growers, and goldsmiths, a city of 1,667 houses, 232 gardens, 165 lots or lots with sheds, and 108 shops. Its six districts had a total population of about 6,000 people; it had suburbs. It had resident strangers, especially from the surrounding areas but also from Rome, Florence, Venice, and particularly from Foligno and Norcia.

In this city of some 1,360 families, about one-third of the wealth was in the hands of some twenty families; and (if the catasto, in this, can be trusted) the value of the property of the richest family (the Sanità, who had come to Sulmona by 1200), who were only less rich (in the richness exposed by the catasto) than the cathedral church, was 107 times that of the property of the average recorded family. The tone of the catasto's

here dependent on its analysis by the careful local historian Elio Mattiocco, particularly in his *Struttura urbana e società della Sulmona medievale* (Sulmona, 1978), but also in his more recent *Sulmona, città e contado nel catasto del 1376* (Sulmona, 1994). Although Don Antonino Chiaverini also permitted me to read the part of the canonization process preserved in Sulmona, I am here following the printed edition in Franz Xaver Seppelt, ed., *Monumenta Coelestiniana: Quellen zur Geschichte des Papstes Coelestin V,* Quellen und Forschungen, Görres-Gesellschaft, 19 (Paderborn, 1921), pp. 209–331. See, for example, documents in Sulmona, Archivio di stato, Cass. II, fasc. 18, nos. 171, 172, 178, 179, and Antonino Chiaverini, *La diocesi di Valva e Sulmona,* vol. 5: *secoli XIV–XV* (Sulmona, 1977).
2. Celidonio, "Una visita," for example, pp. 168–70; MS, fols. 2v–5r. Besides negligence and (reported) sexual activity, there seems to have been much gambling and selling of livestock.

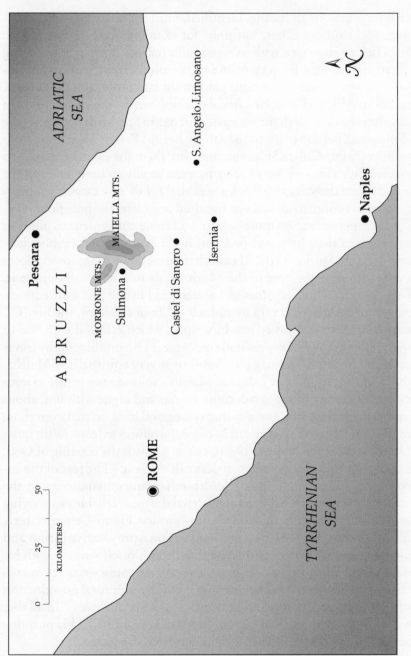

Map 2: Sulmona and Its Environs in the Fourteenth Century

place is suggested by its having, identified, fourteen notaries, eight paper-makers, eight other millers, but only, for example, four bakers. It was, again, a rich enough city, with its water mills for making paper, its raising of silk worms (at least from 1329) and its saffron, its merchant bankers local and foreign, its very noticeable goldsmiths and professionals (doctors, notaries, judges), and its ecclesiastical establishments, the richest of them being, after the cathedral, the monastery of Santo Spirito di Morrone (the old Sulmona-friendly place of the saintly hermit Peter), after it the Poor Claresses of Santa Chiara Sulmona, and after them the Franciscans of San Francesco Sulmona—Peter's Celestini seem locally to have defeated the Franciscans in the competition for wealth.[3] All of this catasto property was, of course, counted almost one hundred years after the holy hermit Peter, in 1293, in order to be more helpful and more convenient to pilgrims from Sulmona than he could be at his high, relatively inaccessible hermitage of Santo Spirito on the Maiella, had come down to the lower, closer Santo Spirito near the base of the Morrone, or to a little cell outside it.

This descent, which is rather elaborately told in the first avowedly external—not purportedly told by himself—life of the saint, the life "C," is not told in Peter's so-called autobiography, which is found with "C" in all the autobiography's early manuscript copies. The autobiography leaves Peter at the height of his airy asceticism on a very spiritualized Maiella. In the autobiography Peter loves the Maiella's solitude too much to leave it; even when many of the *devoti* come to him and argue with him about the difficulty of the place, the way that is long and hard, so that even those from the nearest castro won't want to come, he refuses to leave. With quiet and humble spirit, he replies, "Dearest ones, go with the blessing of God, and then you will come when great desire drives you." The text of the autobiography, for example in the fourteenth-century manuscript in the Vatican archives (which has been considered the most reliable of surviving manuscripts containing the fourteenth-century Pietro-Celestine texts which are collected together), is enclosed within a provocative incipit and explicit, both of which say of the vita that Peter himself wrote it with his own hand and left it in his cell (*quam ipse propria manu scripsit et in cella sua reliquid*). The text itself begins with a floridly scriptural introduction which commences, "Come and hear me . . . ," and concludes, "In all that I say I will speak the truth in Christ, in nothing will I lie." This purports to be very much a Maiella text, very much from the inside.[4]

3. Mattiocco, *Struttura*, particularly pp. 51–88, 205–20, 249–87.
4. For the autobiography I am using the text printed in Arsenio Frugoni, *Celestiniana*, Istituto storico per il medioevo, fasc. 6–7 (Rome, 1954), pp. 56–67, and the manuscript which Frugoni used as his base text, Archivio Segreto Vaticano, A. A. Arm. I–XVIII, 3327, fols. 20r–26v: here particularly, Frugoni, p. 63; Vatican, fol. 24v; Frugoni, pp. 56, 67; Vatican, fols. 20r, 26v. The incipit

The autobiography makes a point in beginning to say it will tell the truth, it (or rather its author) will not lie. The author and the text are anxious to show, or they certainly manage to give the impression that they are anxious to show, their reader and auditor what the real Peter and his life were like before 1293. The autobiography is short, seven double folios, fourteen parchment pages, in the Vatican manuscript, but within it there is a good deal of physical and psychological movement. In the autobiography's grim world of harsh mountains and caves, snow and more snow ("there was much snow and it was then snowing"), and grain, Peter sleeps and dreams; and his is a tale of sleep and dreams, and secrets and phantasms.[5]

The autobiography proper begins: "I will speak first of my parents whose names were Agelerio and Maria." The eleventh of twelve children, or the eleventh of twelve sons, Peter was raised by his widowed mother in conditions of extreme poverty, even famine. One of the miraculous events that the autobiography records of Peter's childhood is a famine story. When finally even bread was lacking for the family, at night the mother prayed to God that he would not let her children die of hunger. In the morning she said to her son, "Son, take up your sickle and go to the field and search within it; perhaps God will show us mercy and we will not die of hunger." The time of harvest was recently past, however, and the son objected and did not want to go. "Why should I go," he asked, "the harvest is over; nothing can come of it." But finally he went; and he found in the middle of the field harvested grain, white and dry, as much as he needed. He collected it, threshed it, and carried it to the mill on the same day, and gave thanks to God.[6]

The autobiography's mother wanted one of her sons to be a clerk and serve God, but Peter's chosen older brother failed. Peter wanted to serve God, and his mother wanted to send him to his letters to make him a clerk. The devil tried to stay the process in various ways, and he tempted the boy's brothers so that they would resist giving him up. "It is enough," they said, "that one of us doesn't work," because in that castro clerks did not work. Also a rich man of the *paese*, who admired this son among the sons of the poor family, wanted to make Peter his heir. But the boy Peter also was given supernatural aid on his way to the priesthood. From their little money the mother took enough to hire a man to teach the boy to

---

and explicit of the Vatican manuscript are in a different hand from (although perhaps the same scribe's hand as) the body of the text; but there is no suggestion that this is an autograph manuscript.

5. Frugoni, p. 60; Vatican, fol. 22v.

6. Frugoni, pp. 56, 58–59; Vatican, fols. 20r, 21v. I have retained, perhaps perversely, the manuscript spelling Agelerius, instead of the more generally accepted, corrected Angelerius.

read, and even when Peter was so small and ignorant that he did not recognize the Mary and John on the sides of a painted crucifix (a not very
likely story) the two saints came down to him and took his psalter from
him and chanted to him.[7]

The autobiography's Peter's desire to follow a path of religion and above
all to become a hermit, an anchorite, led him out of his grain-raising castro in Molise and up mountains in Abruzzo. He ascended through bad
weather, snowy cold, and, occasionally, in summer, blazing heat, through
serpents and insects, like those creatures commonly called *crapolli* (?ticks),
which stuck themselves to his chest, and through sexual temptations and
doubts.[8]

Peter had been afraid to become a hermit "because he did not know
that it was possible to be a hermit with a comrade and thought instead
that he ought always to be alone." He was afraid because of fantastic
dreams and visions that he had at night. And there was not in his neighborhood a servant of God with whom he could take counsel. But after
he had passed his twentieth year and an older young man had begun saying to him, "Let's leave our native place, our *patria,* and travel far in the
service of God, after we have first gone to Rome so that we do everything
with the counsel of the Church," Peter and his comrade finally set off. After one day's journey Peter's companion decided to go back to his place and
his kin. Peter went on alone, after he had told his companion, "Though
you leave me, God does not leave me."[9]

After another day, about noon, Peter came to a "place called Castel
di Sangro." When he entered the castro the air immediately became
disturbed and there was a great tempest of wind and rain although the
weather had been perfect there before he had arrived. Peter wanted to go
on walking in spite of the weather. He came to a bridge over the river
outside the castro, and when he was on the middle of the bridge the wind
tore at him and frightened him so much that he turned back; and at the
foot of the bridge he came to the church of Saint Nicholas and entered
it. There he prayed to God and Saint Nicholas for help. He stayed there

7. Frugoni, p. 57; Vatican, fol. 20v.
8. Frugoni, p. 61; Vatican, fol. 23r. The definitive life of Peter himself is Peter Herde, *Cölestin V.
(1294): Peter vom Morrone, der Engelpapst,* Päpst und Papsttum, 16 (Stuttgart, 1981); Herde has produced a really remarkable summary biography, "Celestino V, papa," in *Dizionario biografico degli
Italiani,* 1979 ed., 23:402–15, which includes an extensive bibliography and a crisp analysis of
the surviving biographies. Now see also Herde's "Celestino V," chapter 2, pp. 93–127 in *La crisi del
Trecento e il papato avignonese (1274–1378),* ed. Diego Quaglioni, vol. II of *Storia della Chiesa,* since
1986 ed. Elio Guerriero. For Peter's life one should go to Herde.
9. Frugoni, p. 59; Vatican, fols. 21v–22r.

for several days and he learned from people's talk that there was a hermit on a nearby mountain.[10]

The storm at Castel di Sangro marked a boundary between two kinds of reality with which the autobiography and its Peter dealt. Peter went up toward the hermit's cell but before he got there the Spirit of the Lord warned him not to tell the hermit his secrets. Since before Peter got to the cell God had, in fact, showed him that the hermit's life was unworthy, Peter only told him that he was going to Rome. Another day Peter went up a mountain to another cell, but before he got there two very beautiful women appeared to him and held him in their hands and said, "Don't go. The hermit is not here. Come with us." Peter slipped out of their hands. He carried bread and fish which he had brought to the cell, and there he found fire and water but no person. It was snowing outside—it was January—and God urged him to stay a while in the cell. Peter remained and kept vigil, but then heavy with sleep he fell on the ground and slept. Then a great crowd of angels and saints appeared to him and in the mouth of each was a red rose, and they flourished their roses delightfully and sang to him; and even after he awoke he heard their song for the length of time it takes to say a Pater Noster.[11]

Peter stayed in the cell for ten days and then found, shown by the Lord, a new place in another mountain, a big rock, under which he dug a space the same size as the rock but so small that it was difficult for him to stand up or stretch himself out. He stayed in the place three years and wonderful things happened to him. He heard the sound of a big bell for the offices of the night; but someone came from another good hermit and told him that that hermit kept a cock that crowed in the night. And he said to Peter, "Since that brother has a cock that crows in the night, why don't you have one?" And a matron who was present said to Peter, "I have a very beautiful cock. If you want it, I will bring it to you." And Peter said, "I want it." The cock came, but he never crowed; and the sound of the bell stopped and never returned, even after Peter had given back the cock—"and he never found again the grace that he had lost."[12]

Peter had dreams or visions. Two very handsome men stood next to him at night. They were dressed like bishops saying Mass, and they said the Psalms with him. Two demons in the forms of very beautiful women, women whom he had earlier seen in the world, and who were delightful, presented themselves frequently to the eyes of his heart. When Peter slept

---

10. Frugoni, pp. 59–60; Vatican, fol. 22r.
11. Frugoni, p. 60; Vatican, fols. 22r–22v.
12. Frugoni, pp. 60–61; Vatican, fol. 22v.

the demon-women came close to him; one of them put her nude body on one side of him, and the other on the other side, and they struggled with him. While he was awake he tucked and secured his robe under his feet, but the demon-women pulled the cloth from under his feet and joined their bodies to his. But God helped him, and they did not prevail.[13]

After three years Peter went to Rome and became a priest. Then he came back and went to the mountain of Morrone near Sulmona where he found a cave which pleased him a lot. On the Morrone he was tempted because of his unworthiness, as he thought, to give up saying Mass. He decided to go to the pope, finally, for his counsel; but the snow was too heavy for him to get down the mountain. Later in a dream or vision a holy abbot said, "Say Mass, son, say Mass." And on the same day a holy monk to whom he was accustomed to confess came to him and told him the same thing.[14]

The autobiography's Peter stayed on the Morrone, where God did many good things for him, for five years. A final, relatively extended but not uncharacteristic, dream-vision ends the autobiography's story of this second, seeking, climbing, tempted, dreaming part of Peter's life. At one time Peter was bothered by a particular temptation: he wondered if, when by accident he had polluted himself in his sleep, he ought on that day to celebrate Mass. He sought advice from religious men; some said yes and some no. So Peter asked God for help. That very night as he slept he seemed to climb to a certain castro which was very high up. He went inside the castro and there he saw a great cloister and, in the middle of the cloister, a great palace and, around the circuit of the cloister, cells and, in the cells, friars or brothers dressed in white clothes. He wanted to go into the palace. He had, however, led with him an ass which he could not get rid of. He began to go up the steps to the palace; the ass climbed them easily. But after he had gone up three or four steps, the bad ass shamefully dirtied himself, as if he had been eating young grass. When Peter saw this, he, ashamed and saddened, stopped on the steps. But he saw at the head of the steps, at the entrance to the palace, three persons, similar and equal, so that they seemed as if they were one; and all of them looked at him. And one of them, who seemed to be Christ, said to Peter, "Come up, come up. Why don't you come up? What the ass did was natural to him, his habit. What does it have to do with you? Come up. Come up."[15]

13. Frugoni, p. 61; Vatican, fols. 22v–23r.
14. Frugoni, pp. 61–62; Vatican, fols. 23r–23v.
15. Frugoni, pp. 62–63; Vatican, fols. 23v–24r.

The autobiography's Peter awoke from his dream full of joy and happiness. On the surface of the text his period of temptation and his five-year stay on the Morrone end together. "Because," according to the autobiography, "Peter always sought solitude, and because the woods around the place had been destroyed by men for cultivating crops, he climbed to the mountain of Maiella, where he found a big cave which pleased him very much." The new place was not pleasing to Peter's companions, except for one of them, nor was it pleasing to some of his friends. After some days, however, they followed him because they loved him so much; but *devoti* came to him and complained about the place, and said others would too, and to Peter's face, had they not been inhibited by the devotion they felt for him. It was then that Peter told them to go and that they would come back when their desire was strong enough.[16]

Peter's life on the Maiella, the third part of the autobiography, is told in different terms, with different sounds and images than were in the other two. The land of grain and sexual torment are left below. Peter's life has entered into its age of the Holy Ghost. There is here, in the autobiography, a dispersal both of plot progression and of the sharp naturalistic and homely detail to which the spiritual descriptions of the earlier part of the work are tied, although there remain in this high spiritual place elements of crude simplicity distorted to fit their function. The bell returns, but multiply. After the brothers had constructed an oratory on the Maiella, Santo Spirito, dedicated to the Holy Ghost (the preferred dedication of the order that Peter had founded), one day the brothers entered it to say nones and then they began to hear the sound of many big bells. The bells continued at the hours of the Office, and all the brothers heard them, although not in the same way: one, for example, heard a bell of particular sweetness when the Corpus Christi was elevated at Mass. The brothers began to hear them wherever they went, outside of the places where laymen lived, except inside towns and castri. They were country bells, desert bells. On the first day of this sounding disturbance of the air, the brothers had come to Peter and asked where they were ringing; they came in tears and fear. And he replied with unusual clarity, "Not far away: non est multum longe." And as the bells rang again and again, the brothers accepted the belief that their sound had come from God.[17]

When the brothers had come to Peter to ask him about the source of the bells' sound, they had come to the brother (ad fratrem). Uncertainty of person in the autobiography's talk of its protagonist, the movement

16. Frugoni, p. 63; Vatican, fols. 24r–24v.
17. Frugoni, p. 64; Vatican, fol. 25r.

from first- to third-person singular has disturbed, unduly, I think, historians who have worked with the text. In the Maiella section, where Arsenio Frugoni has said the story becomes more exactly the story of the monks who live on the mountain than of Peter, Peter's grammatical person surely changes, expands, and becomes less specific: he is repeatedly *iste frater* (that brother) so that he blends in with and is not completely distinguished from the other *fratres: quidam frater, quidam fratrum, alius, omnes fratres* (a certain brother, a certain other brother, all the brothers).[18] In its Maiella stage the autobiography renounces for Peter, in Robert Hanning's phrase, "awareness of the single body's limited spatial extension."[19] Peter has joined the community of the Maiella air. "And many doves are seen in the air above the place"; a dove appears in the beginning of this segment and with his presence announces that this is the realm of the Holy Ghost. Later the signs become explicit. One day after Matins, "that brother" lay asleep on his mat and dreamed of Mass in the oratory, a Mass celebrated by an unknown who seemed to be an abbot; and afterward Peter realized that the abbot saying Mass in the oratory of the Holy Ghost was the Holy Ghost.[20]

The autobiography has two related plots, two progressive narratives, with, in their way, beginnings, middles, and within the frame of the work resolutions. The first of these stories is about religion and religious order. It is the story of a little boy, born with a veil, with a father who was, in his fatherhood, another Jacob, and a mother who wanted him to become a clerk, and who himself wanted to serve God and especially in a hermitage. His mother overcame opposition, and he himself temptation. He became a hermit, a priest, and finally a priest living and celebrating in a hermitage and maintaining its distant eremitical qualities, in spite of, or with the help of, followers and select pilgrims, on the mountains in the snow. The second narrative is connected: it is about sex and culminates in the castro dream. It is about a poor, eventually Abruzzese Anthony, on both sides of whose body the naked beautiful bodies of devilish women, whom he actually remembers from real life, in dream press themselves naked.

But Peter is a victor and victory comes in progressive steps. Neither this patterning, however, nor the presence of much external, sharp, domestic, and rural imagery can delude the autobiography's reader into thinking that its organization is determined by clock or calendar time. In

---

18. Frugoni, pp. 65–67; Vatican, fols. 25v–26v.
19. Robert W. Hanning, *The Individual in Twelfth-Century Romance* (New Haven, Conn., 1977), p. 14.
20. Frugoni, p. 66; Vatican, fol. 26r.

the autobiography we live among feelings and images, and many dreams, in a net of psychic action to which chronology "may or may not adhere." [21] This sensation is sharpened for the reader because in the beginning the autobiography talks of birth and parents, and, in continuing, at least occasionally it suggests a natural order: to go to Rome one must take the road; to become a priest one must first be ordained. As the work progresses the reader feels the force of the delusion, the mocking quality of the initial appearance of order, although from the very beginning the sense of illusion has been suggested by the things the reader was not told: in a life in which Castel di Sangro can be so explicit, the castro of Peter's birth is not named. The holy place which his mother visits is *quemdam sanctum locum* (a certain holy place); a miracle-bearing church, *quamdam ecclesiam Beate Virginis* (a certain church of the Virgin); and there is no description at all of the city of Rome, to which, after some seeking, Peter goes. [22]

That which the autobiography seems to know, the places which it traces with some explicitness, seem to be close to, but not within, Sulmona, as if they were written by someone who had never lived near Isernia or visited Rome but who was really attached to the Maiella, like perhaps the one other who liked the Maiella when Peter went there. But whether the autobiography was written by Peter or by someone else who was attached to the Maiella, it is very local to the high country around Sulmona and it creates the figure of a saint who attracts followers but does not bind them to himself through any sort of elaborate communication. He is a fairly mute holy man. Bells talk for him.

It is certainly arguable that this relatively mute, miracle-bearing, eremitic, mountain saint, the saint of the autobiography, is as close as we can get to the Peter who was seen and desired by the people living in the city beneath his mountains. It was, I think, this Maiella saint whom they wanted, but they wanted him closer, available without the full rigor of the climb to Maiella.

The autobiography does not bring Peter down from Maiella; it leaves him there in his purity. But the almost contemporary, fourteenth-century, "C" life of Peter does, again, bring him down to the Morrone, and in fact makes him pope. The descent to the Morrone is a response to the desires of the *devoti,* to their utility; and in "C" it is justified by rather grandilo-

---

21. The phrase is from Richard Ellman, "Freud and Literary Biography," *American Scholar* 53 (1984): 465–78, 470, a particularly evocative and instructive essay.
22. Frugoni, p. 58; Vatican, fols. 21r–21v. Herde suggests Sant'Angelo Limosano as Peter's place of origin—for example, *La crisi,* p. 99.

quent reference to the submission to utility of very eminent predecessors, Benedict and Paul:

> And he remembered how Saint Benedict moved himself from Subiaco to Monte Cassino, and the blessed Paul, so that he might be of more use to others, had himself lowered from the wall in a basket.[23]

So, "C" continues, Peter, thinking about these examples, returned to the Morrone. For the Peter of "C" the Maiella has become Damascus, and the Morrone, or Sulmona, Jerusalem. He descends in his basket for the greater utility of the devoted notaries and goldsmiths of the city and the other folk of Sulmona's valley—but not, we need assume, without a sense of loss, this "C" Peter who will live on the Morrone in a cell outside the monastery and who will as pope live in a wooden cell within his palatial chamber at Naples.[24]

In fact in a number of ways Peter as pope and saint must have proved a great convenience to Sulmona. Ezio Mattiocco, the historian of medieval Sulmona, in a recent book, has written an effective, condensed description of its political, and other, difficulties in the later thirteenth and early fourteenth centuries, and particularly of its difficulties with the Angevin rulers of the kingdom (in spite of which its turn-of-the-century population burgeoned). Sulmona's Hohenstaufen attachments caused it to suffer under its Angevin rulers. But Angevin attachment to and favoring of Peter of Morrone, and Peter's attachment to and favoring of Sulmona and its people, helped the reconciliation of the city and its rulers.[25]

The autobiography's mountain saint is a distillation of essence, of a selected essence. Its Peter has sheared away from it, or him, important elements and events in Peter's long life which do not fit its essence: the trips to Lyon, Tuscany, and Puglia; the foundation of an order and the obtaining of protection for its very considerable properties; the connection with the Angevin court. This actual Peter has been made most readily available to us by the historian Peter Herde's modern, firm biographical studies.[26] But the Peter of Morrone of the autobiography is echoed by, or echoes, I think, the Peter of the miracle stories collected in 1306 for the

23. "Et recordabatur quomodo sanctus Benedictus se transmutaverat a Subiacu ad montem Cassinum, et beatus Paulus, ut posset alibi magis proficere, fecit sibi sportam dari et per murum deponi": Vatican, 3327, fol. 36v; and see S. Van Ortroy, "S. Pierre Célestin et ses premiers biographes," *Analecta Bollandiana* 16 (1897): 365–487, 413. *Recordabatur* is a word and concept repeatedly used in the autobiography; it is I think a key to understanding the work's structure and composition.
24. Van Ortroy, "S. Pierre Célestin," p. 420.
25. Mattiocco, *Struttura*, pp. 31–43.
26. See above note 8. For Peter's foundations, Anna Moscati, "I monasteri di Pietro Celestino," *Bollettino dell'Istituto storico italiano per il medioevo e Archivio Muratoriano* 68 (1956): 91–163.

process of his canonization. These two Peters are similar; and the miracle stories further define or refine and expand the Peter which the autobiography delineates. Expand is perhaps a mistaken word and idea, because an essential part of this echoing definition is Peter's muteness; but expand seems a just word to describe the miracle stories' amplification of the resonance of Peter's reputation as holy man and, particularly healing and curing, miracle-worker in the valley of Sulmona.

As the stories define the Peter seen from the valley and its city, they also suggest to their reader some elements of the city's society and of the relationships among its denizens not readily available from the catasto or most other documents. They emphasize some of the city's particular qualities.

On 29 May 1306, at Sulmona, master (magister) Benedetto of Sulmona, a medical doctor, a man about sixty years old, appeared as a witness before the archbishop of Naples, who, with the bishop of Valva-Sulmona, had been commissioned by Pope Clement V to conduct the local information-gathering process concerning Peter's life and miracles. Master Benedetto swore that for more than forty years he had observed Peter conducting his holy practices, being holy at his various hermitages, including that cell near Santo Spirito (Morrone) about two miles from Sulmona, but also in various other hermitages during the long period in which Peter stayed in the region of Sulmona. Benedetto swore that he had observed the devotion of people in the parts of the Abruzzi for Peter grow and grow (et crescere et crescere) from day to day (de die in diem); and, so that that devotion might be expressed, he had seen the constant (daily) growth of oratories in which Peter's brethren performed their observances.[27]

But Benedetto was called for a more specific purpose: to testify to the healing miracle performed for his daughter Catania (or Cathania) which had happened before Peter became pope. Of a sudden, Catania had suffered from vertigo and lost her sight. That she had become blind was common knowledge in the whole area of Sulmona. For about nine days she remained blind and her doctors could not help her in any way; and then she had a vision in her sleep in which she discovered that she could only be cured through Peter, and Benedetto knew this because Catania herself had told him. Convinced by her dream, Catania asked her husband, the notary Giovanni Riczardi, to carry her to Peter. Then the notary Giovanni with three other men—magister Raynaldo de Gentile (Gentilis), Jacopo Benevenuti, and Nicola, the son of magister Giovanni of Sulmona—put Catania on a horse and tied her to it and with her took

27. Seppelt, *Monumenta Coelestiniana*, pp. 223–25.

the difficult trail to the cell of San Giovanni de Orfenta on Maiella where Peter was staying. They knew that Peter did not like to have women come to him, so Catania herself did not approach him, but when magister Raynaldo had explained the matter to him, Peter sent a wooden cross to Catania to be placed over her eyes. When the cross was placed on Catania's eyes, immediately she could see (and see even better than before her blindness), and on her own feet, unled, she returned to Sulmona.

Benedetto then added information not characteristic of this collection of miracle stories. After the miracle, Catania's husband, the notary Giovanni, who had led a dissolute enough life, changed his manner of living. He became a better man and for the rest of his life lived laudably. And also, Benedetto said, Catania herself after the miracle lived a better life than she had before.

On the same day Catania herself gave testimony.[28] She was more specific in naming the oratories in which Peter had stayed, and more specific about the time of the miracle, some fifteen years before, so, since she was in 1306 a forty-year-old, it should have happened when she was about twenty-five. She tells more about the coming on of the blindness. She had been sitting one day with neighboring wives spinning (cum mulieribus convicinis suis ad filandum), when suddenly there was such a great turbulence in her head that she could not see those either standing or sitting around her and she could not distinguish their voices. But she could dimly hear voices saying, "Catania, what is it: quid est hoc?" And she said that her head hurt, and she called a girl to lead her into the house of her husband.

Catania was also more specific about her treatment: neither her father nor other doctors (alios medicos) of Sulmona could help her with any of their medicines. She was also more specific about the dream or vision: she was, it seemed, in the church of San Pelino near Sulmona where an old man was saying Mass in clothes which she later recognized as Peter's; and those in the church said to her, "go to him who is standing at the altar, and he will show you the way." She added of her husband that she had repeatedly to ask him to take her to Peter, because he was then a dissolute man and had no devotion for Peter; and she added another *magister* to those who took her to the Maiella oratory, Angelo de Trano. And in Catania's testimony her notary husband was annoyed by Peter's refusal to receive women and talked angrily to Peter. Peter then asked the husband about his mode of life, and he replied that he had not come about his life. Then Peter told Giovanni that he should stop and listen to what he,

28. Ibid., pp. 225–29. One should notice the presence of Catania's maid (*pedisecca*).

Peter, had to say to him, and Peter said to him a number of holy words, and from that hour he changed to a man of prayer and fasting, who frequented churches day and night, did good works, and was a different man. Catania further added evidence about the moments before the miracle: while Peter and her husband were talking she had fallen into a sort of sleep and had a vision in which Peter was carried to her and made a sign over her eyes and spoke to her; and when the vision was over her husband arrived with the cross.

In Catania's mouth the story expanded; and, returned home, she used her cross to help others to get well. Catania's success inspired her sister-in-law Gemma, the wife of Panfilio Riczardi, her husband's brother; Catania and others urged Gemma and her husband to take to Peter their son Bartolomeo, who suffered from a terrible decaying disease throughout his body. They carried Bartolomeo to the Morrone where Peter then was, and he was cured.[29] Gemma, Bartolomeo's mother, a woman of about forty, gave testimony to the archbishop and bishop on the same day as Catania; she confirmed Catania's story.[30] On the next day magister Pietro Thomei, who had been Peter's doctor and later the doctor for his congregation, testified that Catania had found no help from the counsel of medical doctors, not from her father, nor from Raynaldo Gentilis, nor from the witness Pietro himself, nor from others.[31] The eighty-year-old doctor Raynaldo Gentilis also testified, and included in his testimony the fact that after the miracle Catania called to him, saying, "Raynalde, ego video" ("Raynaldo, I see").[32]

The effect of the example of Catania's miracle spread beyond her extended family. Another professional family, that of the two brother judges Leonardo and Filippo of Sulmona and Leonardo's wife Granata and their son, Marino, knowing of Catania's cure, sought similar cures for both Granata and Marino.[33] Granata herself did not approach Peter because he hated the sight of women (*quod feminarum aspectus abhorrebat*), but she approached him through her judge brother-in-law. The judge Filippo also approached Peter about Marino, for whom Peter gave him a small wooden cross to hang about the boy's neck and an apple for the boy to eat, and the boy was cured. These double miracles within one family were not unique; and in Catania's own case and testimony there was another sort of double miracle. The customary bread which Peter gave to those

29. Ibid., p. 228.
30. Ibid., pp. 229–30.
31. Ibid., pp. 231–32.
32. Ibid., pp. 232–35.
33. Ibid., pp. 240–43.

who approached him on the Maiella did not diminish as Catania and her group ate it.[34]

Another kind of professionalism is represented by Sir Alessandro Berardi of Sulmona, a canon of Valva-Sulmona, a man of more than forty years, who had a sister, dompna Gentilucia Berardi, who herself had a daughter, Francessa or Francesca; Francessa, playing with her friends, had struck her left foot on a stone, an injury which developed so that it was thought she might lose the foot. Doctors called the problem a *fistula* and lanced it several times to no avail. The surgeon, magister Riccardo of Sulmona, a fifty-four-year-old witness, who had been called to deal with the fistula, found it incurable and progressive, affecting the girl's bones. Sir Alessandro, knowing Peter's abhorrence of female presence, dressed Francessa in boys' clothes and carried her to the holy man at Santo Spirito, Sulmona (Morrone), where he was staying. The holy man blessed the wound three times with the sign of the cross, and within a few days the girl was walking again.[35]

On 1 June 1306 the goldsmith magister Giffredo, the son of magister Matteo of Sulmona, appeared in the court of inquiry to testify about the cure of his wife dompna Florencia, the daughter of the judge Filippo of Sulmona (perhaps the same judge who was the brother of judge Leonardo).[36] The judge Filippo went to Peter and procured his blessing and a linen cloth to place on his sick daughter, whose life had been despaired of by doctors; and she was cured. And the goldsmith's fifty-year-old mother, dompna Palma, testified, as did his forty-year-old neighbor, a notary of Sulmona, and he testified particularly to the impression that the miracle had made on their neighborhood.[37] On the same day Bartolomea, the widow of the notary Bonuomini of Sulmona, told of the cure of her daughter Helysabeth.[38] Bartolomea had asked the help of a neighbor, the doctor Raynaldo, who was a friend of Peter's, and as a result of his help and advice, and since Helysabeth was a girl, her brother Raynaldo, also the son of the notary Bonuomini, went to Peter and brought back to Helysabeth curing items or agents. A canon of Sulmona, dompno Gualterio, a colleague of Sir Alessandro, testified to the effect on his neighborhood of a neighbor's miraculous cure.[39] Ricco a thirty-six-year-old bar-

---

34. Ibid., pp. 241, 242, 228.
35. Ibid., pp. 246–47, 250–54: the mother and maternal grandmother of Francessa also testify. Alessandro Berardi can be seen in 1311 acting as the bishop's vicar general: Chiaverini, *La Diocesi*, pp. 32, 33.
36. Seppelt, *Monumenta Coelestiniana*, pp. 282–84.
37. Ibid., pp. 304–6, 302–3.
38. Ibid., pp. 277–78.
39. Ibid., pp. 276–77, 307–8.

ber, the son of magister Ruggero of Sulmona, came to testify, as did magister Nicola Berardi, a fifty-year-old *fabricator,* and so did a fifty-eight-year-old archpriest.[40]

Not all of the witnesses who tell of the miracles worked through Peter for the Sulmonesi are identified as magistri (here professionals and skilled artisans) or the wives and children of magistri, but these people do swarm through the accounts of the inquest. They suggest a quite sharp contrast with the saint himself, who generally speaks briefly and dispenses his apple, his cloths, and his wooden crosses. The witnesses seem not unaware of the saint's nature. Sir Alessandro dressed Francessa in boys' clothing. A witness, Sulmontina di Giovanni Petri of Sulmona, a forty-six-year-old woman, testified to a cure and then told of going to Santo Spirito near Sulmona (Morrone) while Peter was celebrating Mass there before a crowd of people among whom was a woman possessed by the devil who cried out, "Petrucius de Murrone debet me liberare" ("Petruccio of Morrone, you should free me").[41] Peter's local cult was, at least in some part, a case of a colloquial, simple Petruccio among, or sought by, the notaries and doctors.

The miracle stories reveal parts of a city not inconsistent with the city that will develop into that of the catasto, a city including a professional class with connections among the professions, a class either conspicuous within the city or conspicuous among the *devoti* of Peter—and he may have been particularly attractive to the magistri (and they good witnesses). The stories also reveal a Peter, although of both Morrone and Maiella, not inconsistent with the Peter of the autobiography and appropriately placed in the rude high outskirts of the diocese that would become the diocese of the visitation. They certainly show the demand for Peter's closeness that the Peter of the autobiography resisted on Maiella and to which the Peter of "C" succumbed in descending from the Damascus of Maiella to the Jerusalem of the Morrone and Sulmona. In his descent to the land of farmed fields, the Peter of the miracle stories did not want to avoid a harsh life. When the witness magister Raynaldo Gentilis went to find him on the Morrone and found his cave empty, he discovered that Peter was out, going around the mountain looking for a harsher place for himself; and Raynaldo said "Wait until the snow falls, and you will find out whether or not this is a harsh place."[42]

In the confrontation of the hermit saint and the notaries and doctors the figures of Catania and her husband Giovanni Riczardi seem to hold

40. Ibid., pp. 294–95, 258, 271–73.
41. Ibid., pp. 249–50.
42. Ibid., p. 233: "Expecta, quod nix cadat, et tunc videbis, si iste est asper locus."

a special place. Catania is the daughter of a doctor and Giovanni is a notary; but Catania is also a visionary, and Peter seems to talk to Giovanni
at relative length and not only to cure Catania but also to change Giovanni's, and also Catania's, way of life. Catania's miracle, moreover, affects a
number of other people, draws them to a Peter cure. This couple and
some of the people around them, like Raynaldo, seem a conducting connection, but particularly Catania seems so, although (?because) a woman,
between the hermit and the magistri.

One should not in noting this connection between Peter and the magistri ignore the fact that witness after witness talks of the attraction of all
the people all over the parts of the Abruzzi to Peter, of his universal local
appeal, of how they all ran to him. But the process's stories certainly show
an attraction that Peter had for the relatively learned and skilled of Sulmona that in some ways recalls the attraction which the cardinals in the
curia felt. The stories reveal a close connection between the healing saint
and the city's medical establishment, including his and his order's own
doctor, Pietro Thomei, and also a connection between the hermit saint
and the city's religious establishment, including the prominent canon,
Alessandro Berardi. The miracle stories allow their reader to penetrate a
bit the Sulmona suggested by the later catasto, to observe the construction and relations of actual families, men and women, and to hear something of the resonance of the neighborhoods in which women were spinning out of doors and in which they lived. The stories suggest that at least
one of these women played a significant role in connecting the hermit
with the city.

Female Religious Experience and Society in Thirteenth-Century Italy

Luigi Pellegrini

The last couple of decades have seen a greater awareness of the problematic of female religious life in Italy.[1] Starting with the 1979 conference in Assisi, "The Female Religious Movement and Franciscanism in the Thirteenth Century," new research methods and fields of inquiry have allowed historians of the religious phenomenon in medieval Italy to place women's role in thirteenth-century Italian religious experience in its proper light.[2] Systematic explorations of the documentation of Lom-

---

1. In fact, after the accurate account by Lilly Zarnke (*Der Anteil des Kardinals Ugolino an der Ausbildung der drei Orden des heiligen Franz,* Beiträge zur Kulturgeschichte des Mittelalters und der Renaissance 42 [Leipzig-Berlin, 1930], pp. 26–77) and the careful reexamination of the situation by Herbert Grundmann (*Religiöse Bewegungen im Mittelalter. Untersuchungen über die geschichtlichen Zusammenhänge zwischen der Ketzerei, den Bettelorden und der religiösen Frauenbewegung im 12. und 13. Jahrhundert und über die geschichtlichen Grundlagen der deutschen Mystik,* Eberings historische Studien 267 [Berlin, 1935; 2d ed. Darmstadt, 1961]), historiographic production has continued to concentrate, as far as Italy is concerned, on reconstructing the origins and development, or rather the diffusion, of the Second Franciscan order with traditional approaches and methods. Even Grundmann (*Ordine francescano e conventi femminili nella prima metà del XIII secolo* [Bologna, 1974], pp. 198–207) inserted his pages dedicated to Italy into a paragraph studying the relationship between the Franciscan Order and female convents in the first half of the thirteenth century. For the rest, half of this voluminous work deals with the female religious movements of the thirteenth century, concentrating mostly on groups that originated and developed in the Germanic realm. It is Grundmann's and Zarnke's merit to have clearly recognized that the "female religious movement" in central-northern Italy had its origins and early institutional development independent of the Franciscans. Brenda Bolton argued along similar lines: "Mulieres sanctae," in *Women in Medieval Society,* ed. Susan Mosher Stuard (Philadelphia, 1976), pp. 141–58.

2. *Movimento religioso femminile e francescanesimo nel secolo XIII.* Atti del VII Convegno internazionale, Assisi, 1–13 ottobre 1979 (Assisi, 1980). The title takes up the expression used by Grundmann in the central chapters of his volume to define the organization of the female religious phenomenon as forms of communal life in some ways autonomous from and alternative to the traditional schemes and ideals of monastic life. Recently some objections have been raised regarding the application of the term "movement" to the diverse religious experiences of the twelfth and

bardy,[3] Veneto,[4] Tuscany,[5] and Umbria[6] have revealed the rich, articulated, and complex reality of the "female religious movement" of central-northern Italy in the thirteenth and fourteenth centuries.

One gains a clear impression that in central-northern Italy in the first half of the thirteenth century female religious initiative assumed characteristics of particular vivacity and originality. We do not know whether or to what extent this female religious initiative may also have been present in southern Italy, or rather we have more than one reason to doubt its presence: the scarcity of documentation on new types of female religious communities there gives the impression of a low profile of this kind of initiative.[7] There is some documented evidence of women's pres-

thirteenth centuries. See Maria Pia Alberzoni, "Chiara di Assisi e il francescanesimo femminile," in *Francesco d'Assisi e il primo secolo di storia francescana* (Turin, 1997), pp. 204–5.

3. Significant for the area of Lombardy are the studies of Maria Pia Alberzoni: a documentary and historiographic survey relating to the female community of S. Apollinare in Milan has been published by this scholar in *Il Francescanesimo in Lombardia. Storia e Arte* (Milan, 1983), pp. 70–73; Alberzoni has since deepened the complex problematic of the origins and institutional development of the Milanese community in *Francescanesimo a Milano nel Duecento* (Milan, 1991), in order then to expand her investigation to other female communities in Lombard territory: "L'Ordine di S. Damiano in Lombardia," *Rivista di storia della Chiesa in Italia* 49 (1995): 1–42; reprinted in *Chiara e il secondo Ordine. Il fenomeno francescano femminile nel Salento*, ed. Giancarlo Andenna and Benedetto Vetere (Galatina, 1997), pp. 117–57.

4. See, in the volume *Minoritismo e centri Veneti nel Duecento*, ed. Giorgio Cracco (Trent, 1983), the contribution by Gian Maria Varanini, "Per la storia dei Minori a Verona nel Duecento," pp. 92–125, as well as the following two articles: Daniela Rando, "Il convento di S. Maria Mater Domini di Conegliano nel Duecento: condizionamenti politici ed esperienza religiosa," pp. 49–64; and Giuseppina De Sandre Gasparini, "Il francescanesimo a Verona nel '200: note dai testamenti," in *Le esperienze minoritiche nel Veneto del Due e Trecento*. Atti del Convegno nazionale di studi francescani (Padova, 28–30 settembre 1984), *Le Venezie francescane*, nuova serie 2 (1985), pp. 121–41.

5. Particularly significant for Tuscany are the studies of Anna Benvenuti Papi: *"In castro poenitentiae": Santità e società femminile nell'Italia medievale*, Italia sacra. Studi e documenti di storia ecclesiastica, 45 (Rome, 1990); and "L'insediamento francescano a Firenze: le origini," in *La presenza francescana nella Toscana del Duecento*, Quaderni di vita e cultura francescana (Florence, 1990), pp. 81–100, particularly pp. 89–91. In English, see her "Mendicant Friars and Female Pinzochere in Tuscany: From Social Marginality to Models of Sanctity," in *Women and Religion in Medieval and Renaissance Italy*, ed. Daniel Bornstein and Roberto Rusconi, trans. Margery J. Schneider (Chicago, 1996), pp. 84–103.

6. See *Il movimento religioso femminile in Umbria nei secolo XIII–XIV*. Atti del Convegno internazionale di studio nell'ambito delle celebrazioni per l'VIII centenario della nascita di S. Francesco d'Assisi (Città di Castello, 27–29 ottobre 1982), ed. Roberto Rusconi (Florence, 1984). Of particular interest for our argument in this volume is Peter Höler, "Il monastero delle Clarisse di Monteluce in Perugia," ibid., pp. 159–82; and "Frauenklöster in einer italienischen Stadt. Zur Wirtschaft- und Sozialgeschichte der Klarissen von Monteluce und der Zisterzienserinnen von S. Giuliana in Perugia (13.–Mitte 15. Jh.)," *Quellen und Forschungen aus italienischen Archiven und Bibliotheken* 67 (1987): 1–107; Mario Sensi, "Incarcerate e recluse in Umbria nei secoli XIII e XIV: un bizzocaggio centro-italiano," in *Mistiche e devote nell'Italia tardomedievale*, ed. D. Bornstein and R. Rusconi (Naples, 1992), and in English translation as "Anchoresses and Penitents in Thirteenth- and Fourteenth-Century Umbria," in *Woman and Religion*, pp. 56–83.

7. We have questionable evidence for the Sicilian monasteries of Palermo and Catania, which Wadding suggests were founded in 1220; but there is no documentation whatsoever of this—see Ric-

ence in the groups of lay people who gathered around new types of monastic foundations, such as the Pulsanesi and Cavensi. Moreover, hagiographic sources describe monastic communities composed of both men
and women, perhaps suggesting the presence of double monasteries.[8]
But, in the end, there is very little evidence of autonomous female communities that were capable of making their own religious choices, independently of male monastic communties.

The signs and documentary evidence regarding alternative forms of
female religious experience that had a following seem to be concentrated
in central-northern Italy, where one finds women taking initiatives independently, in the context of the seething and socially heterogeneous
urban environment. Those responsible for religious society, whether they
were bishops, the papal legate, Cardinal Ugolino, or the Roman Curia itself, had to find adequate outlets for so much religious dynamism. Their
solution to the problem was to direct that dynamism into deliberately and
organically planned institutional channels.

The panorama of southern Italy appears more restricted to traditional
and consolidated forms of religious life. A clear indication of this is the
absence of female communities connected with the new religious orders
up until the middle of the thirteenth century, by which time the new forms
of female religious life appeared to be, and were, solidly incorporated
into community structures that were largely configured on the model of
traditional monasticism.[9] It was a simple transposition of forms of female
monastic life, by which a new religious order, born in the more lively regions of central-northern Italy—the first order in Western history to as-
semble exclusively female communities—was diffused into the southern
regions.[10]

---

cardo Pratesi, *Le Clarisse in Italia,* in *S. Chiara d'Assisi. Studi e cronaca del VII Centenario (1253–
1953)* (Assisi, 1953), p. 347. It is significant that these monasteries do not appear in Cardinal Rainaldo's letter of August 18, 1228, which listed twenty-four female communities, all located in
central-northern Italy, among the "poor monasteries of S. Damian of Assisi": *Escritos de Santa Clara
y documentos conplementarios,* bilingual edition prepared by Ignacio Omaechevarria, Biblioteca de
Autores Cristianos 314 (Madrid, 1993), pp. 362–67.

8. Roberto Paciocco, "Uomini e donne in comunità religiose. Considerazioni in margine al primo
numero dei Quaderni di storia religiosa," *Rassegna storica salernitana* 25 (1995): 285–98.

9. See the tables relating to the emergence of Clarist monasteries in Anna Benvenuti Papi, "La fortuna del movimento damianita in Italia (sec. XIII): propositi per un censimento da fare," in *Chiara
di Assisi.* Atti del XX Convegno internazionale (Assisi, 15–17 ottobre 1992), Società internazionale
di studi francescani (Assisi, 1993), pp. 57–106, esp. 68–102. These tables indicate that only five out
of twenty-seven foundations that took place between 1228 and 1241 were located in the southern
kingdom: the two in Abruzzo, Val dei Varri (Marsica) and Pineto, and those in Napoli, Salerno,
and Rossano Calabro (pp. 91–95).

10. See the recent information and related bibliographic references in Maria Pia Alberzoni, "Papato e nuovi Ordini religiosi femminili," in *Il papato duecentesco e gli Ordini mendicanti.* Atti del
XXV Convegno internazionale di studi (Assisi 13–14 febbraio 1998) (Spoleto, 1998), pp. 205–61.

This is perhaps the reason, or one of the reasons, why the observation of "the blossoming of female sainthood" does not appear at all applicable to the south of Italy. Indeed it seems that southern women remained excluded from the honor of altars and the sacred urn in the last centuries of the Middle Ages. The "feminization of sainthood"[11] that was a characteristic of the religious history of Europe in the last centuries of the Middle Ages, finds verification in southern Italy only in sporadic cases, for which the evidence was preserved in devotional memory and cult two centuries later.[12] Much more characteristic of the south was an ardent devotion to early Christian female saints, whose cults spread from the region during the later Middle Ages. "Female sainthood"—which attains impressive percentages if one counts all the cases of women to whom one or the other urban population of central-northern Italy devoted a cult, though the cult may not have been officially recognized by ecclesiastic authority—is a clear sign of the social prestige attained by women, a recognition of their positive influence on the moral fabric of a society that takes saints—in life and after death—as role models and points of reference.[13] Female saints bring women in their various social roles and different types and choices of life to a height of esteem; it is not by chance that the most privileged religious choices are those which place women outside of the traditional paths of female monasticism.

The nearly complete absence of female sainthood in the regions of the southern kingdom is a phenomenon that parallels perfectly the delay by several decades in the foundation of new types of religious communities in southern Italy. The significant contrast with the great liveliness of female religious initiative, communal as well as individual, and with the large number of cults devoted to female figures in central-northern Italy is a sign of the profound differences in women's role in society, or at least in the estimation of that role in the contemporary mentality. The distribution patterns of the two phenomena in the various regions of Italy appear to mirror each other perfectly: particular density in the regions of central Italy, especially in Umbria and Tuscany, a fair amount in the area

11. André Vauchez, "L'idéal de sainteté dans le mouvement féminin franciscain aux XIIIᵉ et XIVᵉ siècles," in *Movimento religioso femminile e francescanesimo nel secolo XIII.* Atti del VII convegno internazionale (Assisi, 11–13 ottobre 1979), Società internazionale di studi francescani (Assisi, 1980), p. 319.

12. Such was the case with two Sicilian women, Rosalia and Angela of Sciacca.

13. On the cases of women for whom there were central-northern Italian cults, see André Vauchez, *La sainteté en Occident aux derniers siècles du Moyen Âge,* Bibliothèque de l'École Française de Rome 241 (2d ed., Rome, 1988), pp. 315–18, who offers precise percentages, limited, however, to the cases documented in the canonization trials; see the rich case studies relating to Italy, set forth and documented by Benvenuti Papi, *"In castro poenitentiae,"* pp. 101–17.

of Emilia-Romagna and Veneto, progressive scarcity as one descends into the southern regions.[14] By looking at cult practices, one has the clear impression that the infrequency of women's autonomous religious initiative parallels and is symptomatic both of the nonrelevant role they played in some specific Italian regions—particularly in the south—and of their low degree of social consideration.

RADICAL POVERTY AND WOMEN'S INSTITUTIONAL INDEPENDENCE

Radical poverty is the most striking characteristic of the female religious groups in central-northern Italy toward the end of the second decade of the thirteenth century. Here is the precise content of the letter that Honorius III sent to his legate, Ugolino d'Ostia, on August 27, 1218: "Many virgins and other women, to whom nobility [of heritage] promises a prestigious standing in the midst of the instable prosperity of the world . . . desire that some dwellings [*domicilia*] be built for them in which they may live, since they have no possessions under the sky, except these dwellings themselves and the oratories that are to be built inside them."[15] It is difficult to identify the direct beneficiaries of these concessions: the pontifical letter describes the requests of the women in question, but makes no reference to specific cases. However, documentary sources indicate that two communities of women, that of Monticelli near Florence

14. Ibid., pp. 106–13, where individual cases are listed by region. It should nonetheless be noted that the overwhelming majority of new communities are distributed between Umbria and Tuscany, where seventeen out of the twenty-four monasteries listed in Cardinal Rainaldo of S. Eustachio's letter (Omaechevarria, *Escritos de Santa Clara*, pp. 364–65) are located, and that northwestern Italy is not distinguished for density of new female religious communities—though some are attested before 1228 (see Benvenuti, "Fortuna del movimento damianita," pp. 68–102)—nor for women to whom some form of cult is dedicated. The Abruzzan monasteries will be discussed below. Unfortunately, the data in our possession do not permit even an approximate determination of the founding dates of most Apulian monasteries: we can only say that between 1243 (the beginning of the pontificate of Innocent IV) and 1316 (the date of the first series of Franciscan sees with information also about the monasteries of the second order, the so-called *series napolitana*), fourteen female Franciscan monasteries are established in Abruzzo, twenty in Capitanata, and nine in southern Puglia. On the Tyrrhenian side there is a consistent presence of foundations connected to the *Ordo S. Damianii* (and starting from 1263 *Ordo S. Clarae*) only in the region of Campania, with greatest concentration in Naples (4 monasteries) and Salerno (2 monasteries), to which the later foundations of Sorrento, Ravello, and Aversa are joined; see Benvenuti, "Fortuna del movimento damianita," 91–95. Research on individual Apulian foundations has been published in *Chiara d'Assisi e il movimento clariano in Puglia*, ed. Pasquale Corsi and Ferdinando L. Maggiore, Quaderni della biblioteca provinciale Cappuccini di Puglia 2 (Bari, 1996); *Chiara e il secondo Ordine francescano*.

15. In *Bullarium franciscanum*, ed. Joannes Hiacintus Sbaralea (Rome, 1759) (henceforth BF), 1:1–2; see W. R. Thomson, *Checklist of Papal Letters Relating to the Orders of St. Francis: Innocent III–Alexander IV* (Grottaferrata [Rome], 1971), no. 2, p. 14.

and that of Monteluce near Perugia, made such requests. In both cases, as I will discuss below, the women were from elevated social positions. The pontifical letter makes explicit reference to the elevated social background of the women making the requests. Their radical religious choice resulted in the severing of their ties of dependence upon ecclesiastic and lay authorities: "no bishop or ecclesiastic or secular person shall claim any power over them."

This may seem a formulaic phrase, and in fact it goes back to the language of monastic exemption on the part of the Roman Curia. By means of this formula the Curia traditionally precluded any external intervention and claimed for papal authority the direct and exclusive exercise of the power of control. But in the context of this letter the wording takes on a particular significance, inasmuch as it is connected to the choice of poverty by the women in question and to the consequent assumption *in ius et proprietatem Romanae ecclesiae* (as part of the right and property of the Roman church) of the lands for the construction of their dwellings, with the consequent release of such communities from the fiscal burdens imposed by local ecclesiastic authority. In its application to female communities, this is a rather innovative legal device. The assumption by the church of Rome of the property title to their dwellings and liturgical spaces entails the communities' total "immunity" vis-à-vis the exercise of any authority whatsoever, except that of the Apostolic See.

It is therefore not simply a matter of extending to women's religious communities the principle of exemption, by now canonically consolidated and granted to numerous male monastic institutions, though this in itself would be significant. The papal document clearly extends this principle to the women in question, but at the same time carefully distinguishes it from the application on their behalf of a canonical-juridical expedient which the Roman church had used by now for several decades to claim, in opposition to bishops, the absolute and direct dependence on the papacy of monasteries that had been exempted from episcopal authority.[16] In the earlier cases, such exemption had even applied to the patrimonies of the monasteries. Here, however, the exemption clause applied only to the churches and residences of the women, hence excluding other properties which the interested communities had renounced on principle. Thus it provided for the lapse of the clause of exemption should the communities themselves become possessors of immobile properties or

16. See Michele Maccarrone's reference to the monasteries which the *Liber censuum* of Cencio Camerario designated as "*in ius et proprietatem beati Petri et sanctae Romanae ecclesiae*": "Primato romano e monasteri dal principio del secolo XII ad Innocenzo III," *Romana ecclesia, cathedra Petri* vol. 2, ed. P. Zerbi, R. Volpini, and A. Galluzzi (Rome, 1991), pp. 822–27.

the holders of fiscal rights.[17] The juridical expedient thus appears to have been directed toward the safeguarding of the choice of poverty, which had been made by the *mulieres religiosae*.[18]

The customary dependencies on lay founders or donors were thus cut at the roots, eliminating any possibility of using the monastic institution as an instrument for heightening familial power and of transforming it into a security and an enormously expandable repository of family fortune. It was precisely the renunciation of any form of patronage on the part of the donor which characterized the donation deeds made to Ugolino on behalf of the female communities, as will emerge clearly from the analyses of the documents relating to Monteluce. The choice of poverty thus brought with it a drastic rupture with social customs that had become the norm and had been concretized in precise rights regarding the exercise of power and forms of tight economic and fiscal control with respect to individual monasteries, particularly female ones.

Certainly there were elements of continuity with the past, although the same innovations in female religious choices now took place in the context of an economically lively urban society, whose structures and relationships differed sharply from those characterizing feudal society.[19] As far as we know, female religious choice continued to take place within the confines of the monied or even ruling classes, but in a manner quite different from that of the feudal age, when social custom, and indeed the close rapport between monastic institutions and the holders of landed and banal lordship, presupposed that women had a solid dowry at their disposal when they entered the monastery, which became the basis of, or was added to, the monastic patrimony.[20] The very aggregation of adults

17. The text is very clear on this point: after formulating the concession of exemption, it adds significantly: "quandiu quidem fuerint sine possessionibus, decimis, mortuariis, per quae solet locorum Dioecesanis et aliis ecclesiarum praelatis preiudicium generari."

18. It is the pontifical document itself which makes this distinction, by subjecting directly to the Apostolic See the churches to be constructed by the female communities in question. Nonetheless we are not in agreement with those who have recently denied that the assumption in *ius et proprietatem Ecclesiae romanae* of the lands assigned to the *mulieres religiosae* functioned not so much as a safeguard with respect to poverty, but to remove such communities from the power and control of diocesan authority. This position, already held by Höler ("Il monastero," pp. 162–163) has been reasserted by Alberzoni, "Papato e nuovi Ordini," p. 228.

19. Interesting notes on the context and the social implications of female religious choice can be found in Anna Benvenuti Papi, "Donne religiose e francescanesimo nella Valle Reatina," in *Il francescanesimo nella Valle Reatina,* ed. Luigi Pellegrini and Stanislao da Campagnola (Milan, 1993), pp. 196–98.

20. Their origin in the monied and ruling classes is true not only in the case of Clare and of the members of the first Damianite group (see Jacques Guy Bougerol, "Il recrutamento sociale delle Clarisse di Assisi," in *Les ordres mendiants et la ville en Italie centrale [v. 1220–v. 1350],* Mélanges de l'École française de Rome. Moyen Âge—Temps modernes 89 [Rome, 1977], pp. 629–32); the other cases noted by us, which we will examine below, also belong to the ruling classes.

into single monastic entities, by way of *conversio* or *oblatio,* required availability of substantial assets, which were offered to the monastery in return for admission into the community, participation in its spiritual goods, and burial.[21] Even the choices of virginity, chastity, and total religious commitment were at least more easily available to women of high social extraction. Those belonging to the lower and, especially, to the servile classes could not dispose of themselves and their time to the same degree.

Communal poverty, which allowed women to be admitted into the female community without a counter-gift of economic goods, extended to women of lower social classes the possibility of fulfilling a strong socioreligious experience, with the attendant revaluation in terms of social prestige. However, in more than one case this possibility remained at a purely theoretical level, or was translated into the traditional forms of personal oblation, with the consequent social stratification inside the new monasteries, such that for women of lower social class there remained only the roles of *servientes* or *servitiales* (servants).

The choice of communal poverty on the part of female religious groups in the first decades of the thirteenth century tended to disrupt the custom of founding family monasteries for the scions of the feudal nobility, which persisted even in the twelfth century despite the attempts at "liberalization" undertaken by monastic reform movements.[22] As far as the highest and most economically solid classes in the social hierarchy were concerned, the choice of poverty prevented women from becoming a vehicle of investment and exchange in advantageous matrimonial contracts. The strong and even violent resistance put up by the families of such women and strongly emphasized in hagiographic accounts, including those relating to Clare and her sister Agnes,[23] and to Filippa Ma-

---

21. For the problems relating to *conversi, converse,* and adult oblates in the monasteries, see Grado G. Merlo, "Uomini e donne in comunità 'estese'. Indagini su realtà piemontesi tra XII e XIII secolo," in *Uomini e donne in comunità = Quaderni di storia religiosa* 1 (1994), 9–31, which also mentions the respective social implications; Franco Dal Pino, "Oblati e oblate presso gli ordini mendicanti minori," in *Uomini e donne,* pp. 33–67, where one will find further bibliographic citations. Singular and interesting cases are analyzed by Gian Piero Pacini, "Comunità di poveri nel Veneto: esperienze 'religiose' del laicato vicentino dal secolo XII al XIV," in *La conversione alla povertà nell'Italia dei secoli XII–XIV.* Atti del XXVII Convegno storico internazionale (Todi 14–17 ottobre 1990) (Spoleto, 1991), pp. 325–53.

22. See Jean Leclercq, "Il monachesimo femminile nei secoli XII e XIII," in *Movimento religioso femminile e francescanesimo nel secolo XIII* (Assisi, 1980), pp. 61–99; and, "Nobiltà," in *Dizionario degli Istituti di perfezione,* 1980 ed., vol. 6, col. 311–17 and bibliography cited there.

23. See *Legenda sanctae Clarae Assisiensis,* ed. Stefano Brufani, in *Fontes franciscani,* ed. Enrico Menestò and Stefano Brufani (Assisi, 1995), pp. 2415–50, specifically pp. 2420, 2429–31; for problems relating to the text, see Brufani's introduction to pp. 2403–14.

reri,[24] is very significant in this regard. But the act of freeing themselves from any type of dependency on lay potentates and local ecclesiastic authority constituted a breach in the very structure of relationships between female monastic entities and society. The withdrawal from episcopal control, without becoming otherwise directly connected with or actually integrated into a male religious order—as had happened to the nuns of Fontevrault and to those associated with the Cistercian and Premonstratensian orders—certainly represented an absolutely new occurrence. Women became directly responsible for their own choices in society and the primary referents of socio-religious initiative and congregation. This new autonomy brought with it a profound modification of women's relationships to civic and ecclesiastic society and those in charge of it.

The best documented cases furnish excellent evidence on this point. The documents of the Perugian monastery of Monteluce clearly demonstrate the social implications of women's religious choices. On July 31, 1218, Giovanni, bishop of Perugia, gave his consent to the building of a church and a monastery for a group of *converse* (women converted to the religious life), renouncing any rights to the monastery itself.[25] The promoter of the initiative, which was requested by the women, was the papal legate, Ugolino d'Ostia, who received in the same month of July from Glotto di Munaldo the donation of land for the monastery to be constructed.[26] Moreover, by force of his authority Ugolino obtained the concession of immunity from the bishop's authority. The various components of town society became involved at the highest level in the occasion, which signaled the definitive outcome of the original and independent religious choice of "conversion" which this female group had exercised for some time.[27] The donor of the land was a representative of the high urban aristocracy, to which the women in question must have belonged, as may be surmised from the high status of the individuals who witnessed the drawing-up of the deed. Among the witnesses were the *podestà* of Perugia, Andrea di Giacomo dei Montemelini, and as draftsman and legal representative

---

24. See the hagiographic text in Aniceto Chiappini, "Santa Filippa Mareri e il suo monastero di Borgo S. Pietro de Molito nel Cicolano (biografia—liturgia—documenti)," *Miscellanea francescana* 22 (1921): 83.

25. The document is published in *Francesco d'Assisi. Documenti e archivi. Codici e biblioteche. Miniature*. Catalogo della mostra di Perugia (Luglio-novembre 1982) (Milan, 1982), pp. 31–32; for the reconstruction of the history of Monteluce see Höler, "Il monastero delle Clarisse di Monteluce"; Höler, *Frauenkloster in einer italienischen Stadt*.

26. The document is published in *Francesco d'Assisi*, pp. 47–48.

27. In the donation deed it says explicitly that the women are already living on the site "in the service of God."

of the women, the notary of the "sacred imperial palace," Bono. The episcopal concession was drawn up in the monastery of S. Pietro, the most powerful monastic and ecclesiastic entity of the town, in the presence of the abbot and the principal representatives of the monastic community, who functioned as witnesses together with the episcopal deacon. The formalization of the women's religious choice was the center of attention of the ecclesiastic and civic society.

In his donation, Glotto "renounces the benefit of patronage and rule": the combined thrust of the women's will and the authoritative intervention of Ugolino produced an innovation in the social custom that habit or norm had transformed into precise laws. Glotto's declaration in the document is explicit: "renouncing all the clauses, the conditions and the benefits *which are my due by law and by custom.*"[28] Thus is created a female monastery free from the shackles of lay patronage and local ecclesiastic authority. It is a new social condition, officially recognized, for a female community.

Though originating from different religious experiences, the institutionalization of two other groups of religious women in which the cardinal legate took an interest around the same time had similar results. The letters addressed in July 1219 by the papal legate to two previously founded monasteries in Siena and Lucca, which were incorporated into the respective confirmations of Honorius III, give a clear indication of this.[29] The monastery of S. Maria outside Porta Camollia in Siena arose around the chapel of S. Petronilla and the attached *hospitale;* this suggests that the primitive religious community was already present and active in the hospice, which looked out on the street leading from Siena to Rome. The monastery in Lucca, on the other hand, arose in a wooded area (*silva*) in the suburban locality of Gattaiola, which leads us to suppose that it was originally a hermitage. In both cases Ugolino's letter traces the path leading to the establishment of the monastery: first, the women request to be released from dependency on the owners of the land, churches, and dwellings in which they are already conducting their religious activity; next, Ugolino, on the women's behalf, places the properties *in ius et proprietatem Romanae ecclesiae,* but he also decides—and this is the condition posed for his granting the requests of the two female groups—that a monastery is to be founded.[30] Finally, once this condition has been

---

28. "Renuntians," the donor writes in the document, "omnibus exceptionibus, conditionibus ac beneficiis iuris et consuetudinis mihi competentibus."

29. See BF, 1:10–13.

30. In Siena it is the cathedral chapter, in Lucca an influential citizen, who request release from dependency on the owners of the property where the women conduct their religious activities.

accepted, the individual communities request and obtain the "protection of the Apostolic See," establishing a direct connection with pontifical authority.

The groundwork was thus laid for directing free religious initiative into an institutional channel hitherto completely unused by female communities: the creation of an autonomous religious order, directly dependent on the Apostolic See. The innovative choice of poverty on the women's part represented not only the premise but also the indispensable condition for insertion into the new structure. The bishops' formulary prepared by the cardinal for subsequent monastic foundations concludes thus: "If the sisters themselves should reject or not wish to observe the form of such religion, . . . the place will return into our jurisdiction," that is, that of the bishop.[31] This condition refered to the *forma vitae* (way of life) decreed by Ugolino for the already existing monasteries or for those to be founded in the new *religio,* but the independence of individual communities vis-à-vis local ecclesiastic authority was obtained each time by force of the spontaneous and conscious choice of poverty: "as long as they shall remain without possessions, tithes, mortuaries, which things involve an infraction of the rights of the bishops and the other ecclesiastic prelates," as the above-mentioned letter from Honorius III of August 1218 clearly enunciated.

CARDINAL UGOLINO AND THE PROCESS OF NORMALIZATION

The free choice of poverty on the part of female religious groups thus became the basis of a new religious order, conceived and realized by Cardinal Ugolino in order to unite in one homogeneous socio-religious organism the communities that had sprung up in Umbria and Tuscany.[32] This organism was already intended to include communities of different types and objectives that were forming or had already formed elsewhere,

31. This is the tenor of the formula inserted at the end of the Register of Ugolino: "We . . . bishop by grace of God . . . grant to you . . . full authority to establish a monastery in which virgins dedicated to God and other maidservants of Christ serve the Lord in poverty, according to the *forma vitae* of the Poor Ladies of the Valley of Spoleto and of Tuscany, given to them by Ugo, venerable Bishop of Ostia, by authority of the Pope. And we grant to the site itself and to the sisters, both those present and those who will come in the future, the full freedom held by the monasteries of the same religion in Perugia, Siena and Lucca." The formula is inserted in the register of Ugolino as final document: Guido Levi, ed., *Registri dei cardinali Ugolino d'Ostia e Ottaviano degli Ubaldini,* Fonti per la storia d'Italia 8 (Rome, 1890), pp. 153–54; Livarius Oliger, "De origine regularum ordinis S. Clarae," *Archivum franciscanum historicum* 5 (1912): 196.

32. *Pauperes Dominae de Valle Spoliti sive Tuscia* is precisely the name of the new religious Order.

and that by their characteristic of poverty could aspire to join the number of the *pauperes dominae* (literally, "Poor Ladies"). Ugolino's task, then, was one not only of safeguarding the needs of women's religious life, but also of normalization. He pursued this objective by means of a systematic program of claustration which, at least in part, ended up perverting the original character of the female groups and isolating them from the urban society from whose heart they had sprung, and to whose marginalized members they had, in more than one case, dedicated themselves.[33]

Let us follow the development in its successive phases. The papal letter of August 1218 points to the emergence of new situations in the communal religious undertaking of women, which could not be reduced to the traditional modes of organizing female communities. Faced with the proliferation of groups with religious aspirations to which the traditional structures of female monasteries were not able to offer an adequate response, the Cardinal was constrained, already in the course of the first legation to central Italy in 1216–17, to find an innovative solution.[34] The force of such female groups must have been robust and efficacious if it succeeded in getting the papal legate, who had other problems on his hands, involved. Indeed, Ugolino even went so far as to work out, and propose to the highest ecclesiastic authority, legal solutions that were at the very least unusual in their specific application. The return of the leg-

---

33. If in the already mentioned cases of Siena and Penne it is only a matter of a well-founded hypothesis, the case of the Veronese community is clearer and better documented. This community was conceived and realized outside of any relationship with the Franciscan movement, notwithstanding the name *sorores minores,* which first appears in documents in 1224, but with reference to a community whose roots go back to the very first years of the second decade of the thirteenth century. The case has been attentively studied by Gian Maria Varanini ("Per la storia dei Minori a Verona nel Duecento"): the protagonist of the original initiative is a woman, *domina Garzenda,* who avails herself of her daughter's money in order to construct houses for lepers in the locality called *sub Aquario,* near the Adige. The daughter is thus in partnership with her mother in the realization of the project, as is the daughter's husband, whom we very soon find committed to the service of lepers. This initiative, which involves lay people of both sexes, is behind the establishment of a female community, which we find gathered around the church of S. Agata, situated in the above-mentioned locality, together with the lepers, prior to their concentration in 1223 in the nearby hospital of S. Giacomo alla Tomba. Very soon *domina Benvenuta* also joined that community. She was the wife of the brother of that *frater Rudulfus* who was prior of the hospital of S. Giacomo della Tomba in 1218. The female community is identified in a document of January 1224 under the name of *sorores minores.* The community, though undergoing a slow dissolution, succeeded for about thirty years in maintaining its own identity, resisting even the normalizing intervention of the Minorite Friar Leone, who was perhaps that fra Leone Perego who acted as intermediary in 1224 when the *pauperes sorores ordinis de Spolito* took possession of the church of S. Apollinare in Milan.

34. As will be seen, the first documented case is that of the community of Monticelli, already established in the first months of 1218. The analogous acts relative to the soon-to-be-established monasteries of Perugia, Lucca, and Siena date back to this period or, in any case, to before the letter of Honorius III of August 27, which, as we have seen, suggests that there were a number of such cases. Again as we have seen, we have definitive documentation for the Perugian case from July 1218; the other two appear already definitively structured in July 1219.

ate to the papal Curia around 1217 must have constituted the occasion to fine-tune a strategy. Perhaps the earliest stage of that strategy was his response to the community of Monticelli in Florence, which emerged under the direction of Donna Avvegnente, a member of the prestigious Albizzi family.

Monticelli and San Damiano: Two Exceptions to the Rule

On March 19, 1218 Ugolino delegated Berlinghieri de' Girolami to receive, in the name of the Apostolic See, the land which Forese di Mergiullese Bellicozzi destined "for the use of donna Avvegnente di Albizzo and for all the other *sorores* ('sisters') who may in the future wish to live with her in a monastery placed under the invocation of S. Maria *ad Sanctum Sepulcrum,* on the hill of Monticelli," near Florence.[35] At the beginning of 1218, the group of *sorores* that had gathered spontaneously and informally, but autonomously, around the religious choice of a woman of the urban aristocracy was organizing itself as a monastic community. In the following year, after the construction of the monastery, the community obtained official recognition on the part of the Roman Curia, through the intervention of Cardinal Ugolino d'Ostia, who thereby confirmed the institutional evolution brought about by a conscious and spontaneous choice of the group.[36] Indeed, even before the Benedictine rule was imposed on it, the community had adopted the *observantiae regulares iuxta Ordinem Dominarum S. Mariae de S. Damiano de Assisio* (the Rule of St. Damian of Assisi) and had thus associated itself with the group of the Damianites, an alternative to traditional forms of female monastic life, in perfect consistency with the aspirations of the members of the Florentine group.[37] This association was not simply an imitation of the Assisan community; it was the first step in the institutional development which had its beginning in the donation of the property of S. Sepolcro di Monticelli to the papal legate.[38]

Avvegnente is a figure still shrouded in shadow: one can barely make

---

35. Anna Benvenuti Papi, "L'insediamento francescano a Firenze: le origini," in *La presenza francescana nella Toscana del '200,* Quaderni di vita e cultura francescana (Florence, 1990), pp. 81–100, esp. 89–90; precisely this document leads me to place the proposals for solving the problematic relating to the female communities prior to the period between the two legations.

36. In the letter of Honorius III, dated December 9, 1219, there is mention of *monasterio ibi constructo,* whereas in the letter of Cardinal Ugolino d'Ostia, dated July 27, 1219, reference is made to the property on which Avvegnente desires to establish (*dedicare*) the monastery (BF, 1:3–5).

37. The letter by which Ugolino gives official recognition to the Florentine group hastens to make clear that such *observantiae* were fruit of the women's free choice: *vobis voluntarie indixistis* (BF, 1:4).

38. It should be noted that in the letter by which Honorius III confirms the action of his legate, the moment of donation of the property is indicated as preceding the assumption of the canonic rules of the *religio* on the part of Avvegnente: *antequam se ad religionem transferret* (BF, 1:3).

out her contours. A woman of high social extraction, from the Florentine aristocratic family of the Albizzi, she was resolute in her intention of
religious commitment and gifted with sufficient charismatic power to at-
tract other women into the orbit of her own radical choice of life. Those
women, who become her *sorores* and then nuns, had her as a sure guide
on a singular path, one which allowed her community, alone among those
with which the papal legate concerned himself, to ally itself with the
community of S. Damian, which was directed by Clare of Assisi. It was
thus Avvegnente, along with her first nucleus of *sorores,* who allied herself with the community of Clare, thus forming the embryo of what the
letter of the papal legate called the *Ordo Dominarum S. Mariae de S. Damiano de Assisio,*[39] which for several years lent its name to all female monasteries organized under the direction of Ugolino.

Clare and Avvegnente are two female figures who, though coming out
of quite different contexts—Assisi is certainly not comparable to Florence in these first decades of the thirteenth century—ended up becoming closely connected, not only in their common aspiration to break away
from their respective social class in the name of a radical choice of poverty, but also in their spontaneous and stubbornly pursued adhesion to a
practical rule of life—the *observantiae regulares*—which they imposed
upon themselves and which the papal legate ratified.[40]

The existence of *observantiae regulares* at S. Damiano in 1219, with implicit reference to a written text—some form of which was a necessary
prerequisite for ratification by the papal legate—poses more than one
problem. Since it is a matter of *observantiae regulares,* it is absolutely in-
adequate to refer, as is usually done, to the brief document that St. Francis addressed to the community of S. Damiano, all the more since that
text is limited to Francis's assumption, in the name of his friars, of the
commitment to have "diligent care and special concern" for the community of Clares.[41] If Francis had written a true and proper *forma vivendi*
(Rule) for the nuns, it would have had to be rather more extended and
articulated. Perhaps one should not exclude the possibility that even at

---

39. BF, 1:3–5.
40. It is stated explicitly in the letter: *quas ratas habemus,* "which we have ratified" (BF, 1:4).
41. It is the text cited by Clare in chapter VI of her rule and called by her *Forma vivendi* (Omaechevarria, *Escritos de Santa Clara,* pp. 283); how and why that text was so named is a problem that
would need to be addressed from all points of view, including aspects relating to authenticity,
which cannot simply be entrusted to that *scripsit nobis* with which Clare introduces Francis's text
in question; the fact that there is no evidence of such a text in the manuscript tradition is certainly
not enough to throw doubt upon its authenticity, but it is a very significant fact and, nevertheless, it would be necessary on this basis to lay down rigorous and coherent criteria for inserting a
text among the *Scritti* of Francis.

that time the Clarist community availed itself of the first rule, essentially based on evangelical principles, formulated for the male community, adapting it to their own requirements. One may at least surmise that Clare must have used it as a model at a later time when she compiled a rule of her own. Until the last years of the 1220s, when it had to introduce the *formula vitae* of Ugolino, the Assisan female community was not bound to rigorous claustration, a situation which permitted more than one analogy to the corresponding male group, even at the normative level.[42] The sources are not lacking in noteworthy indications of close relationships between the male and the female communities.[43] However, this does not mean that they thereby constituted a double monastery, given that the *sorores minores* (literally, "lesser sisters")—according to what Jacques de Vitry tells us in a testimony which raises more than one problem—had a permanent settlement, which was absolutely unthinkable for *fratres minores* (lesser brothers—the friars) at the time.[44]

In his testimony, Jacques de Vitry furnishes further elements for better defining the *observantiae regulares* of the Damianites. He says of the *sorores* that they live communally "in various hospices close to the cities." The term *hospitia,* in this particular context, indicates a dwelling place of communal organization characterized by temporariness,[45] if one compares it to the expression *conventuales congregationes* which Jacques de Vitry uses for the *Umiliati* and *Umiliate.*[46] Another characteristic is that they "live from the labor of their own hands," and that they rule out donations of any kind (*nihil accipiunt,* "they do not accept anything"). Jacques does not specify the type of labor from which the women live, any more than he does for the *Umiliati* of Milan.[47] However, he under-

---

42. See Maria Pia Alberzoni, *Chiara e il papato* (Milan, 1995), pp. 52–69.

43. See Luigi Pellegrini, "La prima fraternitas francescana: Una rilettura delle fonti," in *Frate Francesco d'Assisi*. Atti del XXI Convegno internazionale (Assisi, 14–16 ottobre 1993) (Spoleto, 1994), pp. 44–47.

44. *Lettres de Jacques de Vitry (1160/70–1240), évêque de Saint-Jean d'Acre*. ed. R. B. C. Huygens (Leiden, 1960), p. 71.

45. The significant coincidence with the already noted contents of the papal letter of August 18, 1218—which makes generic reference to several female groups guided by the unifying intent of living communally their chosen life of poverty in simple habitations (*domicilia*) and without property or income—should induce caution in identifying the *sorores minores* of Jacques de Vitry with the Damianites, or at least exclusively with them.

46. *Lettres de Jacques de Vitry*, pp. 72–73.

47. For the work of the *Umiliate,* spinning and weaving, see Lorenzo Paolini, "Le Umiliate al lavoro. Appunti fra storiografia e storia," *Bullettino dell'Istituto storico italiano per il medioevo e Archivio muratoriano* 97 (1991): 229–65; more generally on this argument see *Donne e lavoro nell'Italia medievale,* ed. M. G. Muzzarelli, P. Galletti, B. Andreolli (Turin, 1991). In the letter of Jacques de Vitry another notable and interesting difference should be remarked: while the movement of the *Umiliati* is circumscribed in the precise confines of the Milanese diocese, for the Minorite movement the expression "in those parts" is used, even though the reference is to the area of Perugia

lines one specific rule: the earning of their subsistence must not come from fixed incomes, from donations, or even from collections, but, at least primarily if not exclusively, from their own labor.[48] The analogy with the first group of Minorites immediately strikes the eye.

Ugolino's *Forma vitae:* Normalization in the North

The *Observantiae* of the group of Clare, chosen by the community of Monticelli and ratified by the papal legate, were precisely the same as those of the Damianites. These distinguish them from the other groups of women animating the civic and religious society of central Italy in this period, which Cardinal Ugolino was directing into an institutional channel that safeguarded the religious choices and autonomy of the emerging female groups and regrouped them into a well-structured religious entity under the direct control of the Apostolic See. To this end he wrote and secured approval of a *forma vitae,* marked by the most rigid claustration, as an alternative to the *observantiae regulares iuxta Ordinem Dominarum S. Mariae de S. Damiano de Assisio,* ratified and granted to S. Damiano and to Monticelli.

The progressive organization of the communities of Clare and Avvegnente, although taking place at the center of conflicting or converging relationships with some noteworthy components of urban society, appeared in its early phases much more in the shadows compared to the interest and attention that this society bestowed on Monteluce and on other cases in the same year or in those immediately following.[49] Another ele-

---

where the encounter between Jacques and the papal Curia had taken place. *In partibus illis,* that is in Umbria, we do not have knowledge of any other communities besides the Damianite group that were in any way affiliated with the Friars Minor. Perhaps Jacques is uniting different communities under a single typology, based on a process of generalization which we see in action in more than one document of the time, and which tends to group under the denomination *sorores minores,* or similar names, various new existing communities.

48. Already Zarnke had noted the tendency on the part of Jacques de Vitry to assimilate the forms of life of the *sorores minores* to those of the Beguines (*Anteil des Kardinal Ugolino,* p. 29). This observation should be kept in mind, but it does not vitiate his information.

49. Of interest in this connection are several cases in the area of Padua between the second decade and the early years of the third decade of the thirteenth century. See Antonio Rigon, "Penitenti e laici devoti fra mondo monastico-canonicale e Ordini mendicanti: Qualche esempio in area veneta e mantovana," *Ricerche di storia religiosa,* n. s., 9 (1980): 51–73; Alberzoni, *L'Ordine di S. Damiano in Lombardia.* That the religious experience of women in the first decades of the thirteenth century placed itself at the center of attention and intervention of civic society at its highest level is well attested also by the documentation of 1233 relating to a female group of penitents in the town of Varese: at the formal establishment of the female community, the *podestà* and the consuls of the newly formed municipality intervene and give their solemn approval. On this point see Alfredo Lucioni, "La società varesina del Duecento. Novità di vita religiosa e inedite sperimentazioni di autonomia amministrativa," in *Sulle tracce degli Umiliati,* ed. Maria Pia Alberzoni, Annamaria Ambrosioni, Alfredo Lucioni (Milan, 1997), pp. 493–602, particularly pp. 508–25.

ment of analogy between the Assisan and the Florentine communities is that they pursued common objectives and seemed not to seek official support and recognition, except as was necessary to attain their particular rule of life. By contrast, the Perugian community and those of Lucca and Siena, organized at around the same time, continued to place themselves in the orbit of Ugolino, who solicited the active presence of civic, ecclesiastic, and lay leadership as a guarantee for their commitment to abstain from future interference, and imposed the *forma vitae* that he himself had prepared.[50]

With the election of Ugolino of Ostia to the papacy in 1227 these two different outcomes gave way to a single institutional organism, in which several dozens of monasteries strewn throughout central-northern Italy, from Terni to Trento, were united. Subject to Ugolino's *forma vitae,* these monasteries were headed, before 1228, by the monastery of S. Damiano, from whence they took their name.[51] The geographic specification, *pauperes dominae de valle Spoleti sive Tuscia* (the Poor Ladies of Umbria and Tuscany), now appeared amply surpassed by reality, but the designation *pauperes moniales reclusae* (poor cloistered nuns) was not,[52] since the whole purpose of Ugolino's *forma vitae* was to ensure the most rigid claustration. The nuns were absolutely forbidden to leave their monasteries, except to found other monasteries, and their contact with the outside world was filtered through a double grill. Access to the monasteries by outsiders was limited to matters of urgent and pressing necessity and to individuals who attained a special papal license. The internal life of the monastery was measured both day and night by liturgical prayer—the only voice that broke the rigorous silence. Ugolino's prologue emphasizes that poverty is a precise choice, carried out by the women themselves.[53] But the body of the text imposes its norms, imprinting every aspect of life in the monastery with the most rigorous austerity—in dress, in diet, in personal and communal furnishings; those regulations are guaranteed, moreover, through the control of the ecclesiastical "visitor."

---

50. See the letters of Ugolino of July 1219, inserted into the pontifical documentation of 1221 for the three monasteries, in BF, 1:10–15.

51. In the letter of Cardinal Rainaldo of Jenne of 1228, he speaks of *conventus pauperum monasteriorum S. Damiani de Assisio* (see note 7); in the papal letter of March 22, 1235, there appears for the first time the designation *Ordo S. Damiani* (BF, 1:149).

52. They are still called this in 1231 in two letters, sent by the bishop of Pamplona to the monastery of S. Grazia and by Gregory IX to that of Monteluce di Perugia (BF, 1:72–73); just as, in his letter addressed the same year to Filippa Mareri, Gregory IX still uses the designation *Pauperes moniales inclusae* (see below, note 63).

53. "Divina vobis gratia inspirante, per arduam viam et arctam, quae ad vitam ducit, incedere et vitam pauperem ducere pro aeternis lucrandis divitiis elegistis," Omaechevarria, *Escritos de Santa Clara,* p. 217.

The Dissemination of the Ugolinian Model in Southern Italy

In the late 1230s the Ugolinian model began to spread into the south of Italy, where, again, ecclesiastical authorities tended to merge distinct religious realities into a single and easily controllable institutional channel. The result of this undertaking was also to direct toward these new and religiously more committed institutions old monasteries needful or (in more than one case) desirous of reform or radical restructuring, as well as newly founded monasteries and autonomously organized groups.

The steps by which the Ugolinian model was diffused in southern Italy speak eloquently to this point. First, several groups that had already been established around charismatic personalities were gathered together. Then new monastic foundations were established as a result of the direct interest of women belonging to families at the pinnacle of local lay society. Finally, the new religious order was drawn upon to invigorate and reform old monasteries. Toward the middle of the century this path reached from the northernmost regions of the southern kingdom to the territories farthest south.

Let us examine several cases in the Abruzzo. The first, in temporal order, is the story of Filippa Mareri,[54] who needs to be studied afresh in the context of the lively religious initiative of women in central Italy, and liberated from the scholarly preoccupation with linking her to the experience of female Franciscanism,[55] which involves an uncritical acceptance not only of the *Legenda* about the meeting between Filippa and Francis, but also of the fable that the Assisan induced her to a religious vocation by telling her about the "conversion" of Clare.[56] A simple mustering of the facts that can be drawn from documents and from the *Legenda* high-

---

54. On Filippa Mareri, see Robert Brentano, "Il movimento religioso femminile a Rieti nei secoli XIII–XIV," in *Movimento religioso femminile in Umbria*, pp. 78–79; and now the contributions of Brentano, Germano Elia Cerafogli, Edith Pásztor, and Henry Romanin, in *Santa Filippa Mareri e il monastero di Borgo S. Pietro nella storia del Cicolano*, Atti del Convegno di Studi di Borgo S. Pietro del 24–26 ottobre 1986 (Borgo S. Pietro, 1989), pp. 27–104.
55. An attempt in this direction has been made by Anna Benvenuti Papi, "Donne religiose e francescanesimo nella Valle Reatina," pp. 189–207.
56. Chiappini gives uncritical credence to the *Legenda*, which speaks of familiar encounters between Francis of Assisi and Filippa; this allows him to emphasize the Franciscan inspiration of the initial religious choice of Mareri: "L'Abruzzo francescano nel secolo XIII," *Rassegna di storia e d'arte d'Abruzzo e Molise* 2 (1926): 47–48. On the poor reliability of the *Legenda*, see Robert Brentano, "Santa Filippa Mareri e il movimento religioso femminile del secolo XIII," in *Santa Filippa Mareri e il monastero di Borgo S. Pietro*, pp. 27–44; see also Edith Pasztor, "Filippa Mareri e Chiara d'Assisi modelli della spiritualità femminile francescana," *L'Italia francescana* 63 (1988): 27–42. Pasztor tends to date the first composition of the *Legenda* earlier than the second half of the thirteenth century, a thesis supported by Alessandra Bartolomei Romagnoli, who actually places the *Legenda* in the first half of the century: "Filippa Mareri: La santità e i miracoli," in *Studi su Filippa Mareri*, ed. Germano Cerafogli (Rome, 1992 — numero monografico of *Frate Francesco* 49 [1992]: 17–32).

lights how the establishment of a monastery joined to the *ordo sancti Damiani* (the Damianites) represented the final stage in a sequence of personal and autonomous religious choices, from which a female religious community progressively came to be formed.[57] The donation document of the church of S. Pietro *de Molito,* dated September 18, 1228, seems, insofar as it can be considered authentic,[58] to represent the attempt on the part of Tommaso Mareri to utilize his sister's personal and communal religious choice, which, according to the liturgic *Legenda,* matured through successive religious experiences.[59] According to the document, Tommaso attempted to channel the new religious community in the direction of establishing a monastery attached to a church under the patronage of the family of the Counts Sinibaldi, which extended its rule over numerous castles of Sabina and Cicolano.[60] At this point Filippa had to find an adequate solution to guarantee the genuineness of her own choice. This effort bore fruit three years later in the granting of exemption by Gregory IX to the monastic community which by now had been established around Filippa,[61] and in its subsequent incorporation, in 1235, into the order of S. Damian.[62] The choice of poverty, emphasized in the pontifical document of November 1236,[63] seems to have taken place in the context of the community's attachment to the order of S. Damian, since the first constitution of the monastery provided for communal possession.[64]

We thus find here a different relationship between the female community and the protagonists of the social context, compared with the cases from Umbria and Tuscany examined above: even at the moment when

57. The texts have been published by Chiappini in an appendix to his piece "Santa Filippa Mareri."

58. Chiappini, who transcribes the document ("Santa Filippa Mareri," pp. 100–1), has no doubts as to its authenticity and attributes the anomalies to errors made by the seventeenth-century transcriber ("Santa Filippa Mareri," p. 92), but too many elements in the formulae lead one to suspect a forgery, or at least a falsification, which might have been constructed to justify the rights of the monastery over the villa of Casardita.

59. See Chiappini, "Santa Filippa Mareri," p. 84.

60. See ibid., pp. 68–69, and Henry Romanin, "La scelta di Filippa Mareri e il monastero di S. Pietro de Molito nella politica equicola del suo tempo," in *Santa Filippa Mareri,* pp. 81–104.

61. Chiappini, "Santa Filippa Mareri," p. 95, but above all the much more critical reconstruction by Romanin, "Scelta di Filippa Mareri," pp. 89–99, and the bibliography cited there.

62. Chiappini, "Santa Filippa Mareri," pp. 95–96; the pontifical letter is addressed "to the abbess and the nuns of S. Pietro de Molet *Ordinis S. Damiani.*"

63. This is what is emphasized as well in the letter of 1236 in which Gregory IX grants indulgence to anyone who will offer the necessary subsidy to the *pauperes moniales* of the community of S. Pietro, who—the letter reads—"have placed in poverty their sustenance (*sufficentia*), such that they sustain themselves only by the alms of the faithful," ibid., p. 96.

64. Even supposing the forgery of the document of Tommaso Mareri, we have the evidence of the 1231 letter of Gregory IX, which takes the possessions of the community under apostolic protection.

the socio-familial class to which Filippa belonged seemed to look favorably on her free religious choice, in actual fact it was attempting to channel that choice into traditional structures which placed monasteries in the precincts of churches under the patronage of families of the feudal nobility. The release from such restrictions took place through incorporation into the institutional organism promoted and put into effect by Ugolino, which created a direct link with the Apostolic See. The story of Filippa is among the first in the territories of the southern kingdom to conclude with the institutional attachment to the order of the *Pauperes Dominae*.

The stories of other female religious communities indicate clearly that the Abruzzo constituted a transitional area, not only because attachment to the Damianite order occured earlier than in other regions of the south, but also because the characteristics of the original religious choice and of its subsequent institutional evolution seem to link such communities to the female reality of central-northern Italy. In the 1230s we already find an independently organized female community in the service of the hospital of S. Spirito in Penne. The designation *pauperes sorores* (poor sisters) leaves little doubt about the characteristics of their religious choice.[65] The completion of the institutional evolution was signaled by an episcopal certificate dated September 1252. In it the female community appeared fully established as a monastery, to which the bishop granted exemption from his own authority, certainly at the request of the community itself, which resolutely sought attachment to the *Ordo S. Damiani* through the mediation of its protector, Cardinal Rainaldo d'Ostia.[66] But the solemn papal privilege confirming the considerable property and possessions with which the monastery was already amply endowed provides evidence that the original choice of poverty had been abandoned, as was the case for the other monasteries of the order as well.

So, too, for the female community of S. Silvestro di Pereto in Marsica, attachment to the order of S. Damian was the completion of the institutional development of a group of women who came together around the religious initiative of Imilla *de Pontibus,* of which nothing more specific is known. The *de Pontibus* family exercised seigneurial rights over the religious house, as is shown by Andrea *de Pontibus*'s deed of renunciation, in favor of his sister Imilla and her community, of real and personal rights

---

65. See Luigi Pellegrini, *Insediamenti francescani nell'Italia del Duecento* (Rome, 1984), p. 89.
66. The Cardinal is the first of the signatories of the pontifical document, which in November 1252 sanctions this attachment (cf. BF, 1:637–39); the episcopal certificate, mentioned above, is incorporated in the papal privilege.

connected with patronage of the church, all assets of the church itself, and all power over persons in any way subject to it.[67] Imilla's group was by this time structured as a monastic community, and the already effective attachment to the order of S. Damian was the instrument by which it was released from the severe restrictions of noble patronage and from dependency on local ecclesiastic authority, in this case the Abbey of Farfa.[68] The whole operation was perfected and sanctioned by Innocent IV between November and December 1243 in two letters confirming the concessions of, respectively, the Abbot of Farfa and Andrea *de Pontibus*. It appears to have been directly and explicitly carried out in order to give renewed religious and economic vigor to an ecclesiastic institution that was "enormously deteriorated from both a spiritual and a material point of view."[69] The establishment of Damianite communities thus turns out to have been instrumental in the reform and invigoration of old ecclesiastic entities. The problem of communal poverty was no longer an issue: the pressures of the Roman Curia to render the Damianite monasteries economically autonomous through secure incomes carried the day.

From now on, other monasteries would follow this same track. Such is the case with the community patronized by Tommasa, marquise of Hoemburg, daughter of Gualtieri *de Palearia*, count of Manoppello, which was the largest and most powerful feudal domain of the Adriatic Abruzzo.[70] In September 1258 the marquise obtained from the abbot of Monte Cassino the church of S. Pietro near Roccamontepiano, in the diocese of Chieti, in order to establish a monastery attached to the new female religious order: here, a noble lay foundation succeeded an old, abandoned female monastery dependent on Monte Cassino.[71]

---

67. BF, 1:320–22: papal letter of December 15, 1243, which transcribes the donation deed of Andrea *de Pontibus*, dated December 27, 1239.

68. On January 15, 1239, the Abbot Matteo, upon the intervention of Cardinal Rainaldo d'Ostia, gave full autonomy to the female monastic community of Imilla; the document of the Abbot of Farfa is cited in the solemn privilege of Innocent IV (cf. BF, 1:314–15).

69. The following is the text of the letter from the Abbot of Farfa: "Agnoscentes judicio evidenti quod Sancti Silvestri ecclesia, quae tam in spiritualibus quam in materialibus enormiter est collapsa, per vos posset redire ad statum prosperitatis" (BF, 1:314–15).

70. Gualtieri is an eminent figure under the Swabians: an expert *condottiere* and able politician, between 1238 and 1262 he played important roles in Italy and in southern France under Frederick II and his successors as *podestà*, imperial vicar, and vicar general: M. Ohlig, *Beamtentum Friedrichs II. in Reichsitalien von 1237–1250 unter besonderer Berücksichtigung der süditalienischen Beamten* (Inaugural diss., Johann Wolfgang Goethe Universität zu Frankfurt am Main, 1936), pp. 98–100.

71. "Quondam ecclesia sancti Petri de monachabus" is written in the document with which the church was granted to Tommasa on November 21, 1258 (Archive of Monte Cassino, caps. XCVII, nr. 8); the designation "of the nuns" is in itself indicative of the former (*quondam*) purpose of the church.

From the middle of the century the society of southern Italy, united for more than a century in a unitary political organism of feudal character, began to look to the new religious order, already existing and structured for thirty years in central-northern Italy, to solve the problems posed by the religious needs of women, whose choices were conditioned by the social structure of the region. It was a matter of taking over a religious model that was already consolidated and that was capable of attracting the devout attention of property donors and funneling into the establishment of new and solid monastic patrimonies considerable, and at times enormous, economic power and assets, brought as dowry by women who chose or were steered toward the monastic life.

The documentary evidence from the Clarist monastery of Roccamontepiano, preserved in the Archive of Monte Cassino, is very eloquent in this regard.[72] The same Tommasa *de Palearia* hastened to consolidate the original monastic patrimony with considerable donations, an operation that was probably not without some concern for dynastic prestige, if one considers that twenty years after the foundation another member of the *de Palearia* family, donna Gemma, would become abbess.[73] The assets, which were at times considerable, brought as dowry by the nuns upon entry into the monastery from the earliest years of its establishment would ultimately consolidate the monastic patrimony.[74]

Another case from the Abruzzo illustrates the definitive turn of the new female religious order toward the more traditional monastic custom of possession, by right and in fact, of landed property. The order's right to landed possession was sanctioned in 1263, in chapter XXI of the Rule of Urban IV,[75] who determined that the various designations previously given the order should be eliminated and it should be called *Ordo Sanctae Clarae*.[76] The monastery of S. Chiara in Sulmona, founded by Flore-

72. Archive of Monte Cassino, Aula II, caps. XCVII: there are fifty-three still unpublished documents; the citations will henceforth simply refer to AM followed by the document number.
73. Gemma is documented as the head of the monastery from 1280 (AM, no. 32).
74. Already in 1261 two sisters, donna Plenacasa and Altadonna, bring as dowry all their goods in Pescara and Ortona (AM, nos. 15, 16, 20); donna Onorata of Pescara on taking the veil brings as her dowry five salt-works and a house, a plot of land, and eighteen ounces of gold (AM, no. 17); on August 26, 1275, the dowry of another future nun, Semeralla, is a mill on the river Foro (AM, no. 30). The documentation relating to the monastery has in part been transcribed and analyzed in two doctoral theses directed by me and defended before the Faculty of Letters and Philosophy of the Università degli Studi "G. D'Annunzio" in Chieti in the academic year 1988–89: F. Pelagalli, *Un gruppo femminile di ispirazione francescana nell'Abruzzo medievale: Il monastero di S. Pietro e S. Chiara in Roccamontepiano;* S. Forchetti, *Il patrimonio di S. Pietro in Roccamontepiano.*
75. Urban's Rule is inserted in the pontifical letter *Beata Clara* of October 18, 1263 (BF 2:517–18).
76. Ibid., p. 509.

senda da Palena between 1268 and 1269, immediately conformed to the traditional typology of an aristocratically founded monastery. It was endowed with goods and possessions by its foundress, who retired there to a monastic life and assumed leadership of the community as its first abbess.[77] The unquestionable personal commitment of the foundress leaves no room for doubt as to the rigorously religious purposes of the foundation, but this in itself highlights the changed climate of female religiosity in the second half of the thirteenth century: the claustral experience, inserted into the mainstream of the Clarist order, was by now justification in itself for aspiring to the most rigorous commitment of Christian life, apart from any radical commitment to religious poverty.

THE *SORORES MINORES:* EXTRA-INSTITUTIONAL FEMALE INITIATIVES IN THE SECOND HALF OF THE THIRTEENTH CENTURY

From the third decade of the century the idea of communal poverty seems to have exhausted its impetus and the new foundations were attached to a female order in which the right to choose poverty represented a "privilege" that was laboriously defended by only a few groups, and that constituted an exceptional situation. Some of the primitive foundations, starting with the community of Clare, obtained the *Privilegium paupertatis* from Gregory IX between 1228 and 1229.[78] By contrast, almost all of the monasteries in central and northern Italy that evolved from female communities that sprang up under the aegis of poverty in the second and third decades of the century tended to accept—and, in more than one case, to promote—communal possession and were well on the way toward the establishment of considerable landed patrimonies.

But the new orientation did not correspond to the basic needs that had stimulated the female religious movement. Proof of this are the extra-institutional experiences that characterized the religious commitment of numerous women throughout the second half of the thirteenth century and the first decades of the fourteenth. One gains the impression of a great diaspora, starting in the fourth decade of the thirteenth century, involving groups of women who did not succeed in entering into

77. See Aniceto Chiappini, "La Beata Floresenda da Palena e il suo monastero di S. Chiara in Sulmona," *Studi francescani* 8 (1922): 118–31.
78. See Alberzoni, *Chiara e il papato,* pp. 52–69; W. Maleczek, *Das "Privilegium paupertatis" Innocenz' III und das Testament der Klara von Assisi,* Bibliotheca seraphico-capuccina 47 (Rome, 1995).

the new monasteries, or who did not want to. The phenomenon was denounced as absolutely irregular by Gregory IX on February 21, 1241.[79] It was branded with even more severe words nine years later by Innocent IV, who gives us another detail: "the usurpation of the name of *sorores minores,* which is not even due the sisters of the order of S. Damian."[80] Over and above the willingness to bring a charge of fraud, the two documents manifest the pressure of religious movements which the recently instituted order was not successful in channeling, or was actually unwilling to accommodate within itself. The phenomenon appears to have been particularly lively in northern Italy, given that Innocent's letter was sent "to the bishops of Lombardy, the Marca Trevigiana, and the provinces of Romagna."[81]

The Damianite order thus acted as a screen for a much larger phenomenon, that of the *sorores minores,* a designation, as we have seen, used by Jacques de Vitry in 1216 to indicate the female component of the group of Minorites. But did the *sorores minores* of Jacques de Vitry represent only the female branch of the *fratres minores,* or were they perhaps a much vaster, more articulated, and more geographically diffuse reality than Jacques de Vitry's information reveals?[82] To reduce everything to the single matrix of minorite-franciscan inspiration is to flatten the complex and heterogeneous reality of the *sorores minores.* Made up of various independently created groups, they were already diffused throughout the various regions of central-northern Italy between the second and third

---

79. "Some women roaming through the cities and the dioceses are deceitful, lying that they are of the Order of S. Damian; in order to extort people's good faith they go barefoot, wearing the habit and the belt of the nuns of S. Damian, for which reason they are called *discalceatae,* or *cordigerae,* or even minorites" (BF, 1:290).

80. "Quaedam mulierculae interius honeratae peccatis, foris tamen sanctitatis, cuius virtutem prorsus abnegant, speciem praetendentes, . . . unde frequenter accidit ut per tales, nomen Sororum Minorum quod nec ipsis etiam sororibus Ordinis S. Damiani ex regula seu formula vitae competit, sibi fallaciter usurpantes, infamiae nubilo dilectorum Fratrum Minorum Ordinis puritas obfuscetur": "Some little women, internally burdened with sins, but outwardly pretending a specious sanctity, whose virtue they completely deny, . . . for which reason it frequently happens that by such women who deceptively usurp the name of *sorores minores,* which is not even due the sisters of the order of S. Damian by virtue of their rule or form of life, the purity of the Order of the beloved Friars Minor is darkened with the cloud of infamy" (BF, 1:541).

81. In 1257 the phenomenon will appear well beyond the confines of Italy, in Gascony and in Aquitaine, as we know from the addressees of the letter of denunciation of Alexander IV (BF, 2:183–184). On the *sorores minores* now see Maria Pia Alberzoni, "Sorores minores e autorità ecclesiastica fino al pontificato di Urbano IV," in *Chiara e la diffusione dell'Ordine delle Clarisse nel secolo XIII,* Atti del Convegno di studi organizzato in occasione del VII centenario della nascita di S. Chiara (Manduria 14–15 dicembre 1994) (Galatina, 1998), pp. 165–94.

82. Already Zarnke had observed: "it is generally thought that Jacques de Vitry in 1216 erroneously considered Franciscan that which in its origin and form had nothing to do with Francis" (*Anteil des Kardinals Ugolino,* p. 30).

decade of the thirteenth century.[83] They shared the same ideal of poverty and evangelic service that animated the vast and vivacious Italian female religious movement, but they developed autonomously, with outcomes as different as the matrices from which they started.

The recriminations of the papal documents allow us to glimpse realities which hardly lent themselves to the normative institutional framework that had been devised by ecclesiastic authorities with the intention of curbing female groups dedicated to poverty in the first decades of the century. The phenomenon, growing larger as the thirteenth century proceeded, assumed various forms and commanded the attention of civic society. One need only think of the hundreds of "incarcerated, secluded hermits" of either sex who constituted the macrophenomenon of the religious life of lay people in the cities of central-northern Italy, or of the phenomenon of the penitents, whether or not connected with the mendicant orders.[84] Among these were women whose religious commitment, consistent to the point of heroism, gained them the attention and veneration of the urban populations. It is significant that from the middle of the century, the case of Clare excepted, one does not find any women belonging to the second order of either the Franciscans or the Dominicans attaining the honors of a saint's cult. It is as though, alongside the development, fixation, and crystallization of the normative institutional process, a concept of sainthood was taking shape outside the monasteries as a phenomenon capable of attracting attention and devout wonder, requiring or at least desiring the exceptional. One has the impression that within the new monastic structures, female individuality was swallowed up by "normality." From now on, venerated women would come from alternative experiences: they would be recluses within the town, or confined to cells, like Gherardesca and Maria of Pisa, Verdiana of Castelfiorentino, Margherita of Cortona, Giovanna of Signa, Giulia of Certaldo, Ugolina of Vercelli, and Sibillina of Pavia. They would be domestic penitents, like Zita of Lucca, Aldobrandesca and Bonizella of Siena, Fina of

83. The group of Verona (see note 33) and that of Penne (see notes 65–66) have already been mentioned. A group of *sorores minores* can be encountered also in Treviso (see *Le Venezie francescane* 29 [1962]: 27–28) and later in Asti and probably in Tortona, the Damianite monastery from which, perhaps, originated the *sorores minores* who went on to found, or to give shape to, the community of Asti (cf. M. P. Alberzoni, "L'ordine di S. Damiano in Lombardia," in *Chiara e il secondo Ordine,* pp. 142–43).

84. For a comprehensive view of the hermits, see Luigi Pellegrini, "A proposito di eremiti laici d'ispirazione francescana," in *I frati minori e il terz'Ordine: Problemi e discussioni storiografiche,* Convegni del Centro di Studi sulla spiritualità medievale 23 (Todi 17–20 ottobre 1982) (Todi 1985), pp. 115–42.

S. Gimignano, and Benvenuta of Cividale in Friuli. They would be women dedicated to the service of society's marginalized and suffering elements, like Tuscana of Verona and Margherita of Cesolo. Certainly there were also Clarists, but they came to the monastery, of which they were the foundresses, only after a religious experience of penitence and of service, as in the case of Chiara of Rimini.

Once again, the regions of the southern kingdom appear to have been absent from this geography of female sainthood for the period between the second half of the thirteenth and the first decades of the fourteenth century. Was it a case of the female figure being assimilated in the "normality" of domestic life or the daily routine of a monastery, even if the monastery was attached to the female branches of the two new mendicant orders? Was it the condition of women that prevented them from gaining religious prominence by taking initiatives and by trying out ways of life that lay outside the current patterns and as such were of "exceptional" character? These are unavoidable questions in the face of an empty picture of female sainthood in thirteenth- and fourteenth-century southern Italy. Here religious women seem to have expressed themselves by directing their generous legacies to the foundation of monasteries which were oriented toward the recent, but by now well-consolidated institutional forms, and which remained bound by multiple ties to the woman from whom the initiative originated. In general such women did not figure as foundresses and charismatic leaders of female communities, but as munificent benefactresses and, in more than one case, patronesses in the traditional sense of the word.

The experience of Clare of Assisi emerged in the context of the fervent and manifold female religious movement that enlivened central-northern Italy in the thirteenth century. From this same soil grew the phenomenon of the *mulier religiosa,* which seems to have resisted not only cataloguing, but any attempt at normalization, which is always in some way deadening. Forms of resistance, both active and passive, in defense of identity and, whenever possible, of the autonomy of religious experience, seem to have characterized the relationships of the *mulieres religiosae* with institutions of authority. At the same time, these women pursued recognition and support, in an ambivalent stance which reflected the ambivalence inherent in the condition of women in the socially and economically most lively areas of Italy and of Europe at that time.

(Translated from the Italian by Megan Weiler)

Saints and Angry Neighbors:
The Politics of Cursing in Irish Hagiography

Lisa M. Bitel

If the books can be believed, early medieval Ireland was clamorous with voices blessing, praying, chanting, poetizing, satirizing, tale-telling, negotiating, murmuring, chattering, gossiping, slandering, insulting, and cursing. The abundant documents left to us from this literate culture tell of a talking people with a reverence for the written word, but also with a traditional dependence on what they could say and hear. Men and women ordered their lives according to legal contracts worked out publicly before witnesses, sworn to by oaths, and rarely recorded in writing. They distributed property not according to charters, but after the collective memory of whose father owned what. People entertained themselves with poems and stories and songs performed before the fire by professionals who spent their entire lives memorizing material. The Irish were famous for praying—loud, long, and in uncomfortable positions. And everyone knew that trouble came from the misuse of the spoken word, whether it was the insidious grumbling of dissident clients, the harsh nagging of women, the slander of evil neighbors, the killing insults of professional satirists, or the curse of a true master of the numinous powers.

For each individual, every day followed a protocol of words, casual and ritual. The importance of the words depended on the context. The time of day and season affected the schedule of words; certain prayers were appropriate for the morning, and certain songs were sung at particular holidays. Places demanded their own words; when a pilgrim visited a shrine, he or she had to speak the language of the patron saint whose relics rested there. Dangerous places, like wild rivers or the battlefield, might call forth specially protective words. And the speaker altered the words to fit his or her function, situation, and status. Kings, peasants, and women all had their own words. Although all Irish spoke one language, the people of Munster pronounced some words unfamiliar to those from northern Ulster. Religious professionals had a language for ritual use and another vocabulary to use with lay folk.

Irish saints, in life and in hagiographic literature, had the most powerful words of all. According to the vitae, the saints' ability to bless, pray, predict, and curse outshone even the speaking powers of other professional talkers, such as the poets and druids. In one sense, this was because the pronouncements of saintly professionals were both explications and enactments of God's will. What a saint heard from God, she or he repeated to other, lesser Christians. Yet it took an extraordinary human to carry out such divine inspiration; hence, saints were also perceived by their hagiographers and devotees as men and women of immense personal power. They could raise the dead and cast down the living. They could heal and sicken, make prosperous and ruin. They could cause havoc and accomplish what kings, lords, and ordinary churchmen fruitlessly strove to do: maintain social and political order—not by force of arms or law, but by vehemence of speech. In a society fractured by small, competing political units and bound by contentious, negotiated law, saints could lay down the last word on truth and justice, which hagiographers then dutifully recorded in written saints' lives.

As with the formal monastic maledictions analyzed by Lester Little, Irish curses had several purposes in both textual and spoken forms.[1] Clerics, who lived in the centuries after their patron saints, read out hagiographic tales of cursing to Christians assembled at saints' feast-day gatherings as a warning against sinning, especially against the destruction of church personnel and property. More generally, cursing episodes taught auditors and readers of the texts the power of the ritually pronounced Christian word. Words from the mouths of saints or their monastic followers were what Little has labeled "speech acts," ritualized social interactions with visible consequences; when saints predicted death and damnation, for instance, they caused these dire events to occur. Hence, the performance of curses and their observed effects also persuaded believers to promote church-sponsored order within Irish politics. Simultaneously, vitae episodes had another purpose: stories of cursing recorded what writers and readers believed to be genuine historical events, earlier real-life

---

1. Lester K. Little, *Benedictine Maledictions: Liturgical Cursing in Romanesque France* (Ithaca, N.Y., 1993); and "Anger in Monastic Curses," in Barbara H. Rosenwein, ed., *Anger's Past: The Social Uses of an Emotion in the Middle Ages* (Ithaca, N.Y., 1998), pp. 9–35.

curses that had brought drastic results. The Irish monastic annals backed up the vitae with historical instances in which curses sent malefactors to perdition. Thus, some of the purposes of Irish religious curses resembled those of Romanesque maledictions; and, as in Continental maledictions, the Irish drew on the same biblical sources for substance and effect. What is more, Irish cursing shared the theology of Continental maledictions. The morality of cursing—particularly the decision regarding when not to curse—derived from the written works of Augustine, Gregory the Great, and other theologians popular throughout early medieval Christendom.

Yet Irish curses—textual and enacted—existed within a larger context of a singing, chanting, and cursing culture unknown elsewhere, and thus had purposes and effects peculiar to that culture. Irish uniqueness has come under historiographical attack in recent years, but in the case of cursing, Ireland was truly different. The conscious hagiographical process of recording once-pronounced saintly curses, based on written biblical examples of earlier spoken prototypes, to be read aloud in later medieval times to audiences familiar with the living practice of ritual cursing imbued Irish curses with overwhelming spiritual force.[2] Continental monks and lords understood that their curses were modeled after the sanction clauses of property contracts and enriched by collective memories of the maledictory psalms of the Hebrew Bible; but so far as we know, Romanesque maledictions did not resonate in secular or non-Christian arenas. By contrast, Irish Christians who heard a biblical curse, or heard tell of a curse imitative of Christ's curses, were conscious of a turbulent Celtic past and a tribal politics based on talking—threat, prophecy, negotiation, and alliance by oath—and on violence. The Irish were specially prepared to hear saintly curses.

Yet, despite the power of the spoken word among the Irish, the story of Irish maledictions comes to us not orally but from the written record of churchmen's curses and blessings. This is not an ironic coincidence. Irish hagiographers were well aware of the immediate force of speech acts, but also of the Christian superiority of the written word. They consciously remodeled the past, Christian and pagan, and made expert use of the tension between the written and the spoken. They drew on the power of the cursing practices of druids, poets, and satirists as well as of biblical fathers. Yet they knew that even collective memory goes astray and that professionals devoted to the maintenance of the *seanchas* (the learned tradition or, in Latin, the *peritia*) could forget the curse—or the story of

2. Walter J. Ong, *Orality and Literacy: The Technologizing of the Word* (London, 1982), esp. pp. 43–45.

the curse—if it were not preserved on vellum. The final say in the war of words belonged to the saints, not only because of their superior verbal powers and divine backing, and not only because they balanced traditions of the Celtic, Israelite, and Christian ancients, but also because their scribal successors recorded, syllable for syllable, the mighty curses of holy men and women. Hagiographers consciously transferred the power of saintly cursing to their own textual creations, in an attempt to maintain at once the performative and the preservative character of the curses.[3] Stories of saints, with curses included intact, thus became scripts for future enactments. Such ritual theater characterized Christian practice in premodern Europe, as Thomas Head has suggested elsewhere in this volume, but nowhere else did the drama focus so consistently on cursing.[4]

The literati's written words allow modern readers to analyze and categorize the curses of Irish saints. Although some cursing stories come from sagas, martyrologies, and annals, most are contained in the scores of Irish vitae composed between about 700 and 1200. While some of the earlier vitae can be securely dated (to the seventh, eighth, or ninth century), all are contained in manuscripts from the twelfth century or later, and most were composed or revised during that later period. Although none were written before the late seventh century, all of them treat the age of the saints in the fifth to the seventh centuries, and much of the material in later vitae derives from earlier recensions. Hagiographers were writing for the ages. Whenever possible, which is not often, historians try to recover layers of historical information: references to the earliest period of saintly action; political recastings from the seventh or eighth centuries when the ur-vita might originally have appeared; and literary and political rewritings from the centuries surrounding the Norman invasions.[5] Although chronological layers are not immediately apparent in the vitae, enough of the texts are datable to demonstrate that the practice and meaning of cursing did not change significantly over the pre-Norman centuries. More important, the hagiography's several positions on saintly curses represented a range of opinions in a many-voiced, relatively literate so-

3. Ibid., pp. 96–101, 112–16.
4. See Chapter 10, below.
5. Richard Sharpe has made the greatest advances in precise dating of the vitae, dating the O'Donoghue group of lives in the *Codex Salmanticensis* to the eighth century: *Medieval Irish Saints' Lives* (Oxford, 1991). But many historians believe that the historical layers of the vitae will never be recovered. Dáibhí Ó Cróinín complains of "no development in this genre; seventh-century texts are practically indistinguishable from twelfth-century ones, and the same tedious formulae recur time after time, often borrowed shamelessly from one Life to another." The vitae are, according to Ó Cróinín, a "dismal swamp of superstition and perverted Christianity" (*Early Ireland, 400–1200* [London, 1997], p. 210).

ciety, where everybody had his or her say on the power of saying. The same literati that wrote of the saints also composed myths of poets and seers and the histories of kings, satirists, and druids—the pagans who remained, in story, the saints' main competition for the loyalty of the laity. The great canon of Irish vernacular literature caught echoes of these other speakers; any hero, hag, or incidental character could lapse into poetry, prophecy, or spellcasting at a moment's notice. The sagas and tales were all punctuated by ritualized versifying.

Our aim must be to catch echoes of the whole complex cacophony from which the maledictions of the saints rang out, and to discover not whether the tradition of Christian cursing changed—it did not—but whether its relation to politics and to other speaking traditions changed.[6] In fact, Irish cursing only lost importance when the political structure, literary tradition, and ecclesiastical organization all began to change at the same time, after the coming of the Normans.

The Politics of Noise

Like monks of the Continent, Irish saints cursed in response to violence. According to hagiographers, saints aimed their words at laymen who threatened them or their property; hagiography recorded the saints' maledictions in order to remind future generations of past displays of saintly protective power. When a king or nobleman took a hostage, abducted women, raised his hand or manhandled someone, insulted a person, or acted ungratefully or ungenerously, he was committing an act of privilege if applied to his legitimate inferiors. But the same act was an outrage when inflicted upon a saint, his or her clerical successors, or dependents. Other kings and nobles responded to such provocations with physical force if they could, or tried negotiation, submission, or ransoms. Mighty men could say what they wanted, at least legally. In Irish society of the pre-Norman centuries, organized around the twin poles of negotiation and violence, the greater the influence of the man, the freer he could be with his words. Faced with fierce deeds or strong oaths, saints responded with words and gestures of prayer or malediction, according to the vitae.

6. The major collections of saints' lives used as evidence for this article are: William W. Heist, ed., *Vitae sanctorum hiberniae*, Subsidia Hagiographica 28 (Brussels, 1965); Charles Plummer, ed., *Vitae sanctorum hiberniae*, 2 vols. (Oxford, 1910); Charles Plummer, ed. and trans., *Bethada Náem nÉrenn*, 2 vols. (Oxford, 1922). For background on the vitae and dating of the texts, see Lisa M. Bitel, *Isle of the Saints: Monastic Settlements and Christian Community in Early Ireland* (Ithaca, N.Y., 1990), esp. pp. 1–13.

Irish saints were famously bad-tempered, but in hagiography their words were rarely angry.[7] "Woe to the man who has as neighbor an angry saint," declared one semi-maledictory poem from a twelfth-century vita of St. Máedóc of Leinster, "to fall out with him is like running up a height."[8] Around the same time, Gerald of Wales mused, "This seems to me a thing to be noticed, that just as the men of [Ireland] are during this mortal life more prone to anger and revenge than any other race, so in eternal death the saints of this land that have been elevated by their merits are more vindictive than the saints of any other region."[9] But Máedóc's hagiographer wanted only to scare off the Ó Raghallaigh (O'Reilly), who had been imposing hospitality dues upon the saint's monastery of Drumlane.[10] Gerald's foreign ear, however, was assaulted by the noise of an entire hostile culture. Much of what he criticized about the saints and the Irish generally was their unintelligible ruckus: they transgressed sworn oaths, they sanctified false treaties with meaningless prayers, they constantly abused the spoken word.[11] What Gerald saw as anger and vindictiveness—and he may have seen more of these traits than other visitors to Ireland, considering the company he kept—was actually a complex system of threats and sanctions which had developed over centuries, was aimed at keeping order, and was expressed in the idiom of blessings and curses. (The Irish disagreed with Gerald that they were noticeably worse-tempered than brothers elsewhere in Christendom; one hagiographer referred to an English monk who seemed ruffled at trivial occurrences *secundum irascibilem Brittonum naturam,* "according to the irascible nature of the Britons."[12])

In fact, contrary to Gerald's notion, Irish hagiographers emphasized the difference between their saints, whom they normally cast as stern but unruffled, and their political opponents, who often were irate, rambunctious warriors and kings. Thus, in the vitae, secular troublemakers did not hesitate to speak *verbis asperis* or *asperis verbis cum ira* (with harsh words or angrily with harsh words), *insanis verbis* (with crazy words), *voce malefica* (in an evil voice), or *in vindictam* (in vindictive anger). They used *verba blasphemie* (blasphemous words), made a *votum malum* (evil

7. Wendy Davies, "Anger and the Celtic Saint," in Rosenwein, *Anger's Past,* pp. 191–202, esp. pp. 195–97.
8. Plummer, *Bethada,* 2:278.
9. John J. O'Meara, trans., *The History and Topography of Ireland: Gerald of Wales,* rev. ed. (New York, 1982), p. 91.
10. Plummer, *Bethada,* 1:284–85.
11. O'Meara, *History and Topography,* 103, 106–9, 112.
12. Plummer, *Vitae,* 1:264.

vow) or *responsum malorum* (response of evilness), or they *multa mala lo-cuti* (said many evil things). They were often *irascentes* (angry) and one even answered *ore pestifero verbisque asperrimis* (in a pestiferous voice and with the harshest words).

Still, the worst the saints usually did in response was *increpare,* to chide or reproach. One or two spoke *ira magna* (in great anger), but only on God's behalf; and one twice cursed a sinner *in vindictam huius sceleris* (in punishment for his crime). But often punishment merely arrived *iuxta verbum* (at the word) of the holy man, not a particularly cranky word. Only occasionally did the saint *maledixit* (Irish *mallaigis*), formally curse. Just as often, the saint merely spoke in the future tense of the terrible things that would happen to a criminal, or gestured with hand or bell, or simply failed to bless an evildoer. Even the mere hope for the downfall of a sinner, expressed aloud by a saint, could bring his doom. The Irish were well aware of the difference between the explosive noisiness of bad guys and the subtly chosen words of their holy men and women, as the Irish glossator on the Wurzburg gospels explained in the eighth century when glossing a familiar sentence in 2 Timothy. St. Paul's verse reads, "Alexander the smith showed many evils to me; may God reward him according to his works." The glossator knew that Alexander would get his just deserts, for Paul's verse "is not a wish but a prophecy."[13] In the hagiographical view, then, the strength of saintly words lay in their discretion, their certainty, and their lack of overtly angry motivation.

Most episodes of Irish cursing emphasized the willingness of the evildoer to ignore the saint or to talk back, or his unwillingness to listen. Episodes followed a typical pattern which began with a man of power committing a hostile misdeed or becoming angry with a saint. At times, as in the following story of St. Munnu (aka Fintan) and the hard-hearted king Guaire mac Eogain, the powerful committed both sins. The story, written around 800, comes from the *Codex Salmanticensis:*

> One day, Guaire mac Eogain, who sought the kingship of Leinster, came and destroyed a settlement in Saint Fintan's neighborhood, and carried off their cattle and arms. Then the widows and orphans of the community came to Fintan and wept before him. So Fintan, calling four men to him, told them, "Go and greet Guaire and tell him in the name of the Lord to send us the cattle that he stole. If he will hear our prayer, tell him that he will be king into his old age and will not be

13. Whitley Stokes and John Strachan, ed., *Thesaurus Palaeohibernicus,* 2 vols. (reprint, Dublin, 1975), 1:697; see also Plummer, *Vitae,* 2:153–54, where St. Máedóc merely "hopes" (*optavit*) that the hand of the killer of Brandub mac Echach will shrivel.

murdered, and his descendants will hold the kingdom of Uí Cheinse-
laig until doomsday. However, I know that hard-hearted [*durus*] man
will not hear you nor send back the cattle of these people; but in the
very hour when you will greet him, he will be getting a haircut before
you, so say to him: If you do not send back to us the people's cattle that
you stole, your head will not be barbered again, but before your hair
grows again on your head you will be slaughtered and your head will
be cut off, and you will not be king." So the messengers went out and
greeted Guaire. And as Fintan said, it was done, and Guaire did not
send back the cattle, and he was killed five days later.[14]

Guaire initiated the hostilities by trying, as any energetic ruler of a small
Irish kingdom might, to devastate the resources of neighboring territorial units, thus bullying their nobles and even their kings into submission
and clientage. It was good politics, but unfortunately Guaire chose to attack not another aggressive kinglet, but a settlement under the protection
of an influential ecclesiastic who did not favor his takeover of the province. Despite the holy man's embassy, the king remained *durus,* difficult
and obstinate, thus proving his unfitness to rule Leinster. Munnu reacted
not as a secular lord might, with angry words or violence, but with a se-
rene prediction of Guaire's sins and resultant fate. Munnu was merely the
voice of God's will in punishing the malefactor and depriving his dynasty
of rule.

In another episode which followed the same pattern, both Munnu and
his opponent were less calm, although the hagiographer made the saint's
role as God's voice even clearer. This time, the setting was a "great council of the Irish people," where both secular and church leaders gathered
to debate the question of the dating of Easter. Munnu was late. Suibne
mac Domnaill, king of Uí Bairrche, made the mistake of demanding tes-
tily, "Why do we await this leprous cleric for so long?" St. Molaisse, who
was Munnu's rival in the debate, cautioned the king to be quiet, "because
whatever you say Fintan hears wherever he is, and you will receive his
vengeance." In fact, when Munnu finally arrived and the nervous Suibne
requested a prayer from him, the saint asked sarcastically, "Why do you
ask a prayer from a leprous cleric?" The saint added, "Whenever you insult me, you have shamed Christ, the right hand of God the father, because I am a true limb of Christ." Munnu predicted that Suibne's kin
would murder him and toss his head in the river Berba which, according
to the hagiographer, is exactly what happened within a month.[15]

The two stories of Munnu illustrate a number of themes common to

14. Heist, *Vitae,* p. 202.
15. Ibid., p. 207.

the cursing episodes in Irish saints' lives. The powerful malefactor threatened or harmed the saint, the saint's allies or dependents, the saint's property, or the saint's reputation. The sinner normally offended in one of a limited number of ways. He raided property or stole, as in the case of Guaire, mentioned earlier. He insulted the saint, as Suibne did. Otherwise, the malefactor might kill or injure an innocent victim or a dependent of the saint. St. Áed mac Bricc, for instance, dealt with the case of the "terrible cruel robbers" who ambushed three religious women and ran off with the women's heads, in good Celtic headhunting fashion. Áed saw everything in a vision, and immediately rushed to the women's community to meet their grieving sisters. Thence he followed the thieves, seeking the heads. The thieves were frozen in flight by an act of God when Áed arrived (a common motif in stories of offenders). The saint *increpavit* (chided) them; the men did penance and asked to be released. The saint went home with the heads, signed the ground to create a miraculous well, washed the heads, reattached them, and revived the women.[16] The whole story attested to the saint's ability to protect women's communities in particular and ecclesiastical property in general against raiders.

Still other offenders took hostages whom they refused to release, despite the pleas of saints. Clerics and nuns throughout Christendom negotiated the release of prisoners and hostages, although not always successfully; the hagiographic episodes in which kings were forced by saints to free their hostages were a lesson for lords who took too lightly the intercession of clerics. Such episodes also demonstrated the churches' disapproval of hostage politics. But in the hands of a master hagiographer, the story of an unruly king and a hostage could become a lesson in the nature of sovereignty, as in one of the most famous cursing stories of Irish hagiography: the contest between St. Ruadán and King Diarmait mac Cerbaill. Every version of Ruadán's life, early and late, contains the episode, and several other texts refer to it as well.[17]

As the story goes, Diarmait was king of Temair, the symbolic capital of Ireland. He had brought about *pacem . . . in tota Hybernia,* peace in all Ireland, which is to say that he had forced other kings to acknowledge his over-kingship. The rhetoric of Temair pervaded Irish literature; the elusive control of the capital represented the ideal of national kingship, but was rarely, if ever, a historical reality.[18] Diarmait's accomplishment was

---

16. Ibid., pp. 172–73.
17. Ibid., pp. 163–65; Plummer, *Vitae,* 2:245–49; Plummer, *Bethada,* 2:312–16; Standish O'-Grady, ed., *Silva Gadelica,* 2 vols. (London, 1892), 1:66–68, 75–78.
18. Francis J. Byrne, *Irish Kings and High-kings* (London, 1973), pp. 46–47; D. A. Binchy, *Celtic and Anglo-Saxon Kingship,* O'Donnell Lectures for 1967–68 (Oxford, 1970), pp. 31–46; Bitel, *Isle of the Saints,* pp. 146–47.

thus admirable, given the divisive clientage system and traditional hostilities among provincial kingdoms that prevented political unification. One of Diarmait's chief men and a herald, who were not so commendable, went out to the province of Connacht to collect dues from the Uí Briuin king, Áed Guaire mac Echach. The herald, to signify Diarmait's power, carelessly brought about the destruction of Áed's fort, after which Áed killed the herald. Áed then fled to sanctuary with Bishop Senach, his maternal uncle; Senach took him to Ruadán, whose sisters had fostered Senach. Despite attempts to hide Áed and curse Diarmait's men, Diarmait was able to extract the Connachtman from Ruadán's settlement and drag him off to Temair.

There the real contest began. Ruadán rounded up other holy men; Diarmait gathered supporters to him. Ruadán rang his bells, fasted, sang psalms, and prayed against Diarmait; Diarmait prayed and fasted as well, although the saints tricked him into eating and sleeping. Ruadán caused the death of Diarmait's twelve fosterlings, although the saint mercifully raised them again. Diarmait had a vision of holy men chopping down a tree that reached to the heavens, and when he awoke, terrified, "the clamor of the synod's psalms . . . filled his ears." Finally, Diarmait went out to challenge Ruadán to a war of words. "I defend the justice of the nation [reipuplice]," he announced to Ruadán, "so that peace may be everywhere; you favor and defend evil. You will receive bloody vengeance from God, for in all Ireland your paruchia [parish] will be first to dwindle and fail." Ruadán responded that Diarmait's kingdom would fail too and none of his seed would reign. "Your settlement will be vacant," the king retorted, adding that pigs would root at the site. Ruadán answered that Temair would be vacant, too. Diarmait predicted that Ruadán would be blemished and would lose an eye; the saint answered that Diarmait would be killed by enemies, and his limbs separated and scattered. "A wild boar will dig your tomb with his teeth," Diarmait replied. Ruadán responded that the very thigh that the king did *not* raise in a gesture of submission to him [a one-kneed kneel] would be separated from Diarmait's body and tossed in a dungheap. Diarmait could manage no worse. As the later Latin life put it, Ruadán "had said the worst" (*peiora dixisset.*) "You defend iniquity, I defend truth," he told the saint. "You have disordered my reign, but God loves you more. So go, take your man, and give me his ransom." Ruadán paid a proper ransom for the captive, but the handsome horses he sent to Diarmait were as ephemeral as the peace brought about by the king: they disappeared into the sea as soon as the saint had gone.

Hagiographers and their medieval audiences, saints and kings, all knew the power of cursing, and of accompanying harsh words with ritual gestures such as fasting. Ruadán had a few tricks unavailable to the king. He had his *cymbalum,* his hand-held bell typical of holy men, which he could ring for added cursing power. Ruadán also had something inexplicable in terms of sense or justice: God's favor. No matter how justified Diarmait's act in capturing Áed, no matter how perfect and moral a ruler he was, the saint's decision overrode that of the good king.

Yet the hagiographer, who agreed with Diarmait about the king's character and accomplishments, was sympathetic to the secular lord. Diarmait resembled the good prince idealized in contemporary Irish gnomic literature and canons. The early-eighth-century *Audacht Moraind* practically gave Diarmait's resumé when describing the perfect ruler: "Let him preserve justice, it will preserve him. Let him raise justice, it will raise him. Let him exalt mercy, it will exalt him. Let him care for his tribes, they will care for him . . . Tell him, it is through the justice of the ruler that plagues and great lightnings are kept from the people . . . It is through the justice of the ruler that he secures peace, tranquility, joy, ease, and comfort . . ." In particular, advised the tract, "Let him estimate the right and justice, truth and law, contract and regulation of every just ruler towards all his clients." [19]

In fact, eighth-century Irish canonists supported the ability of extra-territorial kings to uphold the clientage system, and to punish criminals publicly, as opposed to the rule of Irish law which operated by the negotiation of kin-groups.[20] What is more, the hagiographer made it clear that Ruadán was acting not on behalf of an injured Christian, but for a man connected to him politically through kinship and fosterage. He was behaving, in other words, like the sort of man Diarmait should have been able to coerce and outshout. In the opinion of writers, readers, and rulers, the lawkeeper should have been right, rather than the ecclesiastic. In fact, the hagiographer noted that Diarmait's curse upon Ruadán's eye came to pass; thus Diarmait was justified in calling God's judgment down upon the troublemaking saint, who was not only preventing the king's collection of rightful dues and punishment of a killer, but also subverting his rule.

Yet, as the canonists also pointed out, laymen could not judge clerics.[21] A careful interpreter of the vita understood that Diarmait had indirectly committed an infraction; his herald, whom he should have been able to control, had caused all the trouble in the first place by invading Áed Guaire's fort. Even more important, though, no matter how virtuous the

---

19. Fergus Kelly, ed. and trans., *Audacht Moraind* (Dublin, 1976), pp. 5, 15; see also p. xiii for the other examples of the *Speculum Principum* in Irish literature.
20. H. Wasserschleben, ed., *Die irische Kanonensammlung* (Leipzig, 1885), pp. 63–73, 77; Bitel, *Isle of the Saints,* pp. 145–72, esp. pp. 160–61.
21. Wasserschleben, *Die irische Kanonensammlung,* pp. 72–73.

king, how peace-loving and equitable, God favored his saint and the alternative political order represented by Ruadán. In the end, it was not the balance of faults and virtues, but the cursing contest that determined— or at least, illustrated—who deserved to win the wretched conflict. He who "said the worst things," whose curse was most efficacious, triumphed. The logic of justice and the very kingship supported by churchmen fell to the illogic of spiritual superiority—and kings were not to forget it. What is more, the hagiographer was not merely being petty in referring to Ruadán's own interests (or those of his church) in protecting his ally, Áed Guaire. The political stance of a particular church and its saint overlapped with a larger principle. Although the stance might change— although the political sentiments of the vita's readers and auditors might change through the years—the principle did not, nor did the story in which it was told. Ruadán's hagiographers were sensitive to the seeming injustice of the cursing of Temair, but nonetheless upheld the saint's ability to voice and to work God's inscrutable will.

The story's many redactions attest that the nature of clerical participation in politics continued to be profoundly interesting, as well as debatable, among the Irish. In his earliest vita, Ruadán's conquest may have been the traditional, formerly pagan political center of Ireland, Temair, and its ancient kingship. By the central Middle Ages, when the last version of his vita was written, Ruadán's victim was a more complex provincial kingship of Mide in conflict with the borderlands of Connacht and Munster, where Ruadán's community of Lothra was located. In every version, however, the hagiographer used the saint to promote an ecclesiastical vision of political and social order.

Ruadán's hagiographers were a few voices in a noisy crowd of Irish men and women, for Diarmait mac Cerbaill was not the only antagonist of a churchman to suggest a different script and a different interpretation of justice and order. Not everyone in early medieval Ireland promoted a particular ecclesiastical vision, not even all ecclesiastics. In the seventh century, Adomnán of Iona wrote a biography of St. Columcille (both being kinsmen of Diarmait mac Cerbaill) condemning Diarmait's murderer and praising Diarmait as an ideal king. His killer, himself a king of the Dál nAraidi of Ulster, would "return like a dog to his vomit and he will fall from wood into water, and die by drowning. He had deserved such an end much sooner, who has slaughtered the king of Ireland." [22] Perhaps if Columcille had not fled Ireland to his remote isle off the Scottish coast, Diarmait would have had an easier time with Ruadán.

22. A. O. and M. O. Anderson, eds. and trans., *Adomnán's Life of Columba* (London, 1961), pp. 278–82.

When they had no cleric to protect them, kings and other evildoers tried to stop their own ears to the saints' maledictions and predictions, or shut the saints up by force, or out-curse and out-shout the holy men. Cainnech contended with thieves and robbers who would not listen to his preaching, threatening him harm instead, but the saint humbled and converted them all.[23] A "certain nobleman, or thief" from Osraige had a similar run-in with St. Abbán over some pigs. The pig-thief happened to be a nephew of St. Braccán, abbot of Cluain Immurchuir, so rather than confront him, Abbán went off to negotiate with a man who knew well the rules of cursing. The two went together to the unruly nephew to ask for the pigs, "lest he should incur the malediction of God and his saint." The iniquitous young man raised his hand to strike Abbán but, by the will of God, wounded his own kinsman. He tried again, only to have his hand shrivel up. After watching Abbán heal his uncle and observing his own withered hand, the man prostrated himself at Abbán's feet, doing penance and promising to return the pigs.[24] Here, two clerics worked together to subdue a local authority in the shape of the nasty nephew, but the episode carried other political messages about the relation between Abbán's churches and those of Braccán, the territories they represented, and the people of the neighborhood. Whether Braccán's hagiographer would have told the same story, we cannot know.

The motif of the shriveled arm is common, though. Other kings and warriors watched their arms shriveling when raised against saints, or they were paralyzed in the act of attack or flight, or occasionally swallowed up by the earth, with their horses and henchmen. These well-known codes (which had biblical precedents, as we shall see) did not need to be fully explained in an episode. Once, according to the later Latin life of Máedóc, the mere sound of the saint's bell from afar warned raiders of an imminent curse, and froze them in their tracks.[25]

The arguments of angry kings and noblemen with the saints might well carry echoes of disagreement about political organization and churchmen's role in it. Sometimes kings and others talked back to a saint instead of stopping their ears, or before resorting to violence. But saints and their hagiographers silenced their opponents. In parting, Ciarán of Saigir dealt with a Munster king who spoke angrily to him. He made the king mute and only after the ruler prostrated himself before the saint would Ciarán bless his tongue and return his speech.[26] The

23. Plummer, *Vitae*, 1:153–54, 165–66.
24. Heist, *Vitae*, pp. 269–70; Plummer, *Vitae*, 1:25.
25. Plummer, *Vitae*, 2:147.
26. Ibid., 1:228–29.

hagiographer did not even specify the cause of the king's anger, but another episode in the vita suggested the usual conflict over judgment and rule.[27]

In all such episodes, saints out-argued secular leaders except when kings and nobles had friends at hand, as Áed Guaire did and Diarmait mac Cerbaill did not, among the clerics. For instance, Mochóemóc's hagiographer told, in a later Latin vita, how the saint brokered a peace treaty between two leaders of his mother's people, the Déisi. After one killed the other, the saint came "in great anger to curse [the malefactor] or to call him to penance." But the sinner, Óengus, refused to listen: "I don't care what you do, Mochóemóc," he declared, "because the most holy Cuimmíne Fota son of Fiachna blessed me carefully, and promised me kingship and heaven." Mochóemóc admitted that he could not curse what St. Cuimmíne had blessed. He might have gone for Óengus' wife and son, but they preempted him by seeking his forgiveness. So he destroyed the king's daughter and horse and, what is more, cursed the water around Óengus's island fort, thus drying up the chieftain's defenses. Óengus had to repent, after which the daughter, horse, and water were all restored. The chieftain also offered to build a church for the saint.[28] Although obscured by the fierce feuds of Norman-era chieftains, the principle of ecclesiastical order remained a force in this story; the saintly patronage of Cuimmíne protected Óengus, but only to a point. After that, he had to submit spiritually and politically to Mochóemóc if he wanted to survive.

As the monastic annals vividly showed, kings such as Óengus violated treaties constantly; just to gain the kingship, kinsmen often ignored oaths sworn on sacred relics in Christian sanctuaries in order to kill their cousins and brothers. Yet the annals also recounted with satisfaction the fate of such sinners. In 846, for instance, the king of Munster raided a church belonging to St. Ciarán of Cluain Moccu Nóis. The annalist added that "Ciarán, however, went after him to Munster and thrust his staff into him so that he wounded him in the gut, and so that eventually he died."[29] But Ciarán had been dead for centuries. The annal entry reflected the cursing prayers of ecclesiastics at Cluain, who must have begged their patron to punish the king. They then published their success in the annals. Hence, annalists' texts supported hagiographic stories of Ciarán and Mochóemóc, demonstrating the efficacy of churchmen's words in the acts of judgment, treaty-making, and cursing—so long as their patron saint was

27. Ibid., 1:228.
28. Ibid., 2:180.
29. John O'Donovan, ed. and trans., *The Annals of the Kingdom of Ireland by the Four Masters,* 6 vols. (Dublin, 1848–1851), 1:470; Bitel, *Isle of the Saints,* pp. 152–53.

powerful enough to enforce his hallowed pronouncements, and his words more effective than those of rival saints.

RITUAL WORDS

Whereas saints could count on their insight into cosmic order to empower their political pronouncements and to protect them against the violence of kings and warriors, they had to draw on other skills to counter men of magic. The druids who had once roamed pre-Christian Ireland, and who continued to wander the saints' lives as competitors of Christian men and advisors to disorderly kings, also called down the curses of saints. Plenty of references to druidic curses and rituals appeared in both hagiography and secular texts, not to mention stories of semidivine magicians and shapeshifting hags, both of whose words had magical effect.[30] Some Christian prayers called for God's protection against magical words, such as the "spells of women and smiths and druids."[31] Irish laws ruled against the illegal practice of poetic satire, which could ruin a person's reputation and, literally, his or her face by raising disfiguring blisters; one tract also laid down as a poet's duty the protection of a king from sorcery.[32] Clearly, speech acts had entered Irish consciousness, including legal minds, long before Christianity arrived in Ireland.

The saints came armed with words of their own to fight the magicmakers. St. Patrick (Pátraic) provided the model for later hagiographers in his two seventh-century vitae. He indulged in a "war of words" with druids at the hill of Temair when they tried to hold their annual pagan festival there. He wanted to celebrate Easter, converting king and populace in the process. Although the druids had the gifts of foresight and spellcasting, they were no match for the saint, of whom they had predicted in poetic, insulting words:

> Adze-head will come, the end of his staff bent,
> from his house, with a perforated head, he will chant abomination,
> from his table, in the front of his house,
> all of his household will respond to him, "So be it, so be it."[33]

30. F. N. Robinson, *Satirists and Enchanters in Early Irish Literature* (New York, 1912); Cecile O'Rahilly, ed., *Táin Bó Cúailnge: Recension I* (Dublin, 1976), pp. 57, 62–63; Maria Tymoczko, trans., *Two Death Tales from the Ulster Cycle* (Dublin, 1981), esp. pp. 49–51.
31. Stokes and Strachan, *Thesaurus Palaeohibernicus*, pp. 248–49.
32. Fergus Kelly, *A Guide to Early Irish Law* (Dublin, 1988), pp. 43–44, 50, 137–39.
33. Ludwig Bieler, ed., *The Patrician Texts in the Book of Armagh* (Dublin, 1979), p. 74. On the power of Patrick's words, see Joseph Falaky Nagy's superb study of the relation between the spoken

According to the druids, then, the arrival of Christianity brought new, inexplicable words, disgusting to men of the old ways, and used in weird chants that would ring out through Ireland. ("Adze-head" and "perforated head," the druids' puny attempts at insulting Patrick and his clerics, referred to the clerics' peculiarly Irish tonsure; Irish monks shaved the fronts of their heads and grew out their hair in the back.) The druids were finally disposed of when Patrick begged God to punish men who used the wrong words in the wrong way and, by implication, less skillfully than the saint did: "May this impious one who blasphemes your name be now lifted away and swiftly slain." [34]

Patrick's model pervaded the vitae throughout the pre-Norman centuries, even when druids, as literary characters, came to signify more than just paganism in the texts. Berach, according to his later Latin life, followed a Patrician pattern when he engaged in a long contest with a pesky druid which came down, in the end, to a shouting match. Berach called in outside talent: an angel, who spoke from the heavens with God's own judgment against the *magus*. But the druid would not accept the fantastical voice as anything but an auditory illusion, and replied "full of beastly fury, in contumelious and blasphemous words." Berach responded to the druid's abuse by depriving him of speech: "May that wretched cursing man lose the use of his tongue, lest he should try to offer even more blasphemous words to the true and living God." Offered the chance of penitence, the druid remained silently adamant, and was eventually killed like the beast he imitated with his furious growls.[35] The hagiographer used his druid to epitomize a sinner or backsliding Christian, not a genuine pagan; the later the vita, the more druids came to resemble heretics, magicians, or just troublemakers whose ritual declarations challenged the authority of churchmen but not Christian belief.[36] The druid carried still another meaning, though: traditional pagan pronouncements were literally—with all the connotations of that word—incomprehensible to Bible-toting churchmen and their audiences. In this vita episode, then, only cursers who also knew the *logos* of Christianity made meaningful, audible declarations.

---

and the written in early Ireland, *Conversing with Angels and Ancients: Literary Myths of Medieval Ireland* (Ithaca, N.Y., 1997), esp. pp. 46–49.
34. Bieler, *Patrician Texts*, pp. 88–90.
35. Plummer, *Vitae*, 1:84–85. See Plummer, *Bethada*, 1:33, 2:32, where the offender is called "scholar and chief-master of druidry" (*primh-eicces ocus ardmaigistir druidechta*). In this version, Berach actually puts his hand over the druid's mouth when he begins to satirize the king responsible for judgment.
36. Kim McCone, *Pagan Past and Christian Present in Early Irish Literature* (Maynooth, 1990), pp. 92, 96–98.

No voice sounded more clearly than that of a saint. Neither the blasphemy of druids nor the *incantationes* of sorceresses was any match for the straightforward predictions and maledictions of holy men, even though some writers believed in the power of this earlier generation of speakers and evoked it with their stories.[37] Even the sweet sounds of the poets were bettered by the literate words of versifying clerics, who recorded the bards' lyrics in manuscripts, and made their own little quatrains in the margins. An episode in the life of St. Patrick represented the conversion of memorized poetry symbolically through the poet's own conversion to Christianity. Patrick was able to enhance the pagan arts, which were by definition oral, without losing any of their lyric, spiritual quality. Patrick's triumph was the baptism of Dubthach moccu Lugair, the greatest poet in Ireland, and his companion, Fíacc, who later became bishop of Sléibte.[38]

The hierarchy of words was clear to hagiographers and their audiences: saints' punishing words were more effective than other ritually pronounced words, even identical curses pronounced by the most righteous of Christian monarchs. Ritual words from pagan druids, poets, and satirists had little force in competition with saints' declamations. They were either poor imitations of Christian curses, or wordless growls, or poems coopted and converted by Christian writers. At the bottom of the hierarchy were the petty threats and angry insults of other laymen and women. Various texts depicted voices raised in argument with the authoritative words of the saints, but no one could out-talk them. Everyone had to listen.

SACRA LINGUA

The inherent worth of saintly words was based not on superior native skills or the manipulation of Irish oral traditions, but instead on biblical precedents and Christian theology. Druids' words carried less weight because they came of historical paganism but also because, once pronounced, they vanished into memory—professional, collective memory, to be sure, but fallible human memory nonetheless. Kings' words had a history only in the texts of clerical writers. Irish saints found their words in Christian theology and in the Bible, and their words, often recorded in the *sacra lingua* of Latin, entered history in the precious pages of the vitae.

---

37. Plummer, *Vitae*, 1:78–79.
38. Bieler, *Patrician Texts*, p. 92; Nagy, *Conversing with Angels*, p. 89.

The saints rarely uttered ritual maledictions in the formulaic style of the Continent, but Irish cursers apparently drew upon the same sources as brothers across the waters.[39] The Old Testament provided most of the punishments inflicted upon Irish sinners in hagiography, although the saints selected only a few of the dreadful options available from the Psalms and other books. Death was a popular choice, as exemplified in Psalm 54.16 ("Let death come upon them. And may they descend alive into hell") and similar curses enacted in the stories of kings and prophets. Saints also used Psalm 68.26: "May their homes be deserted. And may no one live in their tents." Diarmait mac Cerbaill was not the only malefactor who lost his fort; St. Eogan predicted an empty fort and barren land for a chieftain who denied him hospitality.[40] Such punishment was, according to Eogan's hagiographer, proof that "whatever the man of God blessed was blessed, and whatever he cursed, his curse was enough for it." Mochuda also deprived a sinner-king of his territory, not to mention salvation. "Look up at heaven, King, and below at the earth," he proclaimed, "you will possess neither earth nor heaven."[41]

Only slightly worse than death and loss of power and place was the Psalmist's curse upon descendants, either to dwindle and disappear or to lose status: "You will destroy their offspring from the earth. And their children from among the sons of men" (Psalm 20.10). St. Patrick, in the seventh-century vita of Tírechán, favored this one: he cursed (*maledixit*) the horse-thieving sons of Ercc and the descendants of Fiachu mac Néill with serving their kinsmen forever, by which he deprived their dynasties of kingship.[42] As usual, the most prestigious of Irish saints set the precedent for later vitae. In a life of several centuries later, St. Gerald of Mag Eó used such a curse upon some thieves.[43] The men of Fir Chell merited the same judgment when they denied Mochuda hospitality, according to the later Irish life of Colmán Ela; not only would they be slain like pigs, according to the saint, but their family would be luckless and short-lived, their women lustful and wanton, and their house without progeny.[44] The numerous episodes in which saints struck dead the children of kings,

---

39. I have found only two references to formal chanting of psalms, both in quite late Irish lives: Plummer, *Bethada*, 2:12 and 314–315. In Irish, the vitae read: *ro chan psalma eascacaine forna demh-naibh* (1:29) and *psalma esccaine ocus innighe . . . shailm chettal na ccleirech* (1:323–24). Earlier versions of the Ruadán episode do not specify the singing of psalms although Plummer, *Vitae*, 2:247 reads: *canebant ieiuni contra regem*.
40. Heist, *Vitae*, pp. 403–4.
41. Plummer, *Vitae*, 1:193.
42. Bieler, *Patrician Texts*, pp. 136, 148.
43. Plummer, *Vitae*, 2:112.
44. Plummer, *Bethada*, 2:174; see also Plummer, *Vitae*, 2:193.

only to revive them after the rulers' submission and penance, also surely referred to the same Patrician, and ultimately biblical, source.

Other saints chose afflictions based not just on Old Testament punishments such as barren land and empty tables, but on an ironic reversal of New Testament blessings. They struck some men and their families with lack of livelihood by making not the land, but the rivers barren. Patrick created the model when he cursed the river Dub. He had asked the fisher-folk for some of their catch and was refused; he cursed the Oengae and Séle because two of his disciples drowned in them.[45] Other saints followed his example. Brendan (Brénainn) cursed fishermen on the Forgus who refused him fish although, unlike Patrick, he did not pronounce the formal curse; as the hagiographer put it, *iudicio factum est* ("by [his] judgment it was done"). The same happened to Énna.[46] No doubt audiences of the stories were to recall the successful, Christ-following fishermen of the New Testament.

Similarly, other saints reversed Jesus' model of healing by dealing disabling punishment to greedy, mocking sinners. When men came to them begging and pretending to be deformed or ill, holy men caused their defects to become real. A man came to Mochuda with his eye closed, pretending to be blind; another grimaced and rattled his lips (blowing a "raspberry"). Both of these beggars ended up permanently crippled.[47] Máedóc, in his twelfth-century Irish life, even employed Jesus, the healer, to visit disease upon anyone who violated the saint's property: "Five diseases the Son of God inflicts on those whom I excommunicate or who outrage me: consumption, cholera, paralysis, sudden death and hell."[48]

But the saints were particularly fond of halting their enemies in the act by shriveling the arms of malefactors, or even causing hands and arms to fall off, as we have seen. Their biblical source for this was not only the Psalms, where the hands of the wicked get broken or withered (10.15, 37.17, 137.5), but a whole Testament full of mighty-versus-maimed hands and arms. Jeroboam (1 Kings 13.4) made the mistake of raising his arm against a prophet and promptly had it shrivel. Job called forth upon himself similar punishment should he ever lift his arm against orphans (Job 31.21–22). Zechariah denounced the shepherd who neglected his flock (Zech. 11.17): "Oh, my worthless shepherd, who deserts the flock! May the sword strike his arm and his right eye! Let his arm be completely

45. Bieler, *Patrician Texts,* p. 160.
46. Plummer, *Vitae,* 1:140; 2:70.
47. Ibid., 1:191–92; see also *Vitae,* 2:147.
48. Plummer, *Bethada,* 2:277.

withered, his right eye utterly blinded!" Compared to the "mighty hand and outstretched arm" of the Lord, who protects the righteous throughout the Old Testament, the lesson was clear to biblical scholars and to all Irish churchmen: the arms of the evil, raised in ungodly acts, were deservedly susceptible to cursing.

Hence, St. Columcille caused the hand of a priest to rot. The cleric had presumptuously ordained as king a man who was not only a sinner, but whom Columcille eventually cursed as the killer of Diarmait mac Cerbaill. The saint pronounced: "That right hand which, contrary to divine law and the law of the church, Findchan has laid upon the head of a son of perdition will presently rot, and after torments of great pain will precede him into the earth in burial; and surviving after his hand has been buried he will live for many years."[49] Such was the punishment of a churchman who chose to patronize the iniquitous, against the better judgment of his ecclesiastical superior. Similarly, when Abbán and his friend Braccán confronted the pig-stealing nephew, the sinner's hand was paralyzed, as we have seen. The killer of King Brandub mac Echach, friend of St. Máedóc, also lost a hand for his misdeed.[50] A fostermother who struck St. Colmán Ela caught a hand-withering curse from St. Cóemgen; the same happened to soldiers who tried to kill a hostage against the will of St. Munnu and to a jealous monk who tried to slay his rival, St. Máedóc.[51]

When it took more than a shriveled hand to stop an attacker, the saints simply froze sinners in their tracks, or caused them to wander in confusion, as the sinful Israelites did for so long in the desert. In a rare instance of a female saint praying for retribution, St. Faenche, sister of St. Énna, struck some bandits with temporary paralysis; after their penance, she released them. The hagiographer felt compelled to explain her powers by referring to Matthew 16.19 ("whatever you shall bind on earth shall be bound in heaven"). But no such similar action from a male saint deserved such explanation.[52] Ciarán of Cluain Moccu Nóis, Abbán, Colmán Ela, Máedóc, and numerous others in vitae spread across the pre-Norman centuries inflicted the freezing curse—often without speaking any specific words—upon evildoers.[53]

The saints could always heal what they had wrought, if they chose. They took Jesus as their model. Hagiographers were well aware of the savior's many healing miracles, which saints commonly imitated, but the

49. Anderson and Anderson, *Adomnán's Life of Columba,* pp. 280–81.
50. Plummer, *Vitae,* 2:157–58.
51. Ibid., 1:158; 2:145, 235.
52. Ibid., 2:62.
53. Heist, *Vitae,* p. 79; Plummer, *Vitae,* 1:23, 263, 264; 2:151.

specific incident in which Christ healed a withered arm on the Sabbath must have been emblematic.[54] The Acts of the Apostles specifically instructed the followers of Jesus to use their healing hands (4.30), and Irish saints did not hesitate, according to the vitae, nor did their successors; many an episode of cursing was followed by an instance of curing, the saint restoring the paralyzed to motion or the dead to life.[55] Followers of the saints could also invoke the protection of a saint's sheltering hand against other harmful arms, or any other aggression, by invoking St. Ultán, according to tenth-century (or later) comments on the *Martyrology of Óengus*. When his right hand was occupied, Ultán raised his left against some oncoming raiders, as a result of which, the commentator wrote, the Irish commonly said "The left hand of Ultán against every evil" (*llamh cle Ulltain anagaid gach uile*) when in danger. But, noted the writer, if the saint had used his mightier right hand, Ireland would have been forever free of foreigners, referring probably to Scandinavians, but no doubt later reinterpreted as Normans.[56]

In stories of cursing and curses reversed, then, the hagiographers relied almost exclusively upon biblical precedents for the actions of the saints, even though the ritual use of negative words had probably been common enough in pre-Christian Ireland. But saints were not practicing poetic satire or casting spells. They cursed mostly by prediction, by ritual gesture, or simply by expressing their disapproval, sometimes merely by the implication of words, or even by patiently awaiting God's judgment upon a sinner. They rarely expressed the kind of anger that drove the insults and hostile action of their opponents. The superiority of their pronouncements lay in their reliance upon the literary models found in the Old Testament, in the orthodoxy of their actions according to Christian theology, and, finally, in the recording of saintly curses in writing. On the page, for all to see (and only the literate few to read), Christian curses were at once historical fact and paradigm for future ecclesiastical participation in politics and society. The force of clerical cursing, which foreign observers such as Gerald of Wales found flourishing in Ireland, depended equally upon the peculiarly Celtic tradition of the magical word and upon the Book.

---

54. Mark 3.1–5; Luke 6.6–10.

55. See Davies, "Anger and the Celtic Saint," pp. 194–95.

56. Whitley Stokes, ed. and trans., *Félire Óengusso Céli Dé* (reprint Dublin, 1984), pp. 200–201. See Plummer, *Vitae*, 2:56. A kind commentator also supplied an Irish translation in the margin for those who could not handle the Latin: "Lamh clé Ultáin it aghhaidh!" Similarly, the simple invocation of St. Crónán's name froze the hand of an attacker of one of the saint's monks. The hagiographer thoughtfully supplied the invocation, in case other devotees should want to use it: "In nomine sancti Cronani dimitte me incolumem abire." See Plummer, *Vitae*, 2:26.

The Hierarchy of Cursing

Saintly curses were superior to the words of others, but not all enacted curses were alike. There were times when saints could not curse, or when their curses did not work. At other times, saints' curses were inefficacious because other cursers or blessers pronounced more words in a more powerful manner. Christianity brought a new kind of spoken word to Ireland, and a new vocabulary of curses. But the converted Irish simply placed Christian curses at the top of a hierarchy of ritualized speaking that had long existed, and which continued to follow many rules solidly rooted in the culture and politics of the island. Saints who outcursed other saints did so not because of superior holiness, but because of specific political situations and how these were reflected in the vitae. Hagiographers knew and used this hierarchy when constructing cursing episodes in the vitae.

As hagiographers told their tales, saints themselves expressed some doubts about cursing. Áed mac Bricc, who rarely did more than *increpare* (chide) villains, once refused to curse an evildoer for a very specific reason. In Áed's vita, a "cruel man" killed a victim near the saint's chariot, violating the saint's protection and the sacred space that surrounded him wherever he went. Áed's charioteer, probably a cleric, declared, "May your hand be wasted and fall from you to the ground." But Áed reproved the charioteer, explaining that the villain would have died instantly but for the cleric's impatience; for God, unlike men, did not want to "take vengeance on that man," and so, given the afflicted hand, had granted the sinner another year to live.[57] St. Daig, likewise, did not wish to "return evil for evil," and forbade a disciple from pronouncing malediction upon some would-be killers, who eventually repented.[58]

Both of these episodes from the *Codex Salmanticensis* echoed established theology. In this case, hagiographers relied on the teachings of Cassian, Benedict of Nursia, and Gregory the Great who preached against anger as a justification for saintly maledictions, or anger generally; if a sinner's penitence could be accomplished by threat of punishment, rather than by the infliction of punishment, so much the better.[59] Throughout the vitae, hagiographers asserted the saints' unassailable authority for their punitive actions. Canonists backed them up by quoting Augustine concerning the four reasons why God waits patiently for the punishment

57. Heist, *Vitae*, p. 177.
58. Ibid., p. 391.
59. Little, *Benedictine Maledictions*, pp. 88–99; Little, "Anger in Monastic Curses," p. 12.

of sinners, rather than acting immediately to correct them: first, to demonstrate his mercy; second, because man is inevitably sinful; third, because the martyrs pray for sinners' forgiveness; and fourth, so that sinners will add to their errors and deserve more fully the torments of hell that await them on judgment day.[60] Canonists also reminded clerics that angry judges were not fit judges, according to Isidore of Seville.[61] Although it was perfectly legitimate for clerics to pray against God's enemies (although not their own personal foes), they were to aim for the offenders' repentance—not injury—as a final result. And although the canonists repeated Deuteronomy's classical maledictions, they also reminded churchmen (in the words of Gregory I) that they were not to pray for the death of evildoers, but only for their repentance.[62]

Hence, if the threat of a curse could do the job, clerics might as well bluster and intimidate rather than actually pronounce the official words of malediction. They would be better saints for it, according to one hagiographer. Munnu once asked an angel why Molua outshone him in sanctity; because, the angel replied, Molua had always been tranquil, never *superbus* (proud) like Munnu. Unlike Munnu, he had "never cursed anyone present or absent"; hence, God wished to humble Munnu by showing his favor to Molua. Munnu could not argue, bad tempered though he was, but could only offer penance—he willingly took the curse of leprosy upon him for the rest of his life.[63] No doubt the hagiographer knew well the theology of limitations upon cursing, as well as the New Testament injunctions against cursing (James 3.8–11, 1 Cor 6.10).[64]

Significantly, most of the instances in which saints decided not to curse occurred in the Salamanca vitae, which are generally earlier than other Irish vitae. In later vitae, saints only occasionally appealed to their colleagues to refrain from cursing. According to the Irish life of Colmán Ela, for instance, an abbot of Dermag sneaked to the saint's settlement to steal some of his prized Roman earth, which he had sprinkled in his cemetery to boost its sacredness. Colmán Ela found the culprit out. The abbot's superior, St. Columcille, came to treat with Colmán Ela, begging him not to curse the other cleric. Colmán Ela compromised: he cursed the abbot, declaring that none of his race would inherit Dermag and that wolves would eat his flesh, but he allowed Columcille to keep the dirt.[65] In the

60. Wasserschleben, *Die irische Kanonensammlung,* p. 91.
61. Ibid., p. 69.
62. Ibid., pp. 227–29.
63. Plummer, *Vitae,* 2:185–86.
64. Little, *Benedictine Maledictions,* pp. 91–94.
65. Plummer, *Bethada,* 2:167.

later life of Déclán, a hagiographer once again used cursing to represent the tension between competing saints and their respective churches and polities. Déclán heard from an angel that St. Patrick was about to curse his kinsmen and his homeland. It seems that Patrick was fasting against a chieftain of Déclán's people who refused to convert. Déclán knew that once Patrick pronounced the words, his own people would be damned forever, like Cain; so he humiliated himself before the greater saint, begging him not to curse. Déclán got the chance to try his preaching powers on the chieftain, but with no success. He went then to the people, asking them to oust their leader and choose a more willing convert, which they did. Together, Patrick and Déclán blessed the new chief and ordained him in his office and, in return, the kinglet offered lots of churches to Patrick.[66] In yet another instance, St. Abbán almost got a curse from his own mentor, St. Ibar, when he tried to go on pilgrimage without permission; only his walking on water convinced the older, wiser saint not to denounce him.[67] Finally, the episode in which a Déisi leader defied St. Mochóemóc, explaining smugly that St. Cuimmíne Fota had already blessed him for protection, showed how a savvy layman might beat the curse of the saints by playing politics with churchmen.

The idea that one saint laid a better curse than another, and that people might seek the help of one cleric against another, came not so much of the theology of maledictions but of politics and the Irish culture of the spoken word. The vitae demonstrated, first, that all saints' words were superior to the protective spells of pagans. The saints' curses had superseded those of druids, as the vitae of Patrick and others plainly showed. How could there be any choice between the pagan magician who brought darkness to the plains around Temair and the saint who not only lifted the darkness but also threw the druid into the air and let him fall to dash out his brains?[68] Vita after vita demonstrated the superior powers of the saints manifested by both gesture and spoken word. Churchmen had mastered and transformed the oral culture of poetry and spell that had characterized Celtic societies before Christianity. The literati had collected and recorded the proof of literary conversion in hagiography and other stories. But the saints' use of Christian curses, drawn from their written scriptures, supplied them with superpowers not available to the old spellcasters of ancient Ireland. The hagiographers were both well aware of Ireland's pagan past and more than willing to make use of both secular tra-

66. Plummer, *Vitae*, 2:45–47.
67. Ibid., 1:9–12.
68. Bieler, *Patrician Texts*, pp. 88–90; see also Whitley Stokes, ed. and trans., *The Tripartite Life of Patrick*, Rolls Series (London, 1887), pp. 44–46.

ditions and biblical precedent in order to reinforce the maledictive skills of the saints (as well as the saints' powers to bless).

But the hagiographers' tales of cursing also referred specifically to Irish politics, in which every saint represented a church, and every church colluded with a secular dynasty. Some dynasties, churches, and saints were more influential than others, but religious communities, like tribes and chiefdoms, were forever negotiating for better places in the hierarchy. Episodes about saints dickering over curses, and deciding when to curse or not curse, referred to this political edifice of holy men and women. Kings were to mind the saints, hagiographers taught, unless they wanted to lose their voices, their arms, their offspring, their kingdoms, and their very lives to Christian curses. Secular lords could not exercise upon the saints the kinds of highhanded privileges they assumed among their clients and tenants. They were not to steal monastic property—which, though held by the monks, properly belonged to the saint who had founded a monastic settlement or church—nor to harm churchmen or their dependents. Kings and lords must not insult or harangue saints or their clerical representatives. They must obey Christian rules.

Nonetheless, if secular leaders found saints willing to patronize and protect them, they might carry out some of their kingly prerogatives without fear of reprisal. They could raid over their borders into another saint's territory if their own patron prevented his colleague's curses. They could collect rightful dues without fear of curse or assassination. The more powerful the saint, the more protection the king was offered, although the saint and his or her church expected healthy donations in return for such services.

Not all hagiographers agreed about the limits of cursing, the need for cursing, or maledictions' effects. In some vitae, rogues were cursed to death, while other villains escaped after penance. Sometimes saints cursed in strict biblical mode, by withering an arm; other times, they worked more creatively, causing the earth to swallow horses, or defensive swamps to dry up. What is more, the debate over the morality of cursing, evident in some saints' refusal to curse when they could, also represented a theological stance consistent with Continental thinking. Finally, Irish sources reveal some development in clerical opinion over time, but in the opposite direction from that of Continental critics. The Salamanca lives contain episodes advising clerical restraint for moral reasons, but the later lives contain no such episodes. The later vitae contain lengthier, more colorful instances of saintly malediction, which rely less upon biblical precedents and more upon folklore and secular poetry for many of their motifs. The most vivid of all is St. Máedóc's curse upon the Ó Raghallaigh who might violate his monastery of Drumlane. In the same maledictory poem, which warned against having an angry saint for a neighbor, St. Máedóc announced:

> I am the serpent destroying hosts,
> I am the fire of blood-red coal,
> I am the lion destroying herds,
> I am the bear in courage.
> I am the bear, a royal course,
> I am mild Máedóc,
> My robbers shall have, a strong course,
> Short life and hell.
> I am the son of the king of great Oriel
> I am a treasury of the canonical Scriptures,
> I am the saint most heavenly in respect of city,
> And noblest in respect of lofty bell.[69]

Although it mentioned a few clerical virtues, the saint's chant sounded much like the poetic boasting of Irish warrior-heroes and magicians, such as Cú Chulainn or Amairgen, one of the mythological invaders of Ireland, who sang famously,

> I am Wind on Sea,
> I am Ocean-wave,
> I am Roar of Sea,
> I am Bull of Seven Fights,
> I am Vulture on Cliff . . .[70]

It is no coincidence that Máedóc's Irish life and the *Lebor Gabála*, which told Amairgen's story, were composed around the same time, when Irish scribes were busy reviving and rewriting their literary traditions, drawing on earlier texts as well as their oral heritage of stories and verses. Indeed, one tale composed in the twelfth century, but securely reliant on older tales of wild kings and cursing saints, was the *Buile Suibhne* (Frenzy of Suibhne), which hinged on the malediction of a sixth-century saint pronounced upon an impetuous ruler. When Suibhne attacked St. Rónán for nothing more than ringing his holy bell, the saint cast a fear of battle upon the warrior; as a result, Suibhne became terrified, grew feathers, and flew away into the treetops, abandoning all that was familiar, and

---

69. Plummer, *Bethada*, 2:277.
70. R. A. S. Macalister, *Lebor Gabála Érenn* (Dublin, 1938–56), 5: 110–13.

all that gave him status and comfort in life. He eventually sought the protection of another saint, Moling, but even that could not reduce the efficacy of Rónán's curse.[71] Suibhne ended his days perched behind a screen of branches, singing heartbreaking poetry that someone—probably a cleric—imagined as the lyrics of his *Buile*.

THE CANON OF CURSING

The change in saintly cursing may have had something to do with the change in politics, both secular and ecclesiastical, brought by Gerald of Wales and his Norman cousins. With the Normans, another set of voices and another political language invaded Ireland. The newcomers immediately began to construct territorial feudal lordships unknown to the Irish, governed by charters and writs from Dublin or across the sea. Yet language traveled in both directions, for the noise of the Irish followed them off the island. By the time Gerald was suffering the bad humor of the Irish saints and their monastic successors, the tradition of saintly maledictions (including negative predictions, failure to bless, and ritual gestures of cursing) had reached the foreign ears of French-speakers. Lester Little has pointed out that Continental maledictions were prevalent where the Irish had proselytized, even though the Irish style of cursing did not travel with the missionaries.[72] Gerald, too, observed the mobility of Irish maledictions in the twelfth century. He once saw an Irish mendicant in Wales wearing around his neck a relic horn of bronze. The horn had been St. Brendan's, and no one was allowed to sound it. A hostile priest named Bernard—obviously not a brother Celt—snatched the horn and blew it, and was immediately struck by the saint, as Gerald told it: "The wretch had a torrent of eloquence before then, and the loose tongue of a tale-bearer, but immediately he lost all use of speech. As a result he was so harmed that he has always had a speech impediment. In addition he went into a coma and immediately lost his memory altogether. He could scarcely remember his name." Neither Brendan nor his devotee had pronounced an audible curse, but Bernard's plight would have been familiar to any reader of Irish saints' lives. The punishment for speaking out against a saint was the curse of a strangled tongue.[73] Just as bad in Irish eyes was the loss of a memorized heritage.

71. J. G. O'Keeffe, ed., *Buile Suibhne* (Dublin, 1975); translated loosely but beautifully by Seamus Heaney, *Sweeney Astray* (Derry, 1983).
72. Little, *Benedictine Maledictions*, pp. 154–85.
73. O'Meara, *History and Topography*, pp. 116–17.

The end of the twelfth century brought the waning of the great literary tradition that produced Irish vitae and written curses. By the time of the Normans' arrival, the flourish of Irish theological creativity, the import of Irish intellectual innovations to the Continent, even the compilatory fervor that had produced a recorded *seanchas* had begun to dwindle. Although the reforming trends of Continental churches came to Ireland just in advance of the Normans, the great exchange of ideas that had begun when the Celts went to Charlemagne's court now slowed. Norman ecclesiastics and native reformers introduced new orders, new churches, new organizations to compete with the old *paruchiae* of the Irish, but not many new saints came with the invaders, nor any new hagiographic styles. No one composed original vitae. Instead, hagiographers revised the old stories of traditional patrons—sometimes elaborating in exciting detail, as in Máedóc's contest with Ó Raghallaigh, but generally sticking to the same reliable formulae of curses.

Perhaps the cacophony of competing words had existed in other early medieval societies, too. Perhaps we hear the Irish only because, paradoxically, they wrote so much down, over so many centuries. Yet they created such a great canon because they transferred so much of the spoken to the written. They were unique not only in their gift of gab, but in their drive to write, and not just in the *sacra lingua* but in the language they spoke. Their poetry, laws, stories, myths, proverbs, as well as theology, hagiography, cosmology, and other imported genres reach us not only in Latin but in the oldest recorded vernacular in Europe. Because of the variety of Irish written material, we can recover a wide range of intellectual opinion on matters including tribal politics, the exercise of power, and the duties of churchmen. We can trace the slow change from tribal kingdoms to provincial lordships and churchmen's consistent participation in secular politics. We can read stories about the noisy debate among churchmen and lay people over the strength of words. We can detect, too, in tales of malediction the literati's sophisticated manipulation of the links between spoken and written words. For seven centuries, the Irish did not progress toward literacy, but maneuvered between pronouncement and inscription, Latin and Irish, performance and preservation. If we imagine echoes of those Irish voices today, it is only because the hagiographers' own literature of cursing lasted even longer than the words of the saints.

III

RETHINKING BINARIES

The Beggar's Body: Intersections of Gender and Social Status in High Medieval Paris

Sharon Farmer

In the past decade or so medievalists who are interested in questions of gender have reached a near consensus on how medieval women were represented in male-authored texts. The central component in that scholarly consensus is the idea that all women were more closely associated with the body and its appetites than were all men. I want to contend that there is a problem with this scholarly position. My working theoretical orientation is informed by multiracial and postcolonial feminists, who have argued that gender categories are never constructed along a single axis—a binary with two simple components, male and female. Rather, gendered categories are always constructed within, and in relationship to, other categories of difference—such as social status or ethnic or religious difference.[1]

I first learned about the social meanings of medieval begging—especially holy begging—in Lester Little's classes at Smith College in the fall of 1973 and the spring of 1974. It is no exaggeration to say that those classes changed my life. This article is dedicated to Lester.

I wish to thank the Institute for Advanced Study for providing me with the time to write this article, Wolfgang Mueller for his help with legal references, and Barbara Rosenwein for her comments on an earlier draft.

1. bell hooks, *Feminist Theory: From Margin to Center* (Boston, 1984); Norma Alarcón, "The Theoretical Subject(s) of This Bridge Called My Back," in Gloria Andalzua, ed., *Making Face, Making Soul/Haciendo Caras: Creative and Critical Perspectives by Feminists of Color* (San Francisco, 1990), pp. 356–69; Nalini Persram, "Politicizing the *Féminine*, Globalizing the Feminist," *Alternatives* 19 (1994): 275–313; Elizabeth Spelman, *Inessential Woman: Problems of Exclusion in Feminist Thought* (Boston, 1988), esp. chap. 7; Patricia Hill Collins, *Black Feminist Thought: Knowledge, Consciousness, and the Politics of Empowerment* (Boston, 1990); Maxine Baca Zinn and Bonnie Thornton Dill, "Theorizing Difference from Multiracial Feminism," *Feminist Studies* 22 (1996): 321–31; Chela Sandoval, "U.S. Third World Feminism: The Theory and Method of Oppositional Consciousness in the Postmodern World," *Genders* 10 (Spring 1991): 1–24; Sharon Farmer and Carol

In order to elucidate how medieval gender categories worked within this larger "grid" of differences, I will focus, in this essay, on the ways in which differences of social status complicated the construction of masculinity, resulting not in one stereotype of maleness, but in several stereotypes. More specifically, I will discuss the stereotypes that thirteenth-century clerical male elites, most of them active in Paris, constructed for men who came from the lowest strata of urban society—that is to say, from the working and the non-working poor—a group that constituted, toward the end of the thirteenth century, about half of Paris' nearly 200,000 people.[2] My argument focuses on three strands of gender scholarship that have emphasized the association of women with the body. What I want to suggest is that elite male authors represented lower status men, as well as lower status women, in ways that fit all three of these strands of the "embodiment" theme. The first strand is the mind/body binary, according to which men were associated with rationality and matters of the spirit while women were associated with irrationality, the body, and lust. Thus, as Caroline Bynum has argued, "Male and female were contrasted and asymmetrically valued as intellect/body, active/passive, rational/irrational, reason/emotion, self-control/lust, judgment/mercy and order/disorder."[3]

The second strand of this scholarship on the association of women with the body concerns the use of cosmetic adornment to distort the true appearance of the individual. Marcia Colish has argued that early Christian and patristic authors simultaneously borrowed and transformed stoic invective against those who altered their natural appearance with depilatories, razors, and other devices. For pagan stoics, Colish argues, this had been a gender-neutral theme, but Christians turned it into an asymmetrical invective against women's adornment and use of makeup.[4] Dyan Elliott has carried that analysis forward into the High Middle Ages, arguing

---

Pasternack, eds., *Differences and Genders in the Middle Ages* (forthcoming). Several medievalists have already analyzed the unique ways in which Jews, Muslims, and peasants were gendered, but they have not suggested that we need to rethink medieval gender categories in general: Steven Kruger, "Becoming Christian, Becoming Male?," *Becoming Male in the Middle Ages,* ed. Jeffrey Jerome Cohen and Bonnie Wheeler (New York, 1997), pp. 21–41; Louise Mirrer, *Women, Jews, and Muslims in the Texts of Reconquest Castile* (Ann Arbor, Mich., 1996); Paul Freedman, *The Image of the Medieval Peasant as Alien and Exemplary* (Stanford, 1999), chaps. 5 and 7.

2. Farmer, "Down and Out and Female in Thirteenth-Century Paris," *American Historical Review* 103 (April 1998): 352.

3. Caroline Bynum, "'And Woman His Humanity': Female Imagery in the Religious Writings of the Later Middle Ages," in *Fragmentation and Redemption: Essays on Gender and the Human Body in Medieval Religion* (New York, 1991), p. 151.

4. Marcia Colish, "Cosmetic Theology: The Transformation of a Stoic Theme," in *Assays: Critical Approaches to Medieval and Renaissance Texts,* ed. Peggy A. Knapp and Michael A. Stugrin (Pittsburgh, 1981), pp. 3–14.

that while medieval Christian authors in the west continued to associate women in an asymmetrical way with the use of unnatural adornment, they sometimes encouraged married matrons to use makeup and other enhancements to their beauty in order to prevent their husbands from falling away into the sin of adultery.[5]

The third strand in the scholarly view of women's association with the body involves the reduction of a woman's character—most especially if she was a saint—to bodily signs. Brigitte Cazelles has argued that in high medieval French translations of the lives of Late Antique saints, female saints were repeatedly disrobed for a voyeuristic audience, and their saintliness was largely reduced to a passive but willing suffering of bodily torments.[6] Similarly Amy Hollywood has argued that in the male-authored lives of high medieval female saints in the west, "the identification of women with the body demands that their sanctification occur in and through that body . . . the medieval hagiographer wants externally sensible *signs* of visionary and mystical experience in order to verify the claims to sanctity of the woman saint."[7] An extreme example of this stress on visible signs is the thirteenth-century mystic Douceline of Digne, whose ecstatic raptures put her into a virtually catatonic state: she was totally unaware of what was going on around her, and her body became completely senseless. Douceline's audience was often more interested in the senseless nature of her body than in the content of her visions, and thus, again and again, people tested her body in order to prove to themselves that it really did become senseless during her raptures. Some of those tests—such as forcing needles under her fingernails, or pouring hot lead over her feet—were so cruel that she remained unable to use her hands or to walk for long periods of time.[8]

I begin, then, with the evidence that subverts the scholarly position that all men were associated with rationality while all women were associated with physicality. My evidence comes from discussions of the different

5. Dyan Elliott, "Dress as Mediator between Inner and Outer Self: The Pious Matron of the High Middle Ages," *Mediaeval Studies* 53 (1991): 279–308.

6. Brigitte Cazelles, *The Lady as Saint: A Collection of French Hagiographic Romances of the Thirteenth Century* (Philadelphia, 1991), pp. 43–61.

7. Amy Hollywood, *The Soul as Virgin Wife: Mechthild of Magdeburg, Marguerite Porete, and Meister Eckhart* (Notre Dame, Indiana, 1995), p. 35.

8. *La vie de Sainte Douceline: Texte provençal du XIVe siècle,* ed. R. Gout (Paris, 1927), pp. 108–9, 115, 126; Claude Carozzi, "Douceline et les autres," *La religion populaire en Languedoc du XIIIe siècle à la moitié du XIVe siècle,* Cahiers de Fanjeaux 11 (Toulouse, 1976), pp. 256–61; Daniel Bornstein, "Violenza al corpo di una santa: Fra agiografia e pornografia," *Quaderni medievali* 39 (1995): 31–46. See also Walter Simons, "Reading a Saint's Body: Rapture and Bodily Movement in the *Vitae* of Thirteenth-Century Beguines," in *Framing Medieval Bodies,* ed. Sarah Kay and Miri Rubin (Manchester, 1994), pp. 16–20.

kinds of work that were appropriate to members of Christian society. Such discussions reached a peak in the third quarter of the thirteenth century, after the secular clergy of Paris attacked the new religious orders— especially the Franciscans and the Dominicans—because they practiced mendicancy, or holy begging, as an aspect of their voluntary poverty.[9] Members of the secular clergy claimed that able-bodied beggars who lived on the alms of the faithful violated Saint Paul's injunction, "if anyone does not wish to work, neither should he eat [2 Thess. 3:10]." Bonaventure, who was master general of the Franciscan order from 1257 to 1274, and one of the leading defenders of the mendicant orders, responded to these criticisms by pointing out that Christians (by which he meant, primarily, Christian men) were not all called upon to practice manual labor. Rather, the work of men could be divided into three categories: inferior or corporeal work (that which was necessary for preparing clothing, food, and so forth); exterior or civil work (such as that of governors, soldiers, and merchants); and finally, spiritual work (that of preachers and priests, for instance). Bonaventure argued that it was valid for the members of the mendicant orders to accept the alms of the faithful because they engaged in this third type of work, "the labor of wisdom," which was superior to corporeal work.[10] Indeed, he went on, there was only one category of men for whom manual labor was a precept—those "poor strong ones who are most fit for corporeal work, and least fit for spiritual work."[11]

9. On the seculars' criticisms of the mendicant orders, see Penn R. Szittya, *The Antifraternal Tradition in Medieval Literature* (Princeton, N.J., 1986), chap. 1; D. L. Douie, *The Conflict between the Seculars and the Mendicants at the University of Paris in the Thirteenth Century,* The Aquinas Society of London, Aquinas Paper 23 (London, 1954); Michel-Marie Dufeil, *Guillaume de St.-Amour et la polémique universitaire parisienne, 1250–1259* (Paris, 1972). For a general discussion of the social meanings of voluntary poverty, see Lester K. Little, *Religious Poverty and the Profit Economy in Medieval Europe* (Ithaca, N.Y., 1978).

10. Bonaventure, "Expositio super regulam fratrum Minorum," c. 5, ed. College of Saint Bonaventure, *Doctoris Seraphici S. Bonaventurae Opera Omnia* (Quaracchi, 1891), 8:420.

11. "Inter membra Christi sunt quaedam maxime idonea ad operationes corporales et minime ad spirituales . . . hinc est quod illis pauperibus validis, qui ad opera corporalia maxime sunt idonei et minime ad spiritualia . . . eis est opus manuale in *praecepto,*" Bonaventure, "Quaestiones disputatae de perfectione evangelica," Quaest. II, art. III, conclusion, ed. College of Saint Bonaventure, *Doctoris Seraphici S. Bonaventurae Opera Omnia,* 5:161. Thomas Aquinas also pointed to a hierarchy of labors in his response to the seculars, but it was less central to his overall argument: "Contra impugnantes Dei cultum et religionem," c. 7, ed. Peter Fiaccadorus, *Sancti Thomae Aquinatis Doctoris Angelici Ordinis Praedicatorum Opera Omnia* (Parma, 1852–1873; reprint: New York, 1950), 15:41. In the sections of the *Summa theologiae* that dealt with whether or not members of religious orders should beg and whether or not they were required to do manual labor, Aquinas avoided constructing a hierarchy of labors, suggesting instead that "manual labor" referred to all forms of useful work for society, including preaching and serving at the altar: *Summa theologiae,* 2a2ae, Quaest. 187, art. 3 and 4, ed. and trans. Blackfriars (London, 1973), 47: 156–57, 160–61, 168–69. Both the Dominican Thomas of Cantimpré (d. 1270) and the early-thirteenth-century churchman Jacques de Vitry

In a different context, Humbert of Romans, who was master general of the Dominican order from 1254 to 1277 and the author of one of the great preaching treatises of the thirteenth century, made a similar mind/body distinction between lower status and elite men.[12] In his sermon material for boys who were studying Latin grammar, Humbert wrote that every occupation involved the acquisition of either mechanical knowledge—which pertained to the body—or the knowledge of letters, which pertained to the soul, and since the soul was more noble than the body, the acquisition of knowledge of letters was more noble than the acquisition of mechanical knowledge.[13]

Both Bonaventure and Humbert of Romans assumed that the male members of the working poor had a stronger association with the body and a weaker association with things pertaining to the soul than did more elite men, especially those who labored for the Lord. This does not imply, however, that Humbert and Bonaventure considered lower status men to be effeminate. Rather, they constructed a hierarchy of "masculinities," which were distinguished from "femininities" not by the difference between mind and body, but by the difference between men's productive labor (that is to say, work in the public sphere) and women's reproductive, or domestic, labor (that is, work in the domestic sphere). Men who worked with their hands were "masculine" because they engaged in productive labor, but their masculinity was inferior to that of prelates and preachers, who engaged in productive labor with their minds rather than with their bodies. Of course, it followed naturally that men who labored with their bodies rather than their minds were less informed about matters of the spirit, and more likely to give in to the rule of their appetites, than were men who labored with their minds. Thus, according to Humbert of Romans, hired laborers were "exceedingly" ignorant of things per-

---

(d. 1240) created a hierarchy of labors with preaching at the top: Thomas of Cantimpré, *Bonum universale de apibus,* 2:10:7 (Douai, 1627), p. 161; Jacques de Vitry, "Sermo XXXV Ad Fratres Minores," ed. J. P. Pitra, *Analecta novissima spicilegii Solesmensis Altera continuatio* (reprint: Farnborough, 1967), 2:400–402.

12. For a discussion of the new preaching, and of Humbert's role in promoting it, see Little, *Religious Poverty,* chap. 11.

13. "Omnis occupatio circa res addiscendas, aut est circa mechanica, et hoc pertinet ad corpus, aut circa litteras, et hoc ad animam, et ideo tanto nobilior est quanto nobilior est anima corpore," Humbert of Romans, "De eruditione religiosorum praedicatorum," bk. 2, tract. 1, c. 63, "Ad scholares in grammatica," ed. Margarin de la Bigne, *Maxima bibliotheca veterum patrum et antiquorum scriptorum ecclesiasticorum* (Lyon, 1677), 25:487. See also bk. 2, tract. 1, c. 56, p. 484, "Ad omnes litteratos," where he compares those with wisdom to the angels and those lacking intellect to beasts; and bk. 2, tract. 1, c. 71, p. 491, "Ad omnes laicos," where he argues that like she-asses, who feed next to the oxen who do the plowing, "simplices"—that is to say, lay people—should be content with the doctrines of their betters—that is to say, the clergy.

taining to their own salvation, and they were prone to drunkenness. He said nothing about these faults in either elite lay men or elite lay women in his sermon material for them.[14]

It was in their sermon material for male and female servants, however, that thirteenth-century clerics most explicitly associated both male and female members of the working poor with the rule of the appetites. Humbert of Romans mentioned sexual sins in his discussion of male and female servants, but not in his sermons for elite lay men.[15] The early-thirteenth-century churchman Jacques de Vitry and the mid-century Franciscan Gilbert of Tournai also mentioned sexual sins in their sermons about servants, and they even went so far as to suggest that elite women, as well as elite men, should assume responsibility for guarding the chastity of both their male and their female servants. Moreover, Gilbert placed the elite matron's responsibility for the behavior of her servants within a context that associated all of her household duties with aspects of "governance": she was to educate her children, humble male servants, and correct female servants.[16]

Gilbert of Tournai's discussion of the role of the matron suggests that clerical authors developed a hierarchy of femininities that paralleled the hierarchy of masculinities. Within that hierarchy, women were all associated with reproductive or domestic labor. However, while the clerical authors dwelt at length on the lustful, and hence bodily, aspects of the reproductive natures of the lower status women (domestic servants and peasant women, for instance), their discussions of elite women's reproductive, or domestic, responsibilities focused more on the intellectual and spiritual aspects of those responsibilities.[17] Gilbert enjoined matrons to govern their households wisely; along similar lines, Humbert urged

14. Humbert, "De eruditione," bk. 2, tract. 1, c. 88, "Ad operarios conductivos," ed. de la Bigne, *Maxima*, 25:500. Humbert's sermon material for elite lay men was in ibid., bk. 2, tract. 1, c. 73, 74, 80–84, pp. 492–93, 495–98; his sermon material for elite lay women was in ibid., bk. 2, tract. 1, c. 95–96, p. 504, reprinted in Casagrande, *Prediche*, pp. 45–48. In his sermon material for peasant women, Humbert included credulity and simplicity among their faults, but not drunkenness: "De eruditione," bk. 2, tract. 1, c. 99, ed. de la Bigne, 25:505; reprinted by Casagrande, pp. 52–53.
15. "Quandoque vero mala familiaritate coniuncti iuvant se inuicem, et zelant in peccatis immunditiae," Humbert, "De eruditione," bk. 2, tract. 1, c. 76, "Ad familiam divitiam in civitatibus," ed. de la Bigne, *Maxima*, 25:494. On sermon material for elite lay men, see the previous note.
16. Jacques de Vitry, "LXIV, Sermo ad servos et ancillas," ed. Jean Longère, "Deux sermons de Jacques de Vitry (d. 1240) *Ad Servos et Ancillas*," in *La femme au moyen-âge*, ed. Michel Rouche and Jean Heuclin (Mauberge, 1990), pp. 278–80; Gilbert of Tournai, "Ad ancillas et servos sermo primus," Paris, Bibliothèque Nationale, ms. lat. 15943, fols. 175–77; Gilbert of Tournai, "Ad coniugatas sermo tercius, ed. Carla Casagrande, *Prediche alle donne del secolo XIII* (Milan, 1978), pp. 93–97.
17. Farmer, "Manual Labor, Begging, and Conflicting Gender Expectations in Thirteenth-Century Paris," in *Differences and Genders in the Middle Ages*, ed. Farmer and Pasternack.

elite girls to learn willingly, so they would know how to recite the Psalter, the Hours of the Virgin, and the Office of the Dead.[18]

In the writings of Jacques de Vitry, Bonaventure, Humbert of Romans, and Gilbert of Tournai, laboring men represented a lower form of masculinity, a masculinity that rested upon the "robust" body, which made a valuable, if inferior, contribution to society. There was a widespread suspicion, however, that many "robust" men of the lower strata of society pretended not to be robust because they preferred the "soft" life of the beggar to the harsh demands of paid labor.[19] While this stereotype of the lazy beggar had been available since the Late Antique period, the suspicion of his ubiquitous presence reached a new intensity in the thirteenth century.[20] Sometime before the middle of the century, the customs of Touraine-Anjou came to include a chapter encouraging justices in towns to banish unemployed, propertyless men who lingered in taverns and led an evil life ["mauvaise vie"].[21] By the early fourteenth century, rulers in Spain and other parts of France followed suit.[22]

18. Humbert, "De eruditione," bk. 2, tract. 1, c. 97, "Ad iuvenculas, sive adolescentulas saeculares," ed. de la Bigne, *Maxima,* 25:504; reprinted by Casagrande, *Prediche,* p. 49.

19. The "De reversione beati Martini a burgundia tractatus," which was probably written between 1137 and 1156, included a story about two cripples who did not wish to be cured of their disabilities because they would have to give up their soft life and go to work. When the prospect of being cured by Saint Martin arose, one of the cripples said to the other, "Behold, brother, we live a life of soft leisure . . . and it is this infirmity by which we are cast down that lays claim to all of this for us. But—God forbid!—if we were to be cured, manual labor, to which we are unaccustomed, would weigh us down by necessity" ["Ecce frater, sub molli otio vivimus. . . . Hoc autem totum nobis vindicat infirmitas haec qua jacemus; quae si curata fuerit, quod absit, necessario nobis incumbet labor manuum insolitus"], ed. André Salmon, *Supplément aux chroniques de Touraine* (Tours, 1856), p. 52. On the date of this text, see Sharon Farmer, *Communities of Saint Martin: Legend and Ritual in Medieval Tours* (Ithaca, N.Y., 1991), pp. 305–6.

20. Jean Batany argued that the years around 1200 marked a turning point toward increasingly negative attitudes toward the poor: "Les pauvres et la pauvreté dans les revues des 'Estats du monde,'" *Études sur l'histoire de la pauvreté,* ed. Michel Mollat, 2 vols. (Paris, 1974), 2:469–86. See also, on negative and ambivalent attitudes toward the poor, Michel Mollat, *The Poor in the Middle Ages,* trans. Arthur Goldhammer (New Haven, Conn., 1986), pp. 71, 109, 111–13, 128, 134; Bronislaw Geremek, *La potence ou la pitié: L'Europe et les pauvres du Moyen Âge à nos jours* (Paris, 1987), pp. 30–46; Jean-Louis Roch, "Le jeu de l'aumône au moyen âge," *Annales: ÉSC* 44 (1989): 505–27; Gerald B. Guest, "A Discourse on the Poor: The Hours of Jeanne d'Evreux," *Viator: Medieval and Renaissance Studies* 26 (1995): 153–80.

21. *Les établissements de Saint Louis,* bk. 1, c. 38, ed. Paul Viollet, 4 vols., Société de l'histoire de France (Paris, 1881), 2:54; trans. F. R. P. Akehurst, *The Établissements de Saint Louis: Thirteenth-Century Law Texts from Tours, Orléans and Paris* (Philadelphia, 1996), p. 27.

22. Pagart d'Hermansart, "Documents inédits contenus dans les archives de Saint-Omer," *Bulletin historique et philologique du comité des travaux historiques et scientifiques* (Année 1900), #47, p. 77 (the statute dates from c. 1319); Luis Revest Corzo, *Hospitales y pobres en el Castellón de otros tiempos* (Castellón de la Plana, 1947), Documents, p. 89 (Statute from Valencia, 1321). Both Jacques de Vitry and Bonaventure made vague references to towns that passed statutes ordering the expulsion of able-bodied beggars: Jacques de Vitry, "Sermo LXI Ad agricolas et alios operarios," ed. Pitra, *Analecta Novissima,* 2:436; Bonaventure, "Apologia pauperum contra calumniatorum," c. 12, ed.

Demographic growth probably provided one of the main stimuli for this renewed suspicion on the part of elites. By the end of the thirteenth century the population of Europe reached a peak which it did not see again until the sixteenth century or later. Underemployment was one of the results of this demographic saturation: mid-thirteenth-century Parisians witnessed disturbing levels of unemployment, and in the last quarter of the century the master dyers of the city complained that there was frequently a fifty-percent unemployment rate among the journeymen of their craft.[23] Medieval intellectuals and rulers did not often analyze poverty in structural terms, and thus, as greater numbers of the un- and underemployed began to seek alms in the streets, elites tended to blame the beggars themselves for their plight.

It is in the rhetoric about false beggars that we encounter the second strand of embodied thought, in which elites accused lower status men of cosmetically distorting the appearance of their bodies. The early-thirteenth-century Parisian moralist, Peter the Chanter, for instance, wrote about beggars who "make themselves tremulous, and putting on the various forms of the sick, change their faces just like Proteus."[24] Similarly, Peter's student, Thomas of Chobham, described beggars who went to church not to hear sermons, but to "extort money through false tears and deceptions and many simulations."[25] Elsewhere, in his influential manual for confessors, Thomas wrote that beggars "frequently transfigure themselves into the appearance of the wretched, so that they seem more destitute than they really are, and thus they deceive others so that

---

College of St. Bonaventure, *Doctoris Seraphici S. Bonaventurae Opera Omnia,* 8:325. For an overview of late medieval vagrancy laws, see Bronislaw Geremek, "La lutte contre le vagabondage à Paris aux XIVe et XVe siècles," *Ricerche storiche ed economiche in memoria di Corrado Barbagallo,* ed. Luigi di Rosa (Naples, 1970), pp. 213–36.

23. The statute of the hosiers' gild in Étienne Boileau's *Livre des métiers* indicates that masters in that craft were being forced to take employment as day laborers: *Le livre des métiers,* ed. René de Lespinasse and François Bonnardot (Paris, 1879), #55, p. 115; Réné de Lespinasse, *Les métiers et corporations de la Ville de Paris,* 3 vols. (Paris, 1886–97), 3:116; cited by Bronislaw Geremek, *Le salariat dans l'artisanat parisien aux XIIIe–XVe siècles,* trans. from the Polish by Anna Posner and Christiane Klapisch-Zuber (Paris, 1962), p. 122. Raymond Cazelles sees in the *Livre des métiers* attempts on the part of King Louis IX and his provost to raise the level of employment by regulating work hours and establishing lengthy apprenticeships: Cazelles, "Le parisien au temps de Saint Louis," *Septième centenaire de la mort de Saint Louis, Actes des Colloques de Royaumont et de Paris (21–27 mai 1970)* (Paris, 1976), p. 103.

24. "Sunt alii omni tempore calamitosi et inimici trivialiter se inflantes, tremulosi, et varias figuras aegrotantium induentes, vultum sicut Protea mutantes," Peter the Chanter, *Verbum abbreviatum,* c. 48, PL 205, col. 152.

25. "[Mendici] numquam enim veniunt ad ecclesia causa orandi uel causa missis audiendi, sed causa extorquendi argentum per falsas lacrimas et per dolos et simulationes multas," Thomas de Chobham, *Summa de arte praedicandi,* c. 3, ed. Franco Morenzoni (Turnhout, 1988), p. 88.

they will receive more."[26] Similarly, the *glossa ordinaria* for Justinian's Code, which was compiled in Bologna in the mid-thirteenth century, described "those who make themselves seem sick, applying herbs or something that causes them to swell."[27]

Elite discussions of the deceits of false beggars can be placed within two interrelated discursive contexts. First, elites expressed a desire to establish "distinguishing signs"[28] that would make known the true nature and status of individuals when they entered the public sphere. Such concern was neither gender nor status specific. Moralists, chroniclers, and legislators expressed the belief that kings and their subjects, clergy and lay people, prostitutes and matrons, Jews and Christians, old women and young should be clearly and hierarchically marked off from one another so that people would know how to conduct themselves in their encounters with each other.[29] The conviction that able-bodied beggars should be clearly distinguishable from disabled beggars fit into this broader set of expressions.

26. "Sepe transfigurant se in habitu miserabili, ut videantur magis egeni quam sunt, et ita decipiunt alios ut plus accipiant," *Thomas de Chobham Summa confessorum*, Art. 5, dist. 4, quaest. 6, ed. F. Broomfield (Louvain, 1968), p. 297.

27. "His qui faciunt se videri aegros apponentes herbam vel aliud per quod tumescunt," *Volumen legum parvum, quod vocant, in quo haec insunt: tres posteriores libri Codicis D. Iustiniani* (Venice, 1583), Codex, bk. ii, tit. 25, gloss to the word *lenitudinem*, col. 146. Other theologians and moralists of the mid-thirteenth and early fourteenth centuries were less specific in their descriptions of the deceits of false beggars. Bonaventure equated the poverty of false beggars ("pauperibus simulatis") with cupidity and that of able-bodied beggars with indolence; Humbert of Romans wrote of the gullibility of village women who gave their goods to "trutannis et falsis quaestoribus"; Gilbert of Tournai advised hospital workers not to receive "ribaldi, vel trutanni, vel hystriones," and the Dominican John of Freiburg (d. 1314) argued that it was better to reprove able-bodied beggars than to give them alms, but he made no mention of their uses of deceit. At least one fifteenth-century Parisian anti-vagrancy law, by contrast, gave lurid descriptions of the deceptive artifices of false beggars: Bonaventure, "Apologia pauperum," c. 12, ed. College of Saint Bonaventure, *Doctoris Seraphici S. Bonaventurae Opera Omnia*, 8:325; Humbert of Romans, "De eruditione," bk. 2, tract. 1., c. 99, "Ad mulieres pauperes in villulis," ed. de la Bigne, *Maxima*, 25:505; Gilbert of Tournai, "Ad servientes et hospitalinos sermo tertius" (actually this is his second sermon to hospital workers—the first sermon given that rubric in the manuscript, at fol. 94ᵛ, was for judges and lawyers), Bibliothèque Nationale, ms. lat. 15943, fol. 99ᵛ; John of Freiburg, *Summa confessorum reverendi patris Joannis de Friburgo*, bk. 3, tit. 8, quaest. 6 (Lyon, 1518), fol. cii; Geremek, "La lutte contre le vagabondage," p. 236.

28. I have borrowed this expression from Diane Owen Hughes, "Distinguishing Signs: Ear-Rings, Jews and Franciscan Rhetoric in the Italian Renaissance City," *Past and Present*, no. 112 (1986), 3–59.

29. On kings and their subjects: Joinville, *The Life of St. Louis*, trans. René Hague (New York, 1955), chap. 6, pp. 30–32; on prostitutes and matrons: Ruth Karras, *Common Women: Prostitution and Sexuality in Medieval England* (New York, 1996), p. 21; on clergy and laity, Jews and Christian: canons 16 and 68 of the Fourth Lateran Council: *Sacrorum conciliorum nova et amplissima collectio*, ed. J. D. Mansi, 53 vols. (Florence, 1759–98; reprint: Graz, 1961), 22:1006, 1055; on old women and young: Stephen of Bourbon, *Tractatus de diversis materiis praedicabilibus*, ed. A. Lecoy de la Marche, *Anecdotes historiques, légendes et apologues tirées du recueil inédit d'Étienne de Bourbon Dominicain du XIIIᵉ siècle* (Paris, 1877), no. 273, 274, 279, pp. 228–29, 231–32.

In most cases, clothing of differing materials and colors provided the required signs to mark off status. In the cases of old women and beggars, however, the body itself was the sign, and the cosmetic transformations of those bodies shared affinities with the shapeshifting of the devil.[30] In their discussions of made-up beggars Peter the Chanter and Thomas of Chobham evoked images of "transfiguration" and of the pagan god Proteus, who had the power to change his shape. Similarly, in his invective against old women who used makeup to look younger, the Dominican preacher Stephen of Bourbon compared them to masked jongleurs and to two-faced images of Janus, which appeared as an old man on one side, and as a youth on the other.[31]

The second discursive context for discussions of false beggars involved the problem of deceit in the marketplace. According to moralists and chroniclers of the thirteenth century, deceit was endemic to urban commerce: craftsmen substituted cheaper materials for costly ones; bakers falsified bread; prostitutes used makeup to transform undesirable bodies and faces into desirable ones.[32]

In their attempts to gain alms under false pretenses, false beggars resembled all men and women who falsified goods in the marketplace. However, because beggars offered up their own bodies as products of charitable consumption, they shared a special affinity with prostitutes, who also placed their bodies on the market. It follows, therefore, that false beggars shared an affinity with those prostitutes who cosmetically transformed their bodies and faces into more desirable products of consumption.

According to Thomas of Chobham and Peter the Chanter, prostitutes transformed licit wages into illicit wages when they falsified their appearance with cosmetics. Thomas argued that while a prostitute's profession was sinful, she licitly earned her living with the labor of her own body, and thus she was allowed to keep her earnings. However, concerning those prostitutes who distorted their appearance with makeup, Thomas thoroughly agreed with Peter the Chanter that such women collected their payments under false pretenses, and should not be allowed to keep their

30. On the devil as the master of deception and transfiguration, see Thomas of Chobham, *Summa de arte praedicandi*, c. 8, ed. Morenzoni, pp. 203–13. On p. 205 Chobham compares the devil's deceptions to those of an ornamented prostitute.

31. Stephen of Bourbon, *Tractatus*, #274, #279, pp. 228–29, 231–32.

32. On craftsmen: Birgit van den Hoven, *Work in Ancient and Medieval Thought: Ancient Philosophers, Medieval Monks and Theologians and Their Concept of Work, Occupation, and Technology* (Amsterdam, 1996), p. 240; on bakers: "Excerpta e Memoriali Historiarum, auctore Johanne Parisiensi," *Recueil des historiens des Gaules et de la France*, ed. M. Bouquet et al., 21:663, trans. William C. Jordan, *The Great Famine: Northern Europe in the Early Fourteenth Century* (Princeton, N.J., 1996), p. 162.

earnings—"because," Thomas asserted, "then the one who hires [such a woman] believes that he has bought an appearance that is not there."[33]

Those who gave alms to false beggars were also, in a sense, buying an appearance that was not really there. Just like the man who gave money to a prostitute, the almsgiver expected an intimate favor in return: the beggar, whom the almsgiver believed to be both needy and unable to work, was supposed to say prayers for the soul of the one from whom he, or she, accepted alms.[34] If the beggar was not truly disabled, then the one giving alms was "buying" prayers, in a sense, from the wrong person.

The deceptive use of cosmetics was not necessarily gender specific. Nevertheless, bodily beauty was more intrinsic to female identity than to male. Not surprisingly, therefore, most of the medieval invective against the deceptive use of beautifying cosmetics was directed against women. There was, moreover, a special anxiety about two categories of women who used cosmetics: old women, because their efforts to look young created status confusion; and prostitutes, because their efforts to make themselves more beautiful created deception in the marketplace.

33. "Item, si meretrix inungit se et ornat se ut decipiat lascivos et mentiatur pulcritudinem suam et speciem quam non habet, quia tunc locator credit emere speciem que ibi non est, peccat meretrix nec licite potest retinere quod sic accipit," Thomas of Chobham, *Summa confessorum*, art. 5, dist. 4, quaest. 5, ed. Broomfield, p. 296. See art. 7, dist. 2, quaest. 6, c. 3, and art. 7, dist. 2, quaest. 20, ed. Broomfield, pp. 352, 403–4, for similar arguments. Chobham's argument about prostitutes being able to keep their earnings was partially based, as was that of Ivo of Chartres (d. 1115), on Justinian's Digest: *Digestum vetus seu Pandectarum Iuris civilis tomus primus* (Venice, 1584), bk. 12, tit. 5, c. 4, col. 1323; Ivo of Chartres, *Decretum*, 8:307, PL 161, col. 651. Chobham was original, however, in stressing the labor of her own body.

For Peter the Chanter's discussions of prostitutes' wages, see "Verbum abbreviatum," PL 205, col. 144; and Pierre le Chantre, *Summa de sacramentis et animae consiliis*, ed. Jean-Albert Dugauquier, 3 vols. (Louvain, 1954, 1957, 1963), 3:170–75. Peter argued (*Summa*, 3:175) that a prostitute should not restore her earnings to the customer, but neither could she licitly keep them—thus she should give them to the church; the church, however, needed to avoid scandal in accepting gifts from such persons. For Peter's discussion of prostitutes who used makeup, see: ibid., 3:172. For a similar argument, that prostitutes who used fraud or deceit had to make restitution, see Aquinas *Summa theologiae*, 2a2ae, quaest. 62, art. 5, resp. ad 2, ed. Blackfriars, 37:116–17.

By the mid-thirteenth century, arguments about prostitutes being able to keep their wages were based on the *glossa ordinaria* to Gratian's *Decretum* (which was last revised c. 1245), which drew on the Codex Justiniani: *Decretum Gratiani emendatum, et notationibus illustratum, una cum glossis Gregorii XIII. pont. max. iussu editum* (Rome, 1588), Prima pars, dist. 86, c. 8, col. 483, gloss to the word *meretricibus; Codicis Dn. Iustiniani Sacratissimi principis pp. Augusti repetitae praelectionis libri XII* (Venice, 1584), bk. 4, tit. 7, col. 733–34, "De conditione ob turpem causam" ("[The payment] given for libidinous motives cannot be demanded back, for in the equivalent motive of turpitude the better circumstance is that of the possessor"; "Datum libidinis causa, non repetitur, cum in pari causa turpitudinis, melior sit conditionis possessoris"); Raimundus de Pennaforte (Master General of the Dominican Order 1237–45; d. 1275), *Summa de iure canonico*, pars 2, tit. 10, ed. Xaverio Ochoa and Aloisio Diez, Universa bibliotheca iuris tome a (Rome, 1975), 86; John of Erfurt (Franciscan, c. 1250–1325), *Summa confessorum*, 1:6:22, ed. Norbert Brieskorn, *Die Summa confessorum des Johannes von Erfurt*, 2:589.

34. Thomas of Chobham, *Summa confessorum*, art. 5., dist. 4, quaest. 6, ed. Broomfield, p. 297.

Most of the invective against the use of cosmetic distortions by beggars was directed against men rather than women. In the rhetoric of clerical elites, male beggars with robust bodies who feigned weakness through deception assimilated themselves to old women and prostitutes, creating, with falsified bodies, both status confusion and deception in the market-place. False beggars also rendered themselves effeminate because they did not fulfill their roles as lower status males, who were expected to work with their hands. Rather, they went to great lengths to assure that, much like "women" (as elite male authors constructed them), they could re-main "soft" and inactive. They placed themselves in great moral danger, and they defrauded their "customers" by deceiving them into believing that they were doing charitable deeds for the truly disabled—and hence, at least in theory, for the deserving poor.

The need to distinguish the able bodied from the disabled poor leads us to the third strand of embodiment—the emphasis on bodily tests in order to establish the true condition of the individual. Our most explicit evidence for the testing of poor people's bodies comes from accounts of saints' miracles, and of the inquests that the church conducted in order to establish that such miracles were really taking place. In order to prove that a miracle had taken place, the churchmen who conducted such in-quests had to establish to their own satisfaction that an individual had been ill, or disabled, that that person had recovered, and that the recov-ery was the result of an appeal to the saint for help. In an effort to pre-vent fraud, the inquisitors almost always interviewed multiple witnesses to a miracle, especially if the principal witness to the miracle was poor. The inquisitors were especially cautious with poor witnesses because it was believed that they were susceptible to bribes, that they might fake ill-nesses in order to enhance their alms, or that they might fake miraculous cures in order to gain notoriety, and perhaps increase their incomes as a result.[35] We know in fact that the churchmen looking into saintly mir-acles occasionally caught people who pretended to have been cured.[36]

Given the suspicions surrounding the testimonies of the poor, it is not at all surprising that William of Canterbury, who was one of the authors of the *Miracles of Thomas Becket,* defended the testimonies of elite wit-

---

35. On the susceptibility of poor witnesses to bribes: Gratian, *Decretum,* secunda pars, causa 4, quaest. 2 et 3, c. 3, *Decretum Gratiani* (Rome, 1588), col. 910. The glossa ordinaria to the *Decretum* argued that poor people could be accepted as witnesses if they were not suspected of anything: Gra-tian, ibid., gloss to the word *locuples.* This point was repeated by John of Erfurt: *Summa confesso-rum,* 2:7:1, ed. Brieskorn, 3:1509. Aquinas acknowledged the position of the gloss, but favored that of Gratian: *Summa theologiae,* 2a2ae, quaest. 70, art. 3, ed. and trans. Blackfriars, 38:138–39.
36. Ronald C. Finucane, *Miracles and Pilgrims: Popular Beliefs in Medieval England* (New York, 1977), pp. 70–71.

nesses, even when there were no corroborating witnesses, on the basis of their social status alone. Concerning the testimony of one noble woman, for instance, he asserted:

> we have heard . . . the woman, and examined her, in the manner proper for her noble birth, and we can presume the truth of her account from her pilgrimage and devotion. For although faith is rare, because many people say many things, nevertheless, just as we conclude that beggars are liars, so we do not at all assume the same of nobles who incline themselves to divine favor by making a pilgrimage.[37]

With this context in mind, I now want to turn to the *Miracles of Saint Louis,* which provides the evidence for the third strand of my argument—that elites were more likely to subject the poor, rather than other elites, to bodily tests in order to establish their actual state, or status. Before I turn to that evidence, however, I need to describe how this source came to be.

The *Miracles of Saint Louis* is an early-fourteenth-century French text that was based on the Latin transcript of an inquest that was conducted by a panel of papally appointed clerics, whose purpose was to inquire into the sanctity of King Louis IX. Between May of 1282 and March of 1283 the archbishop of Rouen, the bishop of Auxerre, and the bishop of Spoleto interviewed around three hundred thirty witnesses to sixty-three posthumous miracles. Another panel apparently went to Parma to interview the witnesses to two additional miracles.[38] Most of the sixty-five miracles were cures that had taken place between 1271 and 1282 at Louis' tomb, which was a few miles outside of Paris, in the basilica of St.-Denis.

Unfortunately, only a fragment of the original transcript of the inquest at St.-Denis has survived.[39] However, Guillaume de Saint-Pathus, a Franciscan friar who had been the confessor of Louis' wife, and who wrote his *Life and Miracles of Saint Louis* around 1303, summarized the evidence from the inquest, and a comparison of his retellings with the surviving fragment of the inquest indicates that he remained quite faithful to

---

37. "Mulierem . . . audivimus, et sicut decuit nobilem examinavimus, et praesumere possumus de veritate relationis ex peregrinatione et devotione referentis. Nam quamvis rara fides est quia multi multa loquuntur, tamen sicut mendicos mendaces, sic nobiles qui sibi divinam propitiationem peregrinando conciliant minime conjicimus." William of Canterbury, *Miraculorum Gloriosi Martyris Thomae, Cantuariensis Archiepiscopi,* Bk. 6, #140, ed. James Craigie Robertson, *Materials for the History of Thomas Becket,* Rerum Britannicarum Medii Aevi Scriptores 67 (London, 1875), 1:524.
38. "Fragments de l'enquête faite à Saint-Denis en 1282 en vue de la canonisation de Saint Louis," ed. H.-François Delaborde, *Mémoires de la Société de l'Histoire de Paris et de l'Île de France* 23 (1896): 4; Louis Carolus-Barré, *Le procès de canonisation de Saint Louis (1272–1297): essai de reconstitution* (Rome, 1994), pp. 20–21.
39. "Fragments de l'enquête," ed. Delaborde.

the original narratives.[40] Guillaume also retained much of the information that the original transcript contained about the civil status of the beneficiaries of the miracles: their place of birth, place of current residence, occupations, and marital status. Because of this detail concerning the background of even the poorest beneficiaries—which we do not find in most canonization inquests—and because the narratives themselves are unusually rich, the *Miracles of Saint Louis* lend themselves to an analysis that takes into account differences of both gender and social status.

My analysis of "bodily inspections" focuses on the fifty-two miracles for which I can establish the social status of the beneficiary, and which were not reported as "secondary" miracles (miracles that witnesses mentioned during the inquest concerning a primary miracle).[41] Fifteen (six female, nine male) of those fifty-two miracles benefited elites (nobles, beneficed clergy, monks, and urban elites), while the other thirty-seven (twenty-two female, fifteen male) benefited poor people—the indigent and those who worked with their hands for a living.[42]

The first noteworthy difference between miracles benefiting elites and those benefiting poor people concerns the locations where the miracles took place: while thirty-five of the thirty-seven poor people received their miraculous assistance from Saint Louis at his tomb in the basilica of St.-Denis, ten of the fifteen elites were in their homes, in the homes of close relatives, at work, or in their own neighborhoods. Of the remaining five, only three had to travel to Louis' tomb in St.-Denis: the other two were cured when the royal entourage bearing Louis' body stopped in their towns in Italy, on their way back to France from Tunisia, where Louis had died.[43] Although many of the elites made post hoc pilgrimages to Louis' tomb in order to fulfill their vows to him, the ten who received help within their homes, work spaces, or neighborhoods were not subjected to the same degree of public scrutiny and physical display, dur-

---

40. Guillaume de Saint-Pathus, *Les miracles de Saint Louis,* ed. Percival B. Fay (Paris, 1913); Carolus-Barré, *Le procès,* 24.
41. I have left out the secondary miracles because many of them involved the same beneficiaries as the primary miracles, and thus they would distort the statistics.
42. Guillaume de Saint-Pathus, *Les miracles.* Elite men/boys: miracles 12, 13, 29, 38, 40, 50, 60, 61, 65. Elite women/girls: miracles 1, 3, 46, 53, 55, 64. Poor men/boys: miracles 7–9, 14, 15, 17, 18, 20, 24, 25, 28, 33, 45, 47, 48. Poor women/girls: miracles 2, 4, 5, 21, 30–32, 34–37, 39, 41–44, 49, 51, 52, 57–59. I have included among the poor a Cistercian *conversa,* two sisters at the Filles Dieu (a house for reformed prostitutes), and an affiliate at the Beguinage of Paris, since all of these women would have come from modest backgrounds.
43. Guillaume de Saint-Pathus, *Les miracles.* For a complete list of miracles involving elite and poor beneficiaries, see the previous note. Poor not at the tomb: miracles 30, 47. Elites at the tomb: miracles 3, 13, 53. Elites in Italy when Louis's relics passed through their towns: miracles 64, 65.

ing their illnesses, that the pilgrims who traveled to Louis' tomb had to endure.[44]

There are multiple reasons for the differences in the locations of the miracles benefiting elites and those benefiting the poor. First, a few of the elites had access to items of clothing that had belonged to Louis. When the prior of the Cistercian abbey of Chaalis fell ill, the sacristan of the abbey brought him a cloak that had belonged to King Louis, which the abbey kept as a relic. The prior kissed the cloak, wrapped himself in it, then slept through the night using it as a blanket. His recovery began during that night.[45] Aelis l'Aveniere, the wife of the former squire of King Louis IX, possessed several feathered hats that had belonged to the king. When her cellars flooded with waters from the Seine, she ordered one of her servants to make the sign of the cross over the waters with one of the hats. The waters then began to recede.[46] Poor people who suffered illnesses or disasters did not have this kind of privileged access to items that had belonged to the king; thus they needed to travel to his tomb in order to make physical contact with his holy powers.

A second reason for the different locations of elite and lower status miracles has to do with the quality and number of witnesses to their diseases. When elites fell ill, even for short periods of time, their houses often filled with people, such as physicians, who would later serve as distinguished and highly credible witnesses. Guillaume de Saint-Pathus mentioned that six out of the fifteen elites (40 percent) consulted physicians. By contrast, he stated that only two of the thirty-seven poor people— 5.4 percent—saw physicians. Another two consulted surgeons, but surgeons were of a much lower social status than physicians.[47] Even under normal circumstances, moreover, elites lived in large households with multiple servants. By contrast, poor people who suffered short-term illnesses—as opposed to long-term disabilities—suffered more privately, in households that were much more limited in numbers. Because their witnesses were less prestigious and less numerous, poor people were probably less confident about coming forward with stories about diseases that were

44. These "at home" miracles are indicative of the growing pattern observed by André Vauchez, of conditional vows—vows that were kept only if a saint came to the individual's assistance. However, Vauchez did not attempt a class analysis of those who were most likely to make, and be helped by, conditional vows: *La sainteté en occident aux derniers siècles du moyen âge* (Rome, 1988), pp. 521–29.
45. Guillaume de Saint-Pathus, *Les miracles,* miracle 12, p. 39.
46. Ibid., miracle 46, pp. 140–41.
47. Ibid. Elites consulting physicians: miracles 38, 40, 50, 60, 64, 65. Poor consulting physicians: miracles 7, 58. Poor consulting surgeons: miracles 21, 33.

relatively short lived and invisible, and officials were probably less willing to include poor people's accounts of such illnesses. Thus, while four of the elite beneficiaries in the *Miracles of Saint Louis* had suffered from short-term fevers, pain, or unconsciousness, not one of the poor people whose story became part of the official record had reported such an ailment.[48]

Elites were much more likely to believe the stories of poor people who had suffered disabilities for a long time—and whose sufferings had thus been observed by the community at large, including, often, the benefi-ciary's parish priest. Moreover, those poor people who traveled to the tomb of the saint submitted to the scrutiny of church authorities at the shrine, and thus the evidence of their appearance, both before and immediately after their cures, was more likely to be a part of official memory.

In the surviving fragment of the inquest into Saint Louis' miracles, for instance, Thomas Hauxton, who had been appointed by the prior of St.-Denis to watch over the infirm people at Louis' tomb, provided an eye-witness account of the dramatic cure of Amelot of Chambly, a woman who had probably been the victim of spinal tuberculosis. For three years, between 1268 and 1271, Amelot had begged in the streets of St.-Denis, moving about town with the aid of an eighteen-inch-long crutch that held her chin off the ground. Like just about everyone else in St.-Denis, Thomas of Hauxton had seen Amelot begging in her pitiful condition. Unlike most others, however, he was standing right next to her when she was cured at Louis' tomb. Thomas told the inquisitors that in 1271, not long after Louis' relics had been placed in their sepulchre at St.-Denis, Amelot visited the tomb for six consecutive days. Then, on the sixth or seventh day, after she had been lying right at Thomas' feet, Amelot stood up, and Thomas heard the bones in her back, which sounded "as if they were being broken and violently shaken." Amelot called out "Lord, Saint Louis," then she cast away her cane, and straightened herself out without any assistance. Thomas ran to get the prior, who then asked Amelot to walk, which she did—from the tomb to the main altar, and back again—without any assistance. Amelot then sat down and cried, calling out her thanks to Saint Louis.[49]

The second difference between miracles benefiting elites and those benefiting the poor concerns bodily examinations at the inquest. In his narratives concerning twelve of the thirty-seven poor people, Guillaume

48. Ibid. Wealthy suffering short-lived fevers, pains, or unconsciousness: miracles 12, 38, 40, 53.
49. "Quasi confringi et concuti videbantur"; "Domine sancte Ludovice!," "Fragment de l'en-quête," ed. Delaborde, pp. 19–20. See also Guillaume de Saint-Pathus, *Les miracles,* miracles 9 and 59 for accounts of the monks' encounters with people who were healed at the tomb.

goes to some trouble to tell us not only about the diseases that these people had suffered, and how they were cured, but also about what the clerics conducting the inquest did during their meetings with the beneficiaries of the miracles. In his discussion of a deaf-mute boy who had been cured, Guillaume described the questions that the inquisitors asked of the beneficiary, but in his narratives about the other eleven poor people (seven female, four male) he described the inquisitors' visual examinations of the beneficiaries' bodies.[50]

One of those eleven was Moriset, a youth who had had a huge oozing tumor on his leg, which forced him to use crutches and smelled so bad that his fellow residents in the public hospital of the town of Saumur did not want him to come near them. Guillaume tells us that after Moriset was cured,

[he] came before the inquisitors and their notaries, and the inquisitors and their notaries saw the place where the tumor had been, where now he had no malady or rupture. And also the traces of the scars were evident, still large and red, as is normal for newly healed and closed wounds.[51]

Guillaume provided a similar description of the inquisitors' visual examination in the case of Ralph the Cobbler, who was crippled for over a year with an oozing infection that had begun with a wound in his foot, but then spread to his knee and up his thigh. Guillaume tells us:

The inquisitors of the said miracle and their notaries saw the said Ralph healed and healthy . . . going about without crutches or any other aid . . . and they saw his right foot and the thigh and the knee and the underside of the knee, and they saw about ten traces of closed wounds of the above mentioned openings, small and large, which were now all closed up and flat.[52]

50. Guillaume de Saint-Pathus, *Les miracles.* Visual inspections of poor men/boys: miracles 7, 14, 20, 47. Visual inspections of poor women/girls: miracles 34, 35, 36, 39, 42, 51, 52. Examination of poor deaf-mute: miracle 15.

51. "Vint le dit Moriset en la presence des inquisiteurs et de leur notaires presenz, et virent les inquisiteurs et leur notaires le lieu de la dite apostume ou il n'avoit point de maladie ne de routure, ainçois aparoient les traces des plaies qui devant avoient esté en cele apostume mout lees et mout rouges, si comme c'est costume de plaie novel guerie et affermee." Ibid., miracle 14, p. 49.

52. "Les inquisiteurs du dit miracle et leur notaires virent le dit Raou gueri et sain . . . alant par soi sanz baston et sanz autre ayde . . . et . . . virent son pié destre et la cuisse et le genoil et neis sus le genoil, et virent dis traces de plaies racloses ou environ des devant diz pertuis, les unes petites et les autres granz, afermees tout a plain." Ibid., miracle 20, p. 70.

Guillaume's discussions of the bodily evidence for the cures of the poor differ strikingly from his discussions of elites. Although his narrative suggests that several of the elites appeared before the inquisitors, he gives us only one direct report of the examination that the inquisitors made of an elite—and that was a verbal examination, in which they asked a girl who had nearly drowned if she had fallen into the water, and why she had approached the water in the first place.[53] In Guillaume's accounts, none of the elites were physically examined by the inquisitors; none had to lift their garments in order to reveal scars on their knees, thighs, or anywhere else on their bodies.

Differences in the kinds of diseases that afflicted the poor and the elite, and that each group bothered to report, may go some way in explaining the inquisitors,' or Guillaume's, greater interest in inspections of the poor. After all, unlike Ralph's and Moriset's oozing tumors, the short-lived fevers, pains, and unconsciousness that four of the elite beneficiaries had endured would have left no visible marks upon their bodies.

Nevertheless, these differences do not explain Guillaume's silence about seven of the elite beneficiaries. One of those seven had had an oozing tumor, much like that of Moriset. Another five had been paralyzed or otherwise unable to use a limb or limbs—much like five of the poor people who were inspected by the inquisitors. Another had suffered from an unsightly facial swelling.[54]

A better explanation for this asymmetrical approach to the bodies of the poor lies, as I have already suggested, in the lack of trust that elites had in the verbal testimonies of the poor. Another explanation probably lies in the greater sense of decorum that elites observed in discussing the intimate details of the illnesses of elites, and in approaching their bodies. The overall effect, however, was to subject both poor men and poor women to a type of voyeurism not unlike the voyeurism in the lives of women saints, and to reinforce the idea that embodiment was more central to the identities of the poor than it was to the identities of elites.

What I have argued, then, is that poor men, as well as poor women, were very much associated with the body. Indeed, elites sometimes paid greater attention to the bodily nature and bodily shortcomings of poor men than they did to the bodily nature and bodily shortcomings of elite women. Of course, the social function of the poor, as viewed by elites,

53. Ibid., miracle 1, p. 7.
54. Ibid. Elite with oozing tumor: miracle 64. Elites who had been paralyzed or unable to use arms or legs: miracles 3, 55, 60, 63, 65. Poor who had been paralyzed or unable to use arms or legs, who were inspected by the inquisitors: miracles 34, 35, 36, 42, 52. Elite with facial swelling: miracle 29.

had a lot to do with this stress on physicality. When poor people's bodies were robust, and when they were willing to work, they—and especially their men—made an important contribution to society. When their bodies became weak or disabled those same people crossed over into the ranks of those who had the right to beg. As members of the deserving (and disabled) poor they played important roles in society by offering elites the opportunity to act charitably, and by providing saints with opportunities to perform posthumous miracles. However, in the minds of elites the poor could not be trusted, and thus they thought it important to scrutinize the bodies of the poor carefully, for the truth of their abilities and disabilities—and hence of their proper roles in society—lay in their bodies, not in their words.

In bringing together the evidence that medieval gender categories were constructed within a grid of other categories of difference I have not meant to denigrate earlier work on medieval gender constructions, to which, in fact, I remain heavily indebted. If we stop at various points along the hierarchy of social status we find, as the work of those scholars suggests, that medieval clerical authors did make statements that drew stronger associations between women and the body than between men and the body: Humbert of Romans said more about the lust of peasant women than he did about the lust of peasant men; Humbert and Jacques de Vitry said more about the lascivious behavior of servant women than about the lascivious behavior of servant men.[55]

Nevertheless, if we ignore the differences between discussions of servants and discussions of elites, or if we fail to notice that Gilbert of Tournai and Jacques de Vitry exhorted elite matrons to control the sexuality of both their male and their female servants, our analysis becomes distorted. Indeed, when we fail to incorporate other categories of difference into our analysis of gender constructions, then it is *we*, and not the authors whom we study, who end up constructing simplistic gender categories that reduce all men, or all women, to a single set of essentialized stereotypes.

55. Jacques de Vitry, "Ad servos et ancillas," ed. Longère, "Deux sermons"; Humbert of Romans, "Ad mulieres pauperes in villulis," "Ad famulas divitum," ed. Casagrande, *Prediche*, pp. 52, 50; Humbert, "De eruditione," bk. 2, tract. 1, c. 76, "Ad familiam diuitum in ciuitatibus," and bk. 2, tract. 1, c. 78, "Ad laicos in villis," ed. de la Bigne, *Maxima*, 25:493–95.

CHAPTER EIGHT

The Leper's Kiss

Catherine Peyroux

Imagine this. One day in 1206 a wealthy merchant's son was out riding on an open plain near his home town when he came upon the thing he "naturally abhorred most among the world's unhappy sights," a leper begging alms.[1] The young man had recently been visited with a vision in which he had been commanded to exchange carnal for spiritual things—"the bitter for the sweet"—and to scorn himself in order to know God.[2] Mindful of this injunction, the youth descended from his horse to give the leper both alms and a kiss. Upon remounting the steed, he looked about to find himself alone in the empty countryside, the leper mysteriously gone. Filled with wonder, he repeated his act, seeking out lepers' dwellings and, after distributing money, kissing each leper's hand and mouth.[3]

Thus did Thomas of Celano, Francis of Assisi's earliest biographer, present the crux of the saint's decisive conversion to an ascetic Christianity whose ethical imperative made continual reference to the material vulnerability of the radically poor. In this, his revised version of the saint's *Life,* Thomas asserted that contact with the leper had "changed [Francis]

Research for this project was supported by a grant from the National Endowment for the Humanities. My thanks are due first to the editors, Barbara Rosenwein and Sharon Farmer, upon whose kind help this essay made excessive demands, and to William C. Jordan, Susan Thorne, Matthew Price, and the anonymous readers of Cornell University Press.

1. "Nam inter omnia infelicia monstra mundi Franciscus leprosos naturaliter abhorrens, leprosum die quadam obvium habuit, cum iuxta Assisium equitaret," Thomas of Celano, *Vita secunda sancti Francisci Assisiensis,* 5, ed. College of Saint Bonaventure, Analecta Franciscana 10 (Quaracchi, 1927), p. 14. Translations are my own unless otherwise noted.
2. "'Francise,' inquit illi Deus in spiritu, 'pro carnaliter et vane dilectis, iam spiritualia commutato, et amara pro dulcibus sumens, contemne te ipsum, me si velis agnoscere.'" Ibid.
3. Ibid., pp. 14–15.

perfectly in heart";[4] having undertaken the bitter embrace of medieval Europe's social outcasts, Francis henceforth set his path irrevocably in step with the most wretched portion of humanity. The tale suggests that Francis's first, "carnal" response in this important encounter was the natural one, and that his horror at finding a leper was to be expected. In the logic of inversion dictated by Francis's vision, a contrary, spiritual response necessitated some acceptance of the figure before him. Thomas of Celano's narrative makes the sign of this acceptance a kiss. While Thomas does not comment on its meaning, in context the action signals at the very least the experience of intimacy and perhaps as well a performance of affection, even reverence, from the wealthy youth for the diseased vagrant. In this telling, the leper's mysterious disappearance implies a miraculous result and suggests that the leper was a divine tool who facilitated the realization of Francis's spiritual growth. The drama of the depicted moment invites curiosity about what it meant for medieval people to kiss a leper, and how readers of Thomas's account might have perceived that gesture.

By the time of Thomas's writing in the early thirteenth century, depictions of a holy person's embrace of the leprous had attained the venerable familiarity of great age. As Michel Mollat has noted, the kissing of lepers was a motif that belonged to the folklore of medieval charity.[5] The gesture had appeared in diverse stories since the end of the fourth century in contexts so various as to impede the tracing of a single path of transmission between texts. Widely distributed though it was, by no means had the image of a leper's kiss calcified into a hagiographical cliché; its telling was reworked over the centuries to yield a host of interpretations, some mutually contradictory. In telling and retelling this story hagiographers confronted, from different vantage points, the constant problem of determining what the fortunate owed to the desperate. A comparison of such representations allows us to tap a vein of social commentary that twisted its way through medieval hagiography, and so to trace changing perceptions of the poor. History as a discipline has been traditionally eager to find reliable narrators in its quest to discover the "what really happened" of the past. In pondering tales of holy men and women who kissed lepers, it is the "unreliable" narrators who hold our attention. These storytellers reveal not what certainly occurred, but what it was felt to be necessary to say when rendering the spectacular meeting between an exemplar of virtue and a figure of utterly abject misery and loss. Their

4. "Mutatus perfecte iam corde." Ibid., p. 15.
5. Michel Mollat, "Conclusions," Assistance et charité: Cahiers de Fanjeaux 13 (1978): 396.

"unreliable" narratives are both mirrors and guides to their contemporaries' perceptions about the relationship between power and poverty.

As Thomas's portrayal indicates, lepers occupied a highly charged and profoundly ambiguous position in medieval society. From the moment when a person was judged to be leprous by a recognized local authority (who might be variously a civic official, a cleric, or a physician), he or she was rhetorically, socially, and in some places juridically separated from humankind in an act that imaginatively excised the leprous from full concourse with the body of Latin Christendom. The rhetoric that supported the exclusion of such individuals from full participation in society construed their continued existence as at best a tolerable calamity and at worst a pernicious threat to the common good. Rites for the separation and claustration of lepers, laws limiting their capacity to transact business or own property, royal ordinances and ecclesiastical decrees requiring their removal from common space, as well as trial records of lepers accused of poisoning wells and so consigned to brutal deaths: all of these sources document clearly the precarious purchase the leprous had on the social continuum. Much historical investigation has explored leprosy's symbolic association with moral corruption in the minds of medieval Europeans.[6] Recent scholarly attention to the consequent violence inflicted on people who were categorized as lepers has well demonstrated the interconnections between leprosy as a personal catastrophe and the role of the diseased as subjects of the expanding purview of state and ecclesiastical power.[7]

Yet the forces that excluded lepers did not eliminate them from the daily life of medieval Europeans. Instead, the leprous underwent a change in social status by which those who were officially excised became completely and permanently dependent upon the good will and material beneficence of members of the surrounding society. In fact this beneficence often flowed forth lavishly, as extensive archival and archaeological records of institutions dedicated to the care of the leprous testify.[8] The founda-

6. Attributions of leprosy as a sign of sin and heresy in the Middle Ages are collected in Saul Brody, *The Disease of the Soul: Leprosy in Medieval Literature* (Ithaca, N.Y., 1974); Robert I. Moore, *The Origins of European Dissent* (Oxford, 1977), pp. 246–50.

7. Notable among an abundance of recent studies are Robert I. Moore, *The Formation of a Persecuting Society* (Oxford, 1987); Françoise Bériac, *Histoire des lépreux au Moyen Âge: Une société d'exclus* (Paris, 1988); Mark Pegg, "Le corps et l'autorité: La lèpre de Baudouin IV," *Annales: ÉSC* 2 (1990): 265–87; Carlo Ginzburg, *Ecstacies: Deciphering the Witches' Sabbath* (New York, 1991); Jeffrey Richards, *Sex, Dissidence, and Damnation: Minority Groups in the Middle Ages* (London, 1991); and David Nirenberg, *Communities of Violence: Persecution of Minorities in the Middle Ages* (Princeton, N.J., 1996).

8. Local and regional institutional histories of leper houses are too numerous to mention; an excellent introduction to the literature is to be found in François-Olivier Touati's *Archives de la lèpre: Atlas des léproseries entre Loire et Marne au Moyen Âge* (Paris, 1996).

tion and support of lepers' houses became a focal point of civic participation in the growing urban centers of the High Middle Ages.[9] The
quasi-religious character of such institutions, whose diseased inhabitants were mandated to lead lives regulated on the monastic model,
caused their benefactors to solicit the prayers of the leprous inmates for
the donors' souls.[10]

From at least the twelfth century, the leper hospital was a feature of
urban life: it has been estimated that "there was scarcely a little townlet
without at least one, and outside the great cities they were numerous."[11]
Contemporaries evidently perceived themselves as moving across a land-
scape thick with such communities: in his will of 1225, Louis VIII famously estimated some 2,000 lepers' houses within his kingdom, and
Matthew Paris reckoned that by 1244 there were some 19,000 in Latin
Christendom.[12] The situation of the typical lepers' hostel, nestled just
outside the walls on an important route into a town, facilitated the collection of donations from passers-by in alms-boxes attached to the side
of the building even when the leprous themselves were not out collecting face-to-face.[13] That lepers often were out and about begging is well
attested by incidental evidence in narratives like Thomas's *Life* of Francis, by the elaborate apparatus of their begging equipment (the clappers
and bells used to warn the healthy of the leper's approach), and by the
very existence of the many regulations that sought to limit their movement among the well.[14] Indeed, as Malcolm Barber has noted, "the alleged leper's plot of 1321 [in which lepers in southern France were widely
accused of poisoning wells] would not have been possible even in people's
imaginations had not the leper on the roads of France been a common

9. Indeed, Isabelle Cochelin has found that the maintenance of a leprosarium was so important to
the civic identity of the burgher class at Liège that a hospital was founded there at a time when few
lepers were there to be tended: "Bourgeoisie et léproseries de la principauté de Liège (fin XIIe–
début XIIIe siècles)," *Sources: Travaux Historiques* 13 (1988): 16.

10. Françoise Bériac describes the functional similarity of monasteries and leper-houses in "Les
fraternités de lépreux et lépreuses," in Kaspar Elm and Michel Parisse, eds., *Doppelklöster und
andere Formen der Symbiose männlicher und weiblicher Religiosen im Mittelalter* (Berlin, 1992),
pp. 203–11.

11. Michel Mollat, *Les pauvres au Moyen Âge* (Paris, 1978), p. 178.

12. These numbers were predictably exaggerated: Touati has identified some 395 certainly attested
houses flourishing between the twelfth and fourteenth centuries in the region of Northern and
Eastern France that covers a wide swath stretching from the Breton coast to Lyons, *Archives de la
lèpre*, p. 235. The figure for contemporary England seems to have been at least 270: Donald Ortner, Keith Manchester, and Frances Lee, "Metastatic Carcinoma in a Leper Skeleton from a Medieval Cemetery in Chichester, England," *International Journal of Osteoarchaeology* 1 (1991):92.

13. Piera Borradori, "Être lépreux autour de 1300," in Agostino Bagliani, Piera Borradori, and Na-
dia Pollini, eds., *Le pays de Vaud vers 1300* (Lausanne, 1992), p. 108.

14. Carole Rawcliffe, *Medicine and Society in Later Medieval England* (Stroud, Gloucestershire,
1995), pp. 16–17; Peter Richards, *The Medieval Leper and His Northern Heir* (New York, 1977),
pp. 48–61.

sight." [15] While lepers in the Middle Ages faced exclusion from full membership in society, they nonetheless remained a relentless presence in the social life of the West as participants in the sub-economies of institutionalized religious public charity and the far more dimly recorded underground of the indigent.

Throughout the Middle Ages, the leper figured doubly as an archetype of medical and material vulnerability, and both dimensions of the disease must be considered in order to put stories about embracing lepers into historical context. As a disease event, medieval leprosy presents the modern investigator with a mutable and mysterious subject of exploration. The illness is caused by a single bacillus, *mycobacterium leprae*, that produces widely varied effects among different subjects and over the course of the disease. Moreover, because the category "leprous" existed as a condition of ritual impurity in biblical texts before the disease caused by *m. leprae* became widespread in Europe, the term leprous was not used in the Middle Ages solely as the clinical description of a single medical pathology.[16] It evidently referred in biblical times to the presence of scaly dermatitis and was only transferred over the course of the early Middle Ages to signify the disease we now identify as leprosy. However, in attempting to reconstruct a medieval phenomenon, we may work from modern clinical descriptions, matching them when possible with osteopathic evidence of the disease's presence and comparing the known disease with medieval diagnoses and descriptions.

Leprosy is a chronic, infectious, degenerative disease that principally affects the skin, the peripheral nervous system, including subcutaneous nerves, and the skeleton, especially the extremities and the skull.[17] In modern clinical observation, leprosy takes a diversity of forms, depending on the immune response of the host. The incubation period varies from a matter of months to twenty or more years. In its early stage leprosy may appear as macules of discolored skin accompanied by, for example, tingling of nerves under the skin, or loss of sensation. After this point if the disease progresses it will be expressed in symptoms that sig-

---

15. Malcolm Barber, "The Order of Saint Lazarus and the Crusades," *Catholic Historical Review* 80 (1994): 456.

16. Leviticus 13.2–46 speaks of skin lesions that made the sufferer ritually impure, and that necessitated the afflicted person's separation from the community; the term was translated in the Vulgate as *lepra*.

17. My summary of the medical data is drawn from Robert G. Cochrane and T. Davey, eds., *Leprosy in Theory and Practice*, 2d ed. (Bristol, 1964); R. H. Thangaraj and S. J. Yawalkar, *Leprosy for Medical Practitioners and Paramedical Workers*, 2d ed. (Basle, 1987); and John M. Grange, *Mycobacteria and Human Disease* (London, 1988). A standard general historical overview of leprosy in Western Europe is to be found in Mirko Grmek, *Les malades à l'aube de la civilisation occidentale* (Paris, 1983).

nal varying stages of leprosy's severity. A less severe type (tuberculoid) is characterized by skin discoloration and skin lesions. If the disease progresses the affected skin becomes thoroughly anesthetized; the lesions may ulcerate, then scar. The ulceration may further progress to the more severe type of leprosy (lepromatous). Lepromatous leprosy is recognized by the presence of variously sized nodules under the skin, especially on the face at the brow, causing the so-called "facies leonina" in which the face reddens, the facial hair drops out, and the shape of the visage changes due to swelling.[18]

Thus far I have been describing the effect upon the skin. Leprosy also attacks the subject's cartilage and bones, causing the absorption into the body of the toes, digits, and nose. In advanced cases the larynx is afflicted, producing a rasping voice, and ulcerations in the mouth cavity and infections in the mucous membranes cause a foul-smelling discharge. Damage to the nervous system may paralyse the muscles, with an ensuing deformation due to chronic contraction of a claw foot or hand. Blindness, also, may result from the spread of the face-nodules and infections about the mucous membranes. Two points concern us in examining the medical profile of leprosy. First, although the early stages of the disease might be confused with other conditions, in its more severe form leprosy presented a quite distinct aspect to its medieval observers. Second, it becomes clear that above and beyond the stigma inherited from biblical injunctions to separate that which is labeled as leprous from the clean, medieval people had genuine reason to fear this disfiguring, incapacitating, and, before the age of microscopy, inexplicably transmitted illness, whose effect on the body in the final stages mimicked walking death, or life animating a rotting corpse.

Leprosy's mortality rate in medieval Europe is now uncertain and likely to remain so. Scholars have ventured estimates of infection ranging from one in two hundred persons to five percent of the European population at leprosy's peak of virulence in the late twelfth and thirteenth centuries.[19] All estimates can rest only upon extrapolated assumptions about the capacity of leprosaria, and textual sources indicate that throughout the Middle Ages an undefinable number of lepers circulated as beggars and pilgrims outside the centers of institutionalized charity. Yet, if the historian's ability to measure the prevalence of the disease is compromised by the limitations of our sources, it is overly skeptical to suggest,

18. A third form, labeled indeterminate or borderline, has the characteristics of both other types.
19. Calvin Wells offers the figure of one in two hundred in *Bones, Bodies, and Disease* (New York, 1964), p. 94. Robert Delort has suggested that 1–5 percent of the population was infected, in *La vie au Moyen Âge* (Paris, 1982), p. 53.

as some have done, that the disease itself was of negligible epidemiological force.[20] Osteoarchaeological evidence garnered from cemeteries dedicated to the use of the leprous indicates that the bulk of the inhabitants of leper hostels were indeed lepers, a fact which suggests that medieval diagnosticians were generally successful in recognizing leprosy. In one well-excavated site, seventy percent of the cemetery remains showed characteristic bone changes specific to the advanced stages of the ailment.[21] Whatever the actual mortality figures were, the epidemic as a whole followed a discernible pattern. Leprosy is a sparsely attested phenomenon in the early medieval period. In the eleventh through thirteenth centuries, however, osteoarchaeological, institutional, legal, and literary evidence piles up to indicate a substantial increase in the prevalence of infection, only to be followed by leprosy's swift disappearance from most of Europe in the later Middle Ages.[22]

The physical vulnerability of the leper overlapped a condition of material vulnerability in ways both literal and ideological. There is reason to believe that leprosy preyed with particular frequency on the poor and malnourished. Leprous skeletons excavated from the cemetery of a Scandinavian leper house displayed signs of a markedly higher rate of childhood malnutrition than did those from a comparable cemetery for the non-leprous; one inference is that the lepers were disproportionately drawn from an economically deprived sector of the population.[23] Of course, any person judged to be stricken with leprosy was prone to experience a diminishment of civil status that might range from restrictions

---

20. Pegg, "Corps," pp. 270–71; Mary Douglas, "Witchcraft and Leprosy: Two Strategies of Exclusion," *Man* 26 (1991): 724.

21. Keith Manchester, "Tuberculosis and Leprosy: Evidence for the Interaction of Disease," in Donald J. Ortner and Arthur C. Aufderheide, eds., *Human Paleopathology: Current Syntheses and Future Options* (Washington, D.C., 1991), p. 31. Further, medieval clinical diagnoses of leprosy are substantially in accord with modern descriptions (which is not to say that they describe leprosy in the terms now employed). For example, Stephen Ell has argued that the thirteenth-century medical writer Theoderic of Cervia, like most medieval physicians, was likely to encounter the leprous at an advanced stage of the disease, and that as a consequence his medical writings reflect accurate if conservative diagnostic practice, in "Three Times, Three Places, Three Authors, and One Perspective on Leprosy in Medieval and Early Modern Europe," *International Journal of Leprosy and Other Mycobacterial Diseases* 57 (1989): 825–33.

22. Charlotte Roberts and Keith Manchester, *The Archaeology of Disease,* 2d ed. (Ithaca, N.Y., 1995), pp. 146–50. Elsewhere, Keith Manchester has offered a persuasive and comprehensive explanation for leprosy's medieval trajectory, in "Tuberculosis and Leprosy," pp. 30–34; the burden of proof now rests on those who doubt the case for a substantial increase in the disease during the High Middle Ages.

23. Keith Manchester, "Leprosy: The Origin and Development of the Disease in Antiquity," in Danielle Gourevitch, ed., *Maladie et maladies: Histoire et conceptualisation* (Geneva, 1992), p. 45. Certainly in modern times the disease is concentrated and spreads most rapidly among the poor: Grange, *Mycobacteria,* p. 99.

in the capacity to dispose of property to the social death of removal to a leper house.[24] Because a formal diagnosis of leprosy forced its carriers to reside in a negative social space, lepers were by definition reliant on the benefactions of the fortunate.

In medieval European society, poverty was situationally defined as an absence of power and privilege.[25] Not surprisingly, since it was also a society where "embodiment was more central to the identities of the poor," the lepers' predicament of being perpetually at risk as trespassers on the terrain of the healthy was their signal attribute.[26] Thus the common, everyday terms for a leper referred not to the disease per se, but to conditions of poverty: *mesel* (and its variants), a vernacular translation of the pejorative diminutive *misellus*, from *miser,* wretched, afflicted; and the other common appellation, *ladre/lazar,* from Lazarus, the man who lay starving, friendless, and full of sores before the table of the wealthy man (Luke 16.19–31). Although nowhere in the Gospel is Lazarus identified specifically as leprous, from the early Middle Ages lepers were consigned to his care, as at the seventh-century leprosarium at Rome dedicated to St. Lazarus.[27] Lazarus's story dramatized the promise that diseased indigence so desperate as to result in death might yet be redeemed by God.[28] By the High Middle Ages, when the Lazarus and Dives narrative was widely depicted in ecclesiastical sculptural programs from Avila to Lincoln, leprosy's evolving association with the wretched and maculate beggar made the leper a living icon of medieval poverty.

Not surprisingly, these potent symbols of weakness were "good to think with" when hagiographers sought to articulate the power wielded

---

24. The limitations imposed on lepers' civil capacity are detailed in Jean Imbert, *Les hôpitaux en droit canonique* (Paris, 1947), pp. 183–86. This phenomenon was specific to Western Europe; research on the Near East demonstrates that there leprosy was regarded as a devastating but not dissociating ailment: Shulamith Shahar, "Des lépreux pas comme les autres: l'Ordre de Saint-Lazare dans le Royaume Latin de Jérusalem," *Revue Historique* 267 (1982): 19–41; Michael Dols, "The Leper in Medieval Islamic Society," *Speculum* 58 (1983): 891–916.

25. The multiformity and the situated quality of medieval definitions of poverty are discussed in Michel Mollat, *Les pauvres au Moyen Âge* (Paris, 1978), pp. 11–13, and Bronislaw Geremek, *Poverty: A History,* trans. Agnieszka Kolakowska (Oxford, 1994), pp. 17–22.

26. See Chapter 7, above, with quote on p. 170.

27. Grmek, *Malades à l'aube,* p. 254. Of course, Lazarus was not alone as the protector of lepers; most notably, the names of St. Julian the Hospitaller and St. Mary Magdalen were also used by founders of leprosaria to signify the sort of refuge the hospices promised.

28. The cult of Lazarus has a more than usually complex history, in that the Lazarus *plenus ulceribus* of Luke was confused, or better, conflated with St. Lazarus of Bethany, the Lazarus *amicus Christi* whom Christ raised from the dead in the Gospel of John 11.1–44. As Françoise Bériac notes, in *Histoire des lépreux,* pp. 127–28, the consolidation of the two figures into one cult associated with leprosy is not simply evidence of a careless understanding of the Gospels: both Lazaruses represent instances of God's victory over death.

by their saintly subjects. Gospel texts offered a ready model for lepers as objects of divine charity in the stories in which Jesus healed their suffering. However, no mention of a kiss appeared in those accounts, where Jesus' curative action was described using only the verb of touching, *tangere* (Mark 1.41, Matt. 8.3). The shift to a verb of kissing (*osculari*) implies a different register of interaction for the moment in which the holy person turned his or her attention to the leprous. Jean-Claude Schmitt has pointed out the way in which medieval figurations of the kiss made it a gesture that incorporated mutually respectful intimacy, a gesture that united the participants in a notional community: the "feudal" kiss of the vassal and lord, the monk's mystic vision of kissing Christ, the kiss of peace between the clergy and the faithful.[29] In the successive iterations of a saint's voluntary embrace of a leper, the narrators returned, fascinated, to explore their holy protagonists' capacity to create that brief, impossible community through a kiss.

When in the late fourth century Sulpicius Severus came to tell of the wonders of his hero-saint, Martin of Tours, his depiction of the miracle by which Martin cleansed a nameless leper of his disease was brief. "One day, passing through the city gates of Paris in the midst of a great crowd, to the horror of all he kissed the piteous face of a leper and blessed him; the man was cured instantly and appeared, his skin glowing, at church the next day to give thanks for his healing."[30] Sulpicius placed this episode late in a long inventory of healing miracles, tucking it in between Martin's interrogation of a demoniac and a notice alluding to frequent miracles worked by threads from the saint's clothing. No attention was paid to the leper's wider identity or social status; indeed, the incident drew minimal embellishment from its chronicler, for whom the noteworthy aspects of the event were limited to the miserableness of the leper's face and the horror felt by the crowd who witnessed the kiss. It was, then, a straightforward thaumaturgic act, one of many in a like series in that section of the *Life,* where the disease itself appeared only as one of very many undesirable conditions from which Martin was wont to free unhappy souls. The arresting detail in the saint's intervention, which Sulpicius marked by noting the crowd's horror, lay in Martin's having put his lips to the ravaged face of an unfortunate sufferer. For Sulpicius and

---

29. Jean-Claude Schmitt, *La raison des gestes dans l'occident médiéval* (Paris, 1990), pp. 297–98.
30. "Apud Parisios vero, dum portam civitatis illius magnis secum turbis euntibus introiret, leprosum miserabili facie horrentibus cunctis osculatus est atque benedixit. Statimque omni malo emundatus, postero die ad ecclesiam veniens nitenti cute gratias pro sanitate, quam receperat, agebat," Sulpicius Severus, *Vita sancti Martini,* 18, 3, ed. and trans. Jacques Fontaine, *Vie de Saint Martin,* 3 vols., Sources Chrétiennes 133, 134, 135 (Paris, 1967), 1:292.

his audience that act, so transgressive of prevailing values, authenticated the accompanying curative miracle and made indisputably manifest Martin's all-conquering grace.

The transgression of social values, not leprosy's holy cure, was precisely what was at stake two centuries later when Venantius Fortunatus sought to portray the marvelous humility of the saintly Radegund, the Thuringian princess who had rejected her royal marriage to found a house of nuns at Poitiers. According to Venantius's *Life of Holy Radegund,* the saint rendered hospitality to groups of lepers who came to her monastery for charity. Having provided food and drink, she went among them and embraced the women who were spotted with leprosy "and kissed even their faces, loving them with her whole soul."[31] The saint cared for their sores and as the lepers left she bestowed gifts upon them. When a servant scolded the holy woman for her intimacy with the diseased, asking Radegund who would kiss her when she had embraced lepers, she "replied kindly, 'Truly, if you will not kiss me, it is no care of mine.'"[32] Venantius made no mention of a cure in this context, though he was at pains to claim healing miracles for Radegund in other parts of the *Life*. Rather, the miracle worth the telling lay in the fact that the noble Radegund was able to abase herself so thoroughly that she could kiss and take leprous beggars in her arms and not count the consequences of others' rejection of her. It was a feat worthy of wonder: Venantius invites his readers to shudder with him at her actions.[33]

These two *Lives* represent two very different models for thinking about intimate contact with lepers. In Martin's case, the saint acted as a triumphant thaumaturgic healer for whom even the leper's kiss held no peril. Radegund's *Life* presented a paradigm of humility in which the holy woman's close communion with the leprous had no therapeutic effect on the ill, but rather served as part of the saint's dual program of tireless self-mortification and charity to the poor. Later references to Martin's healing kiss indicate that his model was the better known in the

---

31. "Cum leprosi venientes signo facto se proderent, iubebat adminiculae, ut unde vel quanti essent pia cura requireret. Qua sibi renuntiante, parata mensa, missorium, cocleares, cultellos, cannas, potum et calices scola subsequente intromittebatur furtim, quo se nemo perciperet. Ipsa tamen mulieres variis leprae maculis conprehendens in amplexu, osculabatur et vultum toto diligens animo." Venantius Fortunatus, *Vita sanctae Radegundis,* 19, ed. Bruno Krusch, MGH AA 4, 2:43.

32. "Deinde posita mensa ferens aquam calidam, facies lavabat, manus, ungues et ulcera et rursus administrabat ipsa pascens per singula. Recedentibus praebebat auri vel vestimenti vix una teste munuscula. Ministra tamen praesumebat et blandimentis sic appellare: Sanctissima domina, quis te osculetur quae sic leprosos amplecteris? Illa respondit benivole: Vere si me non osculeris, hinc mihi cura nec ulla est." Ibid.

33. "Hanc quoque rem intremescendam qua peragebat dulcedine." Ibid.

Middle Ages, as might be expected in the case of so prominent a *Life*. Gregory of Tours suggested that the legend of Martin's kiss had an enduring reputation among the people of Paris, where two centuries after the saint's death a monument marking his miraculous gesture stood at the city gates.[34]

Its career was longer still in medieval texts. Venantius Fortunatus and Alcuin both retained it in their respective reworkings of the *Life* of Martin, as did Bernard of Clairvaux in the sermon he wrote for Martin's feast day.[35] So common a cliché of sanctity had Martin's tale become by the twelfth century that Gerald of Wales placed an ironic reference to Martin's healing kiss in the mouth of Saint Hugh of Lincoln. When Hugh was teased on his inability to cure lepers by kissing them, Hugh replied that "Martin, by kissing the leper, cured him in body, but the leper with a kiss has healed me in soul."[36] It seems likely that Martin's thaumaturgic model had greater cultural salience during the early Middle Ages, when leprosy was closely associated with heresy and sin as an affliction that carried no redeeming qualities for the sufferer.[37] However, when in later centuries writers such as Gerald came to tell about a saintly person who met the leprous in a kiss, they revised the earlier narrative by elaborating the possibilities for redemptive, even theophanic elements in such encounters. Exploring the sanctity to be found in debasement, hagiogra-

34. Gregory tells of an oratory of Martin constructed some time previously: "eo quod ibi lepram maculosi hominis osculo depulisset." Gregory of Tours, *Decem libri historiarum,* 8.33, ed. Bruno Krusch and Wilhelm Levison, MGH SSrerMerov 1:349.

35. Venantius Fortunatus, *Vita sancti Martini,* lib. 1, ed. Frederick Leo, MGH AA 4, 1:312; Alcuin, *Opusculum primum scriptum de vita sancti Martini Turonensis,* 7, PL 101, col. 661; Bernard of Clairvaux, "Sermo in festo sancti Martini," *Bernardi opera,* ed. Jean Leclercq and Henri M. Rochais (Rome, 1968), 5:407.

36. "Testatus est autem magister Willelmus, quem prefatus pontifex in ecclesia sua Lincolniensi canonicum instituit et cancellarium, quod in villa Newerc quemdam leprosum osculatus est episcopus sanctus Hugo, et ne magnum quid se in hoc egisse reputaret episcopus, immo pocius defectum suum in hoc attenderet, quod leprosum deosculando non curaret, dixit ei predictus Willelmus, familiaris eius admodum et dilectus, 'Martinus osculo leprosum mundavit.' Et respondit episcopus, dicti causam intelligens, 'Martinus osculando leprosum curavit eum in corpore. Leprosus autem osculo sanavit me in anima.'" Gerald of Wales, *Life of Saint Hugh of Avalon, Bishop of Lincoln,* 8, ed. and trans. Richard M. Loomis (New York and London, 1985), pp. 30–31; translation of Loomis.

37. Jean-Paul Rassinier has concluded that leprosy had only two functions in the writings of Augustine: either as a physical disease whose cure testified to Christ's redemptive power or as a metaphorical disease that signaled doctrinal error and thus sin. "Miracles et pathologie dans l'oeuvre de saint Augustin," in Bernard Ribémont, *Le corps et ses énigmes au Moyen Âge* (Caen, 1993), p. 148. Geneviève Pichon has compiled a useful survey of the relatively infrequent early medieval references to lepers, from which it becomes clear that with few exceptions the Augustinian understanding of leprosy prevailed in the early Middle Ages; "Essai sur la lèpre du Haut Moyen Âge," *Le Moyen Âge* 3–4 (1984): 331–56.

phers clothed their subjects in the humility of Radegund, rather than in the triumphant thaumaturgy of Martin.

Writing in the twelfth century about the memorable charity of Matilda, the wife of King Henry I of England, Aelred of Rievaulx made use of a story that he claimed to have heard from the mouth of the queen's own brother, King David of Scotland. During his youth at the royal court, David had been called one night by the queen to her own bedchamber, where he found her washing the feet of lepers, and even kissing them.[38] The prince chided his sister, asking her, "My lady, what are you doing? Surely if the king knew of this, your mouth, soiled with the putrefaction of the lepers' feet, would never be worthy to kiss his lips." But Matilda replied, smiling, "Who does not know that the feet of the Eternal King are to be preferred to the lips of a king who must die?"[39] This anecdote seems to have been drawn from Venantius's story of Radegund, another queen who preferred the kiss of lepers to that of a mortal monarch. Yet in a nice rhetorical operation Aelred has effectively raised the stakes of the gesture: by making Christ and the leprous interchangeable, and suggesting that they shared a status above that of kings, the further implication of the tale is that in kissing the leper, one joined in union with God.

Moreover, as hagiographers in the High Middle Ages revalued the effect worked on the soul by the leper's kiss, their descriptions of leprosy's horrific attack upon the body grew more explicit. Gerald of Wales amplified his description of Hugh of Lincoln's holy serenity by recounting the bishop's willingness to kiss even those sufferers severely mutilated by the advanced stages of the disease, whose details he dwelt upon. Hugh was solicitous in visiting lepers ". . . and at his departure he kissed them one by one. No deformity of leprosy, where there was no shape of mouth or lips, but only the teeth projecting outward, could frighten him away from them. Through the great humility of his devotion and the warmth of his

---

38. "Cum, inquit [David], adolescens in curia regia servirem, nocte quadam in hospitio meo cum sociis meis nescio quid agens, ad thalamum reginae ab ipsa vocatus accessi. Et ecce domus plena leprosis et regina in medio stans, depositoque pallio cum se linteo praecinxisset, posita in pelvi aqua coepit lavare pedes eorum et extergere, extersosque utrisque constringere manibus et devotissime osculari." Aelred of Rievaulx, *Genealogia regum anglorum*, PL 195, col. 736. It is striking that in all of these tales, only the women are cast as vulnerable to social rejection due to having "soiled" their lips by kissing lepers. The whole anecdote is repeated in a slightly abbreviated form by Matthew Paris in his *Chronica majora*, ed. Henry R. Luard, Rolls Series 57 (London, 1874), 2:130.

39. "'Quid agis,' inquam, 'O domina mea? Certe si rex sciret ista, nunquam os tuum leprosorum pedum tabe pollutum suis dignaretur labiis osculari.' Tunc ipsa, subridens, 'Pedes,' ait, 'Regis aeterni quis nesciat labiis regis morituri esse praeferendos?'" Aelred of Rievaulx, *Genealogia*, col. 736.

charity, he had no horror of imprinting a kiss on a form more monstrous than human."[40] But, of course, these "monstrous" forms were simultaneously identified as sources of salvation: recall Hugh's insistence that "the leper with a kiss has healed me in soul."[41]

Perhaps the most elaborately imagined account of the sense-experience of placing one's mouth on leprosy's wounds appeared in the *Dialogus Miraculorum*, a compendium of instructive tales written by Caesarius of Heisterbach in the early thirteenth century. Caesarius spun a fable about a nameless bishop whose deep spirituality was expressed by his habitual generosity to lepers begging by the wayside, upon whom he pressed both money and the kiss of peace.[42] One day when out riding he was accosted by a leper who called upon him for pity. The bishop offered him money, but the leper, who was "a sight so horrible, and so gnawed away as if by leprosy, that no human eye could observe him without being tortured," refused it.[43] Not money, but physical care, was the leper's object, and "pointing to a little piece of flesh hanging from his nose, very horrifying and of a great stench," he requested that the bishop "wipe away the putrefaction of his disease."[44] The bishop, "fired by the love of Christ," put out his hand, but the leper refused that also, finding it too rough, and refused in turn the touch of the bishop's fine linen shirt, saying that only the feel of the bishop's tongue could be soft enough for him to endure.[45] Aided by God's grace, the bishop applied his tongue to the leper's diseased face,

---

40. "Ad hec etiam devotissimus erat et frequentissimus in visitando infirmos, et maxime leprosos . . . ipsosque in discessu suo per ordinem osculando, a quo nulla eum lepre deformitas, ubi nec etiam oris seu labiorum forma apparuit ulla, sed tantum dentes extabant et prominebant, absterreri valebat, nec rei monstruose magis quam forme humane osculum inprimere ob nimiam devocionis humilitatem et caritatis ardorem abhorrebat." Gerald of Wales, *Life of Saint Hugh*, 8, pp. 30–31; translation of Loomis.

41. Gerald of Wales, *Life of Saint Hugh*, 8, p. 31; translation of Loomis.

42. "Hic tantae fuit pietatis, misericordiae ac humilitatis, ut equitans in via neminem leprosorum sibi occurrentium sine eleemosyna praeteriret. Saepe etiam de equo descendit, et petentes praeveniens, nummis manibus illorum tanquam Christi gazophilacio immissis, atque deosculatis, iterum ascendit et processit." Caesarius of Heisterbach, *Dialogus miraculorum*, 8, 37, in *Caesarii Heisterbacensis Monachi Ordinis Cisterciensis Dialogus miraculorum*, ed. Joseph Strange, 2 vols. (Cologne, 1851), 2:106.

43. "Erat enim aspectus eius tam horridus, et quasi a lepra tam corrosus, ut oculus humanus non sine cruciatu illum inspicere posset." Ibid.

44. "Ad quem leprosus: Non sunt mihi necessarii nummi tui. Cui Episcopus responderet: Quid ergo vis ut faciam tibi? ille subiunxit: Ut putredinem huius infirmitatis meae abstergas, digito ostendens carunculam de naribus pendentem, magni horroris atque foetoris." Ibid.

45. "Quam cum vir beatus Christi amore succensus, manu tergeret, clamavit ille dicens: Cessa, cessa, asperitatem digitorum tuorum tolerare non valeo. Cumque adhiberet partem camisiae suae quae de panno fuerat, satis subtili, simili clamore prohibitus est. Tunc Episcopus: Si pati non potes manum, si non pannum delicatum, unde vis ut abstergatur? Respondit leprosus: Nihil aliud patiar praeter linctionem linguae tuae." Ibid.

and miraculously received a precious gem from the nostrils of him who had seemed to be a leper but who was now revealed to be Christ, ascending to heaven in glory.[46]

To read these twelfth- and thirteenth-century texts next to their fourth- and sixth-century counterparts is to witness the effect of a spiritual revolution. Instead of relating a wonder-working saint's potent cure, the high medieval variants of the story emphasized the holy humility of the saint and depicted the embrace of a leper as an occasion for self-immolation. The moral of Radegund's story, not Martin's, prevailed, even when Martin's miracle was quoted (as in the case of Hugh of Lincoln). In effect, the relationship between the saint and the leper was being fundamentally reimagined. The two early medieval narratives had frankly celebrated the power of their respective saints and figured the leprous as the passive, debased recipients of the saints' attention. This vision of the holy person's relationship to leprosy generated the simple plot of Sulpicius's brief miracle-tale; it also governed Venantius's description of Radegund, whose self-abnegation was celebrated, not the involuntary lowliness of the diseased.

In contrast, Aelred, Gerald, and Caesarius uniformly inverted the register of sanctity by narrating encounters with the leprous as a saint's experience of the greater sanctity conferred by leprosy's suffering. Each hagiographer more or less explicitly presented the leper as a veiled Christ, with whom the union of a kiss conveyed honor and salvation. For Christian readers, Jerome's *Vulgate* translation of the book of Isaiah had always marked an affinity between Christ and the leprous, but early medieval exegetes had been hard pressed to reconcile the vision of a triumphant God whose body was exalted above the angels with the affliction of leprosy, that most abject of fleshly conditions.[47] In the wake of the twelfth century's deepened interest in the humanity of God and attention to the body as a site of spiritual identity, writers in the High Middle Ages were increasingly primed to see the humble and the vulnerable as Christ, and so to make leprosy a comprehensible catastrophe by balancing it, in an emerging moral economy of misery, with theophany, the revealed splendor of the divine. High medieval tales of the leper's kiss taught that contact with leprosy's suffering might be meaningful

---

46. "Sed gratia Dei cooperante. . . lingua apposuit, et promuscidem elefantinam linxit. Mira res. Mox de naribus eius qui leprosus videbatur, gemma pretiosissima lapsa est in os Episcopi. Et ut ostenderet se esse Christum. . . in oculis eius gloriose coelos ascendit," ibid.

47. The text of Isaiah 53.4 had predicted that the messiah would be perceived "quasi leprosum et percussum a Deo et humiliatum." According to Geneviève Pichon, the early medieval exegetical tradition put heavy weight on the "quasi." Pichon, "Essai sur la lèpre," pp. 354–56.

and indeed salvific for the fortunate. In Aelred's reference to the putre-faction leprosy left upon Matilda's lips by the feet of lepers whom the queen identified with God's eternal sovereignty, in Gerald's description of leprosy's capacity to eat away the face while simultaneously healing Hugh's soul, or in Caesarius's extended meditation on the stinking vul-nerability of leprosy and the loathing it inspired in a bishop who subse-quently recognized his Lord ascending triumphant from the leper's place, these narratives insistently yoked leprosy's gritty physicality to a sublime Christ.

We have seen that Thomas of Celano shared the contemporary interest in exploring a redemption associated with intimate contact with lepers. His portrait of Francis of Assisi's liberation from bitter carnality turned on Francis's embrace of a leper. The gesture appeared in both of Thomas's attempts to write Francis's life story, although the saint himself remem-bered the occasion otherwise. Francis did claim that God had shepherded him among lepers in the saint's own description of the cause of his doing penance, as he called it. But no mention of a kiss appeared in Francis's recollection of the juncture that "changed that which had seemed bitter into sweetness of the soul and body." [48] Perhaps Thomas recorded an oth-erwise lost tradition about Francis's having kissed a leper, or perhaps he borrowed from the "folklore of charity" to articulate his understanding of the saint's experience of a spiritual conversion.

Thomas's own perception of the meaning of that experience changed in the telling. In his first *Life* of the saint, written between 1228 and May of 1230, his account quoted and built directly upon that of Francis. He embellished the saint's own words about having been led by God among the leprous by adding details about Francis's ministry to lepers that emphasized the foulness and corruption of the disease, and by ap-pending Francis's own account of having once so loathed the sight of lep-ers that seeing a leprosarium two miles away would cause him to hold his nostrils. [49] And then one day, as Thomas recounted it, by God's grace prompted to thoughts of holy things, Francis met a leper and, having been

---

48. "Id quod videbatur mihi amarum, conversum fuit mihi in dulcedinem animi et corporis." Saint Francis, "Testament," cited in Francisco M. R. Garcia, *"Videre Leprosos": Contenido y signifi-cado de la experiencia de Francisco de Asís entre los leprosos, según sus escritos,* Theses ad Lauream 302 (Rome, 1989), p. 26.

49. "Diligentissime serviens omnibus propter Deum, et lavans putredinem omnem ab eis, ulce-rum etiam saniem extergebat, sicut ipse in Testamento suo loquitur;" "aliquando [before his spiri-tual conversion] amara ei leprosorum visio exsistebat ut. . . per duo fere milliaria eminus ipsorum domos repiceret, nares suas proprias manibus obtuaret." Thomas of Celano, *Vita prima sancti Francisci Assisiensis,* 1, 7, ed. College of Saint Bonaventure, Analecta Franciscana 10 (Quaracchi, 1926), p. 20.

made stronger than himself, he kissed him.[50] Thomas made no comparison between the leper and Christ in this rendition. If anything, this account recalls the *Lives* of Martin and Radegund in framing the kiss as an act of the holy man's superhuman fortitude upon a passive subject whose suffering functioned in the narrative as the occasion for a display of the saint's prowess.

Some sixteen years later, Thomas was commanded to write a further, expanded version of his biography of Francis. In it he reinterpreted Francis's embrace of the leper in two important ways. As we have seen, in this second *Life* the mysterious disappearance of the leper hinted that the diseased beggar was in fact an agent of the divine or perhaps Christ himself. On that reading, the kiss now marked Francis's embrace of Christ in the semblance of a leprous beggar and further authorized his ministry to the lowly.[51] Simultaneously, however, Thomas restructured the context in which that kiss could be read. Leprosy's violence on the body, which had been plainly and even sensationally represented in contemporary portrayals of the gesture because it was an integral proof of sanctity's manifestation, was now referred to merely as a source of "no little disgust and horror."[52] Instead, Francis's own bodily suffering superseded leprosy's misery in Thomas's narration. The next chapter of the *Life* both signaled the effect of Francis's encounter with the leper and directed the reader's attention to a more meaningful suffering still: the saint who had been "changed perfectly in heart" by his embrace of the leper was "shortly to be changed in body" by his reception of the marks of Christ's crucifixion in a miracle that Thomas insisted to have been "unheard of" in his time.[53] Kneeling before the cross, Francis was "imprinted on his heart" with the signs of Christ's passion; only "a little while later, the love of [Francis's] heart became apparent in the wounds of his body."[54] For Thomas, Francis scarcely needed to meet Christ in the leper; performing as he did a

---

50. "Cum iam gratia et virtute Altissimi sancta et utilia inciperet cogitare . . . leprosum unum obvium habuit die quadam, et semetipso fortior effectus accessit, et osculatus est eum." Ibid., p. 21.
51. Francisco Garcia notes that this reading is, on a literal plane, nowhere in the writings of Francis and scarcely to be found in the biographies, yet it nonetheless informed Franciscan spirituality and christology. Certainly Bonaventure followed it; when he came to compose his own *Life* of Francis less than a generation after Thomas he inserted into this story a quotation from the verse of Isaiah that, in a high medieval Christian reading, refers to Christ as having been esteemed a leper. Garcia, "*Videre Leprosos*," pp. 149, 413.
52. "Taedium non parvum . . . et horrorem." Thomas of Celano, *Vita secunda sancti Francisci Assisiensis*, 5, p. 14.
53. "Mutatus perfecte iam corde, in brevi mutandus et corpore." Ibid., p. 15.
54. "Infigitur ex tunc sanctae animae Crucifixi compassio, et ut pie putari potest, corde eius, licet nondum carni, venerandae stigmata passionis altius imprimuntur. . . . Patuit paulo post amor cordis per vulnera corporis." Ibid., p. 16. In Thomas's first *Life* that "little while" had been eighteen years.

perfect bodily *imitatio Christi*, he met Christ in himself. Lepers, though basic to the course of the narrative, thenceforth simply fade from view. Thomas's was not to be the canonical *Life*, but his focus on the primacy of Francis's bodily suffering in crucifixion persisted in Bonaventure's subsequent authorized version.

In a work singularly alive to the paradoxical legacy left by the flowering of the mendicant orders, Lester Little examined the ironic process by which Franciscans and Dominicans adapted models of voluntary religious poverty to create a new moral order that justified commercial profit.[55] They did so by embracing and emulating the suffering intrinsic to the conditions of involuntary indigence that had themselves been produced by evolving urban economies. So successful were these new movements in soothing the anxieties of the pioneers of the emerging profit economy that within a generation after his death the mendicant Francis, he who had abhorred the very touch of money, could be appropriated as the patron saint of merchants.[56]

The powerful lesson of Little's work is that these developments were the unintended consequences of efforts to realize an authentic Christian spirituality in the transformative conditions of an evolving money economy. This was especially the case for the Franciscans. In seeking to minister to the expanding urban elites, these new avatars of religious poverty domesticated the early, wild identification with the radically poor that had fueled Francis's religious vision. In representing Francis's embrace of the leprous, Thomas of Celano likewise rhetorically domesticated and contained the problem of right action toward the irremediably needy. Thomas's narrative redirected attention away from the agony of the many to valorize the singular and voluntary suffering of Francis. Paradoxically, and assuredly not by design, in the act of seeking to represent the power of Francis's spiritual ideal his first biographer effectively came to displace the experience of those forlorn and desperate bodies who had inspired it.

---

55. Lester K. Little, *Religious Poverty and the Profit Economy in Medieval Europe* (Ithaca, N.Y., 1973).
56. Ibid., pp. 216–17.

The Colonization of Sacred Architecture: The Virgin Mary, Mosques, and Temples in Medieval Spain and Early Sixteenth-Century Mexico

Amy G. Remensnyder

When Cortés and his soldiers arrived in the Mexican peninsula, they came face to face not only with people of alien religious beliefs but also with places of religious worship that impressed the Spanish as profane houses of demon-devotion and idolatry. The narratives of the Spanish conquest insist on how Cortés attempted to persuade the native peoples to renounce the worship of "demons" in favor of Christianity. But such efforts would be in vain if they did not also include the temples where the "idols" were venerated. Accordingly, the chronicles of the conquest underline how Cortés and his followers claimed these structures for Christianity.[1] After the conquest, the emphasis on the conversion of space as well as of people continued in the form of the establishment of churches on the sites of razed temples.[2]

For their generous comments on various versions of this essay, I thank Anne-Marie Boucher, Pascal Buresi, Carolyn Dean, Sharon Farmer, Kenneth Mills, Barbara Rosenwein, Laura Smoller, the members and faculty of the School of Historical Studies at the Institute for Advanced Study (especially Benjamin Kedar, Sabine MacCormack, and Jorge Cañizares Esguerra) in 1997–98, and the members of the Program in Latin American Studies Workshop at Princeton University.

1. A few examples among many include the temple at Cozumel, the temples at Cempoala, the main temple at Tenochtitlan, and the temple at Tlascala: Bernal Díaz del Castillo, *Historia verdadera de la conquista de la Nueva España*, chaps. 27–28, 77, 92, 107, ed. Miguel León-Portilla, 2 vols. (Madrid, 1984), 1:132–33, 1:271, 1:336, 1:388–89; Petrus Martyr de Angliera, *De orbe novo decades* (Acalá de Henares, 1530; rpt. Rome, 1988), Dec. 4.6, fol. 59v; Francisco Cervantes de Salazar, *Crónica de la Nueva España*, 2.30, 3.24, 4.30, 4.31, ed. Juan Miralles Ostos (Mexico City, 1985), pp. 122, 186, 342, 345.

2. For example, see John McAndrew, *The Open-Air Churches of Sixteenth-Century Mexico: Atrios, Posas, Open Chapels and Other Studies* (Cambridge, Mass., 1965), pp. 185–86; Luis Weckmann, *The Medieval Heritage of Mexico*, trans. Frances López-Morillas (New York, 1992), pp. 186–87. For similar examples from Peru, see Valerie Fraser, *The Architecture of Conquest: Building in the Viceroyalty of Peru, 1535–1635* (Cambridge, 1990), pp. 65–68. I thank Kenneth Mills for this reference.

The actions of these men who attempted to claim Mexico's sacred land-scape for their god had a long and very immediate history in Spain itself. Ever since 711, Christians in the Iberian peninsula had lived in contact and confrontation with members of another religious culture: the Muslims. During the Christian "Reconquest" of the Iberian peninsula, which began in the eleventh century and ended with the fall of the last Muslim stronghold in 1492—a process that was well within the living memory of many of the conquistadores—at stake was the conquest not just of territory, but also of sacred space. Just as Muslims had transformed churches into mosques during their conquest of the Iberian peninsula in the eighth century, so too in the eleventh through the fifteenth centuries triumphant Christian warriors appropriated mosques and made them into churches.[3] Not all mosques of a conquered Muslim community, however, were transformed into churches. Typically the Christian conquerors converted the main or Friday mosque (the *jami'*) into a church or cathedral and seized some of the well-located secondary mosques to use as parish churches.[4] If Muslims retook a city, the mosques that had been made into churches might then be returned to their original status.[5]

3. For an excellent consideration of the political and social significance of the conversion of mosques to churches and vice versa, see Pascal Buresi, "Les conversions d'églises et de mosquées en Espagne aux XIᵉ–XIIIᵉ siècles," in *Ville et religion: Mélanges offerts à Jean-Louis Biget par ses élèves* (forthcoming). For art historical and symbolic aspects of this process, see Julie Harris, "Mosque to Church Conversions in the Reconquest," *Medieval Encounters* 3 (1997): 158–72. For a survey of mosques converted to churches in the eleventh and twelfth centuries, see José Orlandis, "Un problema eclesiástico de la Reconquista española: La conversión de mezquitas en iglesias cristianas," in *Mélanges offerts à Jean Dauvillier* (Toulouse, 1970), pp. 595–604.
4. Harris argues that Christians focused on the Friday mosques because they were aware of the importance of these buildings to Muslim communities: "Mosque to Church Conversions," p. 160. On the *jami'* type of mosque, see Robert Hillenbrand, *Islamic Architecture: Form, Function and Meaning* (New York, 1994), p. 44.
Instances of the conversion of the Friday mosques and more important secondary mosques into churches include the Cid's conquest of Valencia in 1095/96, the thirteenth-century Crusader kingdom of Valencia, and thirteenth-century Seville. See Ramón Menéndez Pidal, *La España del Cid*, 7th ed., 2 vols. (Madrid, 1969), 2:809; Robert Ignatius Burns, *Islam under the Crusaders: Colonial Survival in the Kingdom of Valencia* (Princeton, N.J., 1973), pp. 202–3; and Rafael Cómez Ramos, *Arquitectura alfonsí* (Seville, 1974), pp. 27–28. Lesser and private mosques were retained by Muslims and continued to serve as mosques: Burns, *Islam under the Crusaders*, pp. 191–92, 205; Cómez Ramos, *Arquitectura*, pp. 27–28. The Christian conquerors could also convert these secondary mosques to secular uses: Robert Ignatius Burns, *The Crusader Kingdom of Valencia: Reconstruction on a Thirteenth-Century Frontier*, 2 vols. (Cambridge, Mass., 1967), 1:138–42; Cómez Ramos, *Arquitectura*, pp. 27–28.
5. When the Almoravids retook Talavera in 1109, they returned a mosque which the Christians had apparently used as a church to its original function: 'Ibn 'Idari, *Al-Bayan al-Mugrib: Nuevos fragmentos almorávides y almohades*, trans. Ambrosio Huici Miranda, Textos Medievales 8 (Valencia, 1963), p. 123. When Alfonso VII took Córdoba in the 1140s, he celebrated mass in the mosque, thus implicitly making it a church. See the thirteenth-century chronicle composed by the archbishop of Toledo, Rodrigo Jiménez de Rada, *Historia de rebus sive historia gothica*, 7.8, ed. Juan Fernández Valverde, CCCM 72.1 (Turnhout, 1987), p. 229. Alfonso held the city only briefly and the mosque became again a place of Islamic worship.

The appropriation and conversion of sacred space is of course a phenomenon hardly unique to Spanish soldiers and missionaries during religious confrontation on both sides of the Atlantic.[6] Even in our postmodern world in which the very concept of place as a space charged with meaning has been challenged by what Marc Augé calls the "non-place of supermodernity," attempts by members of one religious group to convert religious sites belonging to rival religions persist.[7] The continuing contest between Arabs and Jews over Jerusalem, and the destruction in 1992 by Hindus of the Babri mosque in Ayodhya, India are only two such examples.[8] Religious sites are the quintessence of place, if place (to borrow Augé's definition) is a locus of identity, relations, and history.[9] The charged nature of such places is heightened in colonial contexts, for colonialism itself involves the disposition of significant space by the colonizer.[10] Very often, as historians have pointed out, such colonization of place involves its restructuring through architectural forms imposed by the colonizer.[11]

But during the colonial context of the Reconquest, the Spanish developed a strategy of actually incorporating the sacred architecture of the defeated Muslims into Christianity, just as they elaborated methods for converting Muslims themselves. It is this colonization of sacred architecture, rather than architecture which was itself colonizing, that I want to explore here. While my focus is medieval Spain, I also consider the colonial situation of early sixteenth-century Mexico. As historians such as Mercedes García-Arenal and Antonio Garrido Aranda have argued, the Spanish exported the evangelizing tactics developed in Iberia to their new colonial enterprise on the other side of the Atlantic.[12] Here I extend this

---

6. The locus classicus in the medieval world for the conversion of religious space that so often accompanied the conversion of people is Gregory the Great's letter to Abbot Mellitus about the conversion of the Anglo-Saxons: Gregory the Great, *Epistolae*, 11.76, PL 77, col. 1215–17.
7. On the concept of "non-place," see Marc Augé, *Non-Places: Introduction to an Anthropology of Supermodernity,* trans. John Howe (London, 1995).
8. On Jerusalem, see Roger Friedland and Richard Hecht, *To Rule Jerusalem* (Cambridge, 1996).
9. For this definition of place, see Augé, *Non-Places,* pp. 42–74. Increasing scholarly attention is being paid to place as a locus of such meanings. See, for example, the articles collected in *The Geography of Identity,* ed. Patricia Yaeger (Ann Arbor, 1996); and in *Place/Culture/Representation,* ed. James Duncan and David Ley (London, 1993).
10. For a very illuminating discussion of the importance of place in colonial contexts, see Susan Slyomovics, *The Object of Memory: Arab and Jew Narrate the Palestinian Village* (Philadelphia, 1998).
11. For example, see: Mia Fuller, "Building Power: Italy's Colonial Architecture and Urbanism, 1923–1940," *Cultural Anthropology* 3 (1988): 455–87; Fraser, *The Architecture of Conquest;* Timothy Mitchell, *Colonising Egypt* (Cambridge, 1988), pp. 44–59.
12. Mercedes García-Arenal, "Moriscos e indios: Para un estudio comparado de métodos de conquista y evangelización," *Chronica Nova* 20 (1992): 153–75; Antonio Garrido Aranda, *Moriscos e Indios: Precedentes hispánicos de la evangelización en México* (Mexico, 1980).

insight to include the conversion of non-Christian space as well as non-Christian peoples. For the method first employed by the Spanish to transform Mexican temples into churches was profoundly influenced by the semiotically complex strategy used to claim mosques for Christianity during the Reconquest.[13]

This was a strategy which in at least its initial stages involved a largely symbolic conversion of Muslim sacred space: Christians often left the Islamic structures architecturally intact for decades, if not centuries, while using them as churches.[14] The main mosque at Toledo, for example, converted to Christian use immediately after Alfonso VI's conquest of the city in 1085, retained its Islamic form for approximately 150 years. Not until the first half of the thirteenth century did the Christians replace it with the present Gothic monstrosity.[15] The great Friday mosque at Córdoba was proclaimed a Christian church in 1236 but its new proprietors hardly altered it until the construction in the sixteenth century of a Gothic cathedral in the midst of its graceful arches.[16] There are so many examples of this pattern that James I of Aragon's attitude toward the main mosque of Valencia, consecrated for Christian use when he conquered the city in 1238, stands out as atypical. For very soon after his victory, James decided to replace the converted mosque with a Gothic cathedral built on the same site. Work began on the project in 1262.[17]

13. Europeans' methods for taking possession of secular space in the New World were also profoundly conditioned by the strategies they had developed in the Old World. See Patricia Seed, *Ceremonies of Possession in Europe's Conquest of the New World, 1492–1640* (Cambridge, 1995).

14. For two different explanations for the timing of the eventual replacement of converted mosques by Christian-built structures, see Buresi, "Les conversions," and Harris, "Mosque to Church Conversions."

15. For Christian accounts of the conversion of the mosque into a church, see Alfonso VI's privilege of 1086 in *Privilegios reales y viejos documentos de Toledo* (Madrid, 1963), Document I, pp. 2–3; and Jiménez de Rada, *Historia de rebus,* 6.24–25, 7.4, pp. 205–208, 225. See the excellent discussion of the political and cultural ramifications of this conversion in Francisco J. Hernández, "La cathédrale, instrument d'assimilation," in *Tolède, XIIᵉ–XIIIᵉ: Musulmans, chrétiens et juifs: Le savoir et la tolérance,* ed. Louis Cardaillac (Paris, 1991), pp. 75–91. On the construction of the Gothic cathedral, see Geneviève Barbé Coquelin de Lisle, "De la grande mosquée à la cathédrale gothique," in *Tolède, XIIᵉ–XIIIᵉ,* pp. 147–57.

16. On the conversion of the mosque into a church, see Jiménez de Rada, *Historia de rebus,* 9.27, p. 299, and *Crónica latina de los reyes de Castilla,* ed. Luis Charlo Brea (Cádiz, 1984), p. 100. On the later Christian architectural alterations of the mosque, see Jerilynn Dodds, "The Great Mosque of Córdoba," in *Al-Andalus: The Art of Islamic Spain,* ed. Jerilynn Dodds (New York, 1992), pp. 24–25.

17. On the rapid replacement of this converted mosque and the building of the Gothic cathedral, see Burns, *Crusader Kingdom,* 1:19–20; and Joaquín Bérchez Gómez and Arturo Zaragozá, "Iglesia Catedral Basílica de Santa María (Valencia)," in *Valencia: Arquitectura Religiosa,* ed. Joaquín Bérchez Gómez, Monumentos de la Comunidad Valenciana, Catálogo de Monumentos y Conjuntos declarados e incoados 10 (Valencia, 1984), pp. 16–27. Burns very plausibly suggests that the small number of Christians relative to the large Muslim population in Valencia in this period was the reason that James felt the need to eliminate the mosque. He also argues that there was an

To be sure, the Christian conquerors often introduced the architectural modifications necessary for a mosque to function as a church—typically hanging bells in the minaret, changing the orientation by placing an altar on the east wall, and in the case of some very important mosques, adding chapels to the interior.[18] But such alterations were hardly radical. They did not efface the visual and formal identity of the mosque. And the language Christians used to talk about these buildings could recognize that identity. Toledo's cathedral was a church "in the form of a mosque," stated the thirteenth-century archbishop Rodrigo Jiménez de Rada, who presided over the substitution of this structure with a Gothic building.[19]

Why did Christians so often use mosques rather than replace them immediately with identifiably Christian architecture? In the case of the mosque of Córdoba at least, aesthetic admiration played a part: Christians recognized the extraordinary beauty of this building.[20] There were practical reasons, too. Building a church, especially a cathedral, was a costly and labor-intensive process that could take many years.[21] The mosques were ready-made places of worship. The practical advantages of converting a mosque into a church were accompanied by less tangible but equally important ones. Using the extant Islamic structures as churches actually offered Christians an opportunity to proclaim symbolically their dominion.[22] Converting a mosque into a church appropriated for Christians the visual language which had been associated with dominant power in the Iberian Peninsula for centuries—the vocabulary of Islamic forms.

---

architectural offensive against Muslims in the form of the many new parish churches built in thirteenth-century Valencia; Burns, *Crusader Kingdom,* 1:19–20, 88–90.

18. See the details in Buresi's remarks in "Les conversions," and below, Appendix.

19. "[T]unc iecerunt primum lapidem rex et archiepiscopus Rodericus in fundamento ecclesiae Toletane, que in forma mezquita a tempore Arabum adhuc stabat," Jiménez de Rada, *Historia de rebus,* 9.13, p. 294. There is a similar statement about the mosque-cathedral in the *Primera crónica general de España que mandó componer Alfonso el Sabio y se continuaba bajo Sancho IV en 1289,* ca. 1037, ed. Ramón Menéndez Pidal, 2d ed., 2 vols. (Madrid, 1955), 2:272.

20. Aesthetic admiration for this building was implied in Alfonso X's concern that "tan noble Eglesia" should not fall into disrepair. See his privileges of 1261 and 1263 relating to repairs and maintenance, Cómez Ramos, ed., *Arquitectura,* pp. 22, 28. When in the early sixteenth century the canons of the cathedral decided to build the Gothic structure that mars the mosque's interior, the town council famously protested; when Charles V saw the results, he deplored the defacing of what had been a unique monument: Dodds, "The Great Mosque," pp. 24–25.

21. Harris argues that it was often only when the Islamic structures began to show signs of physical damage that Christians rebuilt the mosques as churches; see her "Mosque to Church Conversions." For a very different interpretation, see Buresi, "Les conversions."

22. For general remarks, see Harris, "Mosque to Church Conversions." Cf. the use by the Venetians of Byzantine buildings and objects in Crete as discussed by Maria Georgopoulou, "Late Medieval Crete and Venice: An Appropriation of Byzantine Heritage," *Art Bulletin* 77 (1995): 479–96, and in her paper entitled "The Encounter of Venice and Byzantium on the Island of Crete," presented at the New England Medieval Conference (October, 1996).

Like the churches and palaces built in Islamic style for Christian patrons during this period, the mosques made into churches employed that vocabulary for Christian ends.[23]

But if the forms themselves were not always altered significantly, how was it made evident that the language of this architecture now proclaimed Christian rather than Islamic power? If the architecture itself did not express the mosque's conversion, what did? There must have been symbolic means of effecting the transformation of sacred space that physically remained the same. And these means had to be powerful. After all, Christian texts could describe mosques as temples contaminated by the filth of the worship of Muhammed and devils.[24]

In part, the ceremony of the church's consecration, by its nature a purificatory ritual, exorcised the contamination of Islamic devotion; it also transformed profane space into sacred.[25] Texts recounting the conversion of mosques often mention this ritual in just these terms.[26] But often, the ritual's performance is merely implied and the transformation is expressed in other terms: the victorious Christian ruler enters the city in a triumphant *adventus* and hears Mass in the church of the Virgin Mary, explicitly or implicitly identified as the main mosque.[27] Here the dedication to

23. On the significance of the use of Islamic forms in Christian buildings (buildings known under the rubric of Mudejar architecture), see Jerilynn Dodds, "The Mudejar Tradition in Architecture," in *The Legacy of Muslim Spain,* ed. Salma Khadra Jayyusi, 2 vols. (Leiden, 1994), 2:592–98.

24. "Nefanda demonum spurcissimique mahomet colebantur figmenta": consecration charter of main mosque of Huesca, 1097 in *Colección diplomatica de Pedro I de Aragón y Navarra,* ed. Antonio Ubieto Arteta (Saragossa, 1951), no. 30, p. 251. "Spurcicia Machometi": consecration of mosque of Córdoba in Jiménez de Rada, *Historia de rebus,* 9.27, p. 299. "Expulsa Mahometi superstitione vel spurcicia": consecration of mosque of Córdoba in *Crónica latina,* p. 100 (and a similar passage regarding the mosque at Capillo, p. 72). "Domus erepta diabolo": dedication of mosque of Toledo in *Privilegios reales,* Document I, p. 2. See also Harris's discussion in "Mosque to Church Conversions," pp. 162–63.

25. On the power of the ritual of consecration to purify and transform space, see Amy G. Remensnyder, *Remembering Kings Past: Monastic Foundation Legends in Medieval Southern France* (Ithaca, N.Y., 1995), pp. 28–36.

26. For example, the text describing the dedication of Toledo's mosque: *Privilegios reales,* Document I, pp. 2–3. The consecration of the mosque of Córdoba: Jiménez de Rada, *Historia de rebus,* 9.27, p. 299, and *Crónica latina,* p. 100. The dedication of the mosque at Capillo by Ferdinand III: *Crónica latina,* p. 72. The consecration charter of the main mosque of Huesca, 1097: *Colección diplomatica,* no. 30, pp. 251–52. The consecration of the mosque at Lisbon in 1147: Osbern, *De expugnatione Lyxbonensi* in *Itinerarium peregrinorum et gesta Regis Ricardi,* ed. William Stubbs, Rerum Britanicarum Medii Aevi Scriptores 38.1 (London, 1864), p. clxxxi. The texts relating El Cid's conversion of the mosque at Valencia: Menéndez Pidal, *La España del Cid,* 2:868–71.

27. See, for example, the description of the transformation of Murcia's mosque in James I, *Llibre dels feits del rei en Jaume o crònica de Jaume I,* c. 450, in *Els Quatre Grans Cròniques,* ed. Ferrán Soldevila (Barcelona, 1971), p. 160; the transformation of Jaén's by Ferdinand III in the *Primera crónica general,* c. 1071, 2:746–747; Ferdinand III's entrance into Seville as described by the *Primera crónica general,* c. 1129, 2:769; the entrance of Ferdinand and Isabella at Málaga in 1487 in Fernando del Pulgar, *Crónica de los reyes católicos,* c. 222–223, ed. Juan de Mata Carriazo, 2 vols. (Madrid, 1943), 2:333–34.

Mary serves as a form of shorthand expressing the process of the mosque's transformation.

I have found twenty-six instances in which mosques were dedicated to the Virgin Mary, beginning with the first great victory of the Reconquest, the taking of Toledo in 1085, and continuing to the last Christian triumph, the fall of Granada in 1492.[28] Doubtless there are more. This pattern appears to have been so common—or at least renowned—that it has even passed into modern folklore. Tourists are assured by the 1994 edition of *Spain: The Rough Guide* that "all mosques taken from Islam" were consecrated to the Virgin.[29] The *Rough Guide* exaggerates: mosques could be and were dedicated to other saintly patrons.[30] But this guidebook is not entirely wrong. I have found no other holy figure to whom so many mosques were dedicated (although to be sure, in the absence of a comprehensive survey of converted mosques, numbers are tricky).

The dedication of mosques to the Virgin may fit a pattern general to later medieval Europe; some research suggests that from the eleventh century onward, Mary might have been the saintly patron whose name was most often attached to churches.[31] But particular instances of this general pattern (if such it was) have specific meaning according to their context. In medieval Spain, the Christian conquerors ascribed particular

28. See Appendix below. I have limited myself to cases for which I could find solid evidence. Many more instances of mosques dedicated to the Virgin are mentioned in studies that provide no documentation for the claim. It is worth remarking that Christian conquest could be architecturally and symbolically marked by the construction of a newly built church to the Virgin. For example, after the Cid took Almenara in 1097, he apparently ordered that a church of Mary be built (*edificari*) there: *Historia Roderici vel gesta Roderici*, c. 67, ed. Emma Falque in *Chronica Hispana saeculi XII*, ed. Emma Falque, Juan Gil, Antonio Maya, CCCM 71.1 (Turnhout, 1990), p. 92. At Coria and Tortosa, churches to the Virgin may also have been built. But the texts are ambiguous—these could be mosques (see Appendix below).

29. Mark Ellingham and John Fisher, *Spain: The Rough Guide*, 6th ed. (London, 1994), p. 222.

30. As far as I am aware, there has been no comprehensive study of the saintly patrons of converted mosques. For mosques in the kingdom of Valencia not dedicated to the Virgin, see Burns, *Crusader Kingdom*, 1:63, 92–93, 140, 249. A mosque at Capillo was dedicated to Christ and the Cross: *Crónica latina*, p. 72. A mosque at Huesca was dedicated to Christ, Nunilo, and Elodia: *Colección diplomatica*, no. 40, pp. 266–68. A mosque near Granada was dedicated to Joseph by 1494, when the German doctor Hieronymus Münzer saw it: Hieronymus Münzer, "Itinerarium hispanicum," ed. Ludwig Pfandl, *Revue Hispanique* 48 (1920): 50. Mosques at Alhama were dedicated respectively to Mary, James, and Michael (the mosque chosen for Mary was the main mosque and was the first to be converted): Pulgar, *Crónica*, c. 132, 2:24. Secondary mosques at Ronda were dedicated to the Holy Spirit, James, John the Evangelist, and Sebastian (but the main mosque was dedicated to Mary): Pulgar, *Crónica*, c. 172, 2:173–174. At Loxa a mosque was dedicated to James (but one was also dedicated to Mary): Pulgar, *Crónica*, c. 187, 2:227. At Vélez-Málaga, mosques were dedicated to James, the Cross, Andrew, and Stephen, but again the main mosque was dedicated to Mary: Pulgar, *Crónica*, c. 202, 2:279.

31. For example, in England between 1066 and 1216, the most popular dedication for monastic houses was to the Virgin: Alison Binns, *Dedications of Monastic Houses in England and Wales 1066–1216* (Woodbridge, England, 1989), pp. 18, 19, 20–23, 26–27, 31–32.

importance to the Virgin Mary as a symbol of the transformation of sacred space.

Dedications to Mary were seen as fundamentally altering the nature of
sacred space, as is evident in James I of Aragon's proud declaration in a
late-thirteenth-century chronicle of his deeds: "in all the large towns
which God has granted that we take from the Saracens, we have built (*havíem edificada*) a church of Our Lady, Saint Mary."[32] In descriptions of
his victories at Majorca and Murcia, James uses the same verb, insisting
that in both places he "built" a church of the Virgin.[33] "Build" may seem
like an odd verb to use, since at Murcia and Majorca, James I converted
mosques rather than creating new structures as he did at Valencia.[34] But
James's choice of this verb shows just how profound he could understand
the conversion of space to be through its dedication to the Virgin.[35] Consecration to Mary was a process of building that transcended architecture
and appearance; it was a symbolic appropriation so thorough that the
space was constructed as new Christian space.

A legend about the first church ever dedicated to Mary underlines her
power as a symbol of the transformation of space. While not of Spanish
origin, this foundational tale circulated both in Latin and in the vernacular in thirteenth-century Spain.[36] According to the legend, the apostles
bought a synagogue from the Jews and made it into the first church ever
consecrated to the Virgin—or rather, as the Latin version states, they

---

32. "Et quan venc que nós hauem l'església, sempre manam—hi fer l'altar de nostra dona santa
Maria, car en totes les viles que grans fossen, que Déus nos havia donades a guanyar de sarraïns,
havíem edificada església de Nostra Dona sancta Maria." James I, *Llibre dels feits,* c. 450, p. 160.
33. Majorca: "hajam nós aquí edificada església de nostra dona sancta Maria," James I, *Llibre dels
feits,* c. 105, p. 55. Murcia: "l'església que haviem edificada de nostra dona sancta Maria." James I,
Llibre dels feits, c. 450, p. 160.
34. Construction on the Gothic cathedral which replaced Murcia's converted main mosque did
not begin until the mid-fourteenth century, well after James I's death. *Reino frontizero castellano:
Murcia en los siglos XIV–XV,* ed. Juan Torres Fontes et al., Historia de la region murciana 4 (Murcia, 1980), pp. 243–44, 246–79.
35. To be sure, practical considerations could override Mary's symbolic powers of conversion. The
converted mosque at Valencia had been dedicated to the Virgin, yet James felt it necessary to replace it with a purpose-built cathedral (which retained the Marian dedication) in order to affirm
the power of the very small numbers of Christian conquerors in the face of an overwhelmingly
Muslim population; see above at n. 17.
36. For the Latin version known in Spain, see Gil de Zamora, *Liber Mariae,* tract. 16, c. 6, mir. 4,
ed. Fidel Fita, "Cincuenta leyendas por Gil de Zamora, combinadas con las 'Cantigas' de Alfonso
el Sabio," *Boletín de la Real Academia de la Historia* 7 (1885): 89–90. For the vernacular version, see
Alfonso X, el Sabio, *Cantigas de Santa María,* Cantiga 27, ed. Walter Mettmann, 3 vols. (Madrid,
1986–89), 1:126–28. This miracle frequently appeared in the standard western European collections of Marian miracles from the twelfth century onward. See *Liber de miraculis sanctae dei geni-
tricis Mariae,* ed. Thomas Frederick Crane (Ithaca, N.Y., 1925), pp. 23–24; and Adolpho Mussafia,
"Studien zu den mittelalterlichen Marienlegenden I, II, V," *Sitzungsberichte der philosophisch-
historischen Classe der kaiserlichen Akademie der Wissenschaften* 113 (1886): 936–53, 989–90; 115;
(1888): 12–13, 14, 16, 18; 139; (1898): 11.

"built" a church in Mary's honor.[37] But the Jews decided to renege on their agreement and asked the emperor to intervene on their behalf. The emperor ordered that the church be sealed for forty days so that God might indicate who the rightful proprietor of the sacred space was. The apostles implored the patron of the church, the Virgin Mary, for aid, which she promised. After the appointed time had elapsed, the apostles and the Jews entered the building. There they found on the walls a painted image of the Virgin. Terrified by Mary's presence, the Jews renounced their claims in favor of the apostles. The first church dedicated to the Virgin was thus remembered as an appropriated sacred space—and it was the Virgin Mary who had effected the conversion. The title of the vernacular version of this story (one of the famous late-thirteenth-century *Cantigas de Santa María* composed under the aegis of if not with the authorship of Alfonso X) emphasizes her power in this regard: "How the Virgin Mary took a synagogue of the Jews and made it into a church."[38]

To be sure, the building in question in this legend was originally a synagogue and not a mosque. Issues specific to tensions between Jews and Christians may account for the choice of the Virgin as patron in this legend, as they did in fourteenth- and fifteenth-century Germany, where the conversion or destruction of synagogues could be accompanied by the foundation of a church dedicated to Mary.[39] Nonetheless, this legend, like the accounts of the conversion of mosques through dedication to the Virgin, demonstrates the importance of Mary in carving Christian space from non-Christian space.

There are many reasons why this powerful role might have been ascribed to the Virgin. The exorcism of the unclean demons of Muslim worship implied by the ritual of consecration might have been enhanced by the dedication of the space to the paradigm of female purity, the Virgin.[40] The answer can also be found in general allegorical representations of the Virgin. The most obvious perhaps is that the Virgin Mary was of-

---

37. Gil de Zamorra characterizes the apostles as "edificantes domum" and states that the Jews ask the emperor to return the building to them "ut reedificarent synagogam." "Cincuenta leyendas," p. 89.

38. "Esta é como Santa Maria fillou a sinagoga dos judeus e fez dela eigreja." Alfonso X, *Cantigas*, Cantiga 27, 1:126.

39. On the fate of the German synagogues, see Hedwig Röckelein, "Marie, l'église et la synagogue: Culte de la Vierge et lutte contre les Juifs en Allemagne à la fin du Moyen Âge," in *Marie: Le culte de la Vierge dans la société médiévale*, ed. Dominique Iogna-Prat, Eric Palazzo, and Daniel Russo (Paris, 1996), pp. 513–32; and Klaus Schreiner, *Maria: Jungfrau, Mutter, Herrscherin* (Munich and Vienna, 1994), pp. 443–50. Röckelein also proposes reasons specific to the social contexts of each case.

40. Röckelein has found evidence of this emphasis on the purificatory aspects of dedication to the Virgin in texts relating to the conversion and destruction of German synagogues: "Marie, l'église et la synagogue," pp. 527–30. I have found no explicit evidence of this interpretation in Spanish Christian texts.

ten interpreted as the Church (Ecclesia).[41] According to this ecclesiologi-
cal reading, a mosque dedicated to the Virgin very clearly became part of
the church and was claimed for Christianity.

Equally important were allegorical images that explained the special
nature of the Virgin's body. Like other mothers, Mary possessed a body
that was a place of passage.[42] But as the mother of Jesus Christ, her body
was a special place of passage. It was the fulcrum between the old (Judaism) and the new (Christianity). A "bridge," a "road," a "path," an "open
door," as one twelfth-century Spanish manuscript described her, Mary
embodied transition and conversion.[43] She was, this text continued,
placed "between night and day . . . between death and life, between sin and
its remission, between the old law and the new," so that she could bring
sinners from the darkness of the old to the light of the new.[44] A mosque
dedicated to the Virgin therefore made the transition from old to new implied in her maternal body.

But if Mary's body was an open door through which the converted
might pass, it was also a "closed door."[45] According to Christian doc-

41. H. Coathalem, *Le parallélisme entre la sainte Vierge et l'église dans la tradition latine jusqu'à la
fin du XIIe siècle*, Analecta Gregoriana 74 (Rome, 1954); Adolf Katzenellenbogen, *The Sculptural
Programs of Chartres Cathedral: Christ-Mary-Ecclesia* (New York, 1964), pp. 59–65. On the way the
Virgin was increasingly used by the eleventh century to define the space of churches, see Eric Pa-
lazzo, "Marie et l'élaboration d'un espace ecclésial au Haut Moyen Âge," in *Marie: Le culte de la
Vierge*, pp. 313–25.

42. Julia Kristeva speaks of the "fonction transitionelle du Maternel" in "Stabat Mater" in *Histoires
d'amour* (Paris, 1983), p. 297. Mother goddesses are symbolized in many cultures by gates and en-
trances representing the womb as a place of passage. Eric Neumann, *The Great Mother: An Analysis of the Archetype* (Princeton, N.J., 1955), pp. 158–59, 160–62, 170.

43. The author elaborates on each of these characterizations and also describes the Virgin with another image of passage: Jacob's ladder. See "Advocaciones de la Virgen en un códice del siglo XII,"
ed. Atanasio Sinués Ruíz, *Analecta Sacra Tarraconensia: Revista de ciencias histórico-eclesiásticas* 21
(1948): 19 ("via et semita"), 21 ("porta aperta"), 25 ("scala"), 26 ("pons"). Such characterizations of
the Virgin are not original to this author. For a visual representation of the Virgin as the transition
between Old (in this case, Judaism) and New, see Hélène Toubert, "Une fresque de San Pedro de
Sorpe (Catalogne) et le thème iconographique de l'Arbor Bona–Ecclesia, Arbor Mala–Synagoga,"
Cahiers archéologiques 19 (1969): 167–89. In late medieval Byzantium, the Virgin was interpreted
as the "Gate of the Word" and thus images of her were frequently placed over portals. See Anthony
Cutler, *Transformations: Studies in the Dynamics of Byzantine Iconography* (University Park, Penn.,
1975), pp. 16–117.

44. "AURORA Dei genitrix dicitur . . . o mira Dei clementia, que velud auroram beatam Virginem Mariam inter noctem et diem posuit, ut his qui in tenebris et in umbra mortis peccati prime
matris Eve sedebant, diem vere lucis christum ostenderet . . . inter mortem et vitam, inter peccatum et remissionem, inter veteram legem et novam, inter archum et celum, inter reum et eius peccatum, Deus posuit Virginem, ut per eam peccatorem ad remissionem veterem legem ad novam
reum penitenciam lapsos in ore leviatati ad celum transduceret." "Advocaciones," p. 19. There is
much evidence that Mary was imagined by Christians as a particularly effective agent in the conversion of Jews to Christianity.

45. "Porta clausa." "Advocaciones," p. 21.

trine, Mary was a virgin not only before Christ's birth but after it. Her virginal body was thus the quintessential intact, enclosed, inviolate, and even impregnable space, as medieval writers insisted. Thus, as Vincent Ferrer (d. 1419) said, she was a castle which only Christ could enter.[46] Indeed, general exegetical tradition read the Virgin as David's tower (Song of Songs 4.4) and as a fortress.[47] In the Carolingian empire and in high medieval Germany, this valence of the Virgin was rendered concrete in the many castle chapels dedicated to her.[48] And in Byzantine iconography and architecture, the Virgin and churches dedicated to her symbolized protective walls defining and protecting boundaries.[49] Mary was a city protected by walls, one twelfth-century Spanish manuscript proclaimed.[50] The consecration of mosques in her name played on this symbolic register. The mosques became so many defensive towers and the Virgin a rampart defending Christians against their enemies.

In accounts from Christian Spain from at least the eleventh century onward, the Virgin appears as exactly such a defensive patron, a function nicely captured in the illumination for one of the *Cantigas de Santa María*. According to this *Cantiga*, the statue of the Virgin placed on the battlements of a castle under attack by Muslims successfully warded off the enemies.[51] In the illumination, the statue is set into a round tower

46. "[C]om Jesuchrist entrà en la verge Maria, ço és lo castell, en la sua concepció," Vincent Ferrer, *Sermon 64*, in Ferrer, *Sermons,* ed. Josep Sanchis Sivera and Gret Schib, 5 vols. (Barcelona, 1932–84), 3:74.

47. "TURRIS Dei mater dicitur, quia . . . ." "Advocaciones," p. 26. See Klaus Schreiner, "Nobilitas Mariae: Die edelgeborene Gottesmutter und ihre adeligen Verehrer: Soziale Prägungen und politische Funktionen mittelalterlicher Adelsfrömmigkeit," in *Maria in der Welt: Marienverehrung im Kontext der Sozialgeschichte 10.–18. Jahrhundert,* ed. Claudia Opitz, Hedwig Röckelein, Gabriela Signori, Guy P. Marchal (Zurich, 1993), pp. 227–29; and Schreiner, *Maria: Jungfrau, Mutter, Herrscherin,* pp. 371–73.

48. On Carolingian castral chapels in Flanders, see N. Huyghebaert, "Le comte Baudoin II de Flandre et le 'custos' de Steneland: A propos d'un faux précepte de Charles le Chauve pour Saint-Bertin," *Revue Bénédictine* 69 (1959): 64, note 2. On medieval Germany, see Schreiner, "Nobilitas Mariae," pp. 227–29.

49. On the Virgin as protector of Constantinople, see Averil Cameron, "The Theotokos in Sixth-Century Constantinople: A City Finds Its Symbol," *Journal of Theological Studies,* n.s. 29 (1978): 79–108; and Schreiner, *Maria,* pp. 336–40. On the Virgin and her churches as walls, see Cutler, *Transformations,* pp. 113–15, 117–18, 136–41 (citing evidence from the seventh through the fifteenth centuries). Procopius strikingly articulates this aspect of the Virgin, calling churches dedicated to her "invisible defenses to the circuit wall of [Constantinople]," and he describes how Justinian "dedicat[ed] to her the threshold of the Empire" by building a church to her in the fortress at Ceuta, thus rendering "this fortress impregnable for the whole race of mankind." Procopius of Caesarea, *Buildings,* 1.3, 6.7, ed. and trans. H. B. Dewing and Glanville Downey (Cambridge Mass., 1940), pp. 41, 393.

50. "Civitas munita muris . . . ." "Advocaciones," pp. 32–33.

51. Alfonso X, *Cantigas,* Cantiga 185, 2:204–7.

and has melded into the fortifications themselves.[52] The caption emphasizes the Virgin's powers of protection: "How Saint Mary defended the castle well like a very good castellan."[53] Enshrined as the patron of converted mosques located along the shifting frontier of military engagement, the Virgin watched over the perimeter of Christian territory, just as she guarded this castle.

Notice that in this *Cantiga,* it is in the form of a statue that Mary's protective powers are embodied. Often the dedication of mosques to the Virgin seems to have been complemented by the placement of an image of her somewhere in the mosque. The installation of these images could itself stand for the conversion of conquered mosques: one of the *Cantigas* proclaims that each time that great devotee of Mary, Ferdinand III of León-Castile, captured a Muslim city, he placed an image of the Virgin on the portals of the mosque.[54]

Furthermore, according to the *Cantigas,* in the wake of their thirteenth-century victories Christians installed statues of the Virgin in the mosques which became the cathedral of Seville and the royal chapel of Jérez de la Frontera.[55] And in a triumphal procession, James I of Aragon carried an image of the Virgin into the church of the Virgin he "built" at Murcia, which was, as we have seen, a converted mosque.[56] When in the 1470s the marquis of Cádiz, Rodrigo Ponce de León, conquered Alhama, he dedicated the main mosque to the Virgin as she had instructed him to do and placed a richly made image of her on the newly installed altar.[57] As in the legend describing the first church ever dedicated to the Virgin, Mary's image thus participated in the conversion of non-Christian space.

The placement of a statue of the Virgin in the mosques made Mary's presence and saintly patronage concrete. It also ensured that enshrined in

52. The illumination comes from the so-called Codice Rico of the *Cantigas* (Escorial T.I.1, fol. 247r) where the *Cantiga* is numbered 187 rather than 185; see the facsimile published as Alfonso el Sabio, *Cantigas de Santa María: Edición facsímil del Codice Rico T.I.1 de la Biblioteca de San Lorenzo el Real de El Escorial (siglo XIII)* (Madrid, 1979).

53. "Como Santa Maria defendou ben o castelo como muy boa castelyra." Escorial T.I.1, fol. 247r.

54. "E quan' agua cidade de mouros ya gãar, ssa omagen na mezquita põya eno portal." Alfonso X, *Cantigas,* Cantiga 292, 3:78.

55. For the image(s?) in Seville, see Alfonso X, *Cantigas,* Cantigas 292, 324, 3:77–81, 150–51. For the statue in Jérez de la Frontera, see ibid., Cantiga 345, 3:197–201.

56. James describes a procession during what appears to be the consecration of the church: "e ab nostres creus e ab image de Nostra Dona Sancta Maria moguem de l'albergada on nós estàvem en la host, e a peu venguem e entram per la vila entró en l'església que haviem edificada de nostra dona sancta Maria." James I, *Llibre dels feits,* c. 450, p. 160.

57. "Historia de los hechos del marqués de Cádiz," c. 15, *Colección de documentos inéditos para la historia de España* 106:207.

the new church would be the image which in the thirteenth and fourteenth centuries increasingly came to stand for the central truths of Christianity: the Virgin and Child.[58] Statues of the Virgin seem to have been far more numerous in medieval Spain than were crucifixes; extant from medieval Navarre alone are over three hundred statues of the Virgin but only one hundred crucifixes.[59] The statues were thus visible and tangible evidence of Christian ownership of the sacred space.[60] And while they claimed the space for Christianity, the statues were also the means of making it unfit for Muslim worship. Given the Islamic prohibitions on representing the human figure in mosque decoration, Muslims would have interpreted the installation of statues as an act of desecration and profanation—as Christians doubtless intended them to.[61]

58. On the way statues of the Virgin could embody doctrinal truths, see Ilene H. Forsyth, *The Throne of Wisdom: Wood Sculptures of the Madonna in Romanesque France* (Princeton, N.J., 1972), pp. 22–30.

59. Such statues make up more than 70 percent of all medieval statuary from this region; see Clara Fernández-Ladreda, *Imaginería medieval mariana* (Pamplona, 1988), pp. 9, 10. On the ubiquity of images of the Virgin in Europe in this period, see Michael Camille, *The Gothic Idol: Ideology and Image-Making in Medieval Art* (Cambridge, 1989), p. 225. For a study of the emergence of such statues and their popularity in medieval France, see Forsyth, *The Throne of Wisdom*.

60. There are legends which make the statues into statements that the appropriation of the mosques is a reconquest. These legends relate how Visigothic statues of the Virgin were miraculously revealed as hidden somewhere in the fabric of the mosque, indicating that the mosque had originally been a church, and thus justifying its appropriation for Christianity. Some scholars allege that these legends date from the Middle Ages: Angela Muñoz Fernández, "Cultos, devociones y advociones religiosas en los orígenes de la organización eclesiástica cordobesa (siglos XIII–XIV)," in *Andalucía entre Oriente y Occidente (1236–1492): Actas del V Coloquio internacional de historia medieval de Andalucía*, ed. Emilio Cabrera (Córdoba, 1988), pp. 138–39; José Augusto Sánchez Pérez, *El culto mariano en España* (Madrid, 1943). I have not yet, however, found any evidence to support this assertion. The earliest hints of such legends that I have found appear in two texts dating only from the last quarter of the fifteenth century. These texts both relate to statues of the Virgin during Ferdinand III's siege of Seville and neither explicitly makes the mosque originally a church or grants the statue Visigothic origins. See "Historia de los hechos del marqués," c. 2, p. 148, and Münzer, "Itinerarium hispanicum," pp. 78–79. For the later elaboration of these Sevillean legends in text and painting, see Adelaida Cintas del Bot, *Iconografía del Rey San Fernando en la pintura de Sevilla* (Seville, 1991), pp. 16, 53–55, 64–66, plates 2, 10.

61. On the prejudice against representing the human being in Islamic sacred spaces, see Hillenbrand, *Islamic Architecture*, p. 128; and Wheeler M. Thackston, "The Role of Calligraphy," in *The Mosque: History, Architectural Development and Regional Diversity*, ed. Martin Frishman and Hasan-Uddin Khan (London, 1994), pp. 43–44. In the texts describing the transformation of mosques I have found almost no traces of the dynamic Camille has found elsewhere in Europe (Spain is almost absent from his discussion) in which Muslims are depicted as idol worshippers so that stories can be told about the replacement of their false images with the true ones of Christianity: Camille, *Gothic Idol*, pp. 129–64. Perhaps this is because Spanish Christians, after centuries of contact with Muslims, were aware that they did not worship statues. The only hint I have found of accusations of idolatry in these texts appears in the text of 1097 describing Huesca's mosque: "nefanda demonum spurcissimique Mahomet colebantur figmenta," *Colección diplomatica*, no. 30, p. 251. But while *figmentum* can mean an image, it more often means "lie, fiction, forgery." J. F. Niermeyer, *Mediae latinitatis lexicon minus* (Leiden, 1984), p. 425.

The images of Mary could carry more secular layers of meaning, as a legend attached to a statue in the cathedral of Seville makes clear. By at least the last decade of the late fifteenth century, visitors to the church (originally a converted mosque dedicated to Mary) were shown a gorgeously crowned statue of the Virgin. The Muslims had kept this statue in Seville's mosque, the visitors were told. Then during Ferdinand III's siege of the city, the story continued, the king was informed in a vision that he should venerate this image and that he would shortly take Seville. The prophecy of Christian triumph was fulfilled. And from that time on, Ferdinand not only venerated the image but always carried it with him into battle against the Muslims.[62]

The image that is the focus of this legend is perhaps the statue known today by the provocative name of the "Virgen de los Reyes," or perhaps it is the one equally suggestively called the "Virgen de las Batallas" (both of which still grace the altars of Seville's cathedral).[63] But in any case, this legend describes an intimate link between Spanish monarchs and statues of the Virgin, an association evident in many other texts beginning in at least the thirteenth century.[64] Such a link reflects the strong Marian devotion that characterized kings such as Alfonso X and James I of Aragon as well as their Capetian contemporaries.[65] Shaping this fervent

---

62. For this legend, see Münzer's account of his visit to Seville in 1494: "Itinerarium hispanicum," pp. 78–79.

63. It is not clear when the statues received these names; Münzer (see previous note) does not name the statue he describes. For these statues and narration of legends that I have been unable to date any earlier than the seventeenth century and that associate these images in further spectacular ways with Ferdinand III's victories, see Cintas del Bot, *Iconografía;* José Hernández Díaz, *La Virgen de los Reyes, Patrona de Sevilla y de la archdiocesis: Estudio iconográfico* (Seville, 1947); Hernández Díaz, "Estudio de la iconografía mariana hispalense de la época fernandina," *Archivo Hispalense: Revista histórica, literaria y artística,* 2d series, 9 (1948): 174–180; and Enrique Pareja López and Matilde Megía Navarro, *El arte de la Reconquista cristiana* (Seville, 1990), pp. 283–89, figs. 256–58, 261–62.

The name of "Virgen de las Batallas" was also attached, by at least the nineteenth century, to a gorgeous Limoges enamel statue belonging to the abbey of San Pedro de Arlanza. See *The Keir Collection of Medieval Works of Art* (New York, 1997), no. 43, pp. 202–4. I thank Oleg Grabar for drawing my attention to this statue.

64. Thirteenth-century rulers such as Ferdinand III and Alfonso X are depicted as being the patrons of images of the Virgin and as fervently venerating such images; see Alfonso X, *Cantigas,* Cantigas 292, 295, 297, 299, 324, 345, 349, 361, 3:77–81, 85, 90–91, 95–96, 150–51, 197–201, 207–8, 232–33. James II of Aragon in the early fourteenth century had a sumptuous silver image of the Virgin made for the famous Marian shrine of Montserrat. See the texts edited in J. Ernesto Martínez Ferrando, *Jaime II de Aragón: Su vida familar,* 2 vols. (Barcelona, 1948), nos. 224, 232, 237, 2:159–60, 166, 170–71.

65. On, for example, Louis IX of France's Marian devotion, see Jacques Le Goff, *Saint Louis* (Paris, 1996), pp. 538–40, 561–63, 573, 617, 743, 764, 772.

veneration of the royal mother of God, the queen of heaven, by male monarchs was, among other things, a mirroring of heavenly and human royalty (complicated by the difference in gender).[66] This identification is embodied in the association, legendary and actual, between rulers and images of the Virgin. Accordingly, the placement of the images in the mosques was a symbol not only of Mary's patronage, but also of royal presence and royal conquest.

The fifteenth-century legend surrounding the statue of the Virgin that Ferdinand III acquired at Seville suggests something else as well. It proposes the Virgin as Ferdinand III's associate and patron specifically in his wars against the Muslims—the legend relates that he always went into battle accompanied by the image. Even more strikingly, the legend creates an image of the Virgin herself as a military conqueror. Her virtue does not protect Ferdinand in battle so much as it is the source of his military prowess. It is "with her power" (*in virtute eius*) that he vanquishes Muslims.[67] Mary was a military conqueror herself. Nor was this a role she gained only late in the Middle Ages; beginning in at least the eleventh century, Mary was imagined as present at the battles of Spanish Christians against Spanish Muslims.[68] As in Byzantium and on the eastern frontiers of medieval Germany, Mary was an active participant in warfare.[69]

66. Royal devotion to the Virgin had its roots in the earlier periods when Mary began to be imagined as herself royal. See Daniel Russo, "Les représentations mariales dans l'art d'Occident: Essai sur la formation d'une tradition iconographique," in *Marie: Le culte de la Vierge*, pp. 209–32; and Schreiner, "Nobilitas Mariae."

67. "[D]um iret in prelium, semper hanc effigiem cum portali ex argento et auro factam secum duxit et in virtute eius multa fecit . . . eamque imaginem semper in campum duxit . . . et ut plurimum in virtute Beate Virginis Mauros vicit." Münzer, "Itinerarium hispanicum," p. 79.

68. See, for example, the eleventh-century miracle story of the Virgin helping the Catalonians in battle at Torá: Andrew of Fleury, "Miraculorum sancti Benedicti liber quartus," 4.10–11, ed. Eugène de Certain, *Les miracles de Saint Benoît écrits par Adrevald, Aimon, André, Raoul Tortaire, et Hugues de Sainte-Marie, moines de Fleury* (Paris, 1858), pp. 187–91. For details of this battle, see José Goñi Gaztambide, *Historia de la Bula de Cruzada en España* (Vitoria, 1958), p. 33. See also the charter of 1045 describing the Virgin aiding a tenth-century king of Navarre/Pamplona in battle against the Muslims: *Colección diplomatica de Irache*, ed. José María Lacarra, 2 vols. (Saragossa, 1965), no. 8, 1:11–13 (esp. 12).

69. Germany: Marian Dygo, "The Politics of the Cult of the Virgin Mary in Teutonic Prussia in the Fourteenth and Fifteenth Centuries," *Journal of Medieval History* 15 (1989): 63–80; and Schreiner, *Maria: Jungfrau, Mutter, Herrscherin*, pp. 369–409. Byzantium: Cameron, "The Theotokos in Sixth-Century Constantinople"; and Schreiner, *Maria: Jungfrau, Mutter, Herrscherin*, pp. 336–40. On the Virgin in general as a battle patron, see Jaroslav Pelikan, *Mary through the Centuries: Her Place in the History of Culture* (New Haven, Conn., 1996), p. 27. In an otherwise excellent discussion, Guy Philippart erroneously proposes that Marian martial miracles imported from Byzantium had little success in the West: "Le récit miraculaire marial dans l'Occident médiéval," in *Marie: Le culte de la Vierge*, pp. 569–70.

In fact, the Virgin was as much a patron of the Reconquest as were male military saints such as Saint George, Saint Isidore of Seville, Saint Aemilianus, and above all, Saint James (or Santiago).[70] But these male saints have received the lion's share of scholarly attention for this role. While a few medievalists have remarked on Mary's presence on Spanish battlefields, they confine themselves to a sentence or two, a few pages at best.[71] But there are entire articles and books detailing James's potent place in the Reconquest.[72] Perhaps this discrepancy in scholarly attention has its roots in gender. It is easier for us to imagine male saints (even one such as James fantastically transformed from his original identity as humble barefoot apostle) in the realm of warfare, than it is for us to conceive of a saintly woman, especially the feminine and loving mother of God, appearing in the masculine world of battle.

But medieval Spanish Christians apparently had no difficulty locating Mary in this sphere of enterprise. Text after text describes Mary's role as military patron of the Reconquest, as I discuss elsewhere.[73] Here, I just want to point to two of the most flamboyant statements of the complex identification between the Virgin and male warriors' dreams of victory against the Muslims. One appears in the *Cantigas de Santa María. Cantiga 169* describes how the Muslims tried to destroy a church of the Virgin at Murcia but were unable to do so. The poem concludes: "Muhammed will never have power there because she conquered it [sc. the church] and furthermore she will conquer Spain and Morocco and Ceuta and Asila."[74] Here the Virgin is clearly identified with the cherished project of the putative author of these poems, Alfonso X: the Christian conquest of Spain and Morocco. In the process, she is also identified with Alfonso himself. The explicit subject of the verb "to conquer" is the Virgin, but the implicit one is Alfonso. The grammar collapses the two subjects—

70. Aemilianus: *Primera crónica general,* c. 698, 1:400–401. George: James I, *Llibre dels feits,* c. 84, p. 48. Isidore: Lucas de Tuy, *Chronicon mundi,* ed. Andreas Schott, *Hispaniae illustratae,* 4 vols. (Frankfurt, 1603–1608), 4:104, 106, 114, 115; *Primera crónica general,* c. 698, 1:400–401. For James, see the references in note 72 below.

71. For example, see Goñi Gaztambide, *Historia de la Bula,* pp. 33, 95; Klaus Herbers, "Politik und Heiligenverehrung auf der Iberischen Halbinsel: Die Entwicklung des 'politischen Jakobus,'" in *Politik und Heiligenvehrung im Hochmittelalter,* ed. Jürgen Petersohn, Vorträge und Forschungen 42 (Sigmaringen, 1994), pp. 256–59; Angus MacKay, "Religion, Culture, and Ideology on the Late Medieval Castilian-Granadan Frontier," in *Medieval Frontier Societies,* ed. Robert Bartlett and Angus MacKay (Oxford, 1989), pp. 230–31; Muñoz Fernández, "Cultos, devociones y advociones," p. 138.

72. For example, Herbers, "Politik und Heiligenverehrung"; Thomas D. Kendrick, *Saint James in Spain* (London, 1960).

73. This is the central subject of the book I am currently writing.

74. "[N]unca Mafomete poder y averá; ca a conquereu ela e demais conquerrá Espanna e Marrocos e Ceta e Arcilla." Alfonso X, *Cantigas,* Cantiga 169, 2:174.

implicit and explicit, male and female, Alfonso and the Virgin—into one conquering figure in the face of the Muslims.

And when in 1462, the eighteen-year-old hot-blooded marquis of Cádiz, Rodrigo Ponce de León, was filled with longing to find himself in battle against the Muslims, it was to the Virgin that he turned for fulfillment of this desire. He prayed fervently before her image. Sympathetic to his pleas, the Virgin appeared in a vision and assured him that not only would he engage in many battles, but he would always triumph over the Moors.[75] Here the Virgin appears as the kind mother (she refers to her own son). But she nurtures by dispensing victory and the military setting for it. For the marquis, she was the mother of battle.

The Virgin was thus a symbol of the Reconquest and a conqueror herself. The dedication of mosques to the Virgin drew on this reservoir of meanings. It was part of the discourse of Christian conquest with which Mary was so intimately identified. The Islamic forms of the mosques were colonized through the Virgin Mary's name and her presence as the patron of the new churches. But the Christian use of Mary in this fashion was a defiance of a certain ambiguity in the Virgin herself. As Spanish Christians were well aware, inherent to Islam was (and is) a belief in the Virgin Mary, or Maryam, as she is known in the Islamic world.[76] Muslims did not have to be conquered or converted to believe in the Virgin and her power.[77] Certainly the *Cantigas de Santa María* describe the Virgin vanquishing Muslims. But these poems also depict Muslims who, without renouncing their own religion, worship the Virgin Mary in Christian style by praying to her in a Christian church, venerating her statue,

---

75. "Hechos del marqués," c. 3, p. 62.

76. On Maryam, see, for example, the *Qur'an*, Suras 3, 19, 21, 56; J. M. Abd el Jalil, "La vie de Marie selon le Coran et l'Islam," in *Maria: Études sur la Sainte Vierge*, ed. H. du Manoir, 8 vols. (Paris, 1949–1971), 1:183–211; Jane Dammen McAuliffe, "Chosen of All Women: Mary and Fatima in Qur'anic Exegesis," *Islamochristiana* 7 (1981): 19–28; Pelikan, *Mary through the Centuries*, pp. 67–78; A. J. Wensinck and Penelope Johnstone, "Maryam," in *The Encyclopedia of Islam*, new ed., 6:628–631. In his problematic work, Louis Massignon also discusses Maryam: "La notion du voeu et la dévotion musulmane à Fatima" and "L'oratoire de Marie à Aqca, vu sous le voile de deuil de Fatima," both in his *Opera minora: Textes recueillis, classés et présentés avec une bibliographie*, ed. Y. Moubarac, 3 vols. (Paris, 1969), 1:573–91, and 1:592–618. For clear statements that medieval Spanish Christians knew of Muslim belief in Maryam, see Alfonso X, *Cantigas*, Cantiga 329, 3:163; *Castigos e documentos para bien vivir ordenados por el rey Don Sancho IV*, ed. Agapito Rey, c. 21 (Bloomington, Ind., 1952), p. 129; Raymundus Martin, *Pugio fidei adversus Mauros et Judaeos*, 3.3.7.14–15, ed. J. B. Carpzow (Leipzig, 1687; rpt. 1967), pp. 749–50.

77. For some suggestive evidence about devotion to Maryam among Spanish Muslims, see Míkel de Epalza, *Jésus otage: Juifs, chrétiens et musulmans en Espagne (VIᵉ–XVIIᵉ s.)* (Paris, 1987), pp. 170–99; E. Lévi-Provençal, *Histoire de l'Espagne musulmane*, rev. ed., 3 vols. (Paris, 1950–1953), 3:336; Münzer, "Itinerarium hispanicum," pp. 61–62. Spanish Muslims living under Christian rule could use their belief in Mary to their advantage. See David Nirenberg, *Communities of Violence: Persecution of Minorities in the Middle Ages* (Princeton, N.J., 1996), pp. 195–96.

and even taking a banner with her image on it with them into battle against other Muslims.[78]

It has been suggested that these *Cantigas* demonstrate that in the thirteenth century, Christians considered Muslims as political rather than religious enemies.[79] These *Cantigas,* however, project Muslim veneration of Maryam in the mold of Christian devotion to the Virgin. Is there not an implicitly colonizing message here, one of the cooptation of Islamic worship under the rubric of the Christian version of Mary? If so, these *Cantigas* send a veiled message of Christian victory which uses Islamic devotional structures as its vehicle—like the conversion of the mosques in the name of Mary.

Perhaps Spanish Muslims found in the mosques dedicated to the Virgin a place for devotional pilgrimage to Maryam.[80] In the late fifteenth century, a mosque in Saragossa which had been transformed into a chapel dedicated to the Virgin was still the object of veneration by Muslims (to be sure, worshipping in the former mosque did not necessarily imply worshipping the structure's new saintly patron).[81] But it is equally probable that at the same time the Muslims read the conversion of the mosques in the Virgin's name as the message of conquest that the Christians intended. While a fourteenth-century Muslim poet from Granada could celebrate Maryam as one of the three most virtuous women of Islam, he could also write that she was the "lady of [our] enemies."[82] Installed

78. Muslims venerating the Virgin in a church: Alfonso X, *Cantigas,* Cantiga 329, 3: 162–65. Muslims venerating a statue of the Virgin: ibid., Cantiga 183, 2:201–2; also the twelfth-century Latin version of Benedict of Peterborough, *Gesta regis henrici secundi,* ed. William Stubbs, *The Chronicle of the Reigns of Henry II and Richard I,* A.D. 1169–1192, 2 vols., Rerum Britanicarum medii aevi scriptores 49.1–2 (London, 1867), 2:121–22. Muslims using a banner of the Virgin in battle: Alfonso X, *Cantigas,* Cantiga 181, 2:196–97.

79. Mercedes García Arenal, "Los moros en las Cantigas de Alfonso X el Sabio," *Al-Qantara* 6 (1985): 133–51.

80. In pre-twelfth-century al-Andalus, Muslims participated in pilgrimages to Mozarabic churches: Christophe Picard, "Sanctuaires et pèlerinages chrétiens en terre musulmane: L'Occident de l'Andalus (X⁰–XII⁰ siècles)," in *Pèlerinages et croisades: Actes du 118⁰ congrès national annuel des sociétés historiques et scientifiques . . .* (Paris, 1995), pp. 243–44. In the later Middle Ages, both Muslims and Christians prayed for miracles in the frontier church of San Ginés de la Jarra: MacKay, "Religion, Culture, and Ideology," pp. 221–22. In the twelfth century, Muslims (and even some Jews) made pilgrimages to a church of the Virgin near Damascus. See Burchard of Strasbourg's description included in Arnold of Lübeck, "Chronica," MGH SS 21:239–40 (I thank Benjamin Kedar for this reference). Muslim women today make pilgrimages to the cathedral dedicated to the Virgin in Oran, Algeria. See Susan Slyomovics, "Algeria Elsewhere: The Pilgrimage of the Virgin of Santa Cruz in Oran, Algeria and Nîmes, France," in *Folklore Interpreted: Essays in Honor of Alan Dundes,* ed. Regina Bendix and Rosemary Lévy Zumwalt (New York, 1995), p. 351, n. 17.

81. "[I]n ambitu stat una antiquissima et fortissima mesquita, quam Sarraceni intrantes valde venerantur. Licet nunc sit capella Beate Virgini dedicata." Münzer, "Itinerarium hispanicum," p. 138.

82. In Spanish translation (unfortunately I do not read Arabic): "señora de los enemigos." For the Arabic text and modern Spanish translation, see María J. Rubiera Mata, "De nuevo sobre las tres morillas," *Al-Andalus* 37 (1972): 141.

as the saintly patron of converted space, Mary symbolically defined and fixed the frontier in defiance of the realities of the all-too-fluid nature of boundaries between Muslim and Christian territory and between the Christian Virgin and the Muslim Maryam.

When the Spanish Christians transferred their military attentions to nonbelievers located on the other side of the Atlantic in the New World, the Virgin accompanied the conquistadores, even gaining the title of La Conquistadora.[83] During this new enterprise of military conquest, Mary retained her role as a symbol of the definition of Christian space. Cortés and his men, for example, invoked the Virgin when they were faced with the temples of central Mexico (1519–1521). The Spanish believed that just like mosques, these structures sheltered "demon-worship."[84] Thus, in the very earliest years of the conquest of Mexico, the Spanish called the temples mosques[85] and often treated them as such: a space to be claimed for Christianity. Accordingly, conquistadores such as Cortés performed ceremonies of purification, transforming the temples into spaces of Christian worship for the Indians.[86] In the process, the Spanish removed native images from the temple altars and replaced them with Christian ones.[87] The new visual representations of divinity were images of the Virgin Mary and crosses or crucifixes. To be sure, Christ accompanied Mary in the temples' conversion. But Fray Toribio de Motolinía, writing to Charles V in 1555,

83. For a clear formulation of the Virgin as a conqueror in the New World, see, among many other examples, Petrus Martyr, *De orbe novo*, fols. 30r–31r (Dec 2.6) and the texts cited below at nn. 89–94. The term La Conquistadora (sometimes Nuestra Señora de la Conquista) emerged by at least the late sixteenth century. See, for example, the statue in central Mexico described in that period by Bernardino López de Mendoza, *Información jurídica* . . . (Puebla de Los Angeles, 1804); the statue in Guatemala City described in the late seventeenth century by Francisco Antonio de Fuentes y Guzmán, *Recordación Florida: Discurso historial y demostración natural, material, militar y política del Reyno de Guatemala*, 6.2, 3 vols. (Guatemala City, 1932–1933), 1:164–65. See also the statue still venerated today by that title in Santa Fe, New Mexico: Angelico Chavez, *Our Lady of the Conquest* (Santa Fe, 1948).

84. Among the many instances of descriptions of temples as sites of demon worship, see Jerónimo de Mendieta, *Historia Eclesiástica Indiana*, ed. Francisco Solano y Pérez-Lila, Biblioteca de Autores Españoles 260–61 (Madrid, 1973), 2.7, 3.20, 260:53–54, 138; Salazar, *Crónica*, 1.18, p. 35.

85. Serge Gruzinski, *La guerre des images de Christophe Colombe à "Blade Runner" (1492–2019)* (Paris, 1990), p. 59; Weckmann, *Medieval Heritage*, pp. 181–82.

86. Cortés had Mass celebrated with Spaniards present in the purified temples of Cozumel, Tenochtitlan, and Tlascala: McAndrew, *Open-Air Churches*, p. 185; Díaz del Castillo, *Historia*, c. 77, 1:271. It is not, however, clear that the Spanish used such temples for their own worship even in the earliest years of the conquest (1519–1521). But the conquistadores certainly intended the Indians to worship the Christian God in such spaces. On the problem of maintaining Christian worship in converted temples among Indians in the absence of Spanish priests during the conquest, see Richard Trexler, "Aztec Priests for Christian Altars: The Theory and Practice of Reverence in New Spain," in Trexler, *Church and Community, 1200–1600: Studies in the History of Florence and New Spain* (Rome, 1987), pp. 469–92.

87. See the references above in note 1. For an excellent discussion of the replacement of native images by Christian images, see Gruzinski, *La guerre des images*.

could collapse the process into Mary's presence; the friar relates that "when the idols had been destroyed, [Cortés] put there an image of Our Lady."[88] A legend that emerged in Spanish chronicles by the mid-sixteenth century hints that Motolinía was not alone in remembering the conversion of space during the military conquest of Mexico in terms of the Virgin. In this miracle story, Mary eclipses her son as an agent and symbol of the transformation of space, just as she had in medieval Spain.

The setting for this miracle is the attempt of the inhabitants of Tenochtitlan to drive the Spanish from their city which began during Cortés's absence.[89] Part of this effort involved the attempt of the Mexicas to reclaim for their gods the temple of Huitzilipochtli, where the Spanish earlier had installed a cross and a statue of the Virgin. Accordingly, the Mexicas tried to remove the statue of the Virgin from the altar. But it would not budge and they were forced to leave it there—a miracle echoing ones from medieval Europe in which relics cannot be moved against the saint's will. The message was clear: the Virgin had claimed the space and she would not leave (and therefore, neither would the Spanish).

There is no mention of any attempt by the Mexicas to remove the symbol of Christ, the cross or crucifix, from the sacred precincts of the temple. Perhaps the statue of the Virgin was the focus of the Mexicas' wrath because the conquistadores' rhetoric and actions had caused them to see her and not the cross as the distillation of the Spanish religion.[90] In any case, surely the Spanish who wrote of these events shaped them according to the tradition of their homeland. The Virgin Mary was

88. "Destruídos los ídolos, puso allí la imagen de Nuestra Señora," "Carta de Fray Toribio de Motolinía al Emperador Carlos V," in Toribio de Benavente o Motolinía, *Historia de los Indios de la Nueva España,* ed. Edmundo O'Gorman, 3d ed. (Mexico City, 1979), p. 220. During the early years of the conquest of Peru, statues of Mary also seem to have symbolized the appropriation of temples for Christianity. According to a letter of 1525 written by the conquistador Pedrarias Davila, when the Indians saw that lightning struck "ciertas mezquitas donde aun no les avian dado imagenes de nuestra señora," they asked for statues of the Virgin for the temples; see *Las relaciones primitivas de la conquista del Perú,* ed. Raúl Porras Barrenechea (Paris, 1937), p. 61.

89. The earliest account of this legend that I have identified is from 1552 in Francisco López de Gómara, *Historia de la conquista de México,* c. 105, ed. Jorge Gurria Lacroix (Caracas, 1979), pp. 164–65. Later sixteenth-century versions include Díaz del Castillo, *Historia,* c. 125, 1:449; Salazar, *Crónica,* 4.109, p. 473. Petrus Martyr, writing by 1530, relates a non-miraculous version of the statue's role in the fight for the tower during "la Triste Noche": "in ea turre deiectis idolis, Beatae Virginis imaginem locaverunt [i.e., the Spanish]; eam hostes abstulerunt," Peter Martyr, *De orbe novo,* Dec 5.6, fol. 75r.

90. In the early years of the conquest, the Nahuas and other indigenous peoples called the Christian God and all Christian images "Mary." See, among others, Motolinía, *Historia,* 1.4, p. 24. For discussion, see Gruzinski, *Guerre des Images,* pp. 69, 107, 123. This was probably because of the Spaniards' emphasis on her in their preaching. Cortés, for example, apparently tried to convert the Tlascalans by holding up a statue of Mary and explaining Christianity through it. Díaz del Castillo, *Historia,* c. 72, 1:269–70.

the symbol of the conversion of space; hence it would be natural for Spanish writers to make her statue and not the cross the focal point of the story.

The significance of this miracle was reinforced by another and very famous one which immediately followed. During the heated battle of La Triste Noche, the Spanish received celestial aid from the Virgin Mary and that other great patron of Spanish military enterprise, Saint James (Santiago).[91] But while Santiago fought the Indians from his horse, the Virgin fought from the same altar from which she could not be moved.[92] The identification between the Virgin, the altar, and the appropriation of the temple for Christianity apparent in the first miracle was again underlined. And so too was the nexus of the conversion of space and military conquest, both expressed here through the statue of the Virgin.[93]

But this valence of the Virgin was no more fixed in the New World than it had been in the Old, although for different reasons. During the Reconquest, the conversion of mosques did not necessarily coincide with the conversion of Muslims. The converted mosques were intended not for newly converted peoples, but for the Christian conquerors. But after the general conversion of the Muslims beginning in the last years of the fifteenth century, the situation changed. Could Moriscos worship in converted mosques without prejudice to their recently and forcibly acquired Christianity? In some cases, the Christian authorities thought they could, but in other instances Moriscos were prohibited from using their former mosques as churches.[94] And in at least four cases, former mosques were destroyed, so that, as Juan de Ribera said in the late sixteenth century, they

91. For another account (putatively from the perspective of a Nahua warrior) of the Virgin's role in this battle, see Juan de Grijalva, *Crónica de la Orden de N.S.P. Agustín en las provincias de la Nueva España*, 2.14 (Mexico City, 1985), pp. 182–83. A similar miracle involving the Virgin and Saint James occurred during the conquest of Peru at the siege of Cuzco in 1536, according to a legend that is full-blown by the very early seventeenth century: Felipe Guaman Poma de Ayala, *Nueva crónica y buen gobierno*, ed. John V. Murra, Rolena Adorno, and Jorge L. Urioste, 3 vols. (Madrid, 1987), 2:408–10; 2:686–88. On Saint James as the patron of Christian warriors in medieval Spain, see Herbers, "Politik und Heiligenverehrung." For a fascinating discussion of Saint James's military role in New Spain, see William B. Taylor, "Santiago's Horse: Christianity and Colonial Indian Resistance in the Heartland of New Spain," in *Violence, Resistance, and Survival in the Americas: Native Americans and the Legacy of Conquest*, ed. William B. Taylor and Franklin Pease (Washington, D.C., 1994), pp. 153–89. I thank Kenneth Mills for this reference.

92. Salazar, *Crónica*, 4.110, p. 474.

93. After the Spanish triumph, the victors built a church of Our Lady of the Remedies on the ruins of a temple which they had earlier named "The Temple of Victory." Salazar, *Crónica*, 4.126, p. 499.

94. Burns points to three mosques in the kingdom of Valencia which became Morisco churches: *Crusader Kingdom*, 1:63, 85. But a royal privilege for the newly converted Muslims of Uclés states that they may retain "la casa de oraçion que tenían seyendo moros para que la puedan vender e hazer casas de morada en tal manera que no quede casa de oraçion." Text edited by Mercedes García-Arenal, "Dos documentos sobre los moros de Uclés en 1501," *Al-Andalus* 42 (1977): 178.

would not serve as a "bad example," reminding the Moriscos of their former religion.[95]

As de Ribera recognized, newly converted peoples worshipping in newly converted religious spaces created a situation fraught with tension and ambiguity. The familiar architecture which spoke so eloquently of the old religion could sway the fragile faith of the convert. Equally, the continuity in the physical setting for worship might encourage resistance to conversion and the persistence, albeit in a covert form, of the old religion. It was exactly this situation of architectural ambiguity that characterized central Mexico in the 1520s, especially after Cortés's victory in 1521 and the subsequent arrival of Christian missionaries. As the conquistadores had done, the friars converted temples to serve as churches for the newly Christian native population.[96] But despite these conversions, the temples did not necessarily lose their original meaning for the Indians.

This ambiguity tinged even the statues of the Virgin enthroned in the temples. The Nahuas, declared the Franciscan chroniclers, did not always understand the presence of the Virgin (and the crucifix) on the altars as a symbol of Spanish triumph and appropriation of space. Unlike Muslims, the Nahuas possessed an iconic tradition of the sacred. They could thus manipulate the invasive images of Mary in ways that Muslims could not. The Nahuas might mingle the Christian images with their own, whether to add these new figures to their pantheon or to disguise their worship of the old statues behind the new.[97] The Virgin on the altar could not in the end cleanse the temple of "idolatry" and effectively convert it into a church. Thus, the Franciscans came to believe, the temples would have to be destroyed and replaced by structures built as churches.[98] Re-

95. "[C]um mali exemplum sit, et preteriti sceleris recordationem habeat, videtur averti prorsus debere, ut nullum eius supersit vestigium," José Sanchis y Sivera, *Nomenclátor geográfico-eclesiástico de los pueblos de Valencia con los nombres antiguos y modernos de los que existen o han existido, notas históricas y estadísticas . . .* (Valencia, 1922), p. 285 (a text written by Juan de Ribera about the destruction of the mosque at Manises). For similar statements by de Ribera about the destruction of the mosques at Carlet, Paterna, and Petrés, see Sanchis y Sivera, *Nomenclátor*, pp. 177, 334, 341.
96. Diego Valades praises the friars for having the saints' days celebrated "iis locis, quibus diabolus tantam dominationem et tyrannidem execuerat" and goes on to describe the beautiful decorations of the temples on such occasions: *Rhetorica Christiana ad concionandi et orandi usum accomodata . . .* (Perugia, 1579), 4.25, p. 227. I am grateful to Jorge Cañizares Esguerra for this reference.
97. Both are explanations proposed by the Franciscans. See, for example, Mendieta, *Historia*, 3.23, 260:142; and Motolinía, *Historia*, 1.3, p. 22. For analysis of the Mexicas' reaction to and manipulation of Christian images, see Gruzinski, *La guerre des images*, pp. 83–100. See also the subtle argument in Tom Cummins, "The Madonna and the Horse: Becoming Colonial in New Spain and Peru," in *Native Artists and Patrons in Colonial Latin America*, ed. Emily Umberger and Tom Cummins (Tempe, Ariz., 1995), pp. 52–83 (esp. 58–68).
98. On the friars' attitude and efforts, see Mendieta, *Historia*, 3.20–21, 260:137–39; Motolinía, *Historia*, 1.3, p. 22. In 1537, the bishops of New Spain requested permission from the crown to destroy those temples still standing because they were the setting for the Indians' continued "idolatry."

moved from the temples—from the physical setting of idolatry—and placed in explicitly Christian space, the images of Mary (and Christ) would receive proper worship from the Indians, or so Toribio de Motolinía wrote.[99] The practical difficulties of adapting temples for Christian worship probably also fueled the increasing antagonism of the Franciscans toward these buildings. After all, the temples were designed to meet ritual needs very different from those of Christianity.[100] In 1525, the friars initiated a campaign of the methodical and wholesale destruction of temples; by the 1550s, central Mexico was denuded of its temples and covered with newly built Christian churches.[101]

Identifiably Christian architecture was thus intended to resolve the contradictions that the presence of the statue of Mary (and the Cross) on temple altars could not. For as the Spanish used the Virgin to convert religious space in the earliest years of the conquest of Mexico, she herself underwent a process of conversion. The temples in which she was installed rendered her intelligible to the newly converted Indians in ways that the Spanish did not always control. Ambiguous in medieval Spain as the Christian Virgin who converted mosques into churches, yet praised by Muslims as Maryam, Mary was no less a paradoxical presence on the altars of Mexican temples.

Joaquin García Icazbalceta, *Don Fray Juan de Zumárraga primer obispo y arzobispo de México*, ed. Rafael Aguayo Spencer and Antonio Castro Leal, 4 vols. (Mexico City, 1947), Document 32, 3:102.
99. According to Motolinía, after finding images of the Virgin and Christ mingled with "idols," the friars admonished the Indians "si querían tener imágenes de Dios o de Santa María, que les hiciesen iglesia": Motolinía, *Historia*, 1.3, p. 22. His description of the ensuing transition from temple to church shows another kind of conversion of space; that is, the stones of the temples (and of their images) were used to build the churches. He writes that the Indians "al principio . . . comenzaron a . . . hacer algunas ermitas y adoratorios, y después iglesias, y ponían en ellas imágenes [i.e., of the Virgin and Christ], y con todo esto siempre procuraron de guardar sus templos sanos y enteros; aunque después, yendo la cosas adelante para hacer las iglesias comenzaron a echar mano de sus teocallis para sacar de ellos piedra y madera, y de esta manera quedaron desollados y derribados; y los ídolos de piedra . . . no sólo escaparon quebrados y hecho pedazos, pero vinieron a servir de cimientos para las iglesias." Motolinía, *Historia*, 1.3, p. 22–23.
100. McAndrew, *Open-Air Churches*, pp. 187–88.
101. For the wave of destruction which began in 1525, see Mendieta, *Historia*, 3.20–21, 260: 137–39; Motolinía, *Historia*, 1.3, p. 22. On the destruction and subsequent replacement of temples by churches, see McAndrew, *Open-Air Churches*, esp. 33, 121–67, 181–84. For a similar process in Peru, see Fraser, *Architecture of Conquest*, pp. 65–68 (although the Inca temple at Cuzco was used as the main church with only minor alterations for at least thirty years, p. 71).

Mosques Dedicated to Mary

Here I give details about those mosques I have found which were dedicated to the Virgin Mary and, where available, their subsequent architectural histories.

Alcira. By 1244 the secondary mosque was dedicated to the Virgin: Robert Ignatius Burns, *The Crusader Kingdom of Valencia: Reconstruction on a Thirteenth-Century Frontier,* 2 vols. (Cambridge, Mass., 1967), 1:63.

Alhama. According to one text, the main mosque was consecrated to the Virgin at the order of the marquis of Cádiz at the time of his conquest of the city in 1482: "Historia de los hechos del marqués de Cádiz," c. 15, *Colección de documentos inéditos para la historia de España,* 106:207. But according to Fernando del Pulgar, it was Ferdinand and Isabella who conquered the city and who dedicated the mosque to Mary: *Crónica de los reyes católicos,* c. 132, ed. Juan de Mata Carriazo, 2 vols. (Madrid, 1943), 2:24.

The Alhambra. The Alhambra's mosque was dedicated to the Virgin Mary and made into Granada's cathedral in 1492. In 1493 or 1494 it was slightly lengthened. In the early sixteenth century it lost its title as cathedral to another mosque dedicated to Mary, Granada's main mosque (see below). By the late sixteenth century it was suffering from structural problems and in 1576 was torn down. Work began on a church to replace it in 1581. Hieronymus Münzer praised the mosque-cathedral during his 1494 visit to Granada: Hieronymus Münzer, "Itinerarium hispanicum," ed. Ludwig Pfandl, *Revue Hispanique* 48 (1920): 49, 66. On the building's architectural history, see Leopoldo Torres Balbás, "La mezquita real de la Alhambra y el baño frontero," in Torres Balbás, *Obra Dispersa I: Al Andalus, Crónica de la España musulmana,* 3 vols. (Madrid, 1981), 3: 198–201, 201–207.

Almería. This city was taken by the Christians in 1489. According to the surrender agreement, the Muslims retained most mosques, including the main one. But after the city's inhabitants joined the revolt of the Mudejars in 1490, the Christians considered these terms to be void. Thus in January 1491, the main mosque was dedicated to the Virgin. There were only minimal alterations to its structure, since a project of 1521 to make the mosque's three central naves into one was never carried out. An earthquake of 1522 severely damaged the mosque-cathedral

and a new cathedral was built. Münzer provides a detailed and lauda-
tory description of the mosque-cathedral, which he saw in 1494: "Itinerarium hispanicum," p. 38. On the architectural history of the mosque-
cathedral, see Christian Ewert, "El mihrab de la mezquita mayor de
Almería," *Al-Andalus* 36 (1971): 391–460 (esp. 402); and Mª del Rosario
Torres Fernández and Mª del Mar Nicolás Martínez, "Una aportación
a la arqueología medieval almeriense: La mezquita mayor y la primitiva
catedral de Almería," in *Andalucía entre Oriente y Occidente (1236–
1492): Actas del V Coloquio Internacional de historia medieval de Andalucía,* ed. Emilio Cabrera (Córdoba, 1988), pp. 773–85.

Alora. After conquering Alora in 1484, at Ferdinand's behest, the main
mosque was made into a church and then dedicated to the Virgin by
Isabella's command: Pulgar, *Crónica,* c. 160, 2:123.

Córdoba. For accounts of the dedication of the mosque to the Virgin immediately after Ferdinand III's capture of the city in 1236, see: *Crónica
latina de los reyes de Castilla,* ed. Luis Charlo Brea (Cádiz, 1984), p. 100;
Rodrigo Jiménez de Rada, *Historia de rebus sive historia gothica,* 9.27,
ed. Juan Fernández Valverde, CCCM 72.1 (Turnhout, 1987), p. 299;
Lucas de Tuy, *Chronicon mundi,* ed. Andreas Schott, *Hispaniae illustratae,* 4 vols. (Frankfurt, 1603–1608), 4:116. Ferdinand introduced very
few changes to the building; it was only sometime later that chapels
were added and that the mihrab was made into the sacristy. In the first
decade of the sixteenth century, work began on the Gothic choir. See
Teresa Laguna Paul, "Córdoba: Mezquita-catedral," in *La España Gótica,
11: Andalucía,* ed. José Fernández Lopez (Madrid, 1992), pp. 181–229.

Coria (possible). The town was taken by Alfonso VII in the 1130s and
a church was dedicated to the Virgin Mary. The chronicle of the 1140s
which describes these events is ambiguous. It describes a process of the
spiritual cleansing of the city: "mundata est ab immunditia barbarice
gentis et a contaminatione Mahometis et, destructa omnia spurcitia
paganorum civitatis illius et templi sui, dedicaverunt ecclesiam in honore sancte marie semper virginis et omnium sanctorum . . . ," *Chronicon
Adefonsi imperatoris,* 2.66, ed. Antonio Maya Sánchez in *Chronica Hispana saeculi XII,* ed. Emma Falque, Juan Gil, Antonio Maya Sánchez,
CCCM 71.1 (Turnhout, 1990), p. 225. The phrase "destructa omnia
spurcitia . . . templi sui" could mean that the mosque itself was destroyed, or simply that the "filth" of the mosque was exorcised. It seems
probable that the mosque was not destroyed but was used as a church.
In any case, the building history of the Gothic cathedral dedicated to

Mary dates only to the mid-thirteenth or fourteenth century. On the Gothic cathedral, see Teresa Laguna Paul, "Coria: catedral," in *La España Gótica, 14: Extremadura,* ed. José Fernández Lopez and Frederico Javier Pizarro (Madrid, 1995), pp. 138–54.

Granada. The main mosque was dedicated to the Virgin in 1501 as a parish church and proclaimed a cathedral shortly thereafter. Some architectural modifications were made to the arches primarily to change the orientation to the east. In the early sixteenth century, chapels intended as the burial place of Ferdinand and Isabella (and other prominent Christians) were added. The mosque-church lost its title of cathedral and in 1588 the alminar was destroyed to make way for the new cathedral. But the rest of the building stood until structural problems caused its demolition beginning in the 1660s. For the architecural history, see Manuel Gómez-Moreno, *Guía de Granada,* 2 vols. (Granada, 1892; reprinted 1994), 1:284, 287–89; Leopoldo Torres Balbás, "La mezquita mayor de Granada," in his *Obra Dispersa I: Al Andalus, Crónica de la España musulmana,* 3 vols. (Madrid, 1981), 3:84–111 (esp. 94–96).

According to a legend which I have not been able to date, in 1490 an audacious Christian knight, Hernán Pérez del Pulgar, made his way into Muslim Granada and claimed the mosque for the Virgin Mary by tacking to the door a parchment inscribed with the Ave Maria; the legend is recounted by Gómez-Moreno in *Guía de Granada,* 1:281; and Torres Balbás in "La mezquita mayor," p. 94. According to Gómez-Moreno (1:287), the emperor granted Pulgar a burial chapel in the mosque-cathedral; inscribed upon Pulgar's tomb was "aqui está sepultado el mag⁰ cavallero Fernand de Pulgar S. del Salar el qual tomó posesión desta Iglesia siendo esta cibdad de moros. . . ." Pulgar died in 1531, but the date of the inscription itself is not clear. There seems to be an echo of this legend in a nineteenth-century play performed in the church of Vilanova de Alcolea commemorating the Christian victory at Granada. In the course of a verbal and physical duel between a Muslim and a Christian, the Muslim accuses the Christian of having boldly placed in the mosque a banner bearing Mary's name. See the text cited in Joan Amades, *Las danzas de Moros y Cristianos* (Valencia, 1966), pp. 61–66.

Guadix. This city was taken by the Christians in 1489. As at Almería, according to the surrender agreement, the Muslims retained most mosques, including the main one. But after the revolt of the Mudejars in 1490, the Christians considered these terms to be void and appropriated the mosques: Andrés Bernáldez, *Memorias del reinado de los reyes católicos,* c. 98, ed. Manuel Gómez-Moreno and Juan de Mata Carriazo (Madrid, 1962), p. 220. The city's main mosque was then dedicated to the Virgin. When Münzer saw the mosque-cathedral in 1494, it had not yet undergone any major modifications: "Itinerarium hispanicum," p. 43. Sometime soon after 1496, work on a Gothic cathedral began. On the mosque's conversion and its architectural history, see Carlos Asenjo Sedano, *La catedral de Guadix* (Granada, 1977), pp. 13–22.

Huesca. At Huesca, the main mosque was dedicated to Christ, Peter, Mary, and John the Baptist immediately after the city was captured by Peter I of Aragon in 1097; *Colección diplomatica de Pedro I de Aragón y Navarra,* ed. Antonio Ubieto Arteta (Saragossa, 1951), no. 30, p. 251. At least one secondary mosque in Huesca was dedicated solely to the Virgin: *Colección diplomatica de Pedro I,* nos. 28, 37, pp. 247–49, 262– 64 (the editor expresses some doubts about the authenticity of these charters).

Jaén. In 1246, after taking the city, Ferdinand III presided over the main mosque's dedication to Mary: *Primera crónica general de España que mandó componer Alfonso el Sabio y se continuaba bajo Sancho IV en 1289,* c. 1071, ed. Ramón Menéndez Pidal, 2d ed., 2 vols. (Madrid, 1955), 2: 746–47. The mosque-church was not replaced with a new cathedral until 1386: Pedro Galera, "Jaén: Catedral," in *La España Gótica, 11: Andalucía,* ed. José Fernández Lopez (Madrid, 1992), pp. 137–39.

Játiva. The main mosque was dedicated to the Virgin by 1244; Burns, *Crusader Kingdom,* 1:85.

Jérez de la Frontera. By the 1260s, after Ferdinand III's conquest of Jérez and Alfonso's subsequent reconquest, what appears to have been an Almohad palace mosque was consecrated as a royal castral chapel and dedicated to the Virgin. By 1283 it was called "Santa María del Alcázar." See Alfonso X's privilege of that year: *Noticias y documentos referentes al Alcázar de Jerez de la Frontera, en los siglos XIII a XVI,* ed. Mariano Alcocer y Martinez and Hipólito Sancho de Sopranis (Larache, 1940), p. 15. On Alfonso X's patronage of this chapel and the statue of the Virgin Mary it contained, see Alfonso X, *Cantigas,* Cantiga 345, 3:197–201; and *Noticias y documentos,* pp. 9–10, 13–15. Although the Alfonsine texts do not state that the chapel was a converted mosque, architectural evidence does. See Marianne Barucand and Achim Bednorz, *Moorish Architecture in Andalusia* (Cologne, 1992), pp. 158–61; and Alfonso Jiménez, "Arquitectura Gaditana de Epoca Alfonsí," in *Cádiz en el siglo XIII: Actas de las Jornandas Commemorativas del VII Centenario de la muerte de Alfonso X el Sabio* (Cádiz, 1983), pp. 142–43, 150, 155–58. Jiménez argues that Alfonso X made relatively few changes to the building (placing the altar on the east wall, and opening a door with a portico in one wall).

Lisbon. When Lisbon was captured by the Christians in 1147, its mosque was dedicated to Mary: Osbern, *De expugnatione Lyxbonensi,* in *Itinerarium peregrinorum et gesta Regis Ricardi,* ed. William Stubbs, Rerum Britanicarum Medii Aevi Scriptores 38.1 (London, 1864), p. clxxxi.

Loja. Ferdinand and Isabella dedicated a mosque to the Virgin after conquering the city in 1486; Pulgar, *Crónica,* c. 187, 2:227.

Majorca (Palma de). After the Christians took the city in 1229–1230, James I dedicated a church to the Virgin. Although he writes that he "built" this church, the evidence suggests rather that he adapted the city's main mosque: James I, *Llibre dels feits del rei en Jaume o crònica de Jaume I,* c. 105, in Jaume I, Bernat Desclot, Ramon Mutaner, Pere III, *Els Quatre Grans Cròniques,* ed. Ferrán Soldevila (Barcelona, 1971), p. 55. The thirteenth-century alterations to the mosque included adding a bell tower. It was only in the early fourteenth century that major alterations in the mosque's fabric occurred. Parts of the mosque were still standing until 1386. See Xavier Barral y Altet, "Palma: catedral," in *La España Gótica 5: Baleares,* ed. Joan de Sureda Pons (Madrid, 1994), pp. 82–116; and Marcel Durliat, *L'art dans le Royaume de Majorque: Les débuts de l'art gothique en Roussillon, en Cerdagne et aux Baleares* (Toulouse, 1962), pp. 150–67.

Málaga. The city was captured by Isabella and Ferdinand in 1487 and the main mosque dedicated to the Virgin as the city's cathedral: Pulgar, *Crónica,* c. 123, 2:334. In 1498, a door was opened in one of the mosque-cathedral's walls; in 1542 the building of a chapel in the northeast corner destroyed much of the mosque. By 1588, work on an entirely new building had begun. See M. D. Aguilar Garcia, "La Mezquita Mayor de Málaga y la Iglesia Vieja," *Boletín de Arte* 6 (1985): 55–70 (esp. 55–58); María Isabel Calero and Virgilio Martínez Enamorado, *Málaga, ciudad de Al-Andalus* (Málaga, 1995), pp. 174–77.

Murcia. In 1266, James I conquered the city and dedicated its main mosque to the Virgin: James I, *Llibre dels feits,* c. 445, 448–50, pp. 159, 160. The mosque-cathedral stood until the mid-fourteenth century, when it was replaced with a Gothic building: *Reino frontizero castellano: Murcia en los siglos XIV–XV,* ed. Juan Torres Fontes et al., Historia de la region murciana 4 (Murcia, 1980), pp. 243–44, 246–79.

Murviedro (modern Sagunto). Its main mosque was dedicated to the Virgin Mary during the thirteenth-century Christian conquest of the kingdom of Valencia: Burns, *Crusader Kingdom,* 1:86. The mosque-church was totally rebuilt beginning in 1334: Daniel Benito Goerlich, "Sagunto: Santa María," in *La España Gótica, 4: Valencia y Murcia,* ed. Daniel Benito Goerlich (Madrid, 1989), pp. 471–74.

Niebla. When the town was taken by Alfonso X in 1262, he dedicated a mosque to the Virgin Mary to serve as a parish church. He made only the absolutely necessary changes to the building, placing bells in the minaret and changing the orientation (probably by placing the altar on the east wall). It was only in the late fifteenth or early sixteenth century that more significant Gothic additions altered the building's appearance. Ana Marín Fidalgo, *Arquitectura Gótica del sur de la provincia de Huelva* (Huelva, 1982), pp. 60–64, plates 10–17.

Ronda. When Isabella and Ferdinand took the city in 1485, they dedicated one of its mosques to the Virgin: Pulgar, *Crónica,* c. 172, 2:173–74.

Santa María del Puerto. When Alfonso X definitively conquered al-Qanatir in 1264 and gave the town its new Christian name, according to the *Cantigas de Santa María,* he built a church there to the Virgin (see, for example, Alfonso X, el Sabio, *Cantigas de Santa María,* Cantigas 356, 358, 364, 398, ed. Walter Mettmann, 3 vols. [Madrid, 1986–89], 3:225–26, 227–29, 237–39, 297–99.) Although none of the *Cantigas* mention it, this process of building was rather the adaptation of a converted mosque. On these *cantigas* and the architectural evidence that the building was originally a mosque, see Leopoldo Torres Balbás, "La mezquita de Al-Qanatir y el santuario de Alfonso el Sabio en el Puerto Santa María," *Al-Andalus* 7 (1942): 417–37. Although the *Cantigas* depict extensive building, it has been argued recently that the conversion of the mosque involved only relatively minor architectural alterations; Jiménez, "Arquitectura Gaditana," 143–44, 149.

Saragossa. When Münzer visited the city in the 1490s, he described its cathedral complex as embracing a mosque transformed into a chapel dedicated to the Virgin: "Et ecclesia est magna, pulcra. . . . Que olim erat mesquita Sarracenorum, et hodie in ambitu stat una antiquissima et fortissima mesquita, quam Sarraceni intrantes valde venerantur. Licet nunc sit capella Beate Virgini dedicata," "Itinerarium hispanicum," p. 138.

Seville. Ferdinand III took the city in 1248 and had the main mosque dedicated to Mary: *Primera crónica general,* c. 1125, 1129, 2:767, 769. By at least the 1270s, work was being done on the mosque-cathedral in order to install chapels: Rafael Cómez Ramos, *Arquitectura alfonsí* (Seville, 1974), pp. 30, 55–58. The interior of the mosque was divided in two. After earthquake damage in the late fourteenth century, the cathedral chapter decided to build a new cathedral; work began on the Gothic structure in 1402. Rafael Cómez Ramos, "Sevilla: Catedral," in *La España Gótica, 11: Andalucía,* ed. José Fernández Lopez (Madrid, 1992), pp. 290–328 (esp. 290–93). When Münzer visited Seville in 1494, although most of the new building was complete (except for the choir), he was very aware that there had been a mosque on the site: "Itinerarium hispanicum," pp. 74, 75.

Toledo. Shortly after Alfonso VI's conquest of the city, the main mosque was consecrated as a cathedral and dedicated to Mary (1086). For Christian accounts of the conversion of the mosque into a church, see Alfonso VI's privilege of 1086 in *Privilegios reales y viejos documentos de Toledo* (Madrid, 1963), Document I, pp. 2–3; and Jiménez de Rada, *Historia de rebus,* 6.24–25, 7.4, pp. 205–208, 225. On the political and cultural ramifications of this conversion, see Francisco J. Hernández, "La cathédrale, instrument d'assimilation," in *Tolède, XIIᵉ–XIIIᵉ: Musulmans, chrétiens et juifs: Le savoir et la tolérance,* ed. Louis Cardaillac (Paris, 1991), pp. 147–57. It was not until 1226 that work began on a Gothic building to replace the mosque-cathedral. See Jiménez de Rada, *Historia de rebus,* 9.13, p. 294; and *Primera crónica general,* c. 1037, 2:272. On what the mosque may have looked like and on the construction of the Gothic cathedral, see Barbé Coquelin de Lisle, "De la grande mosquée à la cathédrale gothique," in *Tolède, XIIᵉ–XIIIᵉ,* pp. 147–57.

Tortosa (possible). In a privilege of 1224, James I of Aragón describes how Raymond Berenger IV took Tortosa in 1148 and "contulit ... Deo et sancte Marie, episcopo et clericis ibidem degentibus mezquitam maiorem." It is not clear who these clerics are (Mozarabs?). The "contulit . . . Deo et sancte Marie" would seem to imply that the mosque was dedicated to God and Mary. Even if the mosque was dedicated to the Virgin, it was quickly replaced with a Christian-built church. For the privilege then relates in detail how Gaufredus, bishop of Tortosa, built a church in honor of the Virgin which was dedicated in the later twelfth century in the presence of Alfonso II and Sancha of Aragón. See the text in *Documentos de Jaime I de Aragón,* ed. Ambrosio Huici Miranda and María Desamparados Cabanes Pecourt, 5 vols. (Valencia, 1976–1988), no. 52, 1:115–20. The mosque was dedicated to the Virgin in 1151 and the first stone of the new cathedral laid in 1156 (this cathedral, completed within twenty years, was completely rebuilt in the fourteenth century), according to Emma Liaño Martínez, "Tortosa: Catedral," in *La España Gótica, 2: Cataluña, 1,* ed. Joan Sureda Pons (Madrid, 1987), pp. 163–73 (she cites no text for the consecration of the mosque-church).

Valencia: After the Cid took Valencia, he had its mosque consecrated as a church and dedicated to Mary (1098). See *Historia Roderici vel gesta Roderici,* c. 73, ed. Emma Falque in *Chronica Hispana saeculi XII,* ed. Emma Falque, Juan Gil, Antonio Maya Sánchez, CCCM 71.1 (Turnhout, 1990), p. 97; and Ramón Menéndez Pidal, *La España del Cid,* 7th ed., 2 vols. (Madrid, 1969), 2:868–71. When the Muslims recaptured the city in the early twelfth century, this building probably became a mosque again. At James I's conquest of the city in 1238, the main mosque (probably the same one as the Cid had earlier made into a church) was dedicated to Mary and made into a cathedral. But by at least the late 1240s, James had begun to prepare the way for building a new structure on the same site; work on the Gothic cathedral began in 1262. See Burns, *Crusader Kingdom,* 1:19–20; and Joaquín Bérchez Gómez and Arturo Zaragozá, "Iglesia Catedral Basílica de Santa María (Valencia)," in *Valencia: Arquitectura Religiosa,* ed. Joaquín Bérchez Gómez, Monumentos de la Comunidad Valenciana, Catálogo de Monumentos y Conjuntos declarados e incoados 10 (Valencia, 1984), pp. 16–27.

Vélez-Málaga. The city was taken by Ferdinand and Isabella in 1487 and its main mosque dedicated to the Virgin; Bernáldez, *Memorias,* c. 82, p. 176; Mosén Diego de Valera, *Crónica de los reyes católicos,* c. 78, ed. Juan de Mata Carriazo (Madrid, 1927), p. 236; Pulgar, *Crónica,* c. 202, 2:279.

CHAPTER TEN

Saints, Heretics, and Fire: Finding Meaning through the Ordeal

Thomas Head

In 978 Archbishop Egbert of Trier reformed the abbey of St. Eucharius and, as part of his efforts, undertook the renovation of its churches.[1] Built over an early Christian burial ground to the south of Trier, those churches housed the relics of several early bishops of that see. During the construction project, workmen uncovered a well-preserved sarcophagus of unusual antiquity and interest. Monks were summoned to examine the find and to read an inscription in Latin: "To whoever anxiously wishes to learn about this tomb. Here lies the man Celsus [i.e., noble one], who lived up to his name not only in word but also in his actions. God has certainly inscribed this man in the roll of honor, a man who was not lazy, but ever vigorous in his quest for his true fatherland."[2]

At various points in the inception and development of this article, I have relied on the institutional support of Hunter College, the Institute for Advanced Study, Washington University, and Yale University. I have presented earlier versions of parts of this article at a number of conferences, including the Shelby Cullom Davis Seminar at the Department of History of Princeton University in 1993 and the American Historical Association at Seattle in 1998. I would like to thank all those present at these varied occasions for their comments, most particularly Caroline Bynum, Peter Brown, Sharon Farmer, Patrick Geary, William Jordan, Frederick Paxton, Virginia Reinburg, and Barbara Rosenwein (whose grace extended to presenting the paper in question on one occasion in my stead). Robert Bartlett, Philippe Buc, and Margaret Cormack also provided me help in tracking down instances of this ritual which figure in the handlist provided in the Appendix.

1. The evidence for the following incident is to be found in Theodoric of St. Eucharius, *Inventio et miracula s. Celsi,* in *AASS,* February III, pp. 402–10. For fuller detail, see Thomas Head, "Art and Artifice in Ottonian Trier," *Gesta* 36 (1997): 65–82.
2. "Sollicitus quicumque cupis cognoscere tumbam, / Praeclarus iacet hic nomine vel meritis / Celsus, quem Dominus vero insigniuit honore, / Non segnis patriae semper ubique vigens: / Qui genus atque ortium claro de stemmate traxit; / Affectuque pio conditur hoc tumulo." Theodoric of St. Eucharius, *Inventio et miracula s. Celsi,* c. 13, p. 398.

The discovery required interpretation by the archbishop and the monks who lived in the monastic community built over this tomb. Egbert and the monks of St. Eucharius complied quickly, decisively, and—one can surmise—happily. As in any act of interpretation, however, the categories available to them were circumscribed by social, cultural, and material circumstances. They had to provide an interpretation which was plausible in the terms shared by themselves and the audiences whom they wished to convince and impress. Egbert and the monks chose to proclaim Celsus a saint. For Christians of the tenth century, the term *sanctus* not only designated a "holy man," but more specifically served as a title. A saint was a holy man, or more rarely woman, of the past who now lived in the court of heaven and who was worthy of liturgical commemoration in the roll of the greatest heroes and heroines of the Christian church. In such an eschatological context the bodies or relics of the saints served as material bridges between the everyday world and the court of heaven.[3]

The designation was a plausible one. For Celsus had been buried with marks of distinction by his contemporaries near the tomb of Eucharius and other fourth-century bishops of Trier who were already acclaimed by long and hallowed tradition to be saints. The tenth-century clerics assumed that Celsus had been a disciple of Eucharius, perhaps even a bishop in his own right. For them, the church of St. Eucharius was a familiar holy place, not like the mosques of newly-conquered Muslims or the temples of newly-conquered natives described by Amy Remensnyder elsewhere in this volume. In fact, as shown by the work of modern archeologists, the monastery of St. Eucharius had been constructed over a cemetery in which Christians had been buried since the third century and in which a shrine to Trier's holy bishops had stood since at least the fifth century.[4]

There was, however, a problem. No written record of an early Chris-

3. On the development of theological reflection on the fate of the soul and the resurrection of the body in Late Antique Christianity and medieval Christianity, see Caroline Bynum, *The Resurrection of the Body in Western Christianity, 200–1336* (New York, 1995), particularly pp. 104–8 on the relationship of this theology to the cult of saints' relics.

4. The funerary church over the episcopal tombs had become a monastery by the early tenth century, and possibly as early as the eighth century; see Ferdinand Pauly, "Die ältesten Urkunden für die Trierer Kirche St. Eucharius und ihre Bedeutung für die Frühgeschichte der Abtei," *Kurtrierisches Jahrbuch* 7 (1967): 12–20. With the discovery of the alleged relics of an apostle in the twelfth century, the abbey came to be known under the patronage of St. Matthias. An inscription (since lost) recorded how a bishop of Trier named Cyril dedicated an altar to his predecessors, Sts. Eucharius and Valerius, at this spot around the middle of the fifth century; see *Recueil des inscriptions chrétiennes de Gaule. I: Première Belgique*, ed. Nancy Gauthier (Paris, 1975), no. 19. See also the summary of evidence in *Province ecclésiastique de Trèves (Belgica Prima)*, ed. Nancy Gauthier, *Topographie chrétienne des cités de la Gaule des origines au milieu du VIIIᵉ siècle* 1 (Paris, 1986), pp. 27–28.

tian *sanctus* named Celsus had survived, apart from the inscription on the sarcophagus. Egbert therefore set about having the status of this newly discovered patron officially recognized. That is, to use a term anachronistic to the tenth century, he undertook the canonization of Celsus. As a climax to these efforts, the archbishop orchestrated a ritual, called an *inventio*. It was in such an *inventio* (that is, literally, a "discovery") that relics were placed on the high altar of a church, and their cult thus officially commenced, before returning the relics to their shrines, located as they might be on other altars, in the crypt, or elsewhere in the church.

At the high altar of the church of St. Eucharius that day Egbert indulged in a bit of innovative showmanship. As a monk of the abbey named Theodoric described the event:

> The priest of the Lord [Egbert] presumed to undertake an examination as to whether one could say that these relics were actually those of blessed Celsus, lest the matter by chance seem to take place, or to have taken place, in a vacuum. In the eyes of all the clergy, he took a small piece of very thin cloth and he wrapped a piece of a joint from the saint's finger in it. He placed it in the live coals of the thurible in which incense was burned for the space of an hour, during which time he recited the mystical canon [of the mass] in its entirety. The relic remained intact in the fire. . . . After this miracle had been witnessed and the chanting of the mass completed, the archbishop placed that relic, [now shown to be] acceptable to God, on the altar along with the remaining bones in a seemly fashion. Having made a benediction, he dismissed the congregation in peace, giving praise to God, and saying, "Now we know what we have [in these relics]! How good is God! How great is his mercy for us in this world!"[5]

According to Egbert's actions and words—and no less significantly according to Theodoric's text which recorded those actions and words—Celsus's identity as a saint had been confirmed by the ritual application

5. "Finito vero doctrinae sermone, de pulpito rediit ad altare, quatenus Deo omnipotenti ad honorem B. Celsi, obque totius saluationem Christiani populi, nostrae redemptionis hostiam deuota mente offerret. Cumque iam offertorius cantus cum magno iubilationis serio consummatus fuisset, et iam Praesationis ordo instaret; examinationis gratia experiri Sacerdos Domini praesumpsit, quid de B. Celso sentiendum foret neforte in vacuu curreret, aut cucurisset, accepto in oculis totius Cleri panniculo tenuissimi fili, et inuoluit illi articulum de compage digiti sacrati, et inuoluit prunis thuribuli viuis quibus thymiamata incendebantur, et totum illud horae spatium, per quod Canonem mysticum ex integro peregit, illaesum atque ab igne intactum permansit: quatenis Apostolicum illud per ignem materialem B. Celso claresceret euidentius . . . Quo viso miraculo, Missarumque tenore completo, reposuit Episcopus Deo acceptabile pignus, reliquis ossibus super altare decenter locatis: dataque benedictione, dimisit populum in pace, laudantem Deum, ac dicentem: Nunc cognouimus quid habemus, quoniam bonus Dominus, quoniam in seculum misericordia eius." Theodoric of St. Eucharius, *Inventio et miracula s. Celsi*, cc. 22 and 24, p. 400.

of fire to the relics and the subsequent failure of those relics to be consumed by that fire.

Egbert had, with an inspired sense of ritual theatre, cobbled together
a ritual which both authenticated and proclaimed Celsus's sanctity. The
archbishop had in essence taken recourse to the judicial ordeal by fire.[6]
In the secular version of the ordeal, the proband in a court case grasped
a red-hot iron or plunged an arm into a cauldron of boiling water, thus
burning the skin. Although the ritual—and it was most certainly a ritual—was used in secular courts, it required the participation of a cleric
in order to bless the means by which fire was applied. The later appearance of the proband's wound determined the truth of the testimony and
thus the outcome of the case. Courts had recourse to the ordeal in cases
where decisive written proof was lacking and the testimony of witnesses
untrustworthy. The discovery of the bones of a hitherto unrecognized
saint afforded a similar type of contested meaning. Rather than applying
the blessed fire to the living body of a compromised witness, however,
Egbert instead applied it directly to the bones of the presumed saint. The
success of the ritual verified the meaning which Egbert had attached
to the bones on the basis of the ancient inscription. Through this process
the archbishop proved that the tomb uncovered during the renovation
of the abbey church of St. Eucharius contained not the detritus of an ordinary human being, but the relics of a saint.

Archbishop Egbert was probably the first to apply the ordeal by fire
to relics in this manner, but he was far from the last.[7] Over the course of
the next two hundred years, clerics utilized a similar ritual on numerous
occasions to authenticate relics of saints.[8] While this ritual was of great
interest to seventeenth- and eighteenth-century scholars, it has received
scant attention since.[9] Use of the ritual first developed within the circle

6. The best account of the practice of the varied forms of ordeal remains Hermann Nottarp,
Gottesurteilstudien, Bamberger Abhandlungen und Forschungen 2 (Munich, 1956). Overviews
may be found in Jean Gaudemet, "Les ordalies au Moyen Âge: Doctrine, législation et pratique ca-
noniques," *La Preuve,* 4 vols., Recueil de la Société Jean Bodin 17 (Brussels, 1965), 2:99–135
and Robert Bartlett, *Trial by Fire and Water: The Medieval Judicial Ordeal* (Oxford, 1986), pp. 13–
33. An invaluable collection of documents relating to the history and practice of the ordeal may
be found in Peter Browe, *De ordaliis,* 2 vols., Pontificia Universitas Gregoriana, Textus et docu-
menta in usum exercitationum et praelectionum academicarum, series theologica 4 and 11 (Rome,
1932–33).
7. I have analyzed the formation of this ritual process, and the priority of Egbert's use of it, in "The
Genesis of the Ordeal of Relics by Fire (c.980–c.1020)" (forthcoming).
8. See the Appendix for a preliminary handlist.
9. Jean Ferrand, *Disquisitio reliquiarum, sive de suspicienda et suspecta earumdem numero reliquiarum, quae in diversis ecclesiis servantur* (Lyons, 1647), bk. 2, pars prior, chap. 3, art. 1, pp. 460–68;
Luc d'Achéry and Jean Mabillon, eds., *Acta sanctorum ordinis Sancti Benedicti,* first edition, 6 vols.
in 9 (Paris, 1668–1701), praefatio, observatio 45, 6.1:xxvi–xxvii; Ludovico Muratori, *Antiquitates
Italicae medii aevi,* 6 vols. (Milan, 1738–1742), dissertatio 58, 5:9–15; Edmond Martène, *De antiquis ecclesiae ritibus libri tres,* 4 vols. (Antwerp and Venice, 1763–64), 3.8, 2:345–46. The most

of reforming clerics in Ottonian Germany of which Egbert was a member. From there it spread through much of Western Europe, including Scandinavia and the Slavic lands, over the course of the eleventh and early twelfth centuries. The use of fire to authenticate relics, like the judicial use of fire to authenticate the oral testimony of witnesses, was a ritual form of proof: the rubrics of the single surviving *ordo* read "for proving relics" (*ad probandas reliquias*).[10] By the thirteenth century, it had passed out of usage; during the same period clerical participation in the judicial ordeal came to be prohibited.[11] The ritual use of fire was apparently resurrected during the early modern period to test relics not of saints' bodies, but of the true cross.[12]

This ritual served primarily to authenticate newly discovered or newly obtained relics for which no other firm proof existed. Sometimes it was used when there was no reasonable guarantee of authenticity offered with a gift or sale. When Abbot Gauzlin of Fleury purchased a relic of Christ's burial shroud during a visit to Rome in the first years of the eleventh century, he employed the ordeal because "he feared that some fraud on the part of the seller might hide under the veil of a simulated truth."[13] At

---

wide-ranging early modern treatment of the ritual is actually to be found in the tersest account, a subentry for the word "ignis" titled "Ignis judicio probatae reliquiae, veraene essent, an supposititiae" in Charles Du Fresne Du Cange, *Glossarium ad scriptores mediae et infimae latinitatis*, 10 vols. (original edition, Paris, 1678; reprint, Paris, 1937–38), 4:760. Twentieth-century scholars have mostly noted the ritual only in passing while treating other subjects related either to the judicial ordeal or to the cult of saints. The one exception is Nicole Hermann-Mascard, *Les reliques des saints: Formation coutumière d'un droit*, Société d'histoire du droit, Collection d'histoire institutionnelle et sociale 6 (Paris, 1975), pp. 134–36. Hermann-Mascard does little more than to expand, with many innaccuracies, on the information provided by Du Cange and Martène. For brief notations, see Hippolyte Delehaye, *Sanctus: Essai sur le culte des saints dans l'antiquité*, Subsidia hagiographica 17 (Brussels, 1927), p. 205 (citing Du Cange); Eric Kemp, *Canonization and Authority in the Western Church* (Oxford, 1948), p. 49 (citing Delehaye); Bartlett, *Trial by Fire and Water*, p. 22 (citing Herrmann-Mascard).

10. Martène, *De antiquis ecclesiae ritibus libri tres*, 3.8, 2:346. The *ordo* has been reprinted several times, including PL 71:1185–86 and Adolf Franz, *Die kirchlichen Benediktionen im Mittalalter*, 2 vols. (Freiburg, 1909), 2:348–49. The manuscript cited by Martène, allegedly a twelfth-century pontifical from Reims, has been lost: Aimé-Georges Martimort, *La documentation liturgique de Dom Edmond Martène: Étude codicologique*, Studi e testi 279 (Vatican City, 1978), nos. 259–60, p. 183 and no. 903, p. 435.

11. On the passing of the judicial ordeal, see John Baldwin, "The Intellectual Preparation for the Canon of 1215 against Ordeals," *Speculum* 36 (1961): 613–36 and Bartlett, *Trial by Fire and Water*, pp. 70–102.

12. Jaime Villanueva reported having seen a relic of the true cross at the Hieronymite monastery in Valdebron; its label stated that Archbishop Mirrales had undertaken an examination of it through fire in 1530 ("per ignem examinatum fuit"): *Viage literario a las iglesias de España*, 20 vols. (Madrid, 1803–52), 19:41–42. Jean Mabillon reported a use of the ritual proof of relics used on the true cross by an Italian legate in Paris in the seventeenth century: D'Achèry and Mabillon, *Acta sanctorum ordinis Sancti Benedicti*, praefatio, observatio 45, 6.1:xxvi–xxvii.

13. "Cum quibus et reliquias sudarii domini nostri Jhesu Christi omni ornamentorum speciei preponendas, mille solidorum dono adeptas, Floriacensi loco intulit, nonis currentibus januarii; ti-

Troia, a fortress town in Apulia newly conquered from the Greeks, work-men uncovered the tomb of Secundinus while rebuilding the cathedral in the late 1020s.[14] The bishop doubted the authenticity of the relics un-til he was cured of a mysterious disease through the saint's intercession; he then employed the ordeal by fire to celebrate and demonstrate the relics' virtues. In the 1050s the monks of Saint-Riquier sent a bone from the right hand of St. Vigor to the abbey of Cérizey, whose abbot authen-ticated it with fire.[15] Guibert of Nogent told how, around the turn of the twelfth century, an unknown man brought the relic of the arm of St. Ar-nulf to Clermont-en-Beauvaisis.[16] In Guibert's words, the townspeople remained "doubtful" (*ambiguus*) until convinced by the proof through fire. Sometime around 1140, workmen found the tomb of Priscus in a field near Frigento.[17] They reported their discovery to a priest, who in turn informed the local bishop. When the priest enshrined the relics, both his bishop and the archbishop of Benevento objected that there was no certainty that the body was truly that of the saint. On their instruc-tions, the priest undertook to test the relics through the ordeal.

In addition to the suspicion of a mistaken or forged identity for relics, there was another reason why a corpse might not be a true relic worthy of veneration: the person, even if he or she had been venerated for a long time, might actually not be a saint after all. In the 1080s, the new arch-bishop of Canterbury required the monks of Evesham to authenticate the sanctity of two former abbots named Wistan and Credanus. Abbot Wal-ter decided to employ the ordeal by fire for this purpose: "not only were the relics . . . not consumed, but none of the raging fire was able to touch them."[18] In the early twelfth century, clerics in Denmark used an ordeal by fire for the bones of a man named Theodegar as one of the chief means of obtaining episcopal permission for his cult.[19] In the middle decades

mensque ne sub velamine simulatae veritatis quaelibet lateret fraus venditoris, medio ferventium injectis prunarum, ac si aurum fornacis in antrum, inlesae fulgentesque apparuerunt." Andrew of Fleury, *Vita Gauzlini abbatis Floriacensis monasterii,* c. 20, ed. Robert-Henri Bautier and Gillette Labory (Paris, 1969), p. 60.

14. *Historia inventionis corporis s. Secundini,* c. 6 in *AASS,* February II, p. 531 and Waiferius of Monte Cassino, *Inventio corporis s. Secundini,* c. 9 in *AASS,* February II, p. 534.

15. Hariulf, *Chronique de l'abbaye de Saint-Riquier (Vᵉ siècle–1104),* 4.20, ed. Ferdinand Lot, Col-lection de textes pour servir à l'étude et à l'enseignement de l'histoire 17 (Paris, 1894), p. 228.

16. Guibert of Nogent, *Autobiographie,* 3.20, ed. Edmond-René Labande, Les classiques de l'his-toire de France au moyen âge 34 (Paris, 1981), p. 462.

17. *Historia inventionis s. Prisci,* c. 13 in *AASS,* September I, p. 218.

18. Dominic of Evesham, *Translatio et miracula s. Odulfi* in *Chronicon Abbatiae de Evesham ad an-num 1418,* ed. W. D. Macray, Rolls Series 29 (London, 1863), pp. 323–24.

19. *De s. Theodgaro,* c. 6 in *Vitae sanctorum Danorum,* ed. Martin Clarentius Gertz, 4 vols. in 1 (Copenhagen, 1908–12), p. 16.

of the twelfth century, the abbot of Andres in Flanders tested the relics of that monastery's saintly patron, a woman named Rotrudis.[20] The reason for doing so was that many people claimed that she was not a saint in her own right, but merely possessed a mistaken spelling of the name of St. Richtrudis, whose relics were enshrined at the nearby abbey of Marchiennes. Through the ordeal, the identities of two saints, Rotrudis and Richtrudis, were distinguished.

The general lines of the ritual were usually similar to those employed by Egbert. The ritual was preceded by a fast and included the chanting of prayers both before and during the ordeal. The source of fire, usually coals in a liturgical vessel known as a censer or thurible, was blessed. The sole surviving *ordo* specified that, at the climactic moment when the relics were placed in contact with the fire, the celebrants would intone verses from Psalm 16: "Try my heart, visit me by night, test me by fire. No wickedness will be found in me."[21] Despite the language of some texts it would seem that the relics were not put in or near actual flames, but rather were placed on top of hot coals.[22] Usually only a small fragment of the alleged saint's body was involved. Sometimes that was all that was possessed; other times a suitable piece was removed from the corpse. After the fragment was wrapped in linen, it was placed in a censer.[23] The climax of these rituals was the observation that the relic had not been harmed.[24] Such relics were often described as glowing in their linen wrappings. Many authors compared the rite to the refining of gold.[25] The intact state of relics after the ordeal served as miraculous certification of their authenticity.

It should also be noted that, unlike the judicial ordeal by fire, there are no records of relics which failed this form of the ordeal. In other words, no one has recorded an event in which a relic burned within the confines of such a ritual and was thus proven inauthentic. This is not surpris-

---

20. William of Andres, *Chronica Andrensis,* c. 5 in MGH, SS, 24:691–92.

21. Martène, *De antiquis ecclesiae ritibus libri tres,* 2:346.

22. In at least one case, however, the coals were placed on top of the relics. See Hariulf, *Chronique,* 4.20, p. 228.

23. A *thuribulus* is specifically mentioned in Theodoric of St. Eucharius, *Inventio et miracula s. Celsi,* c. 22, p. 406; *Historia inventionis corporis s. Secundini,* c. 6, p. 531; Leo of Ostia, *Chronica monasterii Casinensis,* 2.33, ed. Hartmut Hoffman, MGH, SS, 34:230.

24. Sometimes an extra miracle is added by the author. In two cases the relics leapt off the coals: *Historia inventionis corporis s. Secundini,* c. 6, p. 531 and Guibert of Nogent, *Autobiographie,* 3.20, p. 462. In three cases the coals are reported to have been extinguished: *Vita s. Meinwerci,* c. 111 in *AASS,* June I, p. 540 = c. 209 in MGH, SS, 11:156; *Passio s. Kanuti regis et martiris,* c. 9 in *Vitae sanctorum Danorum,* pp. 70–71; *Historia inventionis s. Prisci,* c. 13, p. 218.

25. See, for example, Theodoric of St. Eucharius, *Inventio s. Celsi,* c. 23, p. 407; Leo of Ostia, *Chronica monasterii Casinensis,* 2.33, pp. 229–30; Andrew of Fleury, *Vita Gauzlini abbatis Floriacensis monasterii,* c. 20, p. 60.

ing given the whiggish character of hagiography as a genre. This fact also reminds us, however, that we are not anthropologists observing a ritual, but rather historians analyzing texts which represent a ritual. The authors certainly provide what they regard as a plausible account, and so we are fully equipped to explore the religious ideology embedded in the ritual. At the same time, removed as we are from the event, we should beware of any materialist analysis which purports to present what really occurred as a result of fakery or manipulation. A warning is provided by the seventeenth-century scholar Jean Ferrand, who, in discussing this ritual, turned to a capitulary issued by Louis the Pious. Ferrand claimed that the Carolingian emperor had forbidden use of the ritual proof of relics as regards pieces of the true cross because unscrupulous merchants had taken to selling bits of petrified wood which were resistant to fire under the guise of such relics. Unfortunately Ferrand based his elegant analysis on a misreading of the text: the *capitulum* in question prohibits the ordeal by the cross, a form of the ordeal in which the litigants stand with arms outstretched.[26] A century later Ludovico Muratori expanded Ferrand's analysis with references to Dioscorides' discussion of asbestos.[27]

Why did the authentic bodies of real saints not burn? Or, more accurately, why were they perceived and described as being resistant to fire? In describing one instance of the ritual, Hariulf of Saint-Riquier put the matter plainly when he stated that the monks who employed it "knew that among other virtues . . . [the relics of the saints] were not in any way harmed by the effects of fire or able to be burned."[28] Relics were the bodily remains of holy people who were now resident in the heavenly court and who would be reunited with those very bodies for eternity on the day

---

26. Ferrand, *Disquisitio reliquiarum*, 2.3.1, pp. 463–64. The text of the original *capitulum* reads: "Sanccitum [*sic*] est, ut nullus deinceps quamlibet examinationem crucis facere praesumat; ne quae Christi passione glorificata est, cuiuslibet temeritate contemptui habeatur." *Capitulare ecclesiasticum*, chap. 27 in MGH, Capit., 1:279.

27. Muratori, *Antiquitates Italicae*, 5:12. Perhaps even more surprisingly, a twentieth-century scholar repeated the misreading of the *capitulum* with an analysis taken directly from Ferrand; see Hermann-Mascard, *Les reliques des saints*, p. 135.

28. "Cum itaque monachi ibidem degentes cum ineffabili gaudio sanctissimi sui patroni reliquias ovanter excepissent, voluerunt experiri utrumnam vere illud os de sancti Vigoris corpore fuisset; sciebant autem quod inter alia dona virtutum, quibus fulserat semper, immo fulgebat, hoc quoque excellentius obtineret, quod nullomodo ignis ardore laedi, aut comburi posset. Itaque struem lini, quod scilicet facile nimis incenditur, faciunt, et brachium illud sanctissimi pontificis superponunt; deinde linum desuper congerunt, et ita aridam et tenuem materiem igne supposito inflammant, et licet Deus omnipotens in sui servi merito tentandus non fuisset, eosdem tamen fratres, qui non quolibet vitio, sed certitudinis capiendae gratia id fecerunt, miraculi ac virtutis eventus non fefellit; nam non solum sancti dexteram ignis ille non laesit, sed etiam linum quod fuerat appositum ab igne permansit intactum." Hariulf, *Chronique*, 4.22, p. 228.

of the final judgment.[29] Those bodies had meaning only within that eschatological framework. It was, of course, an ordinary characteristic of dead bodies to burn, not just in the everyday material world, but in the afterlife as well. Christian writers regularly described the flames which tortured the bodies not only of the damned, but also of those sinners who required purification before entering the kingdom of heaven. Behind such early Christian ideas stood the concept of the posthumous fires of Gehenna which punished the unworthy dead, an idea which was being actively elaborated by Jews in the Second Temple period (538 B.C.–70 C.E.). Hariulf himself recalled these traditions by including in his account a hymn which called St. Vigor a *flammarum domitor* ("a man with power over flames") and asked that he "repress the flames of Gehenna" on behalf of those who sought his aid.[30]

As in so many cases, it was Paul who provided a formulation of these Jewish ideas which was to prove formative for Christian doctrine and practice. In 1 Corinthians 3.10–15, Paul had urged each Christian to build a home—that is, to translate the metaphor, a life—firmly grounded on the Lord which would thus withstand the fire of judgment. Augustine later elaborated this Pauline language into an account of posthumous judgment which, as Jacques LeGoff has noted, became standard in Western Christianity.[31] Unlike Paul, Augustine was being grimly literal. His understanding of this "purgatorial fire," as he usually called it, was firmly linked to his belief in the physical resurrection of each person's own body. In a remarkable passage near the end of the *City of God* Augustine described how this "purgatorial fire" would test all people in the period between their death and the final judgment. The bodies of those judged worthy of eternal punishment would be completely reduced so that nothing remained. The bodies of the elect would either remain unaffected or be effectively purged by the fire so that they could enjoy the eternal bliss of the kingdom of God.

29. Bynum, *Resurrection*, has illuminated the literal quality of Late Antique and medieval beliefs in the physical resurrection and the relationship of these doctrines to the practice of the veneration of relics. Also see, Marc van Uytfanghe, "Platonisme et eschatologie chrétienne: Leur symbiose graduelle dans les Passions et les panégyriques des martyrs et dans les biographies spirituelles (IIe–VIe s.). Première partie: Les Actes et passions *sincères*," in *Fructus centesimus: Mélanges offerts à G. J. M. Bartelink* (Steenbrugge and Dordrecht, 1989), pp. 343–62, and "Platonisme et eschatologie chrétienne: Leur symbiose graduelle dans les Passions et les panégyriques des martyrs et dans les biographies spirituelles (IIe–VIe s.). Deuxième partie: Les Passions tardives" in *De Tertullien aux Mozarabes: Mélanges offerts à Jacques Fontaine,* ed. Louis Holtz and Claude Fredouille (Paris, 1992), pp. 1:69–95.
30. "Sancte Vigor, generas; sacras cui solvimus odas, / Flammarum domitor, qui mundi comprimis ignes, / ne nos exurant, flammas compesce gehennae." Hariulf, *Chronique,* 4.22, p. 228.
31. Jacques LeGoff, *The Birth of Purgatory,* trans. Arthur Goldhammer (Chicago, 1984), pp. 61–85.

Theoderic of St. Eucharius—the monk of Trier who recorded Archbishop Egbert's authentication of the relics of Celsus—provided the most detailed explanation of the efficacy of the ritual offered in any of the contemporary texts. In that explanation, Theodoric consciously combined the Augustinian language of "purgatorial fire" with the Pauline imagery of the house from 1 Corinthians.[32] He began, "Since 'the fire will prove [*probabit*] what sort of work each one has done' [1 Cor. 3.13], the degree to which there was apostolic character in blessed Celsus became most evidently clear by means of material fire, which is generally predicted for all in the time of purgatory."[33] He then went on to cite the example of the three boys saved by God from the fiery furnace in Daniel, before continuing,

> If, due to the magnitude of Celsus' merits, the violence of material and extinguishable fire did not have the power to harm even the linen wrapping, is it then possible that on the day of the wrath of the Lord, when all material elements will be aflame, the purgatorial fire will receive the power of doing any harm to blessed Celsus? For Celsus is the son of the resurrection, who . . . as long as he was in the flesh, lived contrary to the flesh.[34]

According to this reasoning, saints were those who had "liv[ed] contrary to the flesh" and thus made their flesh resistant to Augustine's "purgatorial fire." At the final judgment the bodies of the saints simply would not burn. And so, making the link between the body in the tomb and the body resurrected at the end of time more powerful than Augustine would have dared, Egbert (as represented by this author) assumed that a body which will not burn at the end of time would not burn in the present instance.

The bodies of the saints did not burn for two closely associated reasons. First, the dead body itself still constituted part of the saintly person. The relic was the saint. And, as part of a person worthy of salvation, it was in itself holy. We can see this in a remark of Guibert of Nogent, one

32. Theodoric of St. Eucharius, *Inventio et miracula s. Celsi*, cc. 22–23, p. 406.

33. "[Q]uod de purgatorio generaliter praesagatum est omnibus, quia uniuscuiusque opus quale sit, ignis probabit." Theodoric of St. Eucharius, *Inventio et miracula s. Celsi*, c. 22, p. 400.

34. "Si enim violentia, materialis & extinguibilis ignis non habuit potestatem laedendi illud inuolucrum, ob tantorum meritorum magnitudinem, qui fieri potest, ut in die furoris Domini, elementis ardentibus, potestatem accipit ille ignis purgatorius alicuius laesionis in B. Celso, iam resurrectionis filio qui super fundamentum, quod Paulus architectus posuit, aurum, argentum, lapidesque pretiosos, quoad in carne praeter carnem vixit, aedificare non desiit?" Theodoric of St. Eucharius, *Inventio et miracula s. Celsi*, c. 23, p. 400.

of the authors who described the ritual proof of relics: "If whatever exists is good unless there is sin in it, then bodily members which are in themselves good are, in the absence of sin, holy."[35] Second, the dead body of a saint was to be resurrected in a glorified state at the end of time. As the holy members of a holy person, the parts of the body themselves would never be subject to purgatorial fires. Because it literally incorporated holiness, the body of a saint contained within it the proof of its own authenticity. All that had to be done was to read the body with fire. And not, it should be pointed out, with any fire. To be decisive, it was important that the test be ritually regulated and that the fire be consecrated. For, despite the frequently repeated tradition that relics of saints often miraculously survived fires which destroyed the churches in which they were enshrined, it was also recognized that relics could in certain circumstances burn. Abbo of Fleury, for example, had a metal reliquary constructed for his community's patron specifically in order "to repel fire."[36] In 1131 a fire swept through the church of St. Eucharius in Trier. In its wake, some, but not all, of the bones of St. Agricius were found in the ashes which were all that remained of the reliquary.[37] The monk who recorded the event, probably recalling the *inventio* of Celsus some century and one half earlier, gave two answers in response to those who might object that authentic relics did not perish from fire. First, while admitting that God did sometimes deign to save relics from such fires, he argued that such was not always the case, citing the story of the relics of John the Baptist. Second, he said that the fire itself was a sign of divine vengeance intended to punish the community of St. Eucharius for its sins. God's willingness to save some of the relics of Agricius was in itself a miracle, and a suggestion of God's intended mercy.

The importance of blessing the fire comes to the fore in the vernacular traditions surrounding the testing of the relics of King Olaf Haraldsson of Norway, who died at the hands of Norwegian rebels in the battle of Stiklestad in 1030. There certainly was opposition to the public cult of

---

35. "Si quidquid est, bonum est, nisi ubi peccatum est, membra quae per se bona sunt, cum peccatum non est, sancta sunt." Guibert of Nogent, *Tractatus de incarnatione contra Judaeos,* 2.1 in PL 156:499.

36. "Haec itaque et alia nonnulla sub egregio Patre Abbone in Floriacensi coenobio perfecta sunt, instantia et procuratione honorabilis monachi Gauzfredi, cui ipse sacrorum commiserat custodiam thesaurorum cujus etiam Gauzfredi sollicitudine gazophylacium lapideum est constructum, ad repellendam ignis, si (quod absit) ingrueret, violentiam satis idoneum, eodem de quo loquimur venerabili Patre Abbone sumptus subministrante, de cujus vitae moribus et scriptis, quia multa retulimus, ne fastidiosi in multiloquio simus lectori, stilum ad eijus enarrandum vertamus transitum." Aimo of Fleury, *Vita s. Abbonis,* c. 15 in *Acta sanctorum ordinis Sancti Benedicti,* 5:51.

37. Lambert of St. Eucharius, *Inventio corporis S. Mathiae et miracula,* cc. 10 and 11 in *AASS,* February III, pp. 457–58.

this royal martyr, particularly on the part of the mistress and son of Cnut the Great, who had sent them as emissaries to recover control over Norway for Denmark. According to two vernacular accounts, which actually date to the 1220s, the partisans of Olaf subjected pieces of his hair and beard to the ordeal by fire as the decisive means of authenticating his sanctity. [38] Cnut's mistress Alfifa, in opposing the use of the ordeal by fire, allegedly stated, "learned men were able to consecrate fire in such a way that it did no harm." Even in opposing the ordeal, its ritual efficacy when using blessed fire was thus grudgingly accepted. Ritually blessed, the coals of the thurible became an extension of the fires of God's judgment. By failing to mark the remains of a human body, the fire proved that that body belonged to a saint and thus was destined for eschatological bliss, not punishment.

In applying ritually blessed forms of fire to the presumed relics of saints, clerics such as Egbert of Trier put into action their assumptions concerning the Last Judgment and purgatorial fires. Their ritual practice illuminates the belief system which made such rituals not only possible, but plausible. In analyzing a problematic form of religious expression from this same period, Lester Little employed the ideas of the philosopher J. L. Austin in a manner which is pertinent to the present discussion. [39] Little was interested in demonstrating how the liturgical curses used by monks of the eleventh and twelfth centuries implied the existence of assumed "rules" of religious beliefs. Austin himself described how certain rituals, such as the christening of a ship or a marriage, employed linguistic practices which he termed "performative utterances." [40] He thus emphasized how such ritual actions did not employ metaphor, but literally enacted a

---

38. The earlier of the two is the so-called Legendary Saga. For the text, see *Olafs saga helga,* in *Konunga Sögur,* ed. Gudni Jónsson (Reykjavik, 1957), 1:370–73. For a translation (on which I am dependent), see *Olafs saga hins Helga: Die "Legendarische Saga" über Olaf den heiligen,* c. 89, ed. and trans. Anne Heinrichs, Doris Janshen, Elke Radicke, and Hartmut Röhn (Heidelberg, 1982), pp. 208–11. The "Legendary Saga" is usually given a date in the 1220s and probably comes from Norway. The second text is the *Heimskringla* of the Icelandic chieftain Snorri Sturluson. Once again I depend on a translation: see Snorri Sturluson, *Heimskringla: History of the Kings of Norway,* trans. Lee Hollander (Austin, 1964), chap. 244, pp. 527–30. I thank Margaret Cormack for bringing these texts to my attention.

39. Lester K. Little, *Benedictine Maledictions: Liturgical Cursing in Romanesque France* (Ithaca, N.Y., 1993), pp. 113–18.

40. J. L. Austin, *How to Do Things with Words,* ed. J. O. Urmson and Marina Sbisà (2d ed., Cambridge, Mass., 1962), particularly chap. 1; and "Performative Utterances," in *Philosophical Papers,* ed. J. O. Urmson and G. J. Warneck (3d ed., Oxford, 1979), pp. 232–52. It is heartening to observe that Austin began the latter essay by noting, "You are more than entitled not to know what the word 'performative' means. It is a new word and an ugly word." Stanley Tambiah has offered an important critique of Austin's approach to ritual in "The Magical Power of Words," *Man* 2 (1968): 175–208, and, more explicitly, in "A Performative Approach to Ritual," *Proceedings of the British Academy, 1979,* 65 (1981): 113–69, both reprinted in idem, *Culture, Thought, and Social Action: An Anthropological Perspective* (Cambridge, Mass., 1985), pp. 17–59 and 123–66.

pre-existent state of being. Little usefully summarized his claim thus: "Austin argued that it is absurd to regard [such rituals] as reports of the performance of the actions they mention. Instead, in his view they accomplish these very actions."[41] In the rituals considered here, the blessed forms of fire took the part of "performative utterances." They served as a literal embodiment of the "purgatorial fires" described by Augustine and invoked by Theodoric of St. Eucharius. When Egbert placed the bones of Celsus in the thurible, he—so to speak—"made it so" and enacted the Last Judgment on the altar of the church of St. Eucharius.

When considered from the same eschatological perspective, the more ordinary judicial use of the ordeal by fire makes a good deal of sense. The interpretation of the judicial ordeal has caused a great deal of debate among modern scholars. A once fashionable (and by no means abandoned) interpretation—begun by legal historians of the nineteenth century, such as Henry Charles Lea—held that the judicial ordeal was essentially irrational, an appeal to the miraculous power of God which had been relegated to history's dust-bin through the rediscovery of Roman law.[42] In the 1970s and 1980s historians inspired by the work of anthropologists came to see the ordeal as a ritual which allowed a community to grope its way to consensus and compromise about the hard cases which taxed their judicial institutions.[43] For them Western Christendom in the High Middle Ages was a society in which relationships, not rules, formed the core of law. It was social change, specifically the decline of clan structures, and not intellectual evolution, which doomed the ordeal. In the past decade, however, we have witnessed a reaction to such a reputedly "functionalist" analysis. Robert Bartlett and Talal Asad have, in very different ways, described the ordeal as an expression of religious beliefs and attributed its abandonment to changing political concerns among the ecclesiastical hierarchy.[44]

These analyses—of both a "functionalist" and "post-functionalist" nature—have turned attention to the intellectual, social, or political

41. Little, *Benedictine Maledictions,* pp. 113–14.
42. Henry Charles Lea, *Superstition and Force* (4th ed., Philadelphia, 1892).
43. Colin Morris, "*Judicium Dei:* The Social and Political Significance of the Ordeal in the Eleventh Century," *Studies in Church History* 12 (1975): 95–111; Rebecca Colman, "Reason and Unreason in Early Medieval Law," *Journal of Interdisciplinary History* 4 (1974): 571–91; Peter Brown, "Society and the Supernatural: A Medieval Change," *Daedalus* 104 (1975): 133–51; Paul Hyams, "Trial by Ordeal: The Key to Proof in the Early Common Law," in Morris Arnold et al., eds., *On the Laws and Customs of England: Essays in Honor of Samuel E. Thorne* (Chapel Hill, N.C., 1981), pp. 90–126.
44. Bartlett, *Trial by Fire and Water,* particularly pp. 34–42, and Talal Asad, "Notes on Body Pain and Truth in Medieval Christian Ritual," *Economy and Society* 12 (1983): 287–327, reprinted in a revised form as "Pain and Truth in Medieval Christian Ritual," in his *Genealogies of Religion: Discipline and Reasons of Power in Christianity and Islam* (Baltimore, 1993), pp. 83–124.

frameworks in which the ordeal was used, and thus away from the bodies which lay at the center of the ritual. Those frameworks are, to be sure, important for any satisfactory interpretation. But the work of recent scholars of the ordeal show to bad effect the influence of Clifford Geertz's oft-cited study of the Balinese cockfight. In making that ritual a symbolic theatre in which Balinese society itself takes center stage, Geertz made his audience lose sight of the fact that at the ritual's heart stood a pair of crazed fowls with razor blades attached to their legs.[45] He overlooked what Roy Rappaport has called the "obvious aspects" of a ritual. As Rappaport has written,

> [I]n their eagerness to plumb ritual's dark symbolic or functional depths, to find in ritual more than meets the eye, anthropologists have, perhaps increasingly, tended to overlook ritual's surface, that which does meet the eye . . . the surfaces of ritual are *not* symbolic, or at least not entirely so. Indeed, that ritual is not entirely symbolic seems to me to be one of its most interesting and important characteristics.[46]

And so, *mutatis mutandis,* historians of the ordeal. For they have overlooked the most obvious aspect of the ordeal by fire. In the midst of its ritual theatre, bodies burned. Even more significantly, different bodies burned in different ways, or, to be more precise, they were perceived, recorded, and remembered as having burned in different ways.

The authentication of saintly relics described here provides one important comparison. This ritual, however, was not the only form of conse-

45. Clifford Geertz, "Deep Play: Notes on a Balinese Cockfight," in *The Interpretation of Cultures* (New York, 1973), pp. 412–53.
46. Roy Rappaport, "The Obvious Aspects of Ritual," in idem, *Ecology, Meaning, and Religion* (Berkeley, 1979), pp. 173–221 (here pp. 174–75). I am invoking the work of Rappaport here to reject a number of earlier interpretations of the ordeal by fire, including those which have been deemed by others "functionalist." There has been a good deal of scholarly muddle over this term, confusing debates which would be useless to rehearse here. Let me state, however, without reserve that I intend the present analysis to be a vindication, rather than a rejection, of an approach to the relationship of religion and society which might be called intrinsically Durkheimian and which is of the sort advocated and developed, within the Anglophone history of Late Antique and medieval Christianity at any rate, by Peter Brown (although I have some specific reservations about Brown's long-since published analysis of the ordeal by fire, "Society and the Supernatural"). Several recent attacks by scholars on the Durkheimian model of religious history seem to me both baffling and disturbing; see, for example, Susan Rosa and Dale Van Kley, "Religion and the Historical Discipline: A Reply to Mack Holt and Henry Heller," *French Historical Studies* 21 (1998): 610–29, and Mark Vessey, "The Demise of the Christian Writer and the Remaking of 'Late Antiquity': From H.-I. Marrou's Saint Augustine (1938) to Peter Brown's Holy Man (1983)," *Journal of Early Christian Studies* 6 (1998): 377–410 (one could equally cite the contributions of Susanna Elm and Elizabeth Clark to this volume of the journal, which at once curiously mixes a celebration of the work of Peter Brown with an attack on that very work).

crated fire employed during this period to authenticate the eschatological status of bodies. A neat analogue—albeit importantly one enacted in reverse—of the descriptions of the ritual ordeal of relics may be found in contemporary descriptions of the execution of heretics. In the early eleventh century ecclesiastical and secular authorities began to execute people for the crime of heresy, an unprecedented act in the Latin West. The earliest instance was a trial in Orléans in 1022. One of the bishops who advised King Robert the Pious during the trial was Gauzlin of Fleury, a man who only a few years before had used the ordeal by fire to authenticate a relic which he had purchased.[47] The condemned heretics were executed by burning on a pyre blessed by clerics. Ademar of Chabannes, describing their death, wrote, "They were promptly reduced to ashes, so completely that not a trace of their bones was found."[48] These heretics, according to Ademar, "pretended chastity," unlike saints who, according to Theodoric, "while in the flesh, lived contrary to the flesh."[49] Burning would continue to be the favored means of executing heretics and chroniclers would continue to emphasize that the heretics' bodies were completely consumed by flames. According to Walter Map, for example, a great miracle accompanied the execution of Patarines in Vienne around 1182. The condemned were placed in a house so that they might be burned, but when the fire was brought, the building would not ignite. When the attending crowd burst in to kill the heretics, they discovered that "the bones and flesh of the men had become charcoal and glowing ashes . . . and that the most righteous fire had punished only those who had sinned."[50] The fires of execution became, much like the coals blessed in Archbishop Egbert's thurible, an extension of the fires of hell which would completely consume damned heretics in the next world.

Saints were judged authentic by authors who described the authentication of their relics through fire, which the relics escaped unscathed. Her-

---

47. Andrew of Fleury, *Vita Gauzlini abbatis Floriacensis monasterii*, c. 20, p. 60.

48. "Qui autem flammis judicati sunt supradicti decem cum Lisojo, quem rex valde dilexerat propter sanctitatem, quam eum habere credebat, securi nihil ignem timebant, et a flammis se inlesos exire promittebant, et ridentes in medio ignis igati sunt, et sine mora penitus in cinerem redacti sunt, ut nec de ossibus residuum inveniretur eorum." Ademar of Chabannes, *Chronicon*, 3.59, ed. Jules Chavanon, Collection des textes pour servir à l'étude et à l'enseignement de l'histoire 20 (Paris, 1897), pp. 184–85.

49. "Abstinentes a civis, quasi monachi apparebant et castitatem simulabant, sed inter se ipsos omnem luxuriam exercebant, et nuncii Antichristi erant, multosque a fide exorbitare fecerunt." Ademar of Chabannes, *Chronicon*, 3.49, p. 173.

50. "Depulsis igitur hostiis, in domum irruerunt, et ad postem uenientes carbones et fauillas ex ossibus eorum et carnibus factas inueniunt, unicula uident illesa, postem intactum, et iustissimum ignem in eos solos qui delinquerant animaduertisse." Walter Map, *De nugis curialium: Courtiers' Trifles*, 1.30, ed. and trans. Montague James, revised Christopher Brooke and R. A. B. Mynors (Oxford, 1983), pp. 118–23.

etics were similarly judged by authors who described their execution by fire, in which their bones were completely consumed. These were but the limits of the full spectrum of human virtue. The bodies of ordinary people neither survived a fire nor were completely consumed by it. The judicial ordeal by fire simply used fire to read such ordinary bodies. Proper healing indicated the truth of the testimony. Festering indicated falsehood. By focusing on the obvious—that is, on the actual burned flesh of the litigant—and by comparing the reading of that flesh to the accounts of the ritual proof of relics and the execution of heretics, the inherent logic of the ordeal by fire becomes evident. The red-hot bar carried by the proband is also an extension of the purgatorial fires. Those fires would test the presence, or absence, of guilt which required purgation. The means of proof were once again present in the very body itself, which literally incorporated the moral status of the person. Human bodies—before and after death, in this world and in the next—exhibited the degree of a person's virtue. One particular index of that virtue was a body's resistance to fire. This purifying force of nature would be used by God in the afterlife to cleanse the imperfect among the saved and to punish the damned. That force could be ritually harnessed by humans to demonstrate sanctity or heresy. Simply put, the link between the human body and the soul which inhabited it was so strong that bodies—both living and dead—when tested by fire would reveal a person's eschatological fate and thus that person's relationship to God.

A Preliminary Handlist of Authentications of Relics through the Ordeal

1. Trier (Lotharingia), 978: Archbishop Egbert tests the newly discovered relics of St. Celsus in the church of St. Eucharius. (Theodoric of St. Eucharius, *Inventio et miracula s. Celsi* [BHL 1720–1] in *AASS*, February III, pp. 402–10.)

2. Monte Cassino (central Italy), 1010–23: the monks test a relic of the piece of linen used to wash the feet of Christ at the last supper which has been given to the community as a gift. (Leo of Ostia, *Chronica monasterii Casinensis*, 2.33 ed. Hartmut Hoffman, MGH, SS, 34:229–307.)

3. Fleury (Île-de-France), 1013: Abbot Gauzlin tests a relic of Christ's *sudarium* which he had purchased in Rome. (Andrew of Fleury, *Vita Gauzlini abbatis Floriacensis monasterii*, c. 20, ed. Robert-Henri Bautier and Gillette Labory [Paris: 1969], p. 60.)

4. Troia (Apulia), 1022–34: anonymous bishop tests the newly discovered relic of St. Secundinus. (*Historia inventionis corporis s. Secundini* [BHL 7554–5] in *AASS*, February II, p. 530–31 and Waiferius of Monte Cassino, *Inventio corporis s. Secundini* [BHL 7556] in *AASS*, February II, p. 531–54.)

5. Norway, post-1030: a vernacular tradition dating to the 1220s claims that clerics used the ordeal to test the relics, and thus establish the sanctity, of King Olaf Haraldsson after his death at the battle of Stiklestad. (*Óláfs saga hins helga* in *Konunga Sögur*, ed. Gudni Jónsson [Reykjavik, 1957], 1:370–73.)

6. Paderborn (Saxony), ca. 1032: Archbishop Meinwerk tests relics of St. Felix which had been sent to him by the patriarch of Aquileia as a gift. (*Vita s. Meinwerci* [BHL 5884], c. III in *AASS*, June I, p. 5405 = 209 in MGH, SS, 11:156.)

7. Cérizey (Normandy), ca. 1050: monks test a relic of St. Vigor given to the community by the monks of Saint-Riquier. (Hariulf, *Chronique de l'abbaye de Saint-Riquier (Ve siècle–1104)*, 4.20, ed. Ferdinand Lot, Collection de textes pour servir à l'étude et à l'enseignement de l'histoire [Paris, 1894], p. 228.)

8. Durham (Northumbria), 1057–72: some small relics of Cuthbert in the possession of a priest are tested. (Symeon of Durham, *Historia ecclesiae Dunhelmensis*, 3.7, ed. T. Arnold, Rolls Series 75 [London, 1882], pp. 87–90.)

9. Durham (Northumbria), 1065: relics from the tomb of King Oswine newly rediscovered at the priory of Tynemouth are subjected to the ordeal. This tradition may well be a fabrication invented by hagiographers associated with the abbey of St. Alban's as late as the 1160s. (*Vita, inventio et miracula Oswini regis* [BHL 6382–84] in *Miscellanea biographica,* ed. James Raine, Surtees Society 8 [London, 1838].)

10. Evesham (West Midlands), ca. 1080: Abbot Walter uses the ordeal to test relics of two former abbots of Evesham named Wistan and Credanus. (Dominic of Evesham, *Translatio et miracula s. Odulfi* [BHL 6319–20] in *Chronicon abbatiae de Evesham ad annum 1418,* ed. W. D. Macray, Rolls Series 29 [London, 1863], pp. 323–24.)

11. Prague (Bohemia), ca. 1100: relics of the martyr Ludmila are tested on the insistence of Abbess Windelmuth (Cosmas of Prague, *Chronica Boemorum,* 3.11 in MGH, SRG 2:171–72.)

12. Odense (Norway), ca. 1100: ordeal by fire is used to authenticate the relics and thus the sanctity of King Cnut. (*Passio s. Kanuti regis et martiris* [BHL 1550], c. 9 in *Vitae sanctorum Danorum,* ed. Martin Clarentius Gertz, 4 vols. in 1 [Copenhagen, 1908–12], pp. 70–71.)

13. Clermont (Beauvaisis), ca. 1100: ordeal is used to test relics of St. Arnulph brought to Clermont from an untrustworthy source. (Guibert of Nogent, *Autobiographie,* 3.20, ed. Edmond-René Labande, Les classiques de l'histoire de France au moyen âge 34 [Paris, 1981], p. 462.)

14. Denmark, ca. 1117: ordeal by fire of the relics of Theodgar serves as one of the proofs of this somewhat shadowy figure's sanctity in the face of episcopal opposition to his cult. (*De s. Theodgaro* [BHL 8068], c. 6 in *Vitae sanctorum Danorum,* p. 16.)

15. Orkney, 1120s or 1130s: ordeal is used to test the relics, and thus the sanctity, of Magnus, Earl of Orkney, who had been assassinated in 1117. (*Orkneyinga Saga,* c. 57, ed. Finnbogi Gudmundsson, Islenzk fornrit 34 [Reykjavik, 1965], pp. 122–129.)

16. Schaffhausen (Switzerland), ca. 1125: ordeal is used to test relics of the true cross brought back from the Holy Land. (*Narratio de reliquiis in monasterium Scafhusense translatis* in MGH, SS, 15:954–59.)

17. Andres (Flanders), 1161–95: ordeal is used to authenticate the relics of a saint named Rotrudis and thus, in part, to distinguish

her from a saint named Rictrudis whose relics were enshrined at the nearby abbey of Marchiennes. (William of Andres, *Chronica Andrensis,* c. 5 in MGH, SS, 24:691–92.)

18. Quintodecimo (formerly Aeclanum in the Appenines), 1138–43: ordeal by fire is used by local archpriest, at behest of bishop, to authenticate the newly discovered relics of Priscus. (*Historia inventionis s. Prisci* [BHL 6929] in *AASS,* September I, pp. 216–18.)

19. Zwiefalten (Swabia), ca. 1145: ordeal is used to test some relics of the Eleven Thousand Virgins of Cologne. (Ortlieb of Zwiefalten, *Chronicon,* addimenta 2 in *Die Zwiefalter Chroniken Ortliebs u. Bertholds,* ed. Luitpold Wallach, Erich König, and Karl Otto Müller, Schwäbische chroniken der Stauferzeit 2 [2d ed., Sigmaringen, 1978], pp. 132–34.)

20. Bisceglie (Apulia), 1167: during the formal *inventio* of the newly discovered relics of martyrs named Maurus, Pantalemeon, and Sergius, one priest subjects them to the ordeal. (Amandus of Bisceglie, *Inventio, translationes, et miracula ss. Mauri, Pantalemeonis, et Sergii* [BHL 5792], c. 29 in *AASS,* July VI, p. 363.)

Contributors

Alison I. Beach completed her Ph.D. at Columbia University in 1996. She is currently research assistant to Giles Constable at the Institute for Advanced Study in Princeton, New Jersey. She has recently been Visiting Assistant Professor of Church History at New Brunswick Theological Seminary in New Jersey and Visiting Lecturer in Church History at Union Theological Seminary in New York. Her book, *Women as Scribes: Book Production and Monastic Reform in Twelfth-Century Bavaria,* is forthcoming from Cambridge University Press.

Lisa M. Bitel is Associate Professor of Medieval History and Women's Studies at the University of Kansas. She is the author of *Isle of the Saints: Monastic Settlement and Christian Community in Early Ireland* (1990) and *Land of Women: Tales of Sex and Gender from Early Ireland* (1996), among other publications. She is currently writing a synoptic history of women in medieval Europe.

Robert Brentano is Jane K. Sather Professor of History at the University of California at Berkeley, where he has taught since 1952. His degrees are from Swarthmore and Oxford. His books are: *York Metropolitan Jurisdiction and Papal Judges Delegate (1279–1296)* (1959); *Two Churches: England and Italy in the Thirteenth Century* (1968); *Rome before Avignon: A Social History of Thirteenth-Century Rome* (1974); and *A New World in a Small Place: Church and Religion in the Diocese of Rieti, 1188–1378* (1994). He is currently working on a book about autobiographical statement in thirteenth-century chroniclers.

Sharon Farmer is Associate Professor of History at the University of California, Santa Barbara. She is the author of *Communities of Saint Martin: Legend and Ritual in Medieval Tours* (1991) and of several articles about medieval gender constructs and medieval women, including "Down and Out and Female in Thirteenth-Century Paris," which appeared in *The American Historical Review* in April 1998. She is working on a monograph titled "Gender and Poverty in High Medieval Paris."

Patrick J. Geary is Professor of History and Director of the Medieval Institute at the University of Notre Dame. He received his Ph.D. in Medieval Studies from Yale University and has taught at Princeton University, the University of Florida, and UCLA, where he directed the Center for Medieval and Renaissance Studies. His publications include *Furta Sacra: Thefts of Relics in the Central Middle Ages* (1978); *Aristocracy in Provence: The Rhône Basin at the Dawn of the Carolingian Age* (1985); *Before France and Germany: The Creation and Transformation of the Merovingian World* (1988); *Living with the Dead in the Middle Ages* (1994); and *Phantoms of Remembrance: Memory and Oblivion at the End of the First Millennium* (1994). He is currently completing a study of ethnic formation in the Early Middle Ages.

Thomas Head is Professor of History at Hunter College and the Graduate Center, the City University of New York. He has previously taught at Washington University, Yale University, and the Claremont Colleges. Among his publications are *Hagiography and the Cult of Saints: The Diocese of Orléans, 800–1200* (1990); *The Peace of God: Social Violence and Religious Response in France around the Year 1000* (1992; co-editor with Richard Landes); *Soldiers of Christ: Saints' Lives from Late Antiquity and the Early Middle Ages* (1994; co-editor with Thomas Noble); *Medieval Hagiography: An Anthology* (1999; editor). He is currently at work on two projects: a history of the development of the cult of saints to the twelfth century and a new look at the early Capetian monarchy and ecclesiastical politics.

Luigi Pellegrini is Professor in the Dipartimento di Studi medievali e moderni at the Università d'Annunzio in Chieti, Italy. He is the author and editor of numerous works on the early history of the Franciscans and on the history of the mendicant orders in the thirteenth century, including *L'esperienza Francescana nella società del sec. XIII: Corso di storia francescana* (1974); *Insediamenti francescani nell'Italia del Duecento* (1984); *Il Francescanesimo nella Valle Reatina* (1993; with Stanislao da Campagnola); *"Che sono queste novità?" Le religiones novae nell'Italia meridionale (secoli XIII–XIV)* (1999). He has also published on the history of the Abruzzi, including *Abruzzo medioevale: Un itinerario storico attraverso la documentazione* (1988); *Contributi per una storia dell'Abruzzo adriatico nel medioevo* (1992; co-edited with Roberto Paciocco); *Aspetti della cultura dei laici in area adriatica: Saggi sul Tardo Medioevo e sulla prima Età moderna* (1998; with Roberto Paciocco). He is now preparing three books: "I Mendicanti e l'Europa nel secolo XIII," "Le fonti francescane del secolo XIII," and (with Roberto Paciocco) "I Francescani nelle Marche."

Catherine Peyroux is Assistant Professor of History at Duke University. Her research interests have centered on women and the holy in early medieval Europe and Ireland, and she is completing a book titled, "The Governance of Women: Double Monasteries in Early Medieval Europe." With the essay in this volume, she renews a long-standing interest in medieval leprosy and conceptions of poverty in the Middle Ages.

Amy G. Remensnyder is Associate Professor of History at Brown University. The author of *Remembering Kings Past: Monastic Foundation Legends in Medieval Southern France* (1995), she is working on a book about the Virgin Mary as a symbol of conquest and conversion in Reconquest Spain and sixteenth-century Mexico.

Barbara H. Rosenwein is Professor of History at Loyola University Chicago. Her publications include *Rhinoceros Bound: Cluny in the Tenth Century* (1982); *To Be the Neighbor of Saint Peter: The Social Meaning of Cluny's Property, 909–1049* (1989); *Anger's Past: The Social Meaning of an Emotion in the Middle Ages* (1998; editor); *Debating the Middle Ages: Issues and Readings* (1998; co-editor with Lester K. Little); and *Negotiating Space: Power, Restraint, and Privileges of Immunity in Early Medieval Europe* (1999). She is currently working on a study of emotions in the Early Middle Ages.

INDEX